Computer Exercises
for Paralegals

Computer Exercises for **Paralegals**

Second Edition

Kristen L. Battaile
University of San Diego

Formerly published by
Little, Brown and Company

Aspen Law & Business
A Division of Aspen Publishers, Inc.

This publication is designed to provide accurate and authoritative information in regard to the subject matter covered. It is sold with the understanding that the publisher is not engaged in rendering legal, accounting, or other professional services. If legal advice or other professional advice is required, the services of a competent professional person should be sought.

—From a *Declaration of Principles* jointly adopted by a Committee of the American Bar Association and a Committee of Publishers and associations.

Contents

Preface

This workbook was written as a reference and instructional tool for the paralegal student and the practicing legal professional. It contains instructions and practice exercises in WordPerfect® 5.1 for DOS, Windows word processors, Lotus® 1-2-3® for DOS, Windows electronic spreadsheets, dBASE IV® for DOS, and Windows summary databases.

My intent in creating the workbook was to provide the reader with the fundamentals of each software program, while including some advanced and little-known features for the more experienced user. There are a variety of computer systems and software packages used in the training of paralegals and used by the practicing legal professional. I have attempted to include those software packages most commonly used in paralegal schools and law offices. Chapters 1, 3, and 5 cover the most popular DOS word processor, electronic spreadsheet, and summary database. Chapters 2, 4, and 6 cover the features of Windows-based word processors, electronic spreadsheets, and summary databases. The Windows chapters concentrate on WordPerfect®, Microsoft® Word®, Microsoft® Excel®, Quattro® Pro, Lotus® 1-2-3®, Paradox®, and Microsoft® Access®. At the end of Chapters 2, 4, and 6 are exercises that can be completed in the DOS or Windows version of the applications. These exercises consist of tasks that a paralegal likely will be asked to perform on the job. For example, the word processing exercises include the drafting of a confirmation letter and the preparation of a deposition summary. The electronic spreadsheet exercises include a conservatorship worksheet and a computation of plaintiff damages in a class action lawsuit. The summary database exercises include the creation of a database structure and the entering of evidentiary documents into a database.

The chapters in this workbook were written so that the reader may follow along on the computer, but they are also extensively illustrated to help the reader understand the concepts when not at the computer. Each chapter includes a detailed table of contents and an index for quick access to specific information.

I hope that this workbook will provide the reader with a fundamental understanding of these software programs and the ability to immediately apply the knowledge to work in a legal career.

Kristen L. Battaile

June 1997

Acknowledgments

I am grateful to the companies whose products I have included in this workbook for their generous permission to reprint information about and examples of their products.

All Borland product names are trademarks or registered trademarks of Borland International, Inc.

Corel®, WordPerfect®, Quattro® Pro, and Paradox® are registered trademarks of Corel Corporation Limited.

Lotus® and **1-2-3®** are registered trademarks of Lotus Development Corporation.

Microsoft®, Windows®, Microsoft® Word®, Microsoft® Excel®, and **Microsoft® Access®** are registered trademarks of Microsoft Corporation.

Figures 1.1-1.18, 1.21-1.27, 1.29, 1.30, 1.32, 1.33, 1.35, 1.36 from WordPerfect for DOS version 5.1, copyright © 1989 Corel Corporation Limited. All rights reserved. Reprinted with permission from Corel Corporation Limited.

Figures 2.1, 2.3, 2.5, 2.7, 2.9, 2.10, 2.15, 2.16, 2.23-2.25 from WordPerfect for Windows, copyright © 1991-1996 Corel Corporation Limited. All rights reserved. Reprinted with permission from Corel Corporation Limited.

Figures 2.2, 2.4, 2.6, 2.8, 2.11, 2.13, 2.17, 2.19-2.21, 2.27 copyright © Microsoft Corporation. Screen shots reprinted by permission from Microsoft Corporation.

Figures 3.1-3.33 Copyright © 1993 Lotus Development Corporation. Used with permission of Lotus Development Corporation.

Figures 4.2-4.4, 4.7, 4.16-4.18, 4.21 from Quattro Pro for Windows, copyright © 1996 Corel Corporation Limited. All rights reserved. Reprinted with permission from Corel Corporation Limited.

Figures 4.1, 4.5, 4.6, 4.8-4.15, 4.19, 4.20 copyright © Microsoft Corporation. Screen shots reprinted by permission from Microsoft Corporation.

Figures 5.1-5.40 dBASE IV® is a product of Borland International, Inc. The screen prints from this program are used with the permission of Borland International, Inc.

Figures 6.1, 6.3, 6.4, 6.6, 6.8, 6.10, 6.14, Chapter 6 search examples 1 through 7, 6.20, 6.21,

Computer Exercises
for Paralegals

Word Processing

CHAPTER 1

WORDPERFECT® FOR DOS

Chapter Preface

Corel® WordPerfect® version 5.1 for DOS is the word processing software used by many law offices that continue to run DOS-based computer systems. This chapter will acquaint you with WordPerfect 5.1 for DOS and the features that you will likely use in the law office. The commands used in this chapter are based on version 5.1. However, the majority of these commands will work with all of the DOS versions of WordPerfect. Chapter 2 covers Corel® WordPerfect® for Microsoft® Windows® and other Windows word processors. At the end of Chapter 2, there are several word processing exercises that will give practical experience in using WordPerfect for law office tasks.

Section One—The Basics

A. ENTERING WORDPERFECT

To enter WordPerfect from the DOS prompt, type: **WP [Enter]**

<u>OR</u> select the WordPerfect option from a menu screen or double-click on its icon on the Windows desktop.

Upon entering the program, you will see the WordPerfect screen as shown in Figure 1.1.

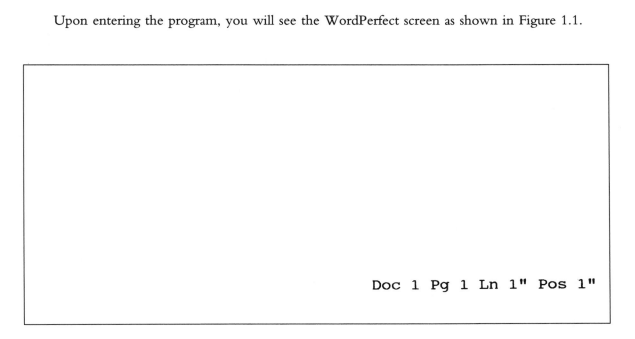

Doc 1 Pg 1 Ln 1" Pos 1"

Figure 1.1 The WordPerfect Screen

B. THE WORDPERFECT ENVIRONMENT

1. The Status Line

When you enter WordPerfect for DOS, you will find a blank screen with a Status Line in the lower right-hand corner. Some screens will also display menus at the top. The Status Line displays the document number (you may be in two at once), the page number and the line, and the position of the cursor in inches or another measurement. If the document currently on the screen has been saved, the location (path) and name of the document will be displayed in the lower left-hand corner of the screen as shown in Figure 1.2.

```
┌─────────────────────────────────────────────────────────────────┐
│                                                                   │
│         SUPERIOR COURT OF THE STATE OF CALIFORNIA                 │
│                                                                   │
│            IN AND FOR THE COUNTY OF SAN DIEGO                     │
│                                                                   │
│  THE ABC CORPORATION, a California  )   Case No. 100111           │
│  Corporation,                       )                             │
│                                     )   ANSWER OF DEFENDANT JOE    │
│                 Plaintiff,          )   SMITH                      │
│                                     )                             │
│           vs.                       )                             │
│                                     )                             │
│  JOE SMITH, and DOES 1 through 50,  )                             │
│                                     )                             │
│                 Defendants.         )                             │
│  _____)                            │
│                                                                   │
│     Comes now Defendant JOE SMITH who responds to the Complaint on │
│                                                                   │
│  file herein as follows:                                          │
│  C:\WORK\SMITH.ANS                       Doc 1 Pg 1 Ln 6" Pos 3.3" │
│                                                                   │
└─────────────────────────────────────────────────────────────────┘
```

Figure 1.2 The document name and Status Line appear at the bottom of the WordPerfect screen

2. Executing Commands

In WordPerfect for DOS, commands are accessed with the function keys or the pull-down menus (versions 5.1 and later). In this chapter, a command will be referenced by its function key or key combination. The function keys are simply a more efficient way to access commands than by using the pull-down menu selections. In WordPerfect for Windows, the pull-down menus are more sophisticated and are a practical alternative to the function keys.

The function keys used to perform a command will be enclosed in brackets. For example, the function key for underlining will be referred to as [F8]. The key combination for centering will be referred to as [Shift] + [F6]. The plus symbol (+) indicates that the [Shift] key is to be held down while pressing [F6]. When a function key or key combination evokes further menu choices, the menu items to be selected will follow the function keystrokes and be separated by commas. For example, to change from single spacing to double spacing you select the Format function with **[Shift] + [F8].** You then must select item **1** from a menu for **Line,** and then item **6** from another menu for **Line Spacing.** Then you type a **2** to change to double spacing. This all would be referred to as:

[Shift] + [F8], 1, 6, 2

Many times when you are finished with commands, you are left at a menu screen. To return to your document, either press the **[Enter]** key until you return to the document screen, or press the Exit key **[F7].**

When a command is shown separated by commas, such as [Home], [Up Arrow], you will press the first key and release it, and then press the next key. WordPerfect will remember that you have pressed the first key.

3. Units of Measure

The line and position measurements within the Status Line are usually set in inches. The inch measurement is based on the actual measurements from the borders of the paper in your printer. This allows you to measure where you would like text placed on a page and then to move the cursor to that measurement to begin typing.

Other units of measure available in WordPerfect are

- centimeters
- points
- 1200ths of an inch
- WordPerfect version 4.2 units

The units of measure can be changed in the Setup, Environment menu: **[Shift] + [F1], 3, 8.**

4. The Function Keys

The function keys are the keys at the top or left-hand side of the keyboard labeled F1 through F10 or F12. WordPerfect utilizes all of these function keys. The keys F1 through F10 each have four separate functions. The F11 and F12 keys each have one function that are repeats of the often-used functions found on the F3 and F4 keys.

The F1 through F10 keys perform one function when pressed by themselves, and others when the [Alt], [Shift], or [Ctrl] keys are held while pressing them. The [Alt], [Shift], and [Ctrl] keys do not perform any task when they are pressed alone.

It is important that when you press a function key, you depress the key and immediately release it. Holding down a function key will cause it to repeat the function. The only keys that should be held down are the [Alt], [Shift], and [Ctrl] keys.

Below is a list of each of the function keys and their corresponding WordPerfect applications.

FUNCTION KEY	[CTRL] +	[ALT] +	[SHIFT] +	ALONE
F1	Shell	Thesaurus	Setup	Cancel
F2	Spell	Replace	Backward Search	Forward Search
F3	Screen	Reveal Codes	Switch	Help
F4	Move	Block	Left, Right Indent	Left Indent
F5	Text In/Out	Mark Text	Date/Outline	List Files

FUNCTION KEY	[CTRL] +	[ALT] +	[SHIFT] +	ALONE
F6	Tab Align	Flush Right	Center	Bold
F7	Footnote	Columns/Table	Print	Exit
F8	Font	Style	Format	Underline
F9	Merge/Sort	Graphics	Merge Codes	End Field
F10	Macro Define	Macro	Retrieve	Save
F11	Reveal Codes			
F12	Block			

> *If your function keys F1 and F3 do not seem to be functioning in the manner consistent with the above commands, the Keyboard Layout may have been set up for* **Alternate**. *The Alternate setup changes the [Esc] key to Cancel, the F1 key to Help, and the F3 key to the function of the [Esc] key. To change back to the* **Enhanced** *keyboard that corresponds to the above command structure, access the Setup menu, select Keyboard Layout, highlight "Enhanced" and press 1:*
>
> **[Shift]+[F1], 5, Enhanced, 1**

5. The Pull-Down Menus

WordPerfect version 5.1 for DOS added pull-down menus that can be accessed with a mouse or the keyboard. These menus offer another way to perform the commands found on the function keys.

The pull-down menus can be displayed or removed from the screen by pressing the mouse's right button or by pressing **[Alt] + [=]**. The WordPerfect screen display may be set up so that the pull-down menus are displayed at the top of the screen at all times. This is done with the Setup function, **[Shift] + [F1], 2, 4, 8.** The pull-down menus are shown in Figure 1.3.

WordPerfect® for DOS

```
File Edit Search Layout Mark Tools Font Graphics Help          (Press F3 for Help)


                    SUPERIOR COURT OF THE STATE OF CALIFORNIA

                    IN AND FOR THE COUNTY OF SAN DIEGO

THE ABC CORPORATION, a California  )     Case No. 100111
Corporation,                       )
                                   )     ANSWER OF DEFENDANT JOE
                Plaintiff,         )     SMITH
                                   )
          vs.                      )
                                   )
JOE SMITH, and DOES 1 through 50,  )
                                   )
                Defendants.        )
_____)

     Comes now Defendant JOE SMITH who responds to the Complaint on

file herein as follows:
C:\WORK\SMITH.ANS                        Doc 1 Pg 1 Ln 6" Pos 3.3"
```

Figure 1.3   The Pull-Down Menus

       To select an option from the pull–down menus using the mouse, move the mouse pointer to the top of the screen where the menus appear. The mouse pointer is a small highlighted square that appears when you move the mouse. Move the mouse pointer to a menu option and press the left mouse button to open the menu. An item within the menu is selected by moving the mouse pointer to the option and pressing the left mouse button. A selection is canceled by pressing the right mouse button or clicking the mouse outside of the menus.

       Using the keyboard, menus may be selected by pressing **[Alt] + [=]** and then using the **[Arrow]** keys to move between, and pull down, the menus. An option is selected by highlighting it and pressing the **[Enter]** key, or by pressing the highlighted letter corresponding to the option. The menus can be closed by pressing the right mouse button, pressing **[Alt] + [=]**, or pressing the **[Esc]** or **[F1]** key. The File menu is shown in Figure 1.4.

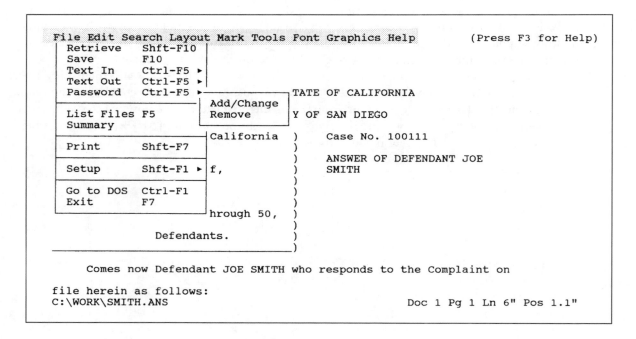

```
File Edit Search Layout Mark Tools Font Graphics Help        (Press F3 for Help)
   Retrieve     Shft-F10
   Save         F10
   Text In      Ctrl-F5 ►
   Text Out     Ctrl-F5 ►
   Password     Ctrl-F5 ► URT OF THE STATE OF CALIFORNIA

   List Files F5           OR THE COUNTY OF SAN DIEGO
   Summary
                           California  )    Case No. 100111
   Print        Shft-F7                )
                                       )    ANSWER OF DEFENDANT JOE
   Setup        Shft-F1 ►  f,          )    SMITH
                                       )
   Go to DOS    Ctrl-F1               )
   Exit         F7                    )
                           hrough 50,  )
                                       )
              Defendants.             )
                                       )

      Comes now Defendant JOE SMITH who responds to the Complaint on

   file herein as follows:
   C:\WORK\SMITH.ANS                        Doc 1 Pg 1 Ln 6" Pos 1.1"
```

Figure 1.4   The File Menu

An arrow to the right of a menu option indicates that there is a submenu to the option. Figure 1.5 displays the submenu of the menu selection: **File, Password.**

```
File Edit Search Layout Mark Tools Font Graphics Help        (Press F3 for Help)
   Retrieve     Shft-F10
   Save         F10
   Text In      Ctrl-F5 ►
   Text Out     Ctrl-F5 ►
   Password     Ctrl-F5 ►           TATE OF CALIFORNIA
                        Add/Change
   List Files F5        Remove      Y OF SAN DIEGO
   Summary
                           California  )    Case No. 100111
   Print        Shft-F7                )
                                       )    ANSWER OF DEFENDANT JOE
   Setup        Shft-F1 ►  f,          )    SMITH
                                       )
   Go to DOS    Ctrl-F1               )
   Exit         F7                    )
                           hrough 50,  )
                                       )
              Defendants.             )
                                       )

      Comes now Defendant JOE SMITH who responds to the Complaint on

   file herein as follows:
   C:\WORK\SMITH.ANS                        Doc 1 Pg 1 Ln 6" Pos 1.1"
```

Figure 1.5   The File, Password Submenu

6. WordPerfect Help

WordPerfect for DOS has one of the best Help facilities available in a word processor. The **[F3]** key accesses WordPerfect's Help menu (the [F1] key in the Alternate keyboard).

While in Help, you can receive help for a particular key or key combination, or you may locate the function keys necessary to perform an action in the Help index. An explanation of an individual key or a key combination is available by pressing the key or keys while in the Help facility. For example, the **[F2]** key, when pressed while in the Help facility, brings up the message shown in Figure 1.6.

```
Search

     Searches forward (F2) or backward (Shift-F2) through your text for a
     specific combination of characters and/or codes.  After entering the
     search text, press Search again to start the search.  If the text is
     found, the cursor will be positioned just after (to the right of) it.
     Lowercase letters in the search text match both lowercase and uppercase.
     Uppercase letters match only uppercase.

     Extended Search
     Pressing Home before pressing Search extends the search into headers,
     footers, footnotes, endnotes, graphics box captions, and text boxes.  To
     continue the extended search, press Home, Search.




Selection: 0                                      (Press ENTER to exit Help)
```

Figure 1.6   WordPerfect's Help for the [F2] Key

To see an index of WordPerfect features and their corresponding key combinations, you can press any letter of the alphabet while in the Help facility. For example, if you cannot remember how to change to double spacing, press the letter "S" for "spacing" while in the Help facility. Further pages of the "S" index can be seen by continuing to press the **[S]** key. "Spacing Lines" is found on the second screen of the "S" index as shown in Figure 1.7. The WordPerfect key for the command, as well as the actual keystrokes necessary to perform the command, are displayed.

To leave the Help facility, press the **[Space Bar]** or the **[Enter]** key. Further help can be obtained in a WordPerfect manual, through WordPerfect on-line message boards, through Corel's Web site at http://www.corel.com, or by calling Corel's WordPerfect user support (800) telephone number.

```
Features [S] (continued)          WordPerfect Key   Keystrokes

Set Tabs                          Format            Shft-F8,1,8
Settings, Initial (Default)       Setup             Shft-F1,4
Setup                             Setup             Shft-F1
Shadow Print                      Font              Ctrl-F8,2,6
Sheet Feeder                      Print             Shft-F7,s,3,3
Sheet Feeder Help                 Print             Shft-F7,s,6,Shft-F3
Shell, Go To                      Shell             Ctrl-F1,1
Short Form                        Mark Text         Alt-F5,4
Short Form, Table of Authorities  Mark Text         Alt-F5,4
Short/Long Filename Display       List              F5,Enter,5
Side-by-side Columns Display      Setup             Shft-F1,2,6,7
Size Attribute Ratios             Setup             Shft-F1,4,8,6
Size of Print (Attributes)        Font              Ctrl-F8,1
Small Capitalized Print           Font              Ctrl-F8,2,7
Small Print                       Font              Ctrl-F8,1,4
Soft Hyphen                       Soft Hyphen       Ctrl,-
Sort                              Merge/Sort        Ctrl-F9,2
Space, Hard                       Space Bar         Home,Space
Spacing Justification Limits      Format            Shft-F8,4,6,4
Spacing Lines                     Format            Shft-F8,1,6
More... Press s to continue.

Selection: 0                              (Press ENTER to exit Help)
```

Figure 1.7   Help for a particular feature can be found in the Help index
by pressing a letter corresponding to the feature

7.   Cursor Movement

The **cursor** is the flashing underline or box that appears on the screen. The cursor shows where characters will be entered as you type them on the keyboard. To practice moving the cursor, type a few lines of text onto the WordPerfect screen.

To move the cursor you may use the **[Arrow]** keys on your keyboard, the [Arrow] keys on the numeric keypad (be sure that [Num Lock] is off), or click on a new location with the mouse. The cursor may be moved to any position in your document, except to a position where you have not yet entered any text, spaces, or returns.

In addition to the [Arrow] keys, the following keystrokes may be used to move the cursor.

<u>KEYSTROKES</u>	<u>ACTION</u>
[End] or **[Home], [Right Arrow]**	To move to the end of a line.
[Home], [Left Arrow]	To move to the beginning of a line.
[Ctrl], [Right or Left Arrow]	To move one word to the left or right.
[Home], [Up Arrow]	To move to the top of the screen.

KEYSTROKES	ACTION
[Home], [Down Arrow]	To move to the bottom of the screen.
[Home], [Home], [Up Arrow]	To move to the top of the document.
[Home], [Home], [Down Arrow]	To move to the bottom of the document.
[Home], [Home], [Home], [Up Arrow]	To move to the top of the document in front of all codes.
[Page Up]	To move up one page.
[Page Down]	To move down one page.
[Ctrl] + [Home]	The Go To key combination. To move to a specific page. You will be prompted for a page number.

8. Insert Versus Typeover

There are two typing modes in WordPerfect, Insert and Typeover. When you enter WordPerfect, the program is in the Insert mode.

In the Insert mode, text that already exists will be pushed to the right as you enter new text. In the Typeover mode, text that is typed will overwrite existing text and spaces.

To "toggle" between Insert and Typeover, press the **[Insert]** key. When you are in the Typeover mode, the word "Typeover" will appear in the lower left corner of your screen.

9. Switching Between Documents

WordPerfect allows you to work on two separate documents simultaneously within the program. You switch between the two documents by pressing **[Shift] + [F3].**

When you first enter WordPerfect, you are in Document 1. You can tell which document you are in by checking the Status Line at the bottom of the screen. You can retrieve a document into Document 1 at this point or begin drafting a new document. When you move to Document 2, with [Shift] + [F3], you may retrieve, or begin drafting, another document. The benefit of having two documents in WordPerfect at the same time is that text can be moved or copied from one document to the other. This feature is useful when you are taking text from an old document to draft a new document. You can be drafting the new document in Document 1 and retrieve the old document into Document 2. Then, text from Document 2 can be copied into Document 1 where it is needed.

C. EDITING A DOCUMENT

1. Deletions

When editing a document, deletions of a character or a group of characters will need to be made. WordPerfect offers a variety of ways to delete text. The two primary keys that perform deletions are **[Delete]** and **[Backspace].**

KEYSTROKES	ACTION
[Delete]	Deletes the character directly above the cursor.
[Backspace]	Deletes the character immediately to the left of the cursor.

To delete more than one character at a time, the **[Delete]** and **[Backspace]** keys may be held down, or the following key combinations may be used.

KEYSTROKES	ACTION
[Ctrl] + [Delete] or **[Ctrl] + [Backspace]**	Deletes the word currently containing the cursor, or the word to the immediate left of the cursor.
[Home], [Backspace]	Deletes to the left of the cursor to the beginning of the previous word.
[Ctrl] + [End]	Deletes all characters from the cursor to the end of the current line.
[Ctrl] + [Page Down]	Deletes all text to the bottom of the current page.

2. Blocking Text

Blocking text is the marking of text prior to performing some action upon the text. Blocking text is a function of **[Alt] + [F4]** or the **[F12]** key. The cursor is moved to the beginning of the text to be blocked, and Block is selected using either function key option. A blinking **Block on** will appear in the lower left-hand corner of the screen. Moving the cursor with the [Arrow] keys will highlight the text to be blocked. When the desired text is highlighted, actions such as moving, copying, deleting, saving, and printing may be performed upon the block.

When highlighting text, the highlighting may be moved with any of the keys you normally use to move the cursor. You may also press any character on the keyboard to move the highlight to the next occurrence of that character within the document. For example, pressing a period will move the highlight block to the end of the sentence. Pressing the **[Enter]** key will move it to the end of a paragraph.

To highlight text using a mouse, move the mouse pointer to the beginning of the text to be highlighted, hold down the left mouse button, and then drag the highlight to cover the desired text.

A highlight can be removed by pressing **[Alt] + [F4], [F12],** or by clicking the left mouse button outside of the highlighted text.

---

*Occasionally you will need to perform more than one action upon a block, such as bolding and underlining a **word or phrase**. To do this, you would block the text once and perform the bold or underline. The same text can then be blocked again by turning on the block function and pressing **[Ctrl]+[Home]** twice. The remaining action, bold or underline, may then be performed.*

---

3. Deleting a Block

If you wish to delete a block of text, highlight the text and press the **[Delete]** key. As a safety feature, WordPerfect will ask you in the lower left-hand corner of the screen if you really wish to delete the block. Select **Y** or **N.**

4. Retrieving Deleted Text (Undelete)

WordPerfect saves you if you have deleted text that you wanted to keep.

The [F1] (Cancel) key will restore any of your three previous deletions. Move the cursor to where you want the text to return and press **[F1].** The text last deleted from the document will appear at the cursor, and the following options will be displayed at the bottom of the screen:

> **Undelete: 1** Restore; **2** Previous Deletion: **0**

Select **1** if the displayed deletion is the one you wish to restore. Select **2** to display the other two previous deletions. Continuing to press **2** will toggle between the three deletions. When the desired deletion is displayed, select **1** to restore it.

5. Canceling a Command

The [F1] (Cancel) key can also be used to cancel a command or back out of a menu or screen. For example, if you have turned on the Block command inadvertently, pressing the **[F1]** key will cancel the Block command.

6. Centering

Centering a word or phrase can be accomplished in a number of ways.

a. *Before Typing Text*

Document titles and pleading headings often need to appear in the center of the printed page. To center text which you will be typing, press **[Shift] + [F6]**. This command places the cursor in the center of the screen. Type the text and press the **[Enter]** key.

b. *After Typing Text*

If the text to be centered has been typed at the left margin, move the cursor to the beginning of the text and press **[Shift] + [F6]**. Use the **[Down Arrow]** key to move down to the next line, or press the **[End]** key to move to the end of the line and press **[Enter]**.

c. *Setting Center Justification*

If you have more than one line that needs to be centered, you may select center justification, **[Shift] + [F8], 1, 3, 2**. You will need to press **[F7]** or the **[Enter]** key twice to return to the WordPerfect screen. All text that you type at this point will be centered. Try turning on the center justification at the left margin and type the text below.

ARTICLES OF INCORPORATION
OF
XYZ CORPORATION

To return to full justification, select **[Shift] + [F8], 1, 3, 4**.

> *Full justification will result in a document with the text aligned against the left and right margins. Left justification will align the text against the left margin and leave the right margin ragged. Right justification will align the text against the right margin and leave the left margin ragged.*

d. *Blocking and Centering*

Another way of center justifying more than one line is to type the lines at the left margin, and then block the lines and press **[Shift] + [F6]**. Try typing the text below, and then block and center the text. WordPerfect will ask you if you wish to center justify; answer yes.

ARTICLES OF INCORPORATION
OF
XYZ CORPORATION

WordPerfect will return you to your selected justification after centering the text.

7. Boldface Type

Occasionally, you will want a word, or sequence of words, to stand out in **boldface type.** For example, a brief can appear more authoritative when the heading for each point stands out from the rest of the text as shown below.

B.
DEFENDANT HAS THE BURDEN OF
SHOWING THAT THE COUNTY IN WHICH
THE ACTION IS BROUGHT IS IMPROPER

It is the Defendant's burden to offer sufficient facts to show to this Court that San Diego County is not the proper court to hear the case. <u>Massae v. Superior Court,</u> 118 Cal. App. 3d 527, 530, 173 Cal. Rptr. 527 (1981).

Boldfacing can be performed while the text is being entered, or later by blocking the text and selecting the Bold command.

a. *Before Typing Text*

To type in boldface print, press **[F6]** prior to typing the text to be boldfaced. With many monitors, you will see the position measurement in the Status Line become brighter when you press **[F6].** When you have finished typing the text that is to be boldfaced, press **[F6]** again.

b. *After Typing Text*

If you have already typed the text you desire to be boldfaced, **Block** the text, and then press **[F6].**

8. Underlining

Underlining is used to <u>emphasize</u> a character, word, or block of text. As you can see in the example from the brief, case names are underlined (or italicized). Underlining is performed in the same manner as boldfacing. Note that if you are using a color monitor, underlining may appear as a highlight. The printed copy will contain the underline.

a. *Before Typing Text*

To underline a word or passage, press **[F8]**, type the text, and then press the **[F8]** key again.

b. *After Typing Text*

If what you wish to be underlined has already been typed, **Block** the text and then press **[F8].**

9. Italicizing

Italicizing is accomplished in the same manner as boldfacing and underlining. The italicizing feature is either activated before typing the text and then turned off at the end of entering the text, or existing text is highlighted and then the italicizing is activated. Italics are used in legal documents as an alternative to underlining. This feature is accessed in WordPerfect with **[Ctrl] + [F8], 2, 4.** The italicized text will appear in a different color on the monitor. To return to a normal type, press **[Ctrl] + [F8], 3.**

PRACTICE EXERCISE

Using some of the commands covered thus far, let us take a portion of an old complaint and conform it to a set of facts for a new case.

The preliminary paragraphs of the old complaint are shown below. These are the paragraphs that can be used to establish the venue for a complaint. Type these paragraphs into WordPerfect. Use the [Tab] key to indent the numbered paragraphs. (You do not need to start with a blank screen to perform this exercise.)

Plaintiff JOHN PORT alleges:

1. Plaintiff, JOHN PORT, is, and at all times herein mentioned was, a resident of Los Angeles County, California.

2. Plaintiff is informed and believes, and on that basis alleges, that Defendant, MARK SAMPSON, is, and at all times herein mentioned was, an individual residing in Los Angeles County, California.

Now, using some of the WordPerfect commands that we learned above, we will revise these opening paragraphs to conform to the new facts. The new facts are that Plaintiff, Joe Smith, is suing ABCD Corporation, a California corporation. The new plaintiff and defendant reside within the same jurisdiction as the old parties.

a) Begin the revision by moving the cursor to the beginning of the first mention of "JOHN PORT." Using the **[Delete]** key, delete the entire name. Then, type the name of our new plaintiff "JOE SMITH" in this space.

b) Next, move to the "J" at the second "JOHN PORT" and use **[Ctrl] + [Backspace]** to remove both words. Then, type in "JOE SMITH."

c) Now, move to paragraph 2 of the complaint and remove the name of the old defendant with **[Ctrl] + [Backspace].** Replace the name with "ABCD CORPORATION."

d) The capacity of this defendant needs to be changed to reflect its status as a corporation. Move to the "a" at the beginning of "an individual" and turn the Block feature on with **[Alt] + [F4]** or **[F12]** so that we may perform a Block Delete. Extend the block highlight to the end of the sentence with the arrow keys or by pressing the period **[.]** key. Then, press the **[Delete]** key and respond with a **Y** for yes.

e) Now, type in the following: "a corporation organized pursuant to the laws of the State of California, having its principal office in Los Angeles County, California."

Your new paragraphs should look as follows:

Plaintiff JOE SMITH alleges:

1. Plaintiff, JOE SMITH, is, and at all times herein mentioned was, a resident of Los Angeles County, California.

2. Plaintiff is informed and believes, and on that basis alleges, that Defendant, ABCD CORPORATION, is, and at all times herein mentioned was, a corporation organized pursuant to the laws of the State of California, having its principal office in Los Angeles County, California.

D. SAVING AND RETRIEVING FILES

To save a document, you must store it on some type of secondary storage device (magnetic disk, tape, etc.), and give it a name. To retrieve a document, you must identify where it is stored and the name of the document. Remember that, as you are typing a document in WordPerfect, the document is temporarily stored in RAM. If your computer is turned off, a power outage occurs, or the computer or network suddenly crashes, your RAM and your document are erased.

There are two methods for saving documents in WordPerfect for DOS, **Save and Continue** and **Save and Exit.**

There are also two methods for retrieving documents, **Retrieve (Open)** and **List Files.** These methods will be discussed below.

1. Save and Continue

The **[F10]** key allows you to save a document and continue working. I recommend that Save and Continue be used often while drafting a document. That way, if there is a loss of power to the computer, you will only lose the text that has not yet been saved. WordPerfect's Automatic Backup feature will also save your document in the event of a loss of power to the computer. However, it should not be relied on so much that you disregard the [F10] key.

AUTOMATIC BACKUP

*WordPerfect versions 5.1 and later offer a feature that automatically backs up your document. This backup occurs according to a time that you have set in the WordPerfect **Setup Menu** under **Environment: [Shift]+[F1], 3, 1** (e.g., every 10 minutes).*

*The backup file that is created is erased if you exit WordPerfect properly using the **[F7]** key. However, in the event that the computer is accidentally turned off, or loses power for any reason, the backup file is saved to the drive and directory indicated in the **Setup Menu** under **Location of Files: [Shift]+[F1], 6, 1** or to the location of the WordPerfect program files. The backup file is given the extension ".**BK1**".*

When you reenter WordPerfect, you will be asked if any other copies of WordPerfect are currently running. You answer "No," if this is the case, and WordPerfect will prompt you to rename the backup file or delete it. Rename the backup file if you want to keep the document.

If your document has never been saved, the following message will appear when the **[F10]** key is pressed.

Document to be saved:

At this point, you enter the drive and directory where you would like the file to be stored, and give the file a name. In WordPerfect the document name can be one to eight characters with an optional period and one- to three-character extension. An example of an appellate brief being stored in the \Smith directory of the C: drive is shown below.

Document to be saved:C:\SMITH\APPELLAT.BRF

If you would like to practice saving your current document, at the "Document to be saved:" prompt, specify where you would like the document to be saved (A:, B:, C:), and give your file a name. You may also simply type in a name for your file without a drive letter. The document will be saved to the default drive and directory designated in the **Setup Menu, [Shift] + [F1], 6, 7,** or to the location of the WordPerfect program files. It is not a good practice to type in a file name without specifying a drive and directory. Many times the files will become commingled with the WordPerfect program files and cause disk organization problems.

After typing the document name, pressing the **[Enter]** key saves the document. The document path and name will be displayed in the lower left-hand corner of the screen.

If the document has previously been saved, pressing the **[F10]** key will display the following message.

Document to be saved:C:\SMITH\APPELLAT.BRF

Pressing the **[Enter]** key to confirm the document name will bring up the next message:

Replace C:\SMITH\APPELLAT.BRF? No (Yes)

Pressing **Y** will replace the stored version of your document with the current document on the screen. It is important that you respond "Yes" here if you wish to save your document. However, if this is a new document that you are saving for the first time, receiving the "Replace" message means that you already have another document with this name. If this is the case, respond "No" and repeat the process giving your document a different name.

2.   Save and Exit

The **[F7]** key allows you to Save your document and exit to a blank WordPerfect screen or to DOS. The messages that you receive are similar to the Save and Continue messages.

When **[F7]** is pressed, a message asking if you wish to save the document appears in the lower left-hand corner of the screen:

Save document? Yes (No)

Pressing the **[Enter]** key, or **Y**, will answer yes to this question.

You will then be prompted with the same messages as with Save and Continue. After responding to these messages, a message asking if you wish to exit WordPerfect will appear:

Exit WP? No (Yes)

Responding with the **[Enter]** key, or **N**, will give you a blank WordPerfect screen to begin a new document. Responding with **Y** will exit the program. Pressing the **[F1]** (Cancel) key will return you to your current document. If you are following along with this Workbook, respond "No" to this prompt so that you may continue working in the program.

3. Retrieve

The **[Shift] + [F10]** key combination allows you to retrieve a document by name. It is important that you have a blank WordPerfect screen before you retrieve a document, unless you intend to retrieve the document into the one in which you are currently working.

The [Shift] + [F10] command will prompt you for the location and name of the document as shown below.

Document to be retrieved:

At this point you will type the drive, directory, and file name of the document and press **[Enter].** For example:

Document to be retrieved:C:\SMITH\APPELLAT.BRF

In newer versions of WordPerfect for DOS, there are two options for retrieving documents: **open** and **retrieve.** The open option will open a document into a blank WordPerfect screen. The retrieve option will insert a document into the current document on the screen.

4. List Files

The **[F5]** key gives you a list of the files located within a specific directory. When this feature is selected, the current default directory (the pre-set storage location) is displayed in the lower left-hand corner of the screen as shown in Figure 1.8.

```
Dir C:\WP51\*.*                              (Type = to change default Dir)
```

Figure 1.8   Pressing [F5], List Files, displays the directory of the files to be listed and allows you to change the directory

If this is the location of the files you wish to see, you may press the **[Enter]** key here. You may also type a different location, such as **"C:\SMITH"**. Pressing the **[Enter]** key will list the files.

If you intend to be working primarily within the SMITH directory, you may wish to change it to the default directory while you are working on the Smith documents. After you have pressed **[F5],** pressing the **[=]** key will let you change the default directory. Typing **"C:\Smith"** and pressing the **[Enter]** key twice will change the default directory and take you to the list of the files as shown in Figure 1.9.

```
01-14-92   01:32p                  Directory C:\SMITH\*.*
Document size:        0  Free:  5,380,096 Used:        12,821      Files:          6

   .     Current   <Dir>             ..     Parent    <Dir>
APPELLAT.BRF         327  01-14-92 01:32p   DEPO    .OTL   2,263  08-09-91 05:21a
INVOICE .DBF         262  11-22-91 07:54p   INVOICE .DBT   2,560  11-22-91 07:54p
INVOICE .MDX       4,096  11-22-91 07:54p   NETWORTH.WK1   3,313  05-07-91 06:10p












 1 Retrieve; 2 Delete; 3 Move/Rename; 4 Print; 5 Short/Long Display;
 6 Look; 7 Other Directory; 8 Copy; 9 Find; N Name Search: 6
```

Figure 1.9   The List Files Screen

In the List Files screen, you may retrieve a file, or perform some other action upon it, by highlighting the file name with the **[Arrow]** keys and selecting the number of an action shown at the bottom of the screen.

You may look at a file before you retrieve it by highlighting the file name and pressing the **[Enter]** key or the number **6.** When you are looking at a document in this manner, the format may be different than when it is actually retrieved into the WordPerfect screen. You may return to List Files from looking at a document by pressing the **[Enter]** key or the **[Space Bar].**

You may perform actions on several files simultaneously by marking the desired file names with an asterisk ([*]). You may mark individual files by highlighting the file names and pressing the **[*]** key. You may mark all of the files by pressing **[Home], [*].** The marks may be removed by highlighting individual file names and again pressing the **[*]** key, or by pressing **[Home], [*].**

If you accidentally return to the WordPerfect screen from List Files before you have completed your selections, you may resume where you left off in List Files by pressing the **[F5]** key twice.

The options available in the List Files screen are explained below.

1 Retrieve		Retrieves the highlighted document into the WordPerfect screen.
2 Delete		Deletes the highlighted document.
3 Move/Rename		Renames the highlighted document (if you wish) and/or moves the file to a new location.
4 Print		Prints the highlighted document without your having to retrieve it into WordPerfect.
5 Short/Long Display		Allows you to switch between short and long document names, if you have elected to use long document names.
6 Look		Lets you look at the highlighted document prior to retrieving. You may not alter the document in Look.
7 Other Directory		Lets you change within List Files to another directory.
8 Copy		Lets you copy the highlighted document to another location.
9 Find		Lets you search the files in the current directory for a specific file name or words or phrases present within the body of a document. This is a valuable feature when you cannot remember what you have named a file.
N Name Search		Highlights the file name that most closely resembles the characters that you enter.

You may leave the List Files screen by pressing the **[Space Bar]** or the **[F7]** or **[F1]** (Cancel) key.

If you would like to permanently change the default directory so that all files will be stored in a certain location unless otherwise specified, you may do this in the **Setup Menu** *under* **Location of Files, [Shift] + [F1], 6, 7.**

E. MOVING AND COPYING TEXT

When editing a document, it is often necessary to move or copy text from one position to another. Moving text removes it from its old location and places it in a new location that you select. In newer versions, this is called "cut and paste." Copying leaves the original text in place and copies that text to a new location. In newer versions, this is called "copy and paste." To move or copy text, you can Block it and then select the Move or Copy command. If you are moving or copying a *sentence*, *paragraph*, or *page*, you can go directly to the command without blocking.

1. Blocking and Moving or Copying

The steps for Blocking and Moving or Copying text are essentially the same.

a) Turn the **Block** on with **[Alt] + [F4]** or the **[F12]** key, and highlight the text to be moved or copied.

b) While the **Block on** is flashing in the lower left-hand corner of the screen, select **[Ctrl] + [F4].** The following options are displayed at the bottom of the screen.

> **Move: 1 B**lock; **2 T**abular Column; **3 R**ectangle: **0**

Even though the options begin with the word "Move," this command is also used for copying.

c) Select **1** for **Block,** because we are moving or copying a block of text. The following options are then displayed.

> **1 M**ove; **2 C**opy; **3 D**elete; **4 A**ppend: **0**

d) Select **1** for **Move,** or **2** for **Copy.** The following instruction is then displayed.

> Move cursor; press **Enter** to retrieve.

e) Move the cursor to where you want the text to be moved or copied, and press the **[Enter]** key.

2. Moving or Copying a Sentence, Paragraph, or Page

WordPerfect saves you the trouble of having to block the text when you are moving or copying a sentence, paragraph, or page. Once again, the steps for moving and copying are essentially the same.

a) Place the cursor within the sentence, paragraph, or page you wish to move or copy.

b) Press **[Ctrl] + [F4].** The following options will be displayed.

> **Move: 1** Sentence; **2 P**aragraph; **3** Page; **4** Retrieve: **0**

Even though the options begin with the word "Move," this command is also used for copying.

c) Select the number corresponding to what you wish to move or copy. The following options are then displayed.

> **1** Move; **2 C**opy; **3 D**elete; **4 A**ppend: **0**

d) Select **1** for **Move,** or **2** for **Copy.** The following instruction is then displayed.

> Move cursor; press **Enter** to retrieve.

e) Move the cursor to where you want the text to be moved or copied and press the **[Enter]** key.

Canceling a Move command. You will have a problem if you cancel a Move command while you are moving the cursor to the new location. Pressing the [F1] (Cancel) key at this point cancels the Move but, since the first part of the move sequence removes the text from the old location, the text is gone. You may retrieve the text by placing the cursor at its original location and using [Ctrl] + [F4], selecting 4 for Retrieve and then 1 for Block: [Ctrl] + [F4], 4, 1.

---

3. Quick Cut and Paste

There is a special feature that will allow you to perform a quick move on a block of text. Block the text you want to move and press **[Backspace], [Y]** to cut it from the document. Move your cursor to the new location and paste the text in by pressing **[F1], [1].** You may paste the same text in other locations by repeating the **[F1], [1]** keystrokes. The steps of this command delete the blocked text and then restore the text in the new location.

Even though this feature is primarily used for the movement of text, it can also be useful for quickly copying a block of text to many different locations. For example, suppose that you are responding to a set of discovery requests and the responses to the first four requests are all to be an objection based on the ground that the information sought is not relevant to the subject matter of the lawsuit. This feature could be used to quickly paste the objection into all four responses. The exercise below will illustrate this process.

On the WordPerfect screen, type the following numbers at the left margin:

1.

2.

3.

4.

Moving your cursor to just after the "1.", press the **[Tab]** key and type the following:

>This responding party objects to this request on the ground that it seeks information that is beyond the scope of permissible discovery. The information sought is not relevant to the subject matter of this litigation and is not likely to lead to the discovery of admissible evidence.

We could perform individual copy commands to copy this text to responses 2, 3, and 4, but it will be quicker to cut the text and then paste it for all four responses. To do this, follow the steps below.

a) Move the cursor to just after the "1." (Make sure that the cursor is in front of the space created by the [Tab] key.)

b) Turn the Block feature on with **[Alt] + [F4]** or **[F12]** and press the period key **[.]** twice to highlight to the end of the objection.

c) Press **[Backspace], [Y].**

d) To paste the text back after the "1.", press **[F1], 1.** To paste the text to responses 2, 3, and 4, move the cursor to just after the period in each response number and press **[F1], 1.**

F. OTHER WORDPERFECT FEATURES

1. Margins and Line Spacing

Margins, line spacing, and a number of other page and document settings are adjusted in the Format screen shown in Figure 1.10. The Format screen is accessed with **[Shift] + [F8].**

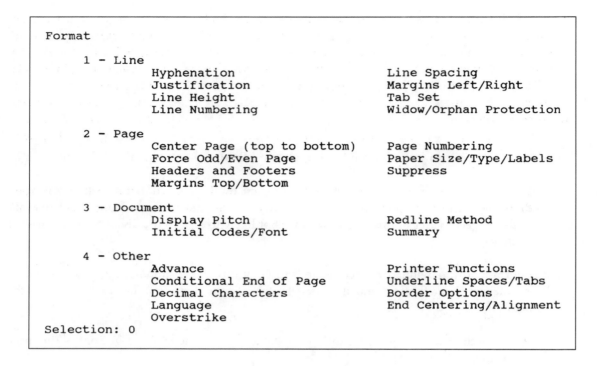

```
Format

    1 - Line
                Hyphenation                     Line Spacing
                Justification                   Margins Left/Right
                Line Height                     Tab Set
                Line Numbering                  Widow/Orphan Protection

    2 - Page
                Center Page (top to bottom)     Page Numbering
                Force Odd/Even Page             Paper Size/Type/Labels
                Headers and Footers             Suppress
                Margins Top/Bottom

    3 - Document
                Display Pitch                   Redline Method
                Initial Codes/Font              Summary

    4 - Other
                Advance                         Printer Functions
                Conditional End of Page         Underline Spaces/Tabs
                Decimal Characters              Border Options
                Language                        End Centering/Alignment
                Overstrike
Selection: 0
```

Figure 1.10   The Format Screen

Left and right margins are adjusted under selection **1–Line.** Top and bottom margins are adjusted under selection **2–Page.** Line spacing is adjusted under selection **1–Line.** You may select single, double, or any other increment of spacing, whether it be 1.25 or 6 lines.

2.   Tabs and Indenting

The [Tab] key and the [F4] key serve the functions of tab and indent, respectively. The spacing for tabbing and indenting is set in the Format screen by selecting **Line** and then **Tab Set: [Shift] + [F8], 1, 8.** Normally the tabs are pre-set to occur every five spaces on the screen.

To change the tabs, access Tab Set with **[Shift] + [F8], 1, 8.** The Tab Set bar is shown in Figure 1.11.

```
L....L....L....L....L....L....L....L....L....L....L....L....L....L....L....L...
|    ^    |    ^    |    ^    |    ^    |    ^    |    ^    |    ^    |    ^
0"        +1"       +2"       +3"       +4"       +5"       +6"       +7"
Ctrl-End (clear tabs); Enter Number (set tab); Del (clear tab);
Type; Left; Center; Right; Decimal; .= Dot Leader; Press Exit when done.
```

Figure 1.11   The Tab Set Bar

The current tab settings are indicated by the letter L. Unwanted tabs may be deleted by moving the cursor to them and pressing the **[Delete]** key. All the current tab settings may be deleted by moving the cursor to the leftmost tab stop and pressing **[Ctrl] + [End].** To set new tabs, move to where you want the tab, with the **[Arrow]** keys or the **[Space Bar],** and press the **[Tab]** key. You may also type a position number and press **[Enter]** to have a tab placed at an exact location. For example, if you need a tab at exactly 3.25 inches, type **3.25** and press **[Enter].** If you want the first tab to begin at one inch and then have tabs every inch after that, you could type **1, 1** and press **[Enter].** You leave the tab screen by pressing the **[F7]** key. Pressing **[F7]** again will return you to the document.

Within your document, you may tab with the **[Tab]** key, or indent with the **[F4]** key. The **[Tab]** key indents the first line of the text to a tab stop. After the first line, the text will word wrap back to the left margin like the text in this paragraph.

The **[F4]** Indent key indents the entire paragraph to the tab stop. The text will word wrap to the tab stop until the **[Enter]** key is pressed at the end of the paragraph.

The **[Shift] + [F4]** key combination indents both the right and left margins to a tab stop. The text will word wrap within the indent until the **[Enter]** key is pressed at the end of a paragraph. This is called a double indent.

The **[F4], [Shift] + [Tab]** key combination leaves the first line of the paragraph at the left margin, and subsequent text word wraps to the tab stop until the **[Enter]** key is pressed at the end of the paragraph. This is called a hanging indent.

The tab and indent features are used frequently when typing legal documents. An example using [Shift] + [F4] and the [Tab] key is shown below. In practice, quoted material of 50 words or more should be indented from both the left and right margins. The material should not be enclosed with quotation marks, and any such marks within the quoted material should remain as they are in the material.

After the double indent in the quotation below, the [Tab] key should be used to tab-in the first line of the quoted paragraph. Try typing the material below to practice these features.

Rule 373 states in pertinent part:

> **In ruling on the motion the court shall consider all matters relevant to a proper determination of the motion, including the court's file in the case and the affidavits and declarations and supporting data submitted by the parties and, where applicable, . . . the diligence of the parties in pursuing discovery or other pretrial proceedings, . . . the nature of any extensions of time or other delay attributable to either party, . . . whether the interests of justice are best served by dismissal or trial of the case; and any other fact or circumstance relevant to a fair determination of the issue.**

The interests of justice would best be served by a trial on the merits in this action. Therefore, plaintiff herein should be allowed to proceed to trial.

3. Reveal Codes

WordPerfect hides its formatting codes to allow you to work with a clean screen. To view the formatting codes, you need to access the **Reveal Codes** feature within **[Alt] + [F3]** or **[F11]**. When accessed, Reveal Codes divides the screen, displaying the normal text at the top and the text with codes at the bottom as shown in Figure 1.12.

Revealing codes is useful when you wish to delete a **bold,** <u>underline</u>, tab, or other code that has been inserted into a document. It is also useful when your document suddenly begins to do something that you did not intend it to do.

```
      Revealing codes is useful when you wish to delete a bold,
underline,      tab or other code which has been inserted into a
document.  It is also useful when your document suddenly
            begins to do
            something that
            you did not
            intend it to
            do.


                                    Doc 2 Pg 1 Ln 1.17" Pos 1"
{   ▲    ▲    ▲    ▲    ▲    ▲    ▲    ▲    ▲    ▲    ▲    ▲    }   ▲
[HRt]
[Tab]Revealing codes is useful when you wish to delete a [BOLD]bold[bold],[SRt]
[UND]underline[und],[Tab]tab or other code which has been inserted into a[SRt]
document.  It is also useful when your document suddenly[HRt]
[L/R Mar:2.5",4.5"]begins to do[SRt]
something that[SRt]
you did not[SRt]
intend it to[SRt]
do.[HRt]
[HRt]

Press Reveal Codes to restore screen
```

Figure 1.12   The hidden codes of a document revealed with Reveal Codes

The Reveal Codes feature, shown in Figure 1.12, displays the actual codes present within the text. You can see that a bolded word is preceded by an uppercase **[BOLD],** and followed by a lowercase **[bold].** This indicates where the bold begins and where it ends. An underlined word is indicated in the same manner with **[UND]** and **[und]** codes. Where the **[Enter]** key has been pressed is indicated by a hard return (**[Hrt]**). A word wrap is indicated by a soft return (**[Srt]**).

Using the **[Arrow]** keys to move the cursor in the upper half of the screen also moves a highlight bar in the lower half of the screen. To remove any of the codes, move the highlight bar to the code and press the **[Delete]** key. With a bold or underline, deleting either the uppercase or lowercase code will remove both codes.

The margin problem with this text begins with a margin code (**[L/R Mar:2.5″,4.5″]**) that has inadvertently made its way into the text. To remove it you would move the highlight bar to the code and press the **[Delete]** key.

Reveal Codes is turned off by again pressing either **[Alt]** + **[F3]** or the **[F11]** key.

4. Page Breaks

When you reach the bottom of a page in your document, a single hashed line will appear across the screen as shown in Figure 1.13. This single hashed line is called a soft page break. WordPerfect automatically ends a page with a soft page break according to the pre-set page length of your document.

```
    WHEREAS, the Directors of the Corporation desire to hold

monthly regular meetings in addition to the annual meeting of the

Board;

    NOW, THEREFORE BE IT RESOLVED, that the Board of Directors of

the corporation shall hold regular meetings on the first Monday of

each month at 1:00 p.m.;

    FURTHER RESOLVED, that Article III, Section 8, of the Bylaws

of the corporation is hereby amended to reflect these changes in

the dates of the meetings of the Board of Directors.  The Secretary

of the corporation is hereby directed to make a notation of this
------------------------------------------------------------------------
change in the Bylaws of the corporation.


C:\WORK\XYZCORP.MIN                          Doc 1 Pg 2 Ln 1.33" Pos 1"
```

Figure 1.13 A single hashed line appears where WordPerfect automatically ends a page

When you wish to end a page in a place other than where the soft page break occurs, you can use a **hard page break.** In the example shown in Figure 1.13 above, a hard page break could be used to make the current page stop after the second paragraph. To create a hard page break, the cursor is placed where you want the new page to begin and **[Ctrl] + [Enter]** is pressed. A double hashed line indicates the location of a hard page break as shown in Figure 1.14.

```
     WHEREAS, the Directors of the Corporation desire to hold

monthly regular meetings in addition to the annual meeting of the

Board;

     NOW, THEREFORE BE IT RESOLVED, that the Board of Directors of

the corporation shall hold regular meetings on the first Monday of

each month at 1:00 p.m.;


===============================================================================
     FURTHER RESOLVED, that Article III, Section 8, of the Bylaws

of the corporation is hereby amended to reflect these changes in

the dates of the meetings of the Board of Directors.  The Secretary

of the corporation is hereby directed to make a notation of this

change in the Bylaws of the corporation.
C:\WORK\XYZCORP.MIN                              Doc 1 Pg 2 Ln 1" Pos 1"
```

Figure 1.14   A hard page break is indicated by a double hashed line

A hard page break is indicated by a **[HPg]** code in Reveal Codes. A soft page break is indicated by a **[SPg]** code.

5.   Text Appearances and Sizes

In addition to bolding and underlining, text may be <u>double underlined</u>, *italicized*, outlined, shadowed, SMALL CAPPED, redlined, or ~~stricken out~~, using different text appearances. Text Appearance is selected with **[Ctrl] + [F8], 2.** The type of appearance is then selected. To turn off the appearance and return to normal typing, press the **[Right Arrow]** key to move outside of the code, or use **[Ctrl] + [F8], 3.** If the text has already been typed, it can be blocked prior to using **[Ctrl] + [F8], 2.**

Text may also be printed in different sizes. The sizes, superscript, subscript, fine, small, large, very large, and extra large, may be selected with **[Ctrl] + [F8], 1.** To turn off the size and return to normal typing, press the **[Right Arrow]** key to move outside of the code, or use **[Ctrl] + [F8], 3.** If the text has already been typed, it can be blocked prior to using **[Ctrl] + [F8], 1.**

6. Changing Fonts

Fonts are the typeface of a document. The initial font of your document, called the "Base Font," is listed in the Format Menu, **[Shift] + [F8], 3, 3.** You may change the Initial Font at this menu. Subsequent font changes in your document may be made in the Base Font screen, using **[Ctrl] + [F8], 4.** At the font screen, highlight the desired font and press **1** to select the font. If you select a scalable font, you will be prompted for a point size. After making a selection, you will be returned to the WordPerfect screen, and further type will be printed in the new font. The type does not change on the screen.

You may notice that your screen margins will change as you change fonts. This is due to the changing size of the type. A code indicating where the new font begins can be seen in Reveal Codes.

7. The Date Feature

WordPerfect provides a way to incorporate the date from your computer's internal clock into documents. The Date feature, **[Shift] + [F5],** allows you to place the current date or a date code within a document. Selecting **1** inserts the current date; selecting **2** inserts a date code. Both options place the current date within a document. The date code, however, will place the current date into the document each time the document is retrieved into WordPerfect.

8. Spell Checking

Checking the spelling within a document is one of the great features of a word processor. The Spell Check feature will read each word within the document and compare it to the words within its dictionary. When it finds a word that does not match, the spell checker will stop and give alternative spellings, and/or allow you to edit your spelling.

It is important that you do a Save and Continue, **[F10],** prior to spell checking your document. The Spell Check feature has been known to freeze computers, requiring that the computer be restarted, thus erasing the RAM where the document is stored.

WordPerfect's Spell Check feature is accessed with **[Ctrl] + [F2].** When you press **[Ctrl] + [F2],** the main options are

1   to check the **Word** containing the cursor

2   to check the current **Page**

3   to check the entire **Document**

When Spell Check finds a word it does not recognize, the list of alternative spellings is supplied on the bottom half of the screen as shown in Figure 1.15. You may select one of these spellings by typing its corresponding letter. If the word is not misspelled, select one of the options at the bottom of the screen to skip the word and continue.

```
    WHEREAS, the Directors of the Corporation desire to hold

monthly regular meetings in adition to the annual meeting of the

Board;

    NOW, THEREFORE BE IT RESOLVED, that the Board of Directors of

                                             Doc 1 Pg 1 Ln 7" Pos 3.8"
{    ▲     ▲     ▲     ▲     ▲     ▲     ▲     ▲     ▲     ▲     ▲     )     ▲     ▲

    A. addition          B. aditio            C. aditios
    D. audition          E. adaption          F. adhesion
    G. adoption          H. edition           I. ideation




Not Found: 1 Skip Once; 2 Skip; 3 Add; 4 Edit; 5 Look Up; 6 Ignore Numbers: 0
```

Figure 1.15   The Spell Check Feature

If a word is found by Spell Check to be misspelled, but the proper spelling is not provided, press **4** to Edit the word, and then press the **[F7]** key to continue the spell checking.

9.   The Thesaurus

WordPerfect contains a thesaurus to assist you in drafting your documents. A thesaurus supplies synonyms for a variety of words. To use the thesaurus feature, place the cursor within a word and press **[Alt] + [F1]**. The thesaurus for the word *desire* is shown in Figure 1.16.

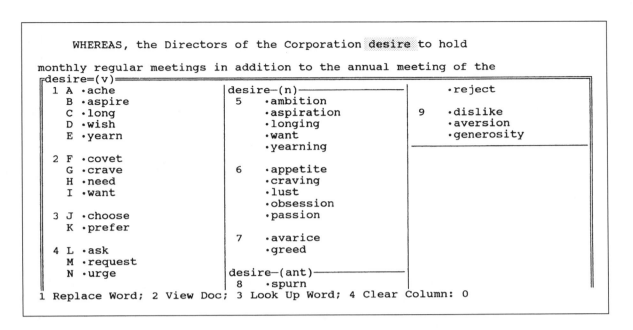

```
   WHEREAS, the Directors of the Corporation desire to hold

monthly regular meetings in addition to the annual meeting of the
┌desire=(v)════════════════╗┌desire─(n)──────────────┐         •reject
   1 A •ache                │  5     •ambition        │
     B •aspire              │        •aspiration       │    9    •dislike
     C •long                │        •longing          │         •aversion
     D •wish                │        •want             │         •generosity
     E •yearn               │        •yearning         │  ──────────────────
                            │                          │
   2 F •covet               │  6     •appetite         │
     G •crave               │        •craving          │
     H •need                │        •lust             │
     I •want                │        •obsession        │
                            │        •passion          │
   3 J •choose              │                          │
     K •prefer              │  7     •avarice          │
                            │        •greed            │
   4 L •ask                 │                          │
     M •request             │desire─(ant)────────────  │
     N •urge                │  8     •spurn            │
1 Replace Word; 2 View Doc; 3 Look Up Word; 4 Clear Column: 0
```

Figure 1.16   WordPerfect's Thesaurus for the word *desire*

Further synonyms may be seen for the words within the synonym list by pressing the letter corresponding to the word. For example, in Figure 1.16, pressing the letter **D** displays the synonyms for the word *wish* in the second column as shown in Figure 1.17.

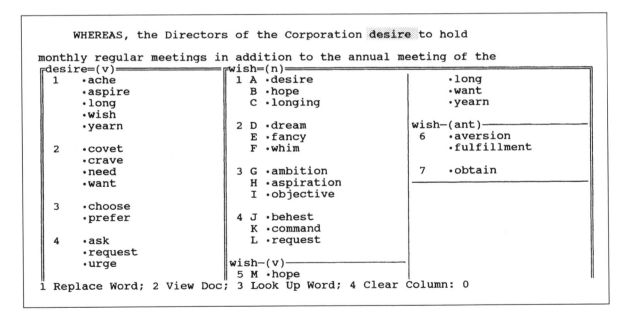

```
   WHEREAS, the Directors of the Corporation desire to hold

monthly regular meetings in addition to the annual meeting of the
┌desire=(v)════════════════╗┌wish=(n)════════════════╗         •long
   1   •ache                │  1 A •desire            │         •want
       •aspire              │    B •hope              │         •yearn
       •long                │    C •longing           │
       •wish                │                         │  wish─(ant)──────────
       •yearn               │  2 D •dream             │    6    •aversion
                            │    E •fancy             │         •fulfillment
   2   •covet               │    F •whim              │
       •crave               │                         │    7    •obtain
       •need                │  3 G •ambition          │  ──────────────────
       •want                │    H •aspiration        │
                            │    I •objective         │
   3   •choose              │                         │
       •prefer              │  4 J •behest            │
                            │    K •command           │
   4   •ask                 │    L •request           │
       •request             │                         │
       •urge                │wish─(v)─────────────────│
                            │  5 M •hope              │
1 Replace Word; 2 View Doc; 3 Look Up Word; 4 Clear Column: 0
```

Figure 1.17   Synonyms for the word *wish*

The letters identifying the selections may be moved from one column to another with the **[Arrow]** keys. You may select a word from the synonyms by selecting **1** for Replace Word and typing the letter corresponding to the new word.

10. Searching

WordPerfect contains a Search feature that can search for a word or group of characters or a WordPerfect code within your document. You may search forward or backward in a document, or perform a Search and Replace to replace a word, phrase, or code with another word, phrase, or code.

a. *Forward Searching*

The [F2] key searches forward in a document. Pressing the **[F2]** key prompts for the word or characters for which you are searching. The word or characters within a search are called the "search term." After entering the search term, press the **[F2]** key again to begin the search. The search will stop at the first instance of the search term. The search can be continued by pressing the **[F2]** key twice. Using lowercase letters in the search term will match both lowercase and uppercase text. Using uppercase letters will only match uppercase letters.

b. *Backward Searching*

If you wish to search backwards toward the top of the document, use **[Shift] + [F2].** The prompts will be the same as with forward searching.

When editing a large document, I find it helpful to mark where I have left off in my editing with three asterisks, ''***''. The next time I enter the document to work on the editing, I simply run a search for ''***''.

---

c. *Search and Replace*

When you wish to replace a word, phrase, or code with another word, phrase or code, use the Search and Replace feature, **[Alt] + [F2].** For example, if you have typed a 25-page legal memorandum and find that you have spelled the Plaintiff's name, "Kerrigan," as "Carrigan" throughout the document, the Search and Replace feature can fix this error very quickly. Pressing **[Alt] + [F2]** accesses Search and Replace, and it asks if you wish the search to stop every time it finds the name in order to confirm the replacement. For this search, we would respond **N.** You are then prompted for the search term. In this case it would be "Carrigan." After typing "Carrigan," you press **[F2]** and are prompted to enter the replace term. The replace term in this example is "Kerrigan." Pressing **[F2]** again begins the Search and Replace.

If you have something currently typed on the WordPerfect screen, try the Search and Replace feature.

G. PRINTING

To receive a hard copy of a document, you must send it to a printer. As a safety measure, use the **[F10]** Save and Continue feature prior to printing your document. Occasionally, a printer problem will freeze your computer.

The **[Shift]** + **[F7]** key combination accesses WordPerfect's Print menu as shown in Figure 1.18.

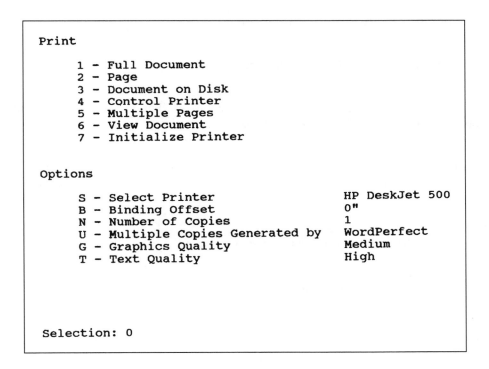

```
Print

     1 - Full Document
     2 - Page
     3 - Document on Disk
     4 - Control Printer
     5 - Multiple Pages
     6 - View Document
     7 - Initialize Printer


Options

     S - Select Printer                      HP DeskJet 500
     B - Binding Offset                      0"
     N - Number of Copies                    1
     U - Multiple Copies Generated by        WordPerfect
     G - Graphics Quality                    Medium
     T - Text Quality                        High




Selection: 0
```

Figure 1.18   The WordPerfect Print Menu

The options available in the print menu are explained below.

1 Prints the entire document.

2 Prints the current page containing the cursor.

3 Prints a document from a disk.

4 Gives you the Control Printer menu where you can cancel and control print jobs.

5 Allows you to print selected pages from the document. For example, 5-10 or 1,3,5-10.

6 Allows you to view how your document will look when printed. This is a very helpful feature when you are using graphics and fonts. Pressing the [Space Bar] returns you to the Print menu.

7 Sends fonts you have designated to be present at the beginning of the print job to the printer.

S Lets you select the type of printer you are using.

B Allows for space for binding the pages of the document if this is required.

N Lets you print more than one copy of the document. The number selected remains during your work session until you change it again.

U If your printer has the ability to print more than one copy of the current print job on its own, this option can be used to have the printer handle the printing of copies. This will print documents faster.

G Determines the quality of the graphics when printed.

T Determines the quality of the text when printed.

H. EXITING WORDPERFECT

Exiting WordPerfect is accomplished with **[F7] Save and Exit.** As was covered in Section D, when you press the **[F7]** key, WordPerfect will display the prompts for saving a document. Respond to these prompts, and then respond **Y** for "yes" when asked if you wish to exit WordPerfect. Responding **N** for "no" will give you a blank WordPerfect screen.

Section Two—Advanced WordPerfect Features

A. BULLETS AND SPECIAL CHARACTERS

There are many special characters, not available on the keyboard, that can be accessed from WordPerfect using the compose key, **[Ctrl] + [V],** or the **[Alt]** key and the number key pad. These keys allow you to use characters found in WordPerfect's character sets. These character sets are shown in the WordPerfect manual, and can also be found in the CHARACTER.DOC file in the WordPerfect program files. To use the compose key, you press **[Ctrl] + [V]** and then type the number of the character set followed by a comma and the number of the character. For example, to create a section symbol, §, use the compose key and type **4, 6** (character set 4, character number 6):

[Ctrl] + [V] 4, 6

You can also create a section symbol using the **[Alt]** key and the numbers on the number key pad as follows:

[Alt] + 21

Releasing the **[Alt]** key inserts the character into your document. Your [Num Lock] key may need to be on in order for this to work. This method will not work with the numbers on the alphanumeric portion of the keyboard.

Bullets and some common characters used in legal documents are shown below with their compose key keystrokes and **[Alt]** keystrokes (where available).

SYMBOL	[CTRL] + [V]	[ALT] +
§	4, 6	21
®	4, 22 or OR	
©	4, 23 or OC	
TM	4, 41 or TM	
SM	4, 42 or SM	
○	4, 37	

SYMBOL	[CTRL] + [V]	[ALT] +
●	4, 44	
○	4, 1	9
●	4, 0 or **	7
•	4, 3	

> *When you create some characters, a box will appear on the screen in place of the character. The character can be seen in the Print menu by viewing the document, or in the printed copy of the document. To view the document, press* **[Shift] + [F7], 6.** *Select the 200% option while viewing to see the characters up close. The* **[Space Bar]** *will return you to your document.*

B. THE ESCAPE KEY

The escape key, **[Esc],** is often used to back out of menus or screens. It has another function, however, that is widely employed by experienced WordPerfect users. This function is that of a repeat key. The [Esc] key will repeat certain functions any number of times that you specify. For example, you may want 20 asterisks, or to repeat a macro 3 times, or to move ahead 5 pages in your document. All of these functions can be accomplished quickly by pressing the **[Esc]** key, typing the desired number of times to repeat (represented by the letter "n"), and selecting the function. A list of some of the functions is shown below.

n (any character)   Repeats the character n times

n (activate macro)   Repeats the macro n times.

n [Page Down]   Moves n pages forward.

n [Page Up]   Moves n pages backward.

n [Up Arrow]   Moves n lines up.

n [Down Arrow]   Moves n lines down.

n [Delete]	Deletes n characters to the right of the cursor.
n [Ctrl] + [Backspace]	Deletes n words to the right of the cursor.
n [Ctrl] + [End]	Deletes n lines following the cursor.

C. MACROS

A **macro** allows you to program a single keystroke combination to play several keystrokes. There are two ways to identify macros: with the **[Alt]** key and a letter of the alphabet, or with a word.

A common macro is one that switches to double-spaced type, something you will do quite frequently when drafting legal documents. The WordPerfect keystrokes necessary to switch from single spacing to double spacing are:

[Shift] + [F8], 1, 6, 2, [Enter], [F7]

You can create a macro that, when you strike a single key combination (e.g., [Alt] + [D]), will perform all of these keystrokes for you.

1. Creating a Macro

Creating a macro in WordPerfect involves the steps set forth below. We will practice creating a macro in the next section.

a) Press **[Ctrl] + [F10].**

b) Define the macro with either a word or by holding down the **[Alt]** key and selecting any letter from A to Z. **[Alt] + [any letter]** is the most common way to store a macro.

> *If WordPerfect says the macro already exists, cancel the command with the* **[F1]** *key. Begin again with Step 1 and try* **[Alt]** *plus another letter.*

c) Enter a brief description of the macro for reference purposes and press **[Enter].** The words **Macro Def** will begin flashing in the lower left-hand corner of the screen. This is to inform you that every key you press at this point will be recorded within the macro.

d) Input the keystrokes you wish to use.

> *[Ctrl] + [Page Up] gives you added features to include within your macro, such as "pause."*

e) Press **[Ctrl] + [F10]** to save the macro.

2. Practicing Macros

Following these steps, we will create a macro for double spacing.

a) Press **[Ctrl] + [F10].**

b) Define the macro. Press **[Alt] + [D].** If WordPerfect says that the macro already exists, try another letter.

c) Enter a brief description. The description of our macro will be "Double Spacing." Press the **[Enter]** key to continue.

d) Input the keystrokes. **Macro Def** will be flashing in the lower left-hand corner of the screen. As we press the keys for our macro, you will see that we move through the WordPerfect menu screens just as though we were working without creating a macro.

> **Press [Shift] + [F8],** select **1** for line, select **6** for line spacing, type **2** for two-line spacing, and press **[Enter].** Now, leave the menu by pressing the **[F7]** key.

e) Press **[Ctrl] + [F10].**

Another use for macros is to record boilerplate language that you need to repeat throughout a document. For example, in responding to a discovery request, you may find yourself using the following objection repeatedly in your responses:

> **Plaintiff objects to this discovery request on the ground that it seeks information that is beyond the scope of permissible discovery. The information sought is not relevant to the subject matter of this litigation and is not likely to lead to the discovery of admissible evidence.**

Creating a macro that will automatically type in this objection can save you a lot of time when drafting the responding document.

To set up this macro, follow steps a through e in Section C1, above. When you input the keystrokes for the macro, type the entire objection. Pressing **[Ctrl] + [F10]** will end the macro creation.

3. Executing a Macro

Executing a macro is accomplished by pressing **[Alt] + [given letter]** or by pressing **[Alt] + [F10]** and typing the macro name. Since we went through the keystrokes to create double spacing in making our **[Alt] + [D]** macro, the document on the screen will be in double spacing. Type a few lines to see the double spacing. Return to single spacing (**[Shift] + [F8], 1, 6, 1, [Enter], [F7]**), and type a few lines. Now execute the macro by pressing **[Alt] + [D]**. Type a few lines to see that you have switched back to double spacing. Many firms also set up a macro for single spacing and call it **[Alt] + [S]**. When these two macros are in place, it is very easy to switch from single to double spacing and back again.

If you create a macro and identify it with a name, instead of using **[Alt] + [any letter]**, the macro is executed by pressing **[Alt] + [F10]**, typing the macro name, and pressing the **[Enter]** key. The macro files are stored with your WordPerfect program files and are available in any document that you create.

> *If you receive the message "**ERROR: File not found—ALTD.WPM**" when you try to execute your macro, you may need to change the location of your macro files in the Setup Menu. Check **[Shift] + [F1], 6,** and look at item **2 Keyboard/ Macro Files**. This will tell you where WordPerfect is looking for the macro files. You may need to change the location to the WordPerfect directory (i.e., C:\wp51) or another directory. Try it yourself and, if the error message continues, seek help from the person in charge of the computer system or telephone WordPerfect's 800 support number.*

4. Editing a Macro

To edit the keystrokes within a macro, follow the steps below:

a) Press **[Ctrl] + [F10]**.

b) Type the macro name or press the keys that correspond to the macro, e.g., [Alt] + [D]. WordPerfect will tell you that the macro already exists and will ask you if you want to replace it or edit it.

c) Select **2** for edit. You may now edit the macro and make any desired corrections.

> *[Ctrl] + [Page Up] will give you access to a number of macro commands that do not correspond to keys—for example, "pause."*
>
> *[Ctrl] + [F10], used within the macro editor, will allow you to add [Enter] symbols and cursor movement characters into the macro. [Ctrl] + [F10], again, returns you to normal editing.*

d) When you are finished editing the macro, press **[F7]** to save your changes.

5. Creating a Memorandum Macro

There are macros that not only execute commands, but also pause and wait for the user to enter information before continuing with their execution.

A memorandum is a document that is created often by legal professionals. It is used to document telephone conferences, record the contents of conversations with witnesses, report on case status, and prepare legal memoranda. A macro can be created to type the memorandum headings and to pause for entry of data, making the memorandum creation process very easy.

Follow the steps below from a blank screen to create the memorandum macro. To get to a blank screen, press **[F7],** respond **Y** or **N** to the prompt and respond **N** to the Exit prompt.

a) Press **[Ctrl] + [F10].**

b) Define the macro as **[Alt] + [M]** by holding down the **[Alt]** key and pressing the letter **M.** If there is already a macro with this letter, try another.

c) Describe the macro as **Memorandum** and press **[Enter]**.

d) Input the keystrokes.

    1) Press **[Shift] + [F6]** to center, **[F6]** to bold, **[F8]** to underline, and the **[Caps Lock]** key.

    2) Type the word **MEMORANDUM** with a space between each letter so that it appears like this:

        <u>**M E M O R A N D U M**</u>

    3) Press **[F8]** again to end the underlining.

    4) Press **[Enter]** three times.

    5) Type **TO:.** Tab twice and press **[Ctrl] + [Page Up]** and select **1** for pause. Press **[Enter]** to end the pause.

    6) Press **[Enter]** twice.

    7) Type **FROM:.** Tab once and press **[Ctrl] + [Page Up]** and select **1** for pause. Press **[Enter]** to end the pause.

    8) Press **[Enter]** twice.

    9) Type **DATE:.** Tab once and press **[Shift] + [F5]** and select **1** (Date Text). This will insert the current date into the memorandum.

    10) Press **[Enter]** twice.

    11) Type **RE:.** Tab twice, press **[Ctrl] + [Page Up],** and select **1** for pause. Press **[Enter]** to end the pause.

12) Press **[Enter]** twice.

13) Press **[F8]** to underline and press the **[Space Bar]** until the position marker reaches the right margin: 7.5″. If you go too far, backspace some of the underline out.

14) Press **[F6]** to end the bold and **[F8]** to end the underline.

15) Press **[Enter]** twice.

16) Press **[Ctrl] + [F10]** to save the macro.

Your completed macro should look like this, but with a different date.

<u>M E M O R A N D U M</u>

TO:

FROM:

DATE: **April 12, 1997**

RE:

_____

To run the memorandum macro, press **[Alt] + [M]** or the name or key combination under which it was recorded. When the macro pauses, enter the appropriate information and press **[Enter]** to continue. Note: If you are underlining something on the "RE:" line, make sure that you turn off the underlining before you press the **[Enter]** key to go on with the macro.

D.   STORING BLOCKS OF TEXT

When creating legal documents, you will often repeat the same phrase or sentence throughout the document. An example would be a deposition summary where you are repeating a person's name throughout the summary.

You could create a macro, but perhaps you only need the recorded text for this document. In this case, storing the block of text would be preferable to a macro because you only need the text for this work session. You may record up to ten blocks of text, consisting of 128 characters or less, for use during a work session (the blocks are erased when you exit WordPerfect).

To illustrate this feature, we will assume that you have been asked to summarize the deposition of an expert witness who is a chemist. In his testimony, the chemist continually refers to the chemical "benzalacet ophenone." It will be to your advantage to store this in a block so that you will not have to struggle to spell it each time it is needed. To record this block of text, you must first type it on the screen. Then, use **[Alt] + [F4]** or the **[F12]** key to block the text, and press **[Ctrl] + [Page Up]**.

You will be prompted for a variable and you may enter a number between 0 and 9, and then press **[Enter]**. When you want to paste this block into your text, you may retrieve it by pressing the **[Alt]** key and the number you gave to the block (e.g., [Alt] + [1]).

When summarizing depositions, I find it beneficial to set up blocks for the witness name and any frequently repeated words or phrases. I then prepare a small piece of paper with the block numbers and the corresponding text and place it next to my keyboard for reference.

E.   FOOTNOTES

Footnotes are used often in the drafting of legal memoranda and pleadings. WordPerfect's footnote feature sequentially numbers the footnotes, and automatically adjusts your page lengths to make room for the footnotes.

To create a footnote within your document follow the steps below.

a) Position the cursor at the point where you would like the reference number of the footnote to appear.

b) Press **[Ctrl] + [F7]**. The following options will appear in the lower left-hand corner of the screen.

> **1 Footnote; 2 Endnote; 3 Endnote Placement: 0**

c) Select **1** for footnote. The following options are then displayed.

> **Footnote: 1 Create; 2 Edit; 3 New Number; 4 Options: 0**

d) Select **1** for Create. A blank edit screen with the footnote number then appears.

e) Type the footnote. When you are finished, the **[F7]** (Exit) key will return you to your document.

The footnote reference number will appear where you placed the cursor when you began. You cannot see the footnote unless you view your document through the Print menu: **[Shift] + [F7], 6.**

F.   COLUMNS

WordPerfect offers three types of columns, Parallel, Parallel with Block Protect, and Newspaper. Parallel columns are used to create pleading captions, deposition summaries, and other documents that require columns of text that can be read from left to right. An example of a deposition summary created using columns is shown in Figure 1.19.

SUMMARY OF THE DEPOSITION OF

HUBERT M. SMITH

Taken November 9, 1997

Page:Line	**Summary**
	EXAMINATION BY MR. GREENE
1:3	Opening statements.
2:4	Mr. Smith was born in Walla Walla, Washington on December 12, 1945. He currently resides at 345 Main Street, Seattle, Washington 00990.
3:27	Mr. Smith obtained a Bachelor of Science degree in Economics from the University of Washington in 1967. He is presently employed by the State of Washington as an economist.

Figure 1.19 Parallel Columns

Parallel with Block Protect columns are parallel columns. However, if any part of a row of column entries continues to the next page of the document, the entire row of entries will be moved to the next page.

Newspaper columns differ from parallel columns in that when the left-most column reaches the bottom of the page, it goes back up to the top of the same page. Instead of reading these columns from left to right, you read the first column to the bottom of the page and then read the second column as shown in Figure 1.20.

Parallel Columns

WordPerfect offers two types of columns, parallel and newspaper. For the most part, legal professionals use parallel columns. This type of column is used to create pleading captions, deposition summaries, and other documents that require columns of text that are read from left to right.

Newspaper Columns

Newspaper columns differ from parallel columns in that when the left-most column reaches the bottom of the page, it goes back up to the top of the same page. Instead of reading these types of columns from left to right, you read the first column to the bottom of the page and then read the second column.

Figure 1.20 Newspaper Columns

To learn about columns, we will use an example of a deposition summary. Deposition summaries can be drafted using parallel columns or the table feature discussed in section G. Follow the steps below from a blank screen to set up a deposition summary using parallel columns.

a) Type in the specifics about the deposition at the top of the document as shown below.

SUMMARY OF THE DEPOSITION OF

HUBERT M. SMITH

Taken November 9, 1997

b) Press the **[Enter]** key to move down a few lines.

c) Access the Columns feature with **[Alt] + [F7].** Select **1** for Columns. Select **3** for Define. We must define the columns before we can use them. The Columns Definition screen is shown in Figure 1.21.

```
Text Column Definition

    1 - Type                                    Newspaper

    2 - Number of Columns                       2

    3 - Distance Between Columns

    4 - Margins

    Column      Left        Right       Column      Left        Right
     1:         1"          4"           13:
     2:         4.5"        7.5"         14:
     3:                                  15:
     4:                                  16:
     5:                                  17:
     6:                                  18:
     7:                                  19:
     8:                                  20:
     9:                                  21:
    10:                                  22:
    11:                                  23:
    12:                                  24:

Selection: 0
```

Figure 1.21 The Columns Definition Screen

A default setting for newspaper columns is already present when you enter the Columns Definition Screen.

d) At the Columns Definition screen, change the type of columns to parallel by selecting **1** for **Type,** and then **2** for **Parallel.** Check to see that item 2, **Number of Columns,** is **2.** If it is not, change it to 2.

e) Define your margins. Select **4** for **Margins** and enter the following margins:

COLUMN	LEFT	RIGHT
1:	1″	2.5″
2:	3″	7.5″

When you have pressed **[Enter]** after the right margin entry for column 2, your cursor will be blinking at the Selection prompt at the bottom of the screen. Press **[Enter]** once to leave this menu.

f) The next screen will display:

Columns: 1 On; 2 Off; 3 Define: 0

Select **1** to turn the columns **On.** When the columns are on, the column number will appear in the Status Line.

g) Type **<u>Page:Line</u>** at the left-hand margin and go to column 2 by pressing **[Ctrl] + [Enter].** Under normal circumstances this would create a hard page break. If you do get a hard page break (= = = = = = = = = = = =), then your columns are not turned on. Check your Reveal Codes to make sure that you are typing after the **[Col On]** code. If you do not see a **[Col On]** code, then you need to turn the columns on with **[Alt] + [F7], 1, 1.**

h) At the second column, type **<u>Summary,</u>** press **[F8]** to turn the underline off, and press **[Ctrl] + [Enter]** to get back to column 1 and begin your summary.

Try entering the summary in Figure 1.19 into your document. To change columns, use **[Ctrl] + [Enter]. [Ctrl] + [Home], [Left Arrow]** and **[Ctrl] + [Home], [Right Arrow]** will move you quickly back and forth between your columns when editing the column text.

When you have finished using Columns in your document, they may be turned off with **[Alt] + [F7], 1, 2.**

G. TABLES

The Table feature in WordPerfect is very similar to an electronic spreadsheet. A table contains columns and rows, the intersection of which forms cells. A cell is identified by its column letter followed by the row number. Text, numbers, or characters are then entered into the cells. Tables can be used in place of parallel or tabbed columns. For example, the deposition summary created using parallel columns in Section F could also be created using a table. The heading would remain the same, and then a table would be created with two columns and four rows (new rows can be added as needed). The result would look exactly like Figure 1.19. The benefit of using a table over parallel columns is the ease of making corrections. When editing text in parallel columns, you can really mess up the document if your cursor is not within the [Col On] and [Col Off] codes. With a table, each section of the text is in a box. You need not worry about whether you are within the proper codes. If the cursor is in the box, you are there.

Another benefit of the Table feature is that you can perform mathematical equations similar to those used in electronic spreadsheets. For example, a billing statement can be created that automatically computes the totals for you. An example is shown in Figure 1.22.

SAMUEL J. COUNSEL
Attorney at Law
43 Main Street
Anywhere, Texas 32008
(909) 555-2945

Haley Corporation
35200 Oil Road
Anywhere, Texas 32008

Re: <u>Haley v. Reaves</u>

LEGAL SERVICES RENDERED:

Date	Description	Time	Amount
12/19/96	Review motion to strike and demurrer. Legal research re statute of limitations on disputed causes of action. Legal research re relation back to original cause of action. Review original complaint. Begin drafting opposition to demurrer.	7.1	$994.00
12/20/96	Draft opposition to demurrer. Begin drafting opposition to motion to strike.	2.9	$406.00
12/21/96	Pull file at courthouse to obtain copy of minute order. Complete motion to strike. Cite check all cases. Prepare table of authorities for opposition to demurrer. Finalize documents.	3.3	$462.00
	TOTAL HOURS AND AMOUNT DUE:	13.3	$1,862.00

Figure 1.22   A billing statement created using a table

1.   Preparing a Table

To set up a table, you need to look at how many columns and approximately how many rows you will need. As an example, we will walk through the creation of the table portion of the billing statement in Figure 1.22. Select the Table Create feature with **[Alt]** + **[F7], 2, 1.** You will be prompted for the number of columns, type **4** and press **[Enter],** and the number of rows, type **5** and press **[Enter].** WordPerfect then takes you to the Table Edit screen shown in Figure 1.23. In this screen you can insert or delete columns and rows, adjust the size of the columns, add or delete border lines, perform math calculations, and execute many other functions. Any time you are working within your table, you may get to this screen with **[Alt] + [F7]**.

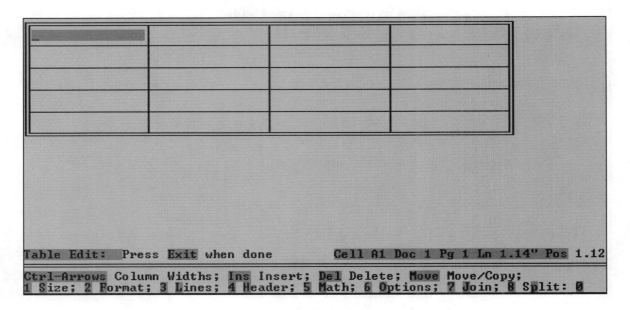

Figure 1.23 The Table Edit Screen

2. Adjusting the Column Size

To adjust the column size you must be in the Table Edit screen. Place the cursor in a cell and use **[Ctrl] +** the **[Left Arrow]** or **[Right Arrow]** key to adjust the size of the four columns. The first column should be approximately 1 inch wide. The third and forth columns should be approximately 3/4 of an inch wide. The second column will be the largest. You will need to move back and forth between the columns making adjustments until you are satisfied with their appearance. The [Arrow] keys will move you from cell to cell. Once you are satisfied with the column widths, press the **[F7]** key to return to your document.

3. Entering Data into the Table

To enter data into the table, you move to the desired cell with the **[Tab]** key or **[Shift] +** **[Tab]** and type the entry. Each cell is like a separate document, so any formatting such as boldfacing or centering must be performed in each cell. For our first row, each of the headings needs to be centered and boldfaced. Move to cell A1, press **[Shift] + [F6]** to center, press **[F6]** to bold, and type the heading. Then move to B1, C1, and D1 and repeat the process with these headings.

In rows 2, 3, and 4, enter the dates, descriptions, and times. Do not enter the amounts.

We will have the table compute them. When you are entering the descriptions, let the text word-wrap within the cell. In the last row, row 5, move to cell B5 and select **[Alt] + [F6]** to select flush right justification, and then type the cell entry.

4.   Using the Table Math Features

To use the Table Math features to compute our billing statement, move the cursor to the amount cell for the 12/19/96 billing item. Select **[Alt] + [F7]** to enter the Table Edit screen. In the Table Edit screen, select **5** (Math) and **2** (Formula). The formula will be the amount of time from column C multiplied by our attorney's billing rate of $140 an hour. Type the formula, **C2*140,** and press **[Enter].** Move down to the amount cell in the next row, select **5, 2,** and type **C3*140,** and press **[Enter].** For the third amount, we are going to copy the formula from cell D3 to cells D4 and D5. With the cursor in D3, select **5** (Math) and **3** (Copy Formula). Select **2** (Down), type **2,** and press **[Enter].** We have not yet entered the total hours and amount due, so your table should look like the one in Figure 1.24.

Date	Description	Time	Amount	
12/19/96	Review motion to strike and demurrer. Legal research re statute of limitations on disputed causes of action. Legal research re relation back to original cause of action. Review original complaint. Begin drafting opposition to demurrer.	7.1	994.00	
12/20/96	Draft opposition to demurrer. Begin drafting opposition to motion to strike.	2.9	406.00	
12/21/96	Pull file at courthouse to obtain copy of minute order. Complete motion to strike. Cite check all cases. Prepare table of authorities for opposition to demurrer. Finalize documents.	3.3	462.00	
	TOTAL HOURS AND AMOUNT DUE:		0.00	

=C5*140   Cell D5 Doc 1 Pg 1 Ln 4.59" POS 6.67"

Ctrl-Arrows Column Widths; Ins Insert; Del Delete; Move Move/Copy;
1 Size; 2 Format; 3 Lines; 4 Header; 5 Math; 6 Options; 7 Join; 8 Split: 0

Figure 1.24   The table after entering the math formulas

To place a "total hours" in cell C5, move the cursor to that cell and select **5** (Math) and **4** (+). This will total column C. To get the amount in cell D5 to calculate, you need to move to cell D5 and select **5** (Math) and **1** (Calculate). If any of the column widths needs adjusting, use [Ctrl] + the [Arrow] keys.

5. Formatting Numbers

Our numbers need a uniform number of decimal places, need to be aligned vertically by their decimal points, and need dollar signs. For column C, all of the numbers need one number beyond the decimal. The number in cell C5 has two numbers beyond the decimal. Place the cursor in C5 and select **2** (Format), **2** (Column), **4** (# Digits), type **1,** and press **[Enter].** You must then select **5** (Math), **1** (Calculate) to have the change take effect.

To align the numbers in columns C and D, begin by highlighting the numbers in column C using the **[F12]** key. Then, select **2** (Format), **1** (Cell), **3** (Justify), **5** (Decimal Align). This will align the numbers on the decimal point. Repeat this process for the numbers in column D.

To place dollar signs in front of the numbers in column D, you must exit the Table Edit screen by pressing the **[F7]** key. Then, move to each individual amount and type a dollar sign in front of it. You may need to go back to the Table Edit screen with [Alt] + [F7] after you have done this in order to edit the column widths.

6. Lines Within a Table

Tables will automatically be created with a double line around the outside and single lines on the inside borders of the cells. The appearance of our current table is shown in Figure 1.25. To change the lines in the table, go to the Table Edit screen with **[Alt] + [F7],** highlight the cells containing the lines that you want to change, and press **3** for line selections.

Date	Description	Time	Amount
12/19/96	Review motion to strike and demurrer. Legal research re statute of limitations on disputed causes of action. Legal research re relation back to original cause of action. Review original complaint. Begin drafting opposition to demurrer.	7.1	$994.00
12/20/96	Draft opposition to demurrer. Begin drafting opposition to motion to strike.	2.9	$406.00
12/21/96	Pull file at courthouse to obtain copy of minute order. Complete motion to strike. Cite check all cases. Prepare table of authorities for opposition to demurrer. Finalize documents.	3.3	$462.00
	TOTAL HOURS AND AMOUNT DUE:	13.3	$1,862.00

Doc 1 Pg 1 Ln 4.8" POS 1"

Figure 1.25   Tables are created with a double line around the outside, and single lines within the table

In our billing statement example, we will begin by removing all of the lines. In the Table Edit screen, place your cursor in cell A1. Turn on the block feature with **[F12]** and highlight down to cell D5. Your entire table should be highlighted. Now, select **3** (Lines), **7** (All), **1** (None). The lines should be removed from the table. Next, we need to underline the column headings. Highlight all of row 1 with **[F12]**. Select **3** (Lines), **4** (Bottom), **2** (Single). The last lines that we need for our table are the single and double lines above and below the totals in cells C5 and D5. Highlight these two cells with **[F12]** and select **3** (Lines), **3** (Top), **2** (Single). Highlight the two cells again and select **3** (Lines), **4** (Bottom), **3** (Double). Press **[F7]** to return to your document. Your table is now complete and should look similar to the one in Figure 1.22.

H. AUTOMATIC SORTING

WordPerfect's Automatic Sort feature allows you to reorder your text and numbers in many different ways. Maybe you need to sort a list of items or names alphabetically or place a list of documents in chronological order. In addition to ordering lists, the Sort feature may be used to find items that meet specific criteria. This feature uses basic summary database searching to locate items within a list.

1. Sorting Basics

The Sort feature can sort single lines of information, paragraphs, information within a table, or secondary merge files. WordPerfect will sort according to the keys that you provide. A key is the criterion for the sort. It identifies the type of data to be sorted and where it is located within the line, paragraph, table, or secondary merge file. More than one key may be needed to sort the data within a document. For example, if you were sorting a list of names and two people had the same last name, you would need two keys. The first key would sort by last name. The second key would sort by first name.

2. Sorting by Line

Line sorts are the most common type of sort. The information within the document is entered on a single line, with fields of information separated by tabs. An example is shown below.

Smith, John	123 Main Street	555–1212
Keefer, Karen	156 Vine Road	555–3040
Smith, Alfred	7686 Apple Lane	555–9030
Armor, Peter	23 Mill Road	555–3219

You may find that you need to adjust your tab settings to get your tabbed columns to align. If you use more than one tab to make your data line up, the lines might not have the information in the correct field. Make sure that your cursor is at the beginning of the list when you change the tab settings.

A key in a line sort will ask whether the data is alphanumeric (words, addresses, and telephone numbers) or numeric (numbers and dates), the field number, and the word number. The fields are separated by the tabs. Words within the fields are normally separated by spaces. If one of the fields contained dates, the slashes in the date (12/31/96) would be treated as spaces and each portion of the date would be a separate word. In the example above, there are three fields. In field number one, containing the names, word number one would be the last name and word number two would be the first name.

To practice a line sort, enter the example shown above into a blank WordPerfect document. Use the **[Tab]** key once between the name and address, and once between the address and telephone number. The columns will not align unless you move the cursor to the top of the document and change the tab settings with **[Shift]** + **[F8]**, **1, 8.** Delete the tab at the 3″ mark. Press **[F7]** twice to return to the document. On the Tab Set bar, tabs can be removed with the **[Delete]** key and added with the **[Enter]** key. When you are finished entering the information, save the document with **[F10]** before you perform the sort.

> *It is always important to save your document prior to performing a sort. This will enable you to retrieve the unsorted document in the event that you sort incorrectly and mess up the document.*

To perform the sort, press **[Ctrl]** + **[F9]**, select **2** (Sort). You will be prompted for the input file. The default is "(Screen)". This is what you want, so press **[Enter].** You will then be prompted for the output file. Press **[Enter]** again to accept the default of "(Screen)". The Sort screen will appear as shown in Figure 1.26.

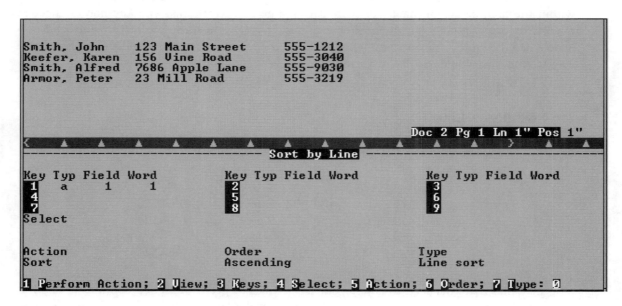

Figure 1.26 The Sort Screen

WordPerfect® for DOS

The first sort that we will perform will be a sort by last name. The default key in the Sort screen is set up to sort an alphanumeric in field number 1, and will sort on word number 1. The order of the sort will be ascending, and it will be a line sort. Select **1** (Perform Action) from the menu at the bottom of the screen to perform the sort. The entries should now appear as shown below.

Armor, Peter	23 Mill Road	555-3219
Keefer, Karen	156 Vine Road	555-3040
Smith, John	123 Main Street	555-1212
Smith, Alfred	7686 Apple Lane	555-9030

To sort this data accurately, we must provide a second key so that it will also sort people with the same last name alphabetically by first name. Press **[Ctrl] + [F9], 2**, and press **[Enter]** twice to return to the Sort screen. Press **3** (Keys) to add a second key. Use the **[Arrow]** keys to move to the second key. The type of information for this key will be alphanumeric, the field number will be 1, and the word will be 2. Press the **[F7]** key when you are finished. Select **1** (Perform Action) to complete the sort. The data should now appear as shown below.

Armor, Peter	23 Mill Road	555-3219
Keefer, Karen	156 Vine Road	555-3040
Smith, Alfred	7686 Apple Lane	555-9030
Smith, John	123 Main Street	555-1212

To practice sorting items by date, exit to a blank WordPerfect screen and enter the following dates and descriptions. You may need to change the tab settings again (**[Shift] + [F8], 1, 8**) to make the columns line up.

2/23/97	Letter to insurance company.
1/2/97	Witness statement.
12/31/96	Police accident report.
1/1/97	Hospital bill.
12/31/96	Ambulance bill.

For this sort, we will need to set up three keys, one for each portion of the date. The slashes in the date are considered as spaces, so field number 1 contains three words.

To begin the sort, go to the Sort screen with **[Ctrl] + [F9], 2, [Enter], [Enter]**. The keys will have to be set up so that the first key sorts by the year, the third word. The second key will sort on the month, and the third key will sort on the day. Select **3** (Keys) and change the first key's type to numeric, field 1, word 3. Move to Key 2 with the **[Arrow]** keys and make it a numeric, field 1, word 1. Move to Key 3 and make it a numeric, field 1, word 2. Press **[F7]** to complete the selections, and press **1** (Perform Action) to perform the sort. This should sort your data in chronological order.

> *If your information has headings at the top of the tabular columns, such as "Date" and "Description," you will need to highlight the data to be sorted with **[F12]** prior to going to the Sort screen.*

3. Sorting by Paragraph

Sorting by paragraph is not really a valuable feature unless you have set up a structure similar to the one shown below.

2/23/97   Letter from plaintiff to his insurance company explaining the nature of the accident and the extent of his injuries.

1/2/97   Statement of Alice Jones. She was driving next to the plaintiff and witnessed the accident.

12/31/96   Police report detailing the circumstances of the accident and noting that both the plaintiff and our client were given citations.

When setting up this kind of list, you must use the **[F4]** (Indent) key to indent the paragraph. You may need to adjust your tab settings to align the information. Also, WordPerfect requires a hard return at the end of the paragraph and before the next item so that it can recognize the end of a record. Therefore, you need to press **[Enter]** at the end of each paragraph and again before typing the next item. To practice sorting by paragraph, type the example into a blank document.

We will sort these items by date. Begin the sort by pressing **[Ctrl]+[F9], 2, [Enter], [Enter].** Change the type of sort from Line sort to Paragraph sort by selecting **7** (Type), **3** (Paragraph). If you performed the date sort in the previous example, the keys will already be set up. You will notice that a line number option has been added to the keys. The default is 1, and that is what we want for this sort. The keys should read as follows:

Key 1: n, 1, 1, 3   Key 2: n, 1, 1, 1   Key 3: n, 1, 1, 2

If you need to adjust the keys, do so by selecting **3** (Keys). To perform the sort, select **1** (Perform Action).

4. Sorting Information in a Table

A table is set up in columns, which makes it a natural for sorting. Table sort keys identify the type of data, cell number, line number, and word number. To practice a table sort, set up the table shown below with **[Alt]+[F7], 2, 1.** Enter three columns and four rows. You will not need to change anything in the Table Edit screen, so you can exit to the document with the **[F7]** key.

Peters, Susan	123 Main Street Constance, GA 10239	(404) 555-1212
Fields, William	2783 Silver Court La Jolla, CA 92810	(619) 555-2345
Fields, John	23 State Street Los Angeles, CA 92009	(213) 555-6849
Hooper, Karen	1920 Poplar Place Phoenix, AZ 83456	(808) 555-1200

Enter the data into the table. We would like to sort this table by the names contained in the first cell of each of the rows. We will use two keys for this sort in case there are duplicate last names.

To begin the sort, make sure that your cursor is within the table. Then, press **[Ctrl] + [F9]**, **2**. Press **3** (Keys) to set up the two keys. They should be as follows:

Key 1: a, 1, 1, 1   Key 2: a, 1, 1, 2

Any other keys should be deleted by moving to them with the **[Arrow]** keys and pressing **[Delete]**. To complete the sort, select **1** (Perform Action). You may find that you lose the line at the bottom of the table and that other lines within the table are in disarray. To correct this, you will need to go to the Table Edit screen with **[Alt] + [F7],** highlight the cells to be changed, and edit the lines.

If the table contained a row of headings, you would need to highlight the area to be sorted prior to pressing **[Ctrl] + [F9].**

5. Sorting a Secondary Merge File

Secondary merge files are set up in fields and contain markings at the end of each record. An example of a secondary merge file is shown in Figure 1.27.

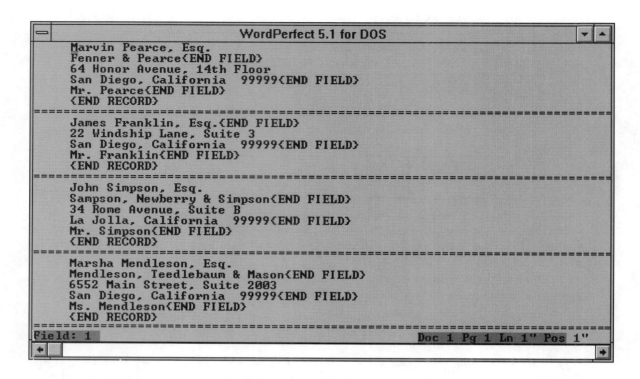

Figure 1.27 A Secondary Merge File

To sort the data in a secondary merge file, you will need to specify the type of data, the field number, the line number, and the word number. After entering the Sort screen, you will need to change the type of sort to Merge. You will then need to enter the keys for the sort. You may want to practice this sort when you complete the secondary merge file in the next section of this chapter.

6. Performing Searches Using Sort

If you have a large amount of data in your document, the Select function in the Sort screen can be used to locate data that meets certain criteria. The search is performed in much the same way as a search in a summary database. The relational or comparative operators are

$$= \quad <> \quad > \quad < \quad >= \quad <=$$

The connectors that connect two or more parts of a search are

$$+ \ (OR) \qquad *(AND)$$

To perform a search, you must first define the keys that you will be looking in for information. Then, you select the data that the key must contain in order to meet your search request. We will use previous examples from this chapter to illustrate these searching methods. It is very important that your database be saved prior to performing a search because the document on the screen will be replaced with the search results.

To locate the address of Alfred Smith in the database shown below, you first need to go to the Sort screen with **[Ctrl] + [F9], 2, [Enter], [Enter]**.

Armor, Peter	23 Mill Road	555-3219
Keefer, Karen	156 Vine Road	555-3040
Smith, Alfred	7686 Apple Lane	555-9030
Smith, John	123 Main Street	555-1212

In the Sort screen, change the sort type to Line sort by pressing **7** (Type), **2** (Line). Next, select **3** (Keys) to set up the keys for the fields you will be searching in. Your keys should be

Key 1: a, 1, 1   Key 2: a, 1, 2

Press the **[F7]** key to complete the editing of the keys.

To perform the search, we will look for Key 1 equal to "Smith" and Key 2 equal to "Alfred". Press **4** (Select) and write the search as follows:

key1 = Smith * key2 = Alfred

There must be a space on either side of the AND or OR connectors. Press **[F7]** to complete the select, and press **1** (Perform Action) to see the results of the search. The results will replace the database on your screen.

Using the next example below, we will perform a search for all documents dated on or before 12/31/96.

2/23/97	Letter to insurance company.
1/2/97	Witness statement.
12/31/96	Police accident report.
1/1/97	Hospital bill.
12/31/96	Ambulance bill.

Remember to save the database with [F10] so that it is not lost when the search is run.

To perform the search for all documents dated on or before 12/31/96, press **[Ctrl] + [F9], 2, [Enter], [Enter]**. The type of sort is a Line sort. Define the date keys by pressing **3** (Keys). The keys should be as follows:

Key 1: n, 1, 3   Key 2: n, 1, 1   Key 3: n, 1, 2

Press **[F7]** when you have finished entering the keys. Next, enter the search criteria by pressing **4** (Select), deleting out any previous information, and typing the following:

key1 < = 96

Press **[F7]** to complete the search information, and **1** (Perform Action) to see the results.

If you needed to locate the documents that were written within a specific year, such as 1996, the search would be

key1 = 96

To locate records within a specific month of a specific year, such as January 1997, the search would be

key1 = 97 * key2 = 1

Parentheses can be used to make sure that some operations are performed together. For example, if you were looking for all documents written between the first and the fifteenth of January 1997, the search would be:

key1 = 97 * key2 = 1 * (key3 > = 1 * key3 < = 15)

A special type of search called a global select will search for something regardless of the field that contains it. You do not need to specify any keys for this sort. To practice a global select, we will use the previous example of documents. If you have saved this list of documents, retrieve it into a blank screen with [Shift] + [F10] or [F5]. To find all documents that refer to "insurance", we will perform the following search:

keyg = insurance

To begin the search, press **[Ctrl] + [F9], 2, [Enter], [Enter].** Press **4** (Select), delete out any previous search information, type in the search, and press **[F7].** Select **1** (Perform Action) to see the results. This type of search is valuable when you would like to find a piece of information that might be contained in several different fields.

I. DOCUMENT MERGING

Mass mailings and frequently used forms can be produced quickly using WordPerfect's merge features.

In a large litigation case, there may be 25 or more opposing counsel. Creating a separate letter for each counsel, inputting their name and address and a salutation, can be very time consuming. It is much easier to create a merge letter and address list than to type each individual letter. By merging the merge letter with the address list, a personalized letter can be created for each individual.

1. Primary and Secondary Files

Merging documents involves the use of primary and secondary files. The primary file is the shell document, into which information will be merged. The secondary file is the list of information to be merged into the primary file document.

For our first example, we will create a simple letter acknowledging an extension of time to respond to a complaint. This letter will be the primary file. The list of addresses for each of the plaintiffs' counsel will be the secondary file.

2. The Merged Document

A merge will combine the information from the primary and secondary files, creating a copy of the primary file for each of the records in the secondary file. After our merge is completed, the merged document will contain a letter for each counsel with a hard page break created between each letter. This makes it easy to send all of the letters to the printer at one time.

3. Example

For our example, we will create a letter and make it into our primary file. Type the letter shown in Figure 1.28 into a blank WordPerfect screen. Use the centering, underline, and bold features where applicable. Use **[Shift] + [F6]** to center the headings and the date. Use **[Shift] + [F5], 1** to insert today's date into the letter. The closing and signature line should not be centered. Use the **[Tab]** key to move the cursor to the middle of the screen to begin typing the closing and signature lines (Pos 4.5"). Use your own name at the signature line.

SMITH AND SMITH
Attorneys at Law
1234 Hampton Avenue
La Jolla, California 99999
(619) 555-1212

January 17, 1997

Opposing Counsel, Esq.
22 Court Boulevard
San Diego, California 99999

Re: <u>Potter, et al. vs. Polluter Co.; Case No. 85549</u>

Dear Mr. Counsel:

Pursuant to a telephone conference of this date, Mr. Johnson of Pote & Tate, on behalf of all plaintiffs in this action, has granted our client, Polluter Co., an extension until May 15, 1997, in which to answer or otherwise respond to the complaint on file in this matter.

Sincerely,

JAMES SMITH
SMITH AND SMITH

Figure 1.28 The Sample Letter

Saving the letter. Before we continue, use the **[F10]** Save and Continue option to save the letter. Remember to specify where you wish to save it (e.g., A: or C:), any directory you wish to place it under, and give the letter the name **EXTEND.LTR.** If you are using a diskette in the A: drive, save the letter as follows: **A:\EXTEND.LTR**

Spell checking. Check the spelling in the letter using the Spell Check feature. Spell checking is accomplished with **[Ctrl] + [F2].** WordPerfect will give you a number of spelling options; choose **3** for **Document.**

4. Creating the Primary File

In creating our primary file, we will be making three fields:

1) Name of the attorney and firm name

2) Firm address

3) The salutation

In order to do this, we must remove some of the text from our letter and place field names where we wish information to be entered from the secondary file.

a) Move the cursor to the "O" in "Opposing Counsel, Esq." Delete to the end of the line using **[Ctrl] + [End].**

b) Press **[Shift] + [F9]** for Merge Codes. Select **1** for **Field.** Type **1** for the field where the name of counsel will be located and press **[Enter].**

c) Remove the entire address by blocking it and pressing the **[Delete]** key.

d) Move the cursor to the beginning of the blank line under the first field that you created, and use **[Shift] + [F9], 1** to create a second field, **2.**

e) The third and final field for our primary file document will be the salutation field. Move the cursor to the "M" in "Mr. Counsel:". Use **[Ctrl] + [End]** to delete to the end of the line. Now, with the cursor remaining after "Dear", use **[Shift] + [F9], 1** to create a third field **3.** Press **[Enter]** and then place a colon after the field reference number.

Your primary file document is now complete and should look like the one in Figure 1.29.

```
SMITH AND SMITH
Attorneys at Law
1234 Hampton Avenue
La Jolla, California  99999
(619) 555-1212


                        January 17, 1997


{FIELD}1~
{FIELD}2~


            Re:   Potter, et al. vs. Polluter Co.; Case No. 85549

Dear {FIELD}3~:

    Pursuant to a telephone conference of this date, Mr. Johnson of Pote & Tate, on behalf
of all plaintiffs in this action, has granted our client, Polluter Co., an extension until May 15,
1997, in which to answer or otherwise respond to the complaint on file in this matter.

                            Sincerely,




                            JAMES SMITH
                            SMITH AND SMITH
```

Figure 1.29 The Primary File

Save this document using **[F7]** (Save). Save it under the same name (**EXTEND.LTR**), respond **Y** when asked if you wish to replace the letter, and respond **N** when asked if you would like to exit.

5. Creating the Secondary File

The secondary file will be the names, addresses, and salutations for each of the persons who will be receiving a letter. We will be able to use the secondary file for this letter and others that we create in the future for this case.

Although the names of several attorneys would likely be included in this secondary file, we will use only four for this example. They are:

Marvin Pearce, Esq.
Fenner & Pearce
64 Honor Avenue, 14th Floor
San Diego, California 99999

James Franklin, Esq.
22 Windship Lane, Suite 3
San Diego, California 99999

John Simpson, Esq.
Sampson, Newberry & Simpson
34 Rome Avenue, Suite B
La Jolla, California 99999

Marsha Mendleson, Esq.
Mendleson, Teedlebaum & Mason
6552 Main Street, Suite 2003
San Diego, California 99999

Remember that there are three fields in this merge letter. The first field is the attorney and firm name, the second is the address, and the third is the salutation.

To create the secondary file we begin with a blank screen and type each field, pressing the **[F9] End Field** key at the end of each field. A group of fields for a single item is called a record. We have four records in our example. At the end of each record, except the last, we will press **[Shift] + [F9], 2** to let WordPerfect know that this is the end of the record.

The first record in our secondary file will be created as follows:

a) Type the name of the first attorney, and the firm name if applicable. Press **[F9].** This puts the merge code **{END FIELD}** at the end of the line and executes a hard return to the next line.

> **Marvin Pearce, Esq.**
> **Fenner & Pearce{END FIELD}**

b) Type the address. At the end of the complete address, after the zip code, press **[F9]** again.

> **64 Honor Avenue, 14th Floor**
> **San Diego, California 99999{END FIELD}**

c) Now, type the salutation.

> **Mr. Pearce**

At the end of the salutation line, press **[F9]**.

d) To tell WordPerfect that you have finished this record, press **[Shift] + [F9], 2.** Your first record should look like the one below.

> **Marvin Pearce, Esq.**
> **Fenner & Pearce{END FIELD}**
> **64 Honor Avenue, 14th Floor**
> **San Diego, California 99999{END FIELD}**
> **Mr. Pearce{END FIELD}**
> **{END RECORD}**
> **= =**

A hard page break will be created at the end of the record. Following these same procedures, input the remaining three records under the first record. When you are finished, your secondary file should look like the one in Figure 1.30.

Marvin Pearce, Esq.
Fenner & Pearce{END FIELD}
64 Honor Avenue, 14th Floor
San Diego, California 99999{END FIELD}
Mr. Pearce{END FIELD}
{END RECORD}

James Franklin, Esq.{END FIELD}
22 Windship Lane, Suite 3
San Diego, California 99999{END FIELD}
Mr. Franklin{END FIELD}
{END RECORD}

John Simpson, Esq.
Sampson, Newberry & Simpson{END FIELD}
34 Rome Avenue, Suite B
La Jolla, California 99999{END FIELD}
Mr. Simpson{END FIELD}
{END RECORD}

Marsha Mendleson, Esq.
Mendleson, Teedlebaum & Mason{END FIELD}
6552 Main Street, Suite 2003
San Diego, California 99999{END FIELD}
Ms. Mendleson{END FIELD}
{END RECORD}

Figure 1.30 The Secondary File

e) Save the secondary file, using the **[F7]** Save, in the same location as your primary file and give it the name **ADDRESS.MRG** to remind us that these are the addresses for our merge. If you are saving the file to your A: drive, the response to "Save as" should be: **A:\ADDRESS.MRG**

Respond **N** to the question of whether you wish to exit.

6. Merging the Primary and Secondary Files

Merging the addresses into our shell letter involves selecting the merge function, identifying the location and name of our primary file, and identifying the location and name of our secondary file. Follow the steps below from a blank screen.

a) Press **[Ctrl] + [F9].** Select **1** for **Merge.**

b) When WordPerfect prompts for the **primary file name,** type the location and name of the primary file and press **[Enter].** Example: **A:\EXTEND.LTR**

c) When WordPerfect prompts for the **secondary file name,** type the location and name of the secondary file and press **[Enter].** Example: **A:\ADDRESS.MRG**

> *If you cannot remember where the file is located, you can find it using [F5]. Selecting 1 (Retrieve) will insert the file name into the primary or secondary file name prompt.*

WordPerfect will then automatically merge the two documents. You should have a merged document with four letters as shown in Figure 1.31.

J. CREATING A PLEADING CAPTION

WordPerfect for DOS contains a Pleading Style and Pleading Macro (March 1992 releases of WordPerfect 5.1 and later) to create pleading paper (line numbers and border lines) on ordinary bond. If you will be printing on plain bond paper, you will want to set up your pleading so that the lines and numbers of pleading paper will be printed on the plain bond along with your document. If you are printing on preprinted pleading bond, you can skip to Section 2 on changing the bottom margin.

SMITH AND SMITH
Attorneys at Law
1234 Hampton Avenue
La Jolla, California 99999
(619) 555-1212

January 17, 1997

Marvin Pearce, Esq.
Fenner & Pearce
64 Honor Avenue, 14th Floor
San Diego, California 99999

Re: <u>Potter, et al. vs. Polluter Co.; Case No. 85549</u>

Dear Mr. Pearce:

   Pursuant to a telephone conference of this date, Mr. Johnson of Pote & Tate, on behalf of all plaintiffs in this action, has granted our client, Polluter Co., an extension until May 15, 1997, in which to answer or otherwise respond to the complaint on file in this matter.

   Sincerely,

   JAMES SMITH
   SMITH AND SMITH

SMITH AND SMITH
Attorneys at Law
1234 Hampton Avenue
La Jolla, California 99999
(619) 555-1212

January 17, 1997

James Franklin, Esq.
22 Windship Lane, Suite 3
San Diego, California 99999

Re: <u>Potter, et al. vs. Polluter Co.; Case No. 85549</u>

Dear Mr. Franklin:

   Pursuant to a telephone conference of this date, Mr. Johnson of Pote & Tate, on behalf of all plaintiffs in this action, has granted our client, Polluter Co., an extension until May 15, 1997, in which to answer or otherwise respond to the complaint on file in this matter.

   Sincerely,

   JAMES SMITH
   SMITH AND SMITH

SMITH AND SMITH
Attorneys at Law
1234 Hampton Avenue
La Jolla, California 99999
(619) 555-1212

January 17, 1997

John Simpson, Esq.
Sampson, Newberry & Simpson
34 Rome Avenue, Suite B
La Jolla, California 99999

Re: <u>Potter, et al. vs. Polluter Co.; Case No. 85549</u>

Dear Mr. Simpson:

   Pursuant to a telephone conference of this date, Mr. Johnson of Pote & Tate, on behalf of all plaintiffs in this action, has granted our client, Polluter Co., an extension until May 15, 1997, in which to answer or otherwise respond to the complaint on file in this matter.

   Sincerely,

   JAMES SMITH
   SMITH AND SMITH

SMITH AND SMITH
Attorneys at Law
1234 Hampton Avenue
La Jolla, California 99999
(619) 555-1212

January 17, 1997

Marsha Mendleson, Esq.
Mendleson, Teedlebaum & Mason
6552 Main Street, Suite 2003
San Diego, California 99999

Re: <u>Potter, et al. vs. Polluter Co.; Case No. 85549</u>

Dear Ms. Mendleson:

   Pursuant to a telephone conference of this date, Mr. Johnson of Pote & Tate, on behalf of all plaintiffs in this action, has granted our client, Polluter Co., an extension until May 15, 1997, in which to answer or otherwise respond to the complaint on file in this matter.

   Sincerely,

   JAMES SMITH
   SMITH AND SMITH

Figure 1.31 The Merged Documents

1. Selecting the Pleading Style or Macro

The Pleading Style in WordPerfect is an option that numbers the lines on your paper from 1 to 28 lines and places a double vertical line on the left side next to the numbers. The problem with the Pleading Style is that it is set up with margins that you can only change if you are an experienced WordPerfect user. The Pleading Macro is a more sophisticated way to set up your pleading paper, and it allows you to create your own style and margins. Both methods are explained below.

Make sure you are at the very top of the first page of a new document by pressing **[Home]**, **[Home]**, **[Home]**, **[Up Arrow]**, and follow part a or b depending on which method will set up your pleading.

a. *Pleading Style*

To choose the Pleading Style for your document, press **[Alt] + [F8]**, move the highlight bar down to **Pleading** and select **1** for **On.** Your document is now set up for pleading paper. You can see the pleading style code with [F11] Reveal Codes.

---

*If you press **[Alt] + [F8]** and no styles are listed on the screen, it may be that the style library has not been set up on your computer. To set it up, select **[Shift] + [F1]**, **6, 5**. You will need to type in where your Style Files are located (usually where your WordPerfect files are located, e.g., C:\WP51). Then you will need to type in the Library file name: **LIBRARY.STY.** Exiting out of this menu with **[F7]**, you will then find that your styles are now listed under **[Alt] + [F8]**.*

---

b. *The Pleading Macro*

The Pleading Macro will allow you to create various pleading styles. The Pleading Macro is accessed by pressing **[Alt] + [F10]**, typing **PLEADING,** and pressing the **[Enter]** key. The screen shown in Figure 1.32 will appear.

```
Pleading Paper Style Macro                          (Press F3 for Help)

    1 - Name                    Pleading

    2 - Top Margin              1"

    3 - Bottom Margin           1"

    4 - Left Margin             1"

    5 - Right Margin            1"

    6 - Left Line (0,1,2)       2

    7 - Right Line (0,1)        0

    8 - Starting Number         1

    9 - Ending Number           28

    0 - Create Style


Selection: 0
```

Figure 1.32 The Pleading Macro Screen

This macro will create a new pleading style called "Pleading." Since one with this name came with my WordPerfect program, I will name this style "Pleading1." Many pleadings require a 1.5″ left margin, so I will make this change. I will also change the right margin to .5″. The left line I will leave as a double line, and I will change the right line to a single line. My screen will now look like the one in Figure 1.33. Pressing the **[Enter]** key will save the new style under **[Alt] + [F8],** and will place it into my document.

If you want to save the new style as part of the style library, in the Styles screen (**[Alt] + [F8]**) select **6** for Save and type the location and file name of the WordPerfect style library (e.g., C:\WP51\LIBRARY.STY).

```
Pleading Paper Style Macro                                    (Press F3 for Help)

      1 - Name                        Pleading1

      2 - Top Margin                  1"

      3 - Bottom Margin               1"

      4 - Left Margin                 1.5"

      5 - Right Margin                0.5"

      6 - Left Line (0,1,2)           2

      7 - Right Line (0,1)            1

      8 - Starting Number             1

      9 - Ending Number               28

      0 - Create Style


Selection: 0
```

Figure 1.33   Changing the Style Settings

2. Changing the Bottom Margin

In order to accommodate page numbers at the bottom of each page, the bottom margin must be changed to .5″. If we had made this change in the Pleading Macro, line 28 would have been placed .5″ from the bottom. We want line 28 to remain 1″ from the bottom and the page number to be placed .5″ from the bottom. The Pleading Style contains a .883″ bottom margin.

To change the bottom margin, make sure that your cursor is after the Pleading Style code in the document using Reveal Codes. Select **[Shift] + [F8]**, **2, 5** and change the bottom margin to **.5″**. Press **[Enter]** and then press **[F7].**

3. Page Numbering

To number the pages of your pleading, select **[Shift] + [F8]**, **2, 6, 4, 6** and press **[F7]**. This will place the page number at the bottom center of your pleading. Your screen will still be blank. You can see what has been done so far in Reveal Codes.

4. Attorney Address

Immediately following your Pleading Style, bottom margin, and page numbering selections, type the attorney's name, state bar number, address, telephone number, and representation designation as shown below. Make sure that the attorney name is on the first line of the document.

Attorney Name
Attorney at Law
State Bar Number
Address
Telephone Number

Attorney for (Plaintiff, Defendant, etc.)

5. Court Designation

Different jurisdictions will have different ways that they want their pleadings to be created. In many jurisdictions, the court designation should begin at line 8 on the pleading paper. This is line 3.33″ if you are using WordPerfect's Pleading Style. If you created a pleading style using the Pleading macro, line 8 of the pleading paper is located at line 3.29″. Press the **[Enter]** key until you reach the correct line. You may use View in the Print Menu (**[Shift] + [F7], 6**) to check to see that the Court Designation begins on line 8.

The court designation should be centered, capitalized, and double spaced. (Use the **[Enter]** key to insert a blank line. Do not change to double spacing.) For example:

SUPERIOR COURT OF THE STATE OF CALIFORNIA

IN AND FOR THE COUNTY OF SAN DIEGO

6. Caption

Move four lines from the Court Designation to begin the caption.

Change the line justification from **Full** to **Left** so that the caption and pleading title are not spread to the right margins. To do this press **[Shift] + [F8], 1, 3, 1** and press **[F7]**.

Prepare three columns following these steps.

a) Press **[Alt] + [F7]**, select **1** for **Columns**, select **3** for **Define**.

b) At the Column Definition Screen, select **1** to change the column type, select **2** for **Parallel.**

c) Select **2** for **Number of Columns**, type **3**, and press **[Enter]**.

d) Select **4** for **Margins** and select one of the following margin settings depending on whether you used the Pleading Style or the Pleading Macro:

WordPerfect Pleading Style

Column 1	1″	4.5″
Column 2	4.5″	4.6″
Column 3	5″	6.5″

Pleading Macro Style with Margins L–1.5″, R–.5″

Column 1	1.5″	4.7″
Column 2	4.7″	4.8″
Column 3	5.3″	8.0″

Press **[Enter]** to exit the Column Definition Screen. Then, select **1** to turn the columns **On.**

In the first column, type the plaintiff and defendant names.

JOHN SMITH and MARY SMITH,

       Plaintiffs,

vs.

**ABCD CORPORATION, and DOES 1
through 100, Inclusive,**

       Defendants.

After typing the word **Defendants,** press the **[Enter]** key to return to the left margin.

Using the underline character **[Shift] + [___],** create an underline from the left margin to the right margin of Column 1 (4.5″ or 4.7″). If you go too far, use the **[Backspace]** key to back up.

Press **[Ctrl] + [Enter]** to move to the second column and insert ")" characters until they are even with the underline in the first column.

```
JOHN SMITH and MARY SMITH,          )
                                    )
            Plaintiffs,             )
                                    )
vs.                                 )
                                    )
ABCD CORPORATION, and DOES 1        )
through 100, Inclusive,             )
                                    )
            Defendants.             )
_____)
```

When the second column is completed, press **[Ctrl] + [Enter]** to move to the third column and enter the case number and pleading name.

```
JOHN SMITH and MARY SMITH,          )   CASE NO. 567320
                                    )
            Plaintiffs,             )   TITLE OF PLEADING AND
                                    )   HEARING INFORMATION IF
vs.                                 )   NECESSARY
                                    )
ABCD CORPORATION, and DOES 1        )
through 100, Inclusive,             )
                                    )
            Defendants.             )
_____)
```

When the third column is completed, turn the columns off by pressing **[Alt] + [F7]**, **1** for **Columns** and **2** for **Off.** This will return you to the left margin.

Turn the full justification back on by pressing:

[Shift] + [F8], 1, 3, 4, [F7]

7.   Text

The text of the pleading should follow the caption and should be double spaced. To make sure that the text will line up with the pleading line numbers on the printed document, your first line of text must begin on a line inch ending in .00, .33, or .67 for the WordPerfect Pleading Style. For the pleading style created with the Pleading Macro, you will need to type some text and View the document in the Print Menu to see if it is aligned (**[Shift] + [F7], 6**).

After positioning the cursor on a correct line, select double spacing with **[Shift] + [F8], 1, 6, 2, [Enter], [F7]**.

You may view your document before you send it to the printer by pressing **[Shift] + [F7], 6.** A sample pleading is shown in Figure 1.34.

```
 1 │ Attorney Name
   │ Attorney at Law
 2 │ State Bar Number
   │ Address
 3 │ Telephone Number

 4 │

 5 │ Attorney for Plaintiff

 6 │

 7 │

 8 │                    SUPERIOR COURT OF THE STATE OF CALIFORNIA

 9 │                      IN AND FOR THE COUNTY OF SAN DIEGO

10 │

11 │ JOHN SMITH and MARY SMITH,          )    CASE NO.  567320
   │                                     )
12 │              Plaintiffs,            )    TITLE OF PLEADING AND
   │                                     )    HEARING INFORMATION IF
13 │ vs.                                 )    NECESSARY
   │                                     )
14 │ ABCD CORPORATION, and DOES 1 through)
   │ 100, Inclusive,                     )
15 │                                     )
   │              Defendants.            )
16 │ _____)

17 │ The text of the pleading will begin here.  Make sure that the line spacing is set at 2, and that the

18 │ justification is full.

19 │

20 │

21 │

22 │

23 │

24 │

25 │

26 │

27 │

28 │
   │                                  - 1 -
```

Figure 1.34   A Sample Pleading

K. PARAGRAPH NUMBERING AND OUTLINE

Paragraph numbering is a feature that will sequentially number items in a document. This feature is beneficial in the creation of discovery requests and contracts. Not only does the feature provide sublevel numbers and letters, but it also will renumber all paragraphs when others are added or removed. The Outline feature is an advanced method of paragraph numbering that automatically generates a new level number each time you press [Enter] or [Tab].

1. Activating Paragraph Numbering

To activate paragraph numbering, press **[Shift] + [F5]** and select **6** (Define) to pick the type of numbering that you desire. The screen shown in Figure 1.35 will appear.

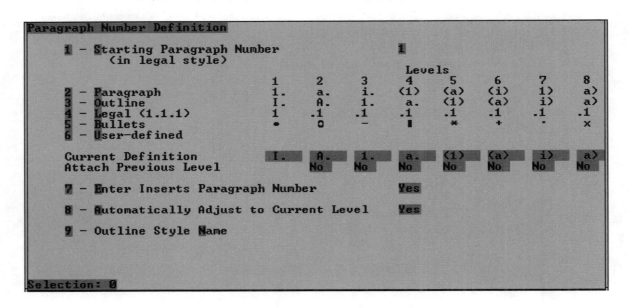

Figure 1.35 The Paragraph Numbering Screen

There are several different styles of paragraph numbering to choose from. The most commonly used styles are

Paragraph		Outline		Legal
1.		I.		1
	a.	A.		1.1
	i.		1.	1.1.1

WordPerfect® for DOS

The different levels occur at successive tab stops. At the Define screen, select **2** (Paragraph) and press **[F7]** to return to the **[Shift] + [F5]** options. Next, select **5** (Para Num) and press **[Enter]** for automatic numbering. You will return to the document and a paragraph number will have been inserted.

Paragraph numbering is a bit primitive when used in this manner in that you must press [Shift] + [F5], 5, [Enter] each time you want a level number or letter inserted. To get a sublevel inserted, you will press the tab key in to the desired level before pressing [Shift] + [F5], 5, [Enter]. Once a level number or letter has been inserted into the document, it can be changed to a different level by placing the cursor under the paragraph number or letter and pressing [F4] (Indent) to move levels to the right, or [Backspace] to move levels to the left. The more sophisticated method of paragraph numbering, the Outline feature, will be discussed below in Section 3.

To practice paragraph numbering, we will enter two discovery requests. If you have not placed a paragraph number into your document follow the steps above to define the type as Paragraph, and insert your first paragraph number. Type the first paragraph below. The [Tab] key will be used to indent this paragraph. The [F4] key will be used to indent the sub-items.

1.   **Plaintiff requests that Defendant produce all records evidencing the existence of a contract between Plaintiff and Defendant including, but not limited to, the following:**

Press **[Enter]** at the end of the paragraph, press the **[Tab]** key to move in one tab stop, and press **[Shift] + [F5], 5, [Enter]** to get the next level letter. Type the following list of items using **[F4]** (Indent) to indent the text, pressing the **[Enter]** key at the end of each paragraph, pressing the **[Tab]** key to move in, and activating the numbering with **[Shift] + [F5], 5, [Enter]**.

a.   **The written contract between the parties.**
b.   **Any correspondence between the parties regarding the contract.**
c.   **All invoices, internal memoranda, or other documents generated as a result of the contract.**
d.   **All documents, spreadsheets, or databases existing in electronic format that evidence the existence of a contract.**

Return to the left margin after the last item, and press **[Enter]** to insert a blank line. The second request is shown below. Insert its paragraph number with **[Shift] + [F5], 5, [Enter]**.

2.   **Plaintiff requests that Defendant produce all accounting records of Defendant corporation for the years 1995, 1996, and 1997.**

The completed paragraphs should look similar to the ones in Figure 1.36.

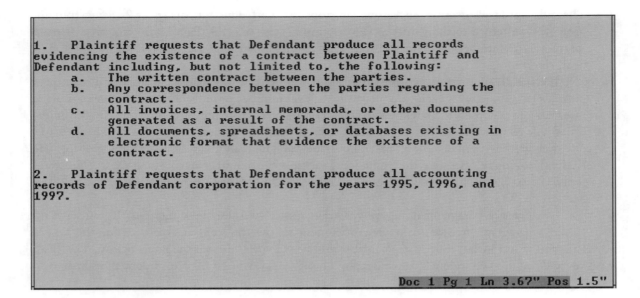

```
1.   Plaintiff requests that Defendant produce all records
evidencing the existence of a contract between Plaintiff and
Defendant including, but not limited to, the following:
     a.   The written contract between the parties.
     b.   Any correspondence between the parties regarding the
          contract.
     c.   All invoices, internal memoranda, or other documents
          generated as a result of the contract.
     d.   All documents, spreadsheets, or databases existing in
          electronic format that evidence the existence of a
          contract.

2.   Plaintiff requests that Defendant produce all accounting
records of Defendant corporation for the years 1995, 1996, and
1997.
```

Doc 1 Pg 1 Ln 3.67" Pos 1.5"

Figure 1.36 Automatically Numbered Paragraphs

2. Inserting, Moving, and Deleting Paragraphs

To insert a new paragraph or level, move the cursor to the end of the paragraph above where you wish to place the inserted paragraph, press the **[Enter]** key and then tab in to the desired level, press **[Shift] + [F5], 5, [Enter],** and type the new item. To practice this, insert a new paragraph after paragraph b in request number 1. It will automatically be labeled as c. As soon as you press the [F4] key to indent the text, the other paragraph numbers will change. The new item c should read:

c.   All addendums or modifications made to the contract.

To move an item, you will move the cursor to the left margin of the document in front of the paragraph number. Next, block it with [F12] to the left margin of the document in front of the next level. Then, press **[Ctrl] + [F4], 1** (Block), **1** (Move). Place the cursor at the left document margin where you would like the item inserted and press **[Enter].** Try changing the order of the subparts of request number 1 using Move.

To delete a paragraph, move to the left document margin in front of the paragraph number and block it to the left document margin of the next paragraph. Then, press **[Delete]** and press **Y** (Yes).

3. The Outline Feature

The Outline feature is a quicker, but somewhat more difficult, way to number your paragraphs. This feature gives you a new line number each time you press the [Enter] key. It

WordPerfect® for DOS

also adjusts the number to the next level when you press the [Tab] key. If you want a tab space to follow the paragraph number, you will need to use [Home], [Tab]. You can also use the [Space Bar] and [F4] (Indent) to create space after the paragraph number.

To demonstrate the Outline feature, we will use the discovery requests from Section 1 above. First, get to a blank document with **[F7], n, n.** Before we activate the Outline feature, we must define the paragraph numbering. Press **[Shift] + [F5], 6** (Define) and press **2** (Paragraph). Press **[F7]** to return to the menu options. Next, press **4** (Outline), **1** (On). The word "Outline" will appear in the bottom corner of the screen. Press the **[Enter]** key to get the first number. Press **[Home], [Tab]** to tab in the first line, and type request number **1.** When you press **[Enter]** at the end of the paragraph, you will be given number 2 at the left document margin. Press the **[Tab]** key once to move the number in one level. Press **[F4]** to indent the item and type the first subpart of this request. Repeat the process until all of the items have been entered. When you press [Enter] at the end of the last item, you will need to use **[Shift] + [Tab]** to move the number one level to the left. Press **[Enter]** to move it down a line.

To insert paragraphs into an outline, you need to move to the end of the line above where you want to insert a new paragraph, and press **[Enter].** Try inserting a new item into request number 1. If a new paragraph number is added inadvertently, you can use the [Backspace] key to back it out. To insert a blank line between any two paragraphs, press **[Enter]** from the end of a line, and then use [Backspace] to remove the number.

When you are finished with the Outline feature, press **[Shift] + [F5], 4** (Outline), **2** (Off).

L. PREPARING A TABLE OF AUTHORITIES

A table of authorities is similar to a table of contents and is included at the beginning of legal briefs and points and authorities to list the statutes, cases, and other materials referenced within the pleading. An example of a table of authorities is shown in Figure 1.37.

There are four steps to creating a table of authorities using WordPerfect for DOS:

1. **Identify the categories of materials** contained within the pleading and the order in which you wish them to appear in the table. The usual order of these materials is
    - Cases
    - Constitutional Provisions
    - Statutes
    - Regulations
    - Court Rules
    - Miscellaneous
2. **Mark each authority** within the document.
3. **Prepare the table of authorities,** identifying where the categories of materials should be listed.
4. **Generate the table.**

TABLE OF AUTHORITIES

CASES

City of Los Angeles v. Gleneagle Development Co.
    62 Cal. App. 3d 543, 133 Cal. Rptr. 212 (1976) 5, 6

Denham v. Superior Court
    2 Cal. 3d 557, 564, 86 Cal. Rptr. 65 (1970) 3, 4, 6

Dunsmuir Masonic Temple v. Superior Court
    12 Cal. App. 3d 17, 22, 90 Cal. Rptr. 405, 408 (1970) 4, 5

Farrar v. McCormick
    25 Cal. App. 3d 701, 705, 102 Cal. Rptr. 190 (1972) 5

Ordway v. Arata
    150 Cal. App. 2d 71, 79, 309 P.2d 919 (1957) 3, 6

Tannatt v. Joblin
    130 Cal. App. 3d 1063, 1070, 182 Cal. Rptr. 112 (1982) 3, 4

STATUTES

Cal. Code Civ. Proc. §583.410 2-5

Cal. Code Civ. Proc. §583.410(a) 2

Cal. Code Civ. Proc. §583.410(b) 2

COURT RULES

Cal. Rules of Court, Rule 373 2

Cal. Rules of Court, Rule 373(a) 5

Figure 1.37   A Table of Authorities

WordPerfect® for DOS

The most time-consuming aspect of this process is the actual marking of each authority. However, when you have completed the marking, you may regenerate the table after making any corrections to the text and have the old table replaced with a new table.

The pleading used in this example is included in Appendix A to this chapter. In order to practice preparing the table of authorities, you will need to type it into WordPerfect yourself, or your instructor will provide it to you on a disk. We will follow the four steps for creating a table of authorities using this pleading.

1. Identifying the Categories of Materials

In reviewing the pleading, we see that it contains cases, statutes, and court rules. Therefore, the categories of authorities that we will use in our table of authorities are cases, statutes, and court rules. Using the common order, the cases section will be Section 1, the statutes section will be Section 2, and the court rules section will be Section 3.

Section 1—Cases
Section 2—Statutes
Section 3—Court Rules

2. Marking the Authorities

Now that we have defined the sections of the table and given them numbers, we must mark the occurrence of each authority. Each authority will be marked in full form at its first occurrence. A short form name, like a nickname, will also be given. Subsequent occurrences of the authority will be marked quickly with the short form name.

The first authority within the text of the pleading, in Part II, is California Code of Civil Procedure, Section 583.410(a). Mark this authority with the following steps.

a. *Full Form Marking*

a) Highlight the entire authority, from "California" through the section number, by blocking it with **[Alt] + [F4]** or **[F12].**

b) Press **[Alt] + [F5], 4.**

c) At the prompt, **type in the table section number** and press **[Enter].** For this authority the number will be 2 because the authority is a statute.

d) The ToA Full Form edit screen will then appear. This is where you will place the full form of the authority as you would like it to appear in the table of authorities. For this authority, we would like the full form to appear as follows:

Cal. Code Civ. Proc. §583.410(a)

Edit the full form and access the section symbol by pressing **[Alt] + 21** using the numbers on the number keypad. (You may need to turn on the [Num Lock] key.) When you have finished the full form, press **[F7]** to exit.

e) When you are prompted for the short form of the authority, type a short name for this authority. This name will be used to identify all occurrences of this authority, so it must be unique. For the first authority we will use the short form:

CCP 583.410(a)

f) Press **[Enter]** to complete the marking.

The next authority is found within the same paragraph. Repeat the steps we used for the previous authority: placing it in Section 2, giving it the full form name "Cal. Code Civ. Proc. §583.410(b)", and giving it the short form name "CCP 583.410(b)".

Mark the next authority using the full form name "Cal. Code Civ. Proc. §583.410" and the short form name "CCP 583.410".

The next authority is a citation to California Rule of Court, Rule 373. This authority will be in Section 3 of the table. Mark this authority with the full form name "Cal. Rules of Court, Rule 373" and the short form name "Rule 373".

b. *Short Form Marking*

The next authority is another reference to California Code of Civil Procedure, Section 583.410. Since we have already identified the full form of this authority, we need only mark this authority and identify its short form name. Follow the steps below.

a) Block the citation to be marked with **[Alt] + [F4]** or **[F12].**

b) Press **[Alt] + [F5], 4** and instead of entering a table section number, press **[Enter].** Type in the short form for the authority. For this authority we used "CCP 583.410".

Mark the next reference to Rule 373 also using the short form method.

After marking the next reference to CCP 583.410 with its short form, you will come to the first case authority.

c. *Marking Cases*

The first case authority is Ordway v. Arata. To mark a case authority, highlight the case name, citation(s), and date. Mark this first reference to this case using the full form method. It will be in Section 1. In the full form edit screen, edit the authority as you would like it to appear in the table. A common method is to place the case name on the first line at the left margin, and the citation(s) on the second line one tab stop in. An example using Ordway is shown below.

Ordway v. Arata
150 Cal.App.2d 71, 79, 309 P.2d 919 (1957)

You will need to decide if you want your case name underlined in your table of authorities. If you want the case name to be underlined, underline it in the full form edit screen. If you do not want the case name underlined, reveal your codes in the edit screen and delete any underline codes. After you have exited the full form screen, give the case the short form name "Ordway".

Mark the next two cases, Denham and Tannatt, using the full form method.

When you come to the next case authority, you will see that it is another reference to Denham. Mark this reference with the short form method by highlighting the case reference, pressing **[Alt] + [F5], 4,** pressing **[Enter],** and giving the short form name "Denham".

Continue on through the pleading, marking new authorities with the full form method, and identifying repeated authorities with the short form method.

3. Preparing the Sections of the Table

After you have marked all of the authorities, it is time to define the table. The pleading in Appendix A has a page already set out for the table of authorities. With other pleadings, you may need to use a hard page break and create this page for your pleading. Move to the page of the pleading where the table is to appear. Space down two or three lines to where you would like the first section of the table, CASES, to appear. Type in the heading at the left margin as shown below.

<u>CASES</u>

Press **[Enter]** twice to double space down. At this point, you will identify where the cases will begin to appear in the table. (Make sure that you have turned off the bold and underline that you used in the section title.)

a) Press **[Alt] + [F5], 5, 4** to define the table. You will be prompted for the table section number. Type **1** for the CASES section and press **[Enter].**

b) After you have identified the section number, you will be prompted to select some options in the table setup. Common tables will have leader dots, no underlining, and a blank line between authorities. Change any of the options and press the **[Enter]** key to return to your document.

To mark the second section, press the **[Enter]** key twice to double space down from where we entered the definition for Section 1, and type **STATUTES** at the left margin. Make sure that you turn the bold and underline off. Double space down and follow the steps above defining the statutes as Section 2. Double space down again and type **COURT RULES** at the left margin. Turn off the bold and underline. Double space down and follow the steps above to define the court rules as Section 3. When you have finished, you are ready to generate the table.

4. Generating the Table

Before you generate the table, the page numbering of the pleading needs to be changed so that the document begins renumbering at the beginning of the text with another page 1. To do this, move to the first page of the text of the pleading and press **[Shift] + [F8], 2, 6,** select **1** to change the page number, type **1,** and press **[Enter].** Press **[F7]** to return to your document. After generating the table, you may want to move to the caption page of the pleading and change the type of page numbering to small roman numerals—for example, i, ii, iii, iv. The text of the pleading will continue to contain arabic numerals.

To generate the table, press **[Alt] + [F5], 6, 5,** and press **Y** for **yes.** Your table of authorities should appear similar to the one in Figure 1.37.

If you have authorities that are listed with an asterisk, they were marked with a short form that did not match the one used when the first reference to the authority was identified. Use Reveal Codes to see how the first reference is marked. Delete the old code, remark the authority using the correct short form, and generate the table again.

The benefit of all the work that went into creating this table of authorities occurs when changes are made to the pleading that result in authorities moving to different pages or being eliminated entirely. If this happens, all that needs to be done is to again follow the steps for generating a table. The new table will write over the existing table. If new authorities are added to the pleading, they should be marked and the table should be generated again.

Summary

WordPerfect 5.1 for DOS is a word processing software program that allows you to create and edit documents. WordPerfect features are accessed through the function keys or the pull-down menus. The pull-down menus may be accessed by pressing the right mouse button or **[Alt] + [=].**

There are two typing modes within WordPerfect, Insert and Typeover. Insert inserts new text at the point of the cursor, pushing existing text to the right. Typeover types over the existing text. You may switch between Insert and Typeover by pressing the **[Insert]** key.

Deleting text can be accomplished with the **[Delete]** or **[Backspace]** key. Blocks of text may be deleted by first blocking the text, and then pressing the **[Delete]** key. A block of text is a group of characters or words that is marked by turning on the Block feature with **[Alt] + [F4]** or **[F12],** and highlighting the text of the block. The marked block may be deleted, copied, moved, printed, bolded, underlined, centered, or acted upon in many other ways.

WordPerfect is equipped with spell check, thesaurus, and search features. Other features allow you to create columns, tables, footnotes, merged documents, macros, pleading captions, tables of authorities, and to automatically sort and number lines and paragraphs. The wide range of features, Corel's user support, and the ease in using the program itself make WordPerfect the leading choice for legal word processing.

Appendix A

The pleading contained in this appendix is to be used with the table of authorities section of this chapter, which begins on page 81.

```
 1   Stephen E. Attorney
     Attorney at Law
 2   State Bar No. 55555
     1234 Santa Fe Drive
 3   Anywhere, California  92444
     (619) 555-1212
 4
 5   Attorney for Plaintiff, JAY P. JONES
 6
 7
 8              SUPERIOR COURT OF THE STATE OF CALIFORNIA
 9                  IN AND FOR THE COUNTY OF SAN DIEGO
10
11   JAY P. JONES,                    )    CASE NO. 56789
                                      )
12             Plaintiff,             )    PLAINTIFF'S RESPONSE TO
                                      )    DEFENDANT'S MOTION TO
13   vs.                             )    DISMISS ACTION
                                      )
14   ABCD CORPORATION, and DOES 1     )    DATE:    DECEMBER 10, 1996
     through 100, Inclusive,          )    TIME:    9:00 A.M.
15                                    )    DEPT:    35
               Defendants.            )
16   _____)
17   /////
18   /////
19   /////
20   /////
21   /////
22   /////
23   /////
24   /////
25   /////
26   /////
27   /////
28   /////
```

1

2

3

4

5

6

7

8

9

10

11

12

13

14

15

16

17

18

19

20

21

22

23

24

25

26

27

28

TABLE OF AUTHORITIES

2

1	<div style="text-align:center">**I**</div>
2	<div style="text-align:center">**INTRODUCTION**</div>
3	This motion is brought by the defendant to dismiss this action
4	for plaintiff's alleged failure to prosecute this action
5	diligently. Yet it is brought three months following the service
6	of the Summons and Complaint, and following months of active
7	discovery by both sides.
8	Plaintiff was injured on February 23, 1991, when he slipped on
9	spilled liquid and fell while demonstrating portable copy machines
10	to the employees of defendant on defendant's premises. The
11	Complaint in this action was filed on June 11, 1991. Plaintiff
12	demonstrates his company's copiers throughout the United States and
13	Europe and travels constantly. The fact that Plaintiff's
14	employment continually moved him from city to city, made
15	communication with his counsel extremely difficult. Any and all
16	communication with plaintiff took considerably more time to
17	effectuate than it would have had plaintiff resided within this
18	county, or even within the state. Consequently, the Complaint was
19	not served upon the defendant, ABCD CORPORATION, for more than two
20	years following its filing.
21	Defendant asserts that this claim is stale, and that witnesses
22	cannot be located, although discovery is ongoing and defendant has
23	been supplied with a witness list. In addition, Defendant was
24	notified of this claim in July of 1991 by its insurance carrier.
25	Although plaintiff did fail to serve the Complaint on
26	defendant ABCD CORPORATION within two years of the commencement of
27	the action, this delay was excusable due to the nature of
28	plaintiff's employment which impeded his communication with his

3

1 counsel.   The court should exercise its discretion and deny

2 defendant's motion to dismiss.

3 <center>II</center>

4 <center>**STATUTORY AUTHORITY**</center>

5 California Code of Civil Procedure, Section 583.410(a)

6 provides that: "The court _may in its discretion_ dismiss an action

7 for delay in prosecution pursuant to this article on its own motion

8 or on motion of the defendant _if_ to do so appears to the court

9 appropriate under the circumstances of the case." (Emphasis added.)

10 Section 583.410(b) of the Code of Civil Procedure provides that

11 dismissal under Code of Civil Procedure, Section 583.410 shall be

12 pursuant to the Judicial Council Rules. Rule 373 of the California

13 Rules of Court sets forth the relevant matters to be considered by

14 the court in ruling on a motion brought under Code of Civil

15 Procedure, Section 583.410.

16   Rule 373 states in pertinent part:

17   In ruling on the motion the court shall consider all

18   matters relevant to a proper determination of the motion,

19   including the court's file in the case and the affidavits

20   and declarations and supporting data submitted by the

21   parties and, where applicable, . . . the diligence of the

22   parties in pursuing discovery or other pretrial

23   proceedings, . . . the nature of any extensions of time

24   or other delay attributable to either party, . . .

25   whether the interests of justice are best served by

26   dismissal or trial of the case; and any other fact or

27   circumstance relevant to a fair determination of the

28   issue.

4

The interests of justice would best be served by a trial on the merits of this action. Therefore, plaintiff should be allowed to proceed to trial.

III

**DISMISSAL PURSUANT TO CODE OF CIVIL PROCEDURE
SECTION 583.410 IS DISCRETIONARY**

The discretion of the trial court to dismiss an action pursuant to Section 583.410 of the Code of Civil Procedure is not arbitrary or capricious, but is controlled by legal principles and is to be exercised in accordance with the spirit of the law and with a view towards serving rather than defeating the ends of justice. Ordway v. Arata, 150 Cal. App. 2d 71, 79, 309 P.2d 919 (1957). This type of discretionary dismissal is not proper if there is any basis for a showing of good cause by plaintiff for the delay and no injustice will result from denying the motion to dismiss. Denham v. Superior Court, 2 Cal. 3d 557, 564, 86 Cal. Rptr. 65 (1970); Tannatt v. Joblin, 130 Cal. App. 3d 1063, 1070, 182 Cal. Rptr. 112 (1982).

Plaintiff's employment kept him moving throughout the United States and Europe. Several times when plaintiff's counsel attempted to contact him it required telephone calls to numerous foreign countries and numerous cities before plaintiff could actually be reached. Oftentimes, plaintiff was unreachable and plaintiff's counsel was unable to communicate with him whatsoever. The complication of communication between plaintiff and his counsel resulted in the delay in serving defendant ABCD CORPORATION.

Dismissal is only mandated when there is an entire absence of any showing of good cause for delay. Denham v. Superior Court,

5

1 _supra_.

2   The policy underlying Code of Civil Procedure, Section

3 583.410, which seeks to prevent unreasonable delays in litigation,

4 must sometimes yield to the more powerful policy that seeks to

5 dispose of litigation on the merits. _Dunsmuir Masonic Temple v._

6 _Superior Court_, 12 Cal. App. 3d 17, 22, 90 Cal. Rptr. 405, 408

7 (1970). "[T]he probability of a miscarriage of justice is more

8 when a trial on the merits is denied than it is where plaintiff is

9 permitted to proceed." _Tannatt v. Joblin_, _supra_, at 1069.

10   **IV**

11 **DEFENDANT'S OWN CONDUCT HAS RESULTED IN DELAYS**
    IN BRINGING THIS CASE TO TRIAL AND IS

12 **ANOTHER FACTOR JUSTIFYING DENIAL**
    OF DEFENDANT'S MOTION TO DISMISS

13

14   Defendant cites _Dunsmuir v. Superior Court_, _supra_, as being

15 directly on point with the action herein. However, _Dunsmuir_ is

16 distinctly different on two crucial points:

17   1.   In _Dunsmuir_ the defendant filed his motion to dismiss

18   within three weeks of service upon him of the Complaint;

19   and

20   2.   "No handicap to communication between attorney and client

21   [was] even hinted."

22   In the within action, defendant has requested extensions to

23 answer, has answered, and both parties have engaged in discovery.

24 With discovery nearly completed, plaintiff's attorney has requested

25 that defendant's counsel sign a Joint At-Issue Memorandum.

26 Defendant's counsel has refused and continues to refuse.

27   In _City of Los Angeles v. Gleneagle Development Co._, 62 Cal.

28 App. 3d 543, 133 Cal. Rptr. 212 (1976), the appellate court

6

1 reversed the trial court's dismissal noting that the plaintiff had
2 filed interrogatories, filed an At-Issue Memorandum, and given
3 other reasons for the delay in prosecution.

4 The unusual nature of the notice procedure for this type of
5 motion to dismiss sheds light on its nature, purpose, and function.
6 Rule 373(a) of the California Rules of Court requires at least 45
7 days' notice on a motion to dismiss pursuant to Code of Civil
8 Procedure, Section 583.410. This extended notice period is: ". . .
9 intended to afford a plaintiff ample time within which to
10 complete any necessary preparation and move to set the case for
11 trial. . . ." Farrar v. McCormick, 25 Cal. App. 3d 701, 705, 102
12 Cal. Rptr. 190 (1972); City of Los Angeles v. Gleneagle, supra.
13 In this action, those steps were taken before any such motion was
14 filed. Any delay that occurred was due to the handicapped
15 communication between plaintiff and his counsel. In Dunsmuir,
16 relied on by defendant in its motion, the plaintiff was bedridden
17 and somewhat immobile, but the court ruled that this did not
18 constitute good cause for delay in service where she was at all
19 times represented by counsel and there was no handicap in
20 communication.

21 In support of its arguments, defendant cites three cases
22 decided before 1920 and one 1962 case in which excuses for delay
23 were not sufficient. The Supreme Court and the appellate courts
24 have more recently upheld the discretion of the trial court in
25 refusing dismissal in a number of cases where reasonable excuses
26 were given. In Denham v. Superior Court, supra, the personnel
27 turnover in a small law firm resulted in an increased workload and
28 pressure on the attorneys remaining in the firm. In City of Los

7

1   <u>Angeles v. Gleneagle Development Co.</u>, <u>supra</u>, understaffing in a
2   large law office with a heavy and demanding caseload resulted in
3   several attorneys handling the file and constituted sufficient
4   excuse for delay in setting the case for trial. Finally, in <u>Ordway</u>
5   <u>v. Arata</u>, <u>supra</u>, the illness and subsequent death of one of the
6   plaintiffs and its disruptive effect on the family and business
7   affairs constituted good cause for delay in the service of Summons.
8   The court in <u>Ordway</u> stated: "As a matter of sound public policy
9   litigation should be disposed of upon substantial rather than
10   technical grounds." <u>Id.</u> at 79.
11   Plaintiff's employment created a hardship in communication
12   between him and his counsel. His action should not be allowed to
13   be dismissed as a result of this hardship.
14   DATED: December 1, 1996.
15   Respectfully submitted,
16
17
18   _____
19   STEPHEN E. ATTORNEY
20
21
22
23
24
25
26
27
28

8

Chapter Index

CHAPTER 2

WINDOWS WORD PROCESSORS

Chapter Preface

Windows-based word processors all utilize menus, buttons, and key combinations in a graphical environment for the creation of documents. This chapter will cover the basics of using a Windows-based word processor and many advanced features that take advantage of the power of these applications. The figures used to illustrate the features of these programs are shown in the Microsoft® Windows® 95 operating system. The instructions in this chapter will apply to programs used in Microsoft Windows or Windows 95. The primary Windows word processors used to demonstrate these features will be Microsoft® Word® and Corel®'s WordPerfect®, the two word processors most often used in the law office environment. There are many versions of these programs in use; the steps covered in this chapter are geared toward the newest versions. However, many of the features discussed are available in all versions. The only difference may be the menu from which a feature is selected or the dialog box where choices are made. Wherever a difference in versions occurs, I have tried to show the alternative methods of accessing the feature. For example, in instances where newer versions of WordPerfect refer to the "Format" menu, I have placed the name of the older version of that menu, "Layout," in parentheses.

Section One—The Basics

A. THE WINDOWS WORD PROCESSOR ENVIRONMENT

1. Entering the Application

To enter an application in Windows, double-click on the application's icon. To enter a Windows 95 application, either double-click on its icon on the desktop or click the Start button, point to Programs, point to the word processor's program group, and click on the program name. Upon entering the program, you will see the main window of the word processor. The main windows of WordPerfect and Word are shown in Figures 2.1 and 2.2.

2. The Word Processor Window

The main screen of a Windows-based word processor is a window. A window has a Title Bar, a Control Menu button, Minimize and Maximize buttons (and a Close button in Windows 95), Menus, and Scroll Bars.

- The **Title Bar** is at the top of the window and will display the application name and the name of the document that you are working on.
- The **Control Menu** button, in the upper left-hand corner of the window, will give you options to minimize, maximize, or close the window. In Windows this button will look like a file drawer. In Windows 95, this button is represented by the application's icon.

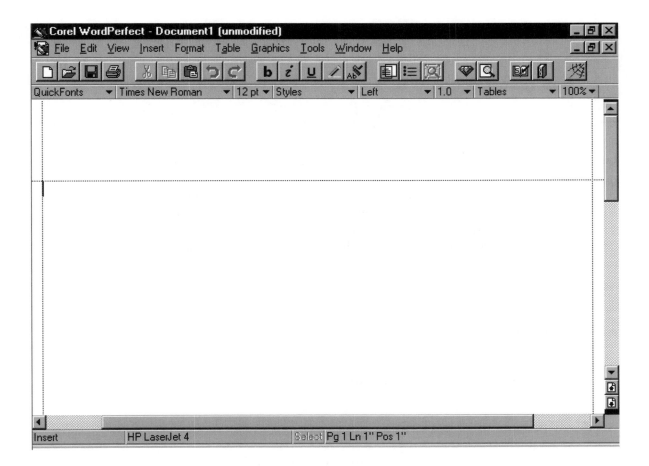

Figure 2.1 The Main Window of Corel® WordPerfect®

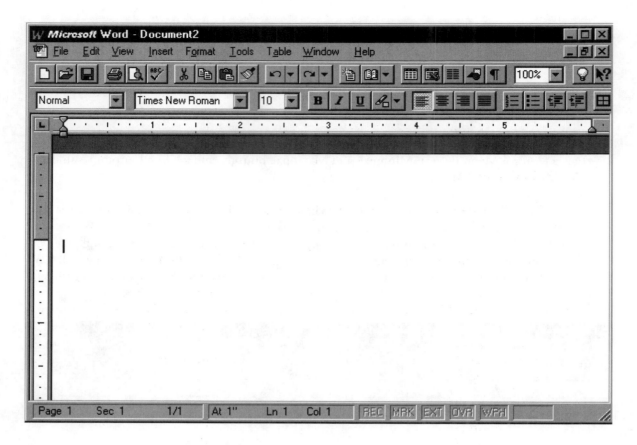

Figure 2.2 The Main Window of Microsoft® Word®

- The **Minimize** and **Maximize** buttons, in the upper right-hand corner of the window, will change the size of the application's window. The Minimize button will take the window down to an icon. The Maximize button will take the window to the full screen. When a window is maximized, the maximize button will turn into a button that will take the window to a mid-size window. In Windows, these buttons are represented by up and down arrows. In Windows 95, they are represented by icons that look like windows. Also in Windows 95 you will find a button with an "X" that will close the application.
- **Menus** under the Title Bar activate the options available in the window.
- **Scroll Bars** are found in some windows at the right and/or bottom of the windows. Clicking on the up or down arrows, or dragging the square scroll box, will move the contents of the window up, down, or from side to side.

3. Toolbars and Status Bars

Windows-based word processors have Toolbars at the top of the window and Status Bars at the bottom of the window. Toolbars consist of buttons that activate frequently used features.

These features are also available through the menus. The lower of the two Toolbars is used to change the formatting of your document. WordPerfect calls this the "Power Bar." Word calls it the "Formatting Toolbar." The Toolbars can be removed from, or added to, the word processor window through selections in the View menu. Alternatives to the standard Toolbar can also be chosen from a list that is activated by pointing at a Toolbar and clicking the right mouse button.

The Status Bar at the bottom of the screen displays the page number, cursor position, and other information concerning the document you are creating.

4. Pull-Down Menus

The pull-down menus at the top of the word processor window can be accessed with a mouse or the keyboard. These menus contain the many features available within the word processor. To access a menu with the mouse, click on the menu name and then click on the desired option. To use the keyboard to access a menu, hold down the **[Alt]** key and press the underlined letter in the menu name and the letter for a menu option. For example, to print you can access the File menu with **[Alt] + [F],** and then select print by pressing the **[P]** key. You can also press the **[Alt]** key and then use the gray arrow keys on the keyboard to move among the menu options. A menu can be closed by clicking the mouse outside of the menu or by pressing the **[Alt]** key or the **[Esc]** key.

The menus available within the word processor will vary between programs. The menus commonly found in WordPerfect and Word are File, Edit, View, Insert, Format (Layout), Table, Window, and Help.

- The **File menu** contains the options that open, close, save, and print your files. It also contains the option to exit the program. You will notice that there are two save options, Save and Save As. The Save As option will prompt you for a file name. The Save option is used after your file has a name to quickly save the file.
- The **Edit menu** contains options to undo mistakes that you have made, to cut or copy and paste, to find and replace text, and to go to a specific page of the document.
- The **View menu** changes the appearance of your word processing screen. Within this menu are options to add or remove the Toolbars, to change to a different page layout, and to zoom in to view a portion of the document or zoom out to see the entire page.
- The **Insert menu** gives you the options to insert special characters, the date, footnotes, files, and spreadsheets or databases into your document.
- The **Format (Layout) menu** will allow you to change the format of your document by giving you options to change your font (typeface) and the layout of your lines, paragraphs, and pages.
- The **Table menu** contains all of the options needed to create and edit a table. A table is a wonderful alternative to tabular columns. It is made up of columns and rows and looks and acts like an electronic spreadsheet. The intersection of a column and row forms a cell where you can enter text or numbers.
- The **Window menu** lists the documents that you currently have open in the word processor and allows you to set up ways to view them simultaneously on the screen. You can switch between your documents by clicking on the desired document name in this menu. A check is placed next to the current document on the screen. Switching between

documents becomes useful when you are drafting a new document from one or more old documents. Text can be moved or copied from the old documents and then pasted into the new document. Moving and copying text will be covered in a later section.

• The **Help menu** can contain tutorials, Coaches, and Wizards. Each of these features will teach you how to perform different functions. You can also search for a specific topic or look through an index or a list of contents. If you cannot find the appropriate information in the Help menu, check the software manual or contact the company's technical support department by telephone or on-line.

5. Function Keys

The Function keys are the keys at the top or left-hand side of the keyboard labeled F1 through F10 or F12. A Function key can be pressed by itself or in combination with the **[Alt]**, **[Shift]**, or **[Ctrl]** key. The features activated by the Function keys can be found in the Help menu. In WordPerfect, you have the option to choose between keyboard setups—the standard CUA keyboard and a DOS keyboard that is similar to that of WordPerfect for DOS. Changes in the WordPerfect keyboard setup can be made in the Preferences option of the File or Edit menu. Users who are accustomed to the WordPerfect for DOS key combinations should change to the DOS keyboard.

6. Keystroke Combinations

Many features can also be activated by combining the **[Alt]**, **[Shift]**, or **[Ctrl]** keys in combination with a letter key, an arrow key, or the special keys (Insert, Home, etc.). For example, italics can be activated by pressing **[Ctrl] + [I]**, and a word can be deleted with **[Ctrl] + [Backspace]**. These keystroke combinations will differ between programs. A complete list of these keystroke combinations can be found in the Help menu.

7. Cursor Movement

The cursor is the flashing bar that appears on the screen. The cursor indicates where characters will be entered as you type them on the keyboard. The mouse pointer will appear as a large capital I when pointing within a document. It will appear as an arrow when pointing at menu selections and as a hand or as other graphics in other places within the word processor. The mouse pointer is moved by moving the mouse.

To move the cursor within a document, you can use the arrow keys on the keyboard, a special key, a keystroke combination, or the mouse. The cursor may be moved to any position in your document, except to a position where you have not yet entered any text. Below is a list of special keys and keystroke combinations that will move the cursor within your document. The columns display the keystroke combinations for the WordPerfect for DOS keyboard template, and the WordPerfect CUA keyboard template and Word keys.

ACTION	WORDPERFECT (DOS)	WORDPERFECT (CUA) AND WORD
Previous page	[Page Up]	WP: [Alt] + [Page Up] Word: [Ctrl] + [Alt] + [Page Up]
Next page	[Page Down]	WP: [Alt] + [Page Down] Word: [Ctrl] + [Alt] + [Page Down]
Move to top of screen	[Home], [Up Arrow]	[Page Up]
Move to bottom of screen	[Home], [Down Arrow]	[Page Down]
Move to top of document	[Home], [Home], [Up Arrow]	[Ctrl] + [Home]
Move to bottom of document	[Home], [Home], [Down Arrow]	[Ctrl] + [End]
Move to beginning of line	[Home], [Left Arrow]	[Home]
Move to end of line	[End]	[End]
Go to a specific page	[Ctrl] + [Home]	[Ctrl] + [G]
Move one word left or right	[Ctrl], [Lft. or Rt. Arrow]	[Ctrl], [Lft. or Rt. Arrow]

8. Insert Versus Typeover

There are two typing modes in most word processors, insert and typeover. When you enter the program, it is usually in the insert mode. In the insert mode, text that already exists will be pushed to the right as you enter new text. In the typeover mode, text that is typed will overwrite existing text and spaces. To toggle between insert and typeover, press the **[Insert]** key. Your typing mode will be indicated on the Status Bar at the bottom of the screen.

B.   CREATING AND EDITING A DOCUMENT

To create a document, you will need to type in the text or insert graphics, sound, or special characters. To edit a document, you will need to know how to highlight text, delete text, and move and copy text.

1. Setting the Margins

A new document will have margins that have been pre-set by the word processor. In WordPerfect, the margins can be changed in the **Format (Layout) menu.** In Word, the margins are changed in the **File menu** under **Page Setup.** Position the cursor where you want the margin changes to take effect within a document. If there is a particular portion of the document that needs different margins, highlight the text and then make the margin change.

2. Justification

Justification is the positioning of the text in relation to the left and right margins of the page. The word processor will begin a new document with either left or full justification. **Left justification** positions the text flush against the left margin and leaves a jagged right margin. **Full justification** positions the text flush against both the left and right margins. Other justification selections include right and center. **Right justification** positions the text flush against the right margin and leaves a jagged left margin. **Center justification** centers the text between the margins of the page. You can switch between justifications within a document, or highlight a block of text and select a justification feature for that block. Justification selections can be found on the Toolbar or in the Format (Layout) menu.

3. Tabbing and Indenting

Tabbing and indenting are two different ways to bring in the left margin of a paragraph to a tab stop. Word processors have tab stops that are pre-set at approximately every half inch. Pressing the **[Tab]** key or selecting an indent option will bring the text in to the first tab stop. If you press the **[Tab]** key or select an indent option multiple times, the text will be brought in that number of tab stops.

The **[Tab]** key is used to indent the first line of a paragraph or to indent a heading or other item. At the beginning of a paragraph, you will press the **[Tab]** key to indent the first line to the first tab stop. As you type the remainder of the paragraph, the text will word wrap back to the left margin.

Indenting will indent the entire text of a paragraph. There are several types of indents. A left indent will indent the left side of a paragraph. A double indent will indent both sides of the paragraph. A hanging indent will indent all of the paragraph except for the first line. Hanging indents are commonly used in bibliographies. You can indent a paragraph by pressing the function key that activates the indent feature, selecting a button on the Toolbar, or by selecting an indent option from the menu selection **Format (Layout), Paragraph.**

The tab stops within a document can be adjusted using the Ruler. The **Ruler** can be added below your Toolbar by selecting it from the View menu. A tab stop is moved by dragging it with the mouse. A tab stop can be added by clicking your mouse button where you would like the tab to appear. A tab stop can be removed by dragging it off the Ruler. It is important to note that your tab changes occur from the position of the cursor forward. So, if you want the changes to apply to the entire document, place the cursor at the top of the document before you make them.

4. Line Spacing

The most common settings for line spacing are single and double. Most word processors are pre-set at single spacing. To change the line spacing in a document, you can use a button on the Toolbar or use the Format (Layout) menu. In Word, you can also highlight a section, or move to the beginning of a paragraph, and press **[Ctrl] + 1** or **[Ctrl] + 2.**

5. Adding Emphasis with Bold, Italics, and Underlining

Emphasis can be added within the text of your document by **boldfacing,** *italicizing*, or underlining. You may also use a combination of these styles. To add this emphasis to your document, you turn on the feature prior to typing the text, type the text, and then turn it off. These features are turned on and off by clicking on the appropriate button on the Toolbar or by using the following keystroke combinations:

Bold	**[Ctrl] + [B]**
Italics	**[Ctrl] + [I]**
Underline	**[Ctrl] + [U]**

If you have already typed the text, you can highlight it and then activate the feature.

6. Centering Text

Centering text can be accomplished by selecting a centering option and then typing the text, or by typing the text at the left margin and then selecting the centering option. Centering options can either be for a single line or for multiple lines (center justification.)

In WordPerfect, you can center a single line of text with **Format (Layout), Line, Center,** or by clicking the right mouse button and selecting the Center option. After typing the text, pressing the **[Enter]** key will return you to the left margin.

In both WordPerfect and Word, you can center multiple lines by changing to center justification on the Toolbar. Pressing the **[Enter]** key will keep returning you to the center of the page. After you have typed the last line to be centered, press the **[Enter]** key to go to the next line, and select another justification option such as left or full (termed "Justify" in Word).

7. Highlighting Text

Highlighting text is the marking of text prior to performing some action upon the text. Text can be highlighted with the mouse, or with the **[Shift]** key and the **[Arrow]** keys on the keyboard.

To highlight text using the mouse, move the mouse pointer to the beginning of the text to be highlighted, click and hold the left mouse button, and drag the highlighting to the end of the portion of text to be highlighted. You can then perform an action upon the highlighted text. To turn the highlight off, you can click the mouse anywhere else in the document. You can also use multiple clicks of the left mouse button to select a word, sentence, or paragraph as shown below.

Select a word:	**Double click**
Select a sentence:	**WordPerfect Only: Triple click**
Select a paragraph:	**WordPerfect: Quadruple click** **Word: Triple click**

Clicking outside of the highlight will remove the highlight.

When you are first learning to use the mouse to highlight text, it can be frustrating because it is hard to get the highlight to begin and end exactly where you want. An alternative to using the mouse to highlight text is to use the **[Shift]** key in combination with the **[Arrow]** keys. You can also use the **[Page Up]** and **[Page Down]** keys in combination with the **[Shift]** key to highlight a lot of text quickly. Moving the cursor after you have released the **[Shift]** key will remove the highlight.

8. Deletions

When editing a document, deletions of a character or a group of characters will need to be made. The two keys that delete one character at a time are **[Delete]** and **[Backspace].** To delete more than one character at a time, you can highlight the text and press the **[Delete]** key or use a keystroke combination. Deletions that can be performed, and the keys or keystroke combinations that perform them, are listed below. To restore text that has been mistakenly deleted, use **Undo** or **Undelete** from the **Edit menu.**

ACTION	KEY OR KEYSTROKE COMBO
Delete the character to the right of the cursor, or delete highlighted text.	**[Delete]**
Delete the character to the left of the cursor.	**[Backspace]**
Delete the word containing the cursor.	WordPerfect: **[Ctrl] + [Backspace]** Word: **[Ctrl] + [Backspace], [Ctrl] + [Delete]**
Delete to the end of the line.	WordPerfect (DOS): **[Ctrl] + [End]** WordPerfect (CUA): **[Ctrl] + [Delete]** Word: **[Shift] + [End], [Delete]**

ACTION	KEY OR KEYSTROKE COMBO
Delete to the bottom of the page.	WordPerfect (DOS): **[Ctrl] + [Page Down]** WordPerfect (CUA): **[Ctrl] + [Shift] + [Delete]** Word: **[Shift] + [Down Arrow] (to the bottom of the page), [Delete]**

PRACTICE EXERCISES

Type the following samples of text using some of the features that have been covered so far. You do not need to use a new document for each one.

Sample 1

B.

DEFENDANT HAS THE BURDEN OF SHOWING THAT THE COUNTY IN WHICH THE ACTION IS BROUGHT IS IMPROPER

It is the Defendant's burden to offer sufficient facts to show to this Court that San Diego County is not the proper court to hear the case. *Massae v. Superior Court* 118 Cal. App. 3d 527, 530, 173 Cal. Rptr. 527 (1981).

Sample 2

Plaintiff alleges:

    1.   This Court is the proper court to hear this matter because Defendant, MARK SAMPSON, resides in this jurisdiction.

    2.   Plaintiff is informed and believes, and on that basis alleges, that Defendant, MARK SAMPSON, is, and at all times herein mentioned was, an individual residing in San Diego County, California, within the North County Judicial District.

Using the commands that were covered above, edit Sample 2 to conform to the facts of a new case. In the new case, our client Joe Smith is suing ABCD Corporation, a California corporation. The new defendant resides in the same jurisdiction as the old defendant.

    a) Begin the revision by deleting Mark Sampson's name in the first paragraph with the **[Delete]** key. Replace his name with the name of our new defendant, ABCD Corporation. Note that in most pleadings the names of the parties will always be in capital letters. Also, substitute "resides" with "has its principal office".

b) Next, move to paragraph 2 and remove "Mark Sampson" using **[Ctrl] + [Backspace].** If you are using Word, you will need to also use **[Ctrl] + [Delete]** to complete the task. Insert the new defendant's name, ABCD Corporation, in that spot.

c) Now, use the mouse to highlight the phrase "an individual residing" and press the **[Delete]** key to remove it. Replace this text with the following: "a corporation organized pursuant to the laws of the State of California, having its principal office".

Your new paragraphs should look as follows:

Plaintiff alleges:

    1.   This Court is the proper court to hear this matter because Defendant, ABCD CORPORA-TION, has its principal office in this jurisdiction.

    2.   Plaintiff is informed and believes, and on that basis alleges, that Defendant, ABCD COR-PORATION, is, and at all times herein mentioned was, a corporation organized pursuant to the laws of the State of California, having its principal office in San Diego County, California, within the North County Judicial District.

C.   SAVING AND OPENING DOCUMENTS

To save a document, you must store it on a magnetic disk, optical disk, or magnetic tape by identifying the storage location and giving it a name. There are three menu options found in the File menu that will save your documents; **Save As, Save,** and **Close.**

To open a document, you must identify its location and its name. There are two menu options in the File menu that will open documents. The **New** option will open a new document. The **Open** option will open an existing document from a disk or tape. To insert a document from disk or tape into the document you are creating on the screen, you will use an option from the Insert menu to insert an existing file into your document.

1. Save As

The Save As option opens a dialog box that prompts you for a location and name for your document. An example of this type of Save As dialog box is shown in Figure 2.3.

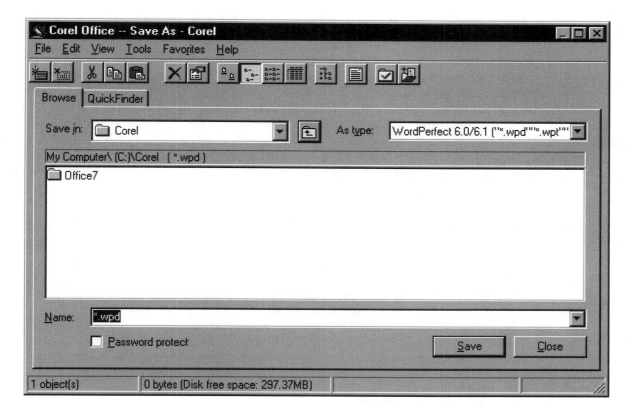

Figure 2.3 A Save As Dialog Box

In this dialog box, you can type the drive letter, folder, and file name in the space indicated for the file name. You can also change the default directory to the drive letter and folder in which you want to save the document by clicking on drive and folder icons. Then, you can place just the file name in the space indicated. If you would like to save the file in a word processor format that is different from the word processor that you are using, you can also make this change in the dialog box. Pressing the **[Enter]** key or clicking on a **Save** or **OK** button will complete the process of saving the document.

2. Save

The Save option stores changes in a document without opening a dialog box or otherwise prompting you. This option is used after you have given the document a file name. If the document does not yet have a name, you will be prompted with the Save As dialog box. You should use this option often when creating a document. This will prevent you from losing most of your document in the event of power loss to your computer.

3. Close

The Close option is used to exit from the document you are working on and leave you in the word processing program. If all changes in the document have been saved, this option will close the document. If all changes have not yet been saved, you will be prompted to save the changes. Responding "yes" to the prompt asking if you wish to save the changes will save them, and you can exit from the document. If the document has not yet been given a name, the Save As dialog box will appear.

4. Automatic Backup

Most word processors have an automatic backup feature that saves the document you are working on at a set interval of minutes. This feature saves the document in a special format that will allow for its retrieval in the event that your word processor freezes or your computer loses power. When you reenter the word processor, you will be asked whether you would like to open the automatically saved document. Responding in the affirmative will retrieve the documents with the changes made as of the last automatic save.

To adjust the time interval for the automatic backup feature, select **Edit, Preferences, File** in WordPerfect, or **File, Save As, Options** in Word.

5. Opening a New Document

The **New** option in the **File menu** will open a new document on the screen. You can also use the New Document button on the Toolbar. When you first enter the word processor, you will have a new document on your screen. It is only when you want a new document to work in, or when you have closed the document on the screen, that you will need to use this option. When the New option has been selected, you will be prompted in many word processors to select a document template. The default template is a blank document, but you can choose from among templates or Word Wizards for memoranda, letters, legal documents, and many other categories of documents.

6. Open a Document from a Disk or Tape

The **Open** option in the **File menu** allows you to open a document file that has been saved to a disk or to tape. When this option is selected, the Open dialog box will appear on the screen and prompt you for the name of the file. An example of one of these dialog boxes is shown in Figure 2.4. You can type the drive, folder (directory), and file name in the space for the file name, or you can open drives and folders to find the file by clicking on their icons. When you have found the file, you click on the file name. Clicking on the **Open** or **OK** button will complete the process.

Most word processors now have the ability to open documents created in other word processing programs. If the word processor does not recognize the document as one of its own, you will be prompted to select the type of word processor it was created in and the document will be converted.

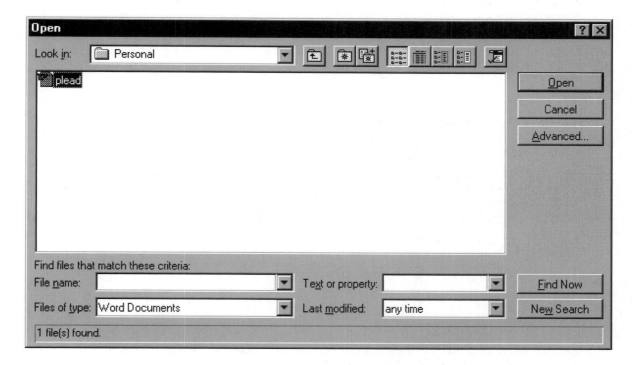

Figure 2.4   The Open Dialog Box in Word

7.   Inserting a File into a Document

There will be times when you want to insert a stored document into the document you are working on. If it is a word processing document file, you will select **Insert, File.** (In WordPerfect 5.2 for Windows, you will select File, Retrieve.) You then will be prompted with a dialog box similar to the Open dialog box in Figure 2.4. If you want to insert a database or spreadsheet file into your document, you can select an option for inserting databases or spreadsheets from the Insert menu.

D.   MOVING AND COPYING TEXT

When editing a document it is often necessary to move or copy text from one position to another. You can move and copy text within the current document on the screen, between documents open in the word processor, and to other Windows programs. Moving text is called "cutting and pasting" in Windows programs. Cutting text removes it from its old location. You then move the cursor to the new location and paste the text there. Copying leaves the original text in place. You then move the cursor to the new location and paste the text. You can move or copy text using the Edit menu, the Toolbar, or the mouse.

1. Within the Current Document

Most moving and copying occurs within the current document on the screen. To select the text to be moved or copied, highlight it with the keyboard or mouse. To use the Edit menu to move or copy the highlighted text, select **Edit, Cut** or **Edit, Copy.** Then move the cursor to the new location and select **Edit, Paste.**

To use the Toolbar to move or copy the highlighted text, click on the **Cut** button (scissors) or the **Copy** button (two documents). Then move the cursor to the new location and click on the **Paste** button (paste jar or clipboard).

To use the mouse to move text, highlight the text, point the mouse arrow within the highlight, and drag it to a new location. To copy the text, hold down the **[Ctrl]** key prior to dropping the text in the new location.

2. Between Documents

To move or copy text between documents, you follow the steps in Section 1 above, and then switch to or open another document, and paste the text in the desired location.

3. Between Windows Programs

Windows programs have the ability to move and copy text between each other because moved or copied text is placed on the Windows Clipboard. The Clipboard is a part of Windows and is used by all Windows-based programs to hold text so it can be pasted in new locations. The Clipboard can hold only one entry, so when other text is selected to be moved or copied, it replaces the text previously held by the Clipboard. Not all text moved or copied from one Windows-based program can be read by another program, but many can.

To move or copy text from one program to another, highlight the text, select **Edit, Cut** or **Edit, Copy,** move to the other program, and select **Edit, Paste.**

---

*You may restore text that you have cut out of the document by pasting it back in the same location, or by selecting **Edit, Undo**.*

E. OTHER WORD PROCESSING FEATURES

1. Document Codes

Document codes are the formatting codes that show you where a formatting feature begins and ends. WordPerfect has a feature called "Reveal Codes" that splits the screen to display the normal text at the top and the same text with its formatting codes at the bottom. The Reveal Codes feature is shown in Figure 2.5. The codes can be removed by moving the cursor to them and using either the **[Delete]** or **[Backspace]** key. You can also alter the formatting of a section of text by highlighting it and activating formatting features.

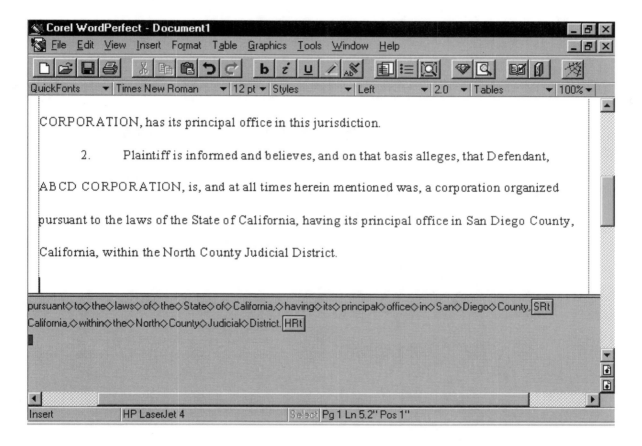

Figure 2.5   The WordPerfect Reveal Codes feature displays the text and codes at the lower part of the screen

In Word, a user can see the codes present within a document by clicking on the **Show/Hide** button (the button containing a paragraph symbol) on the Toolbar. To change the format of a portion of the text, move the cursor in front of the text and activate the feature. Another method is to highlight the text and activate the formatting feature.

2. Fonts and Text Appearances

Using different fonts and text appearances can add emphasis, significance, and originality to your documents. Fonts are typefaces, and there are many available in word processing features. The primary fonts used in legal documents are Courier and Times Roman. The font size is the size of the character. The larger the number, the larger the character. The primary font size used in legal documents is 12 point. Check your local rules of court for the fonts and font sizes permitted in pleadings. Attributes are features like **boldfacing,** *italicizing*, and underlining, and include SMALL CAPS and ~~strikeout~~. Small caps are often found in law review articles in place of italicizing or underlining. Strikeout is used when displaying changes to documents such as legislation or contracts. The strikeout shows text and provisions that have been deleted from the original document. Many of these features can be found on the Toolbar, but to find all of the possible features, you must select **Format, Font.** An example of the Font dialog box is shown in Figure 2.6.

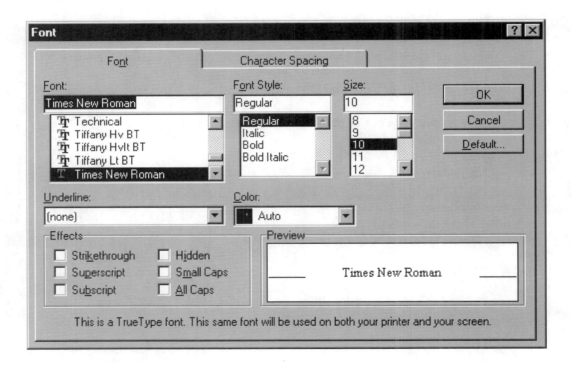

Figure 2.6   The Font Dialog Box in Word

These features can be activated before typing the text, or after by highlighting the text and selecting the feature.

3. Special Characters

There are many special characters not available on the keyboard that can be accessed in the **Insert menu.** In WordPerfect, the **Insert menu** option is **Character.** The feature can also be activated by pressing **[Ctrl] + [W].** Characters from different character sets can be seen by clicking and holding on the button in the Set box, highlighting the desired set, and releasing the mouse button. Most of the characters used in legal documents can be found in the Typographic Symbols character set. The WordPerfect characters dialog box is shown in Figure 2.7.

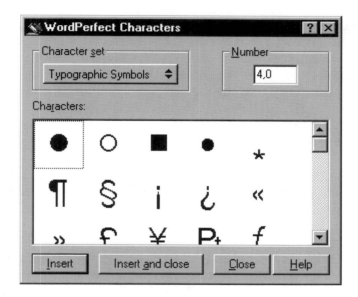

Figure 2.7   An example of the special characters available in WordPerfect

In Word, the menu selection is **Insert, Symbol.** The symbols from many different font sets can be accessed in the Font selection box. These font sets include the WordPerfect Typographic Symbols set. Common typographic symbols can also be found on the Special Characters page of the Symbol dialog box.

To insert a character into your document, place the cursor where you would like the character to appear, activate the special characters dialog box, select the font or character set, click on the desired character, and click on the Insert button.

---

*To quickly place a section symbol (§) in your document, use **[Alt] + 21.** The "21" must be typed on the number keypad at the right of the keyboard, and the **[Num Lock]** key must be on. This will work in both WordPerfect and Word.*

---

4. Page Breaks

When you reach the bottom of a page in your document, a single line or page bottom graphic will appear across the screen. This type of page break is called a **soft page break.** Word processors automatically end a page with a soft page break according to the pre-set page length of your document.

When you wish to end a page in a place other than where the soft page break occurs, you will use a **hard (manual) page break.** To create a hard page break, place the insertion point where you want the page to end and a new page to begin. Pressing **[Ctrl] + [Enter]** will place the hard page break into the document. In some word processors the bottom of a page will look different when a hard page break has been used. For example, in WordPerfect 7, a soft page break leaves a thin line graphic at the bottom of the page. A hard page break leaves a thick line graphic. In other word processors there will not be a difference in the appearance of the bottom of the page. In those instances, you will need to reveal codes in WordPerfect. A hard page break is indicated by a **[HPg]** code in Reveal Codes. A soft page break is indicated by a **[SPg]** code. In Word, you will need to choose **Edit, Find, Special** to locate a manual page break.

5. The Date Feature

Word processors provide a way to incorporate the date from your computer's internal clock into your documents. The feature is accessed with **Insert, Date.** In WordPerfect, selecting **Date Text** will place the current date within the document. In Word, you will select the date format you desire, and click on the **OK** button. Word also allows you to enter the time into your document.

Both WordPerfect and Word also have an option to place the current date within the document each time it is opened. This is beneficial in creating form documents. In WordPerfect, you select **Insert, Date, Date Code.** In Word, after you have selected the date format, you will click the selection to have the date automatically updated.

6. Page Numbering

When inserting page numbers into a document, you will need to select where the page numbers will go and what type of numbers you desire. Although you can usually activate this feature anywhere within the document, it is a good idea to place the cursor at the top of the document when you select page numbering. In WordPerfect, select **Format (Layout), Page, Numbering** or **Format, Page Numbering** depending on the version of the program that you are using. In Word, select **Insert, Page Numbers.**

7. Spell Checking

Checking the spelling within a document is important and is one of the great features of a word processor. The spell checking feature will read each word within a document and compare it to the words contained within its dictionary. When the spell check feature finds a word that does not match a word in the dictionary, it will stop and give you alternative spellings or allow you to edit the word. The spelling dialog box is shown in Figure 2.8. The spell checker is found in the **Tools menu** in both WordPerfect and Word.

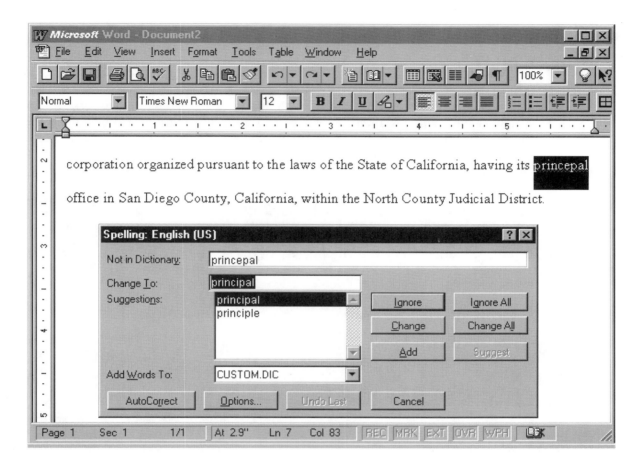

Figure 2.8   The Spelling Dialog Box in Word

The newest versions of WordPerfect and Word also have a feature that automatically underlines a word that is misspelled as you are typing. Misspelled words can then be clicked on with the right mouse button for correct spelling options. WordPerfect calls this feature "Spell-as-you-go." Word calls it "Automatic spell checking." Both can be activated in the Tools menu. Word's feature is found as an option in the Tools, Spelling dialog box.

WordPerfect and Word also have features that automatically correct commonly misspelled words as you type. For example, typing "teh" and pressing the [Space Bar] will automatically become "the." WordPerfect calls this feature "QuickCorrect" and it can be found in the Tools menu. Word calls this feature "AutoCorrect." A great advantage of this feature is that you can add words that you commonly misspell, or add abbreviations for words that you use frequently. For example, if you were working on a case that continually used the term "hydrogen chloride," you could add "hc" to the correcting feature and have it automatically replace it with "hydrogen chloride." The WordPerfect feature can be turned off by deselecting "Replace words as you type" in the QuickCorrect dialog box. The Word feature can be turned off by deselecting it in the Options dialog box of the Spelling dialog box.

8.   The Thesaurus

Word processors often contain a thesaurus to assist you in drafting your documents. A thesaurus supplies synonyms for a variety of words. To use the thesaurus feature, place the insertion point within a word and select **Thesaurus** from the **Tools menu.** The thesaurus for the word "**press**" is shown in Figure 2.9.

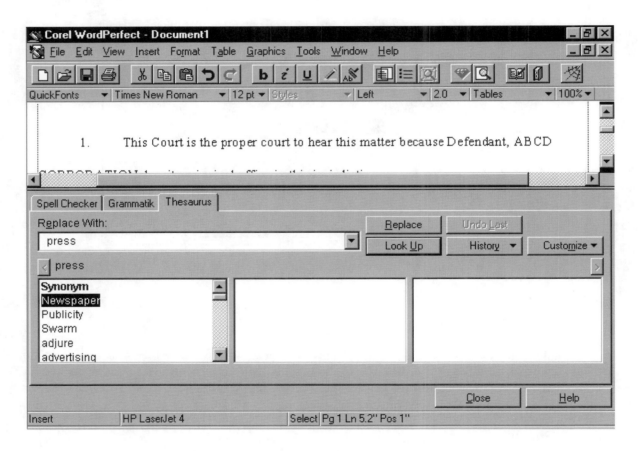

Figure 2.9   The WordPerfect thesaurus displaying alternatives for the word "press"

Further synonyms for words listed under "press" can be seen by double-clicking on the desired word. You may select any one of the synonyms shown by clicking on it and pressing the **Replace** button.

9. Finding Text or Codes

Word processors contain features that find or search for text or codes within a document. An additional feature will replace found text or codes with nothing at all or other text or codes. Find is found in the **Edit menu.** Some programs have the Find and Replace feature as a separate menu item, while others include it within the Find menu option. To begin a search, select the Find option from the Edit menu. A dialog box will then appear that is similar to the one in Figure 2.10.

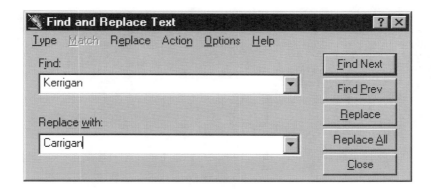

Figure 2.10   The Find Dialog Box in WordPerfect

A word or text can be entered into the Find dialog box and then clicking on a button will proceed to find the word or text within the document. To find a code, the code must be selected from a menu of codes found within the dialog box. Options within the Find dialog box will allow you to begin from the top of the document or forward or backward from the position of the cursor.

The Replace portion of a Find is used when you wish to replace a word, text, or code with a different word, text, or code throughout the document. For example, you have typed a 25-page legal memorandum and find that you have spelled the Plaintiff's name, "**Carrigan**," as "**Kerrigan**" throughout the document. The Find and Replace feature can fix this error very quickly. You can choose from an option to replace all occurrences, or to replace them one at a time giving you the option not to replace in certain instances.

F. PRINTING

To receive a hard copy of a document, you must send it to a printer. Save your document prior to printing as a safety measure. Occasionally, a printer problem will freeze your computer. There are many options available when printing a document. The most commonly used are the options to print the entire document, multiple pages of the document, or the current page that you are viewing. To access the Print dialog box, you should select **Print** from the **File menu.** The printer button available on most Toolbars may simply send the entire document to the printer without prompting you for options with a dialog box. A sample print dialog box is shown in Figure 2.11.

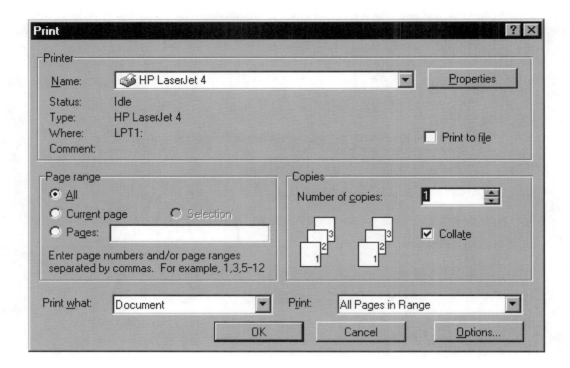

Figure 2.11   The Print Dialog Box in Word

After selecting the desired options, clicking on the appropriate button will send the document to the printer.

To view a document prior to sending it to the printer, many word processors have a Print Preview option available in the File menu or in the Print dialog box. In programs that do not contain this option, you can view what the page will look like when printed by zooming out to the full page with an option from the Toolbar or in the View menu.

G.   EXITING WINDOWS WORD PROCESSORS

Exiting Windows word processors is accomplished by selecting **File, Exit.** If any documents are currently open, you will be asked if you would like to save them. It is a good idea to close all of your documents before you exit.

Section Two—Advanced Word Processing Features

A. MACROS

A **macro** allows you to program a single keystroke combination or file name to play several keystrokes or create entire documents. For example, you may have paragraphs that you include within every complaint that you type similar to those shown below.

> Plaintiff is ignorant of the true names and capacities of Defendants sued herein as DOES 1 through __, inclusive, and therefore sues these Defendants by such fictitious names. Plaintiff will amend this complaint to allege their true names and capacities when ascertained. Plaintiff is informed and believes and thereon alleges that each of the fictitiously named Defendants is negligently responsible in some manner for the occurrences herein alleged, and that Plaintiff's injuries as herein alleged were proximately caused by that negligence.
>
> Plaintiff is informed and believes and thereon alleges that at all times herein mentioned each of the Defendants was the agent and employee of the remaining Defendants, and in doing the things hereinafter alleged, was acting within the course and scope of such agency and employment.

Rather than repeatedly typing these paragraphs, you can record them within a macro so that they may be replayed when you need them.

1. Creating a Macro

When you create a macro, you may identify it with a key combination such as **[Ctrl] + [any letter]** or **[Ctrl] + [Shift] + [any letter],** or give it a name. Word only allows you to use a name. If you use the key combination in WordPerfect, the macro will be played by pressing the key combination. If you have given the macro a name, you will play the macro by selecting **Tools, Macro, Play.** You will be prompted for the name of the macro. Selecting a play or run option will play the macro.

To record a macro, select **Tools, Macro,** give it a name, and select **Record.** When you are recording a macro the macro records both keystrokes and mouse actions. However, to position the cursor you must use the keyboard instead of the mouse. If you need to pause at any point there are options to pause the recording. There are also options to add special features to the macro such as command lines or prompts. When you have completed the macro, you will click on a stop button that contains the word "stop" or the recording symbol for stop "■". The first time you play a macro, the word processor will take a few seconds to compile it. When you use the macro thereafter, it will operate much faster. Some word processors include helpful macros with their program. You will find them listed in the Macro dialog box.

2. Editing a Macro

Macros are edited in the same manner as ordinary documents. You can access the edit feature in the Macro dialog box using **Tools, Macro.** When you are finished editing, save the changes and select **File, Close.** Try creating a macro to record the sample paragraphs shown above.

B. TEMPLATE DOCUMENTS

Many newer word processors contain document templates. In Word, many of these are called Wizards. Document templates are preformatted documents for frequently used forms. Templates that accompany the word processors include memoranda, resumes, pleading paper, fax cover sheets, brochures, newsletters, and the like. They often prompt you for the necessary information and generate most of the document for you. You can use the templates that come with the program, make your own templates, or modify the program's templates to suit your own needs.

To access the templates, select **File, New.** A list of the available templates will be presented. In the dialog box that appears you will be given the option to select one of the program's templates, create a new template, or edit an existing template. When you select a template, it will prompt you for the necessary information and create your document. If you create a new template, you can add it to the template selections for frequent use.

C. FOOTNOTES

Footnotes are used often in the drafting of legal memoranda and pleadings. The footnote features in Windows word processors sequentially number the footnotes and automatically adjust the page lengths to make room for the footnotes.

To create a footnote within a document, place the cursor where you want the reference number for the footnote to appear. Next, select **Footnote** from the **Insert menu** (or other menu) and follow the instructions within the dialog box. Some programs, like WordPerfect, will give you an edit screen in which to type the footnote contents. You must close this edit screen when you finish typing the footnote using the Close button from the button bar that appears. In other programs, such as Word, you can just move back up to your document with the [Arrow] keys or the mouse. In very old programs, you will only be able to see the footnote in a print preview option. Newer word processors display the entire page with headers, footers, page numbers, and footnotes.

To practice creating a footnote, type the sentence below into a document.

The parents of a legitimate unmarried minor child, acting jointly, may maintain an action for injury to such child caused by the wrongful act or neglect of another.

This is a quote from California Code of Civil Procedure, Section 376. To reference this section with a footnote, follow the steps below.

a) **Position the insertion point** at the space just after the period in the sentence.

b) **Select Insert, Footnote,** and follow the instructions in the dialog box.

c) **Type the text of the footnote.** For our footnote the text will be **CCP Section 376.** When you are finished, click on the **Close** button (WordPerfect) or use the **[Arrow]** keys (Word) to return to your document.

You will see the footnote number at the end of the sentence. The footnote contents will be at the bottom of the page.

D.   COLUMNS

Columns are used to split a page vertically, creating columns of text. Columns can be read from left to right (parallel) or read sequentially (newspaper). With newspaper columns, you read the first column to the bottom of the page and then read the second column as shown in the newspaper column example in Section 1 below.

Word offers only the newspaper columns feature. In Word, if you want to create parallel columns, you will use a table. WordPerfect offers three types of columns, Parallel, Parallel with Block Protect, and Newspaper. Parallel columns are used to create pleading captions, deposition summaries, and other documents that require columns of text that are read from left to right. An example of a deposition summary created using parallel columns is shown in Figure 2.12.

SUMMARY OF THE DEPOSITION OF

HUBERT M. SMITH

Taken November 9, 1997

Page:Line	**Summary**
	EXAMINATION BY MR. GREENE
1:3	Opening statements.
2:4	Mr. Smith was born in Walla Walla, Washington on December 12, 1945. He currently resides at 345 Main Street, Seattle, Washington 00990.
3:27	Mr. Smith obtained a Bachelor of Science degree in Economics from the University of Washington in 1967. He is presently employed by the State of Washington as an economist.

Figure 2.12   Deposition summaries can be created using parallel columns or a table

Parallel with Block Protect columns are parallel columns. However, if any part of a row of column entries continues to the next page of the document, the entire row of entries will be moved to the next page.

1. Newspaper Columns

To practice creating newspaper columns, we will type the following news article:

The Internet is a network of networks that began as a government project connecting university computers for quick access to information resources. Today, the Internet consists of universities, government agencies, businesses, and organizations that connect their networks to the Internet to provide reference materials, information, and communications to Internet users.

The Internet can be accessed by anyone with a modem and an account with an Internet provider. If your university, school, or law firm has an Internet address, you can usually obtain an Internet account from them at no cost. If you cannot obtain a free account, you will need to subscribe to one of the commercial Internet access providers.

To begin the newspaper columns, place the cursor at the left margin where you would like the columns to begin and access the **Columns** feature from the **Format (Layout) menu.** You will first need to define the columns before you can begin typing. A columns definition dialog box is shown in Figure 2.13.

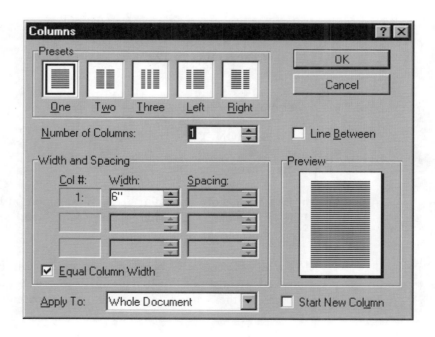

Figure 2.13 A Columns Definition Dialog Box

In the box designated for the number of columns, select **2.** If you are using WordPerfect, you will also need to designate that you want newspaper columns. If you are using Word, you may need to indicate that the columns occur from this point forward. Clicking on the **OK** button will send you back to your document with the columns set up for you. When you are typing in newspaper columns, you will not move to the second column until you reach the bottom of the page. To move before that, you can insert a break. A break is inserted by placing the cursor where you want to break the column, and in WordPerfect pressing **[Ctrl] + [Enter]** or in Word selecting **Insert, Break, Column Break.** Type the news article shown above and practice breaking the columns after the sentence that ends "communications to Internet users."

When you are finished typing in columns, you will need to turn them off. In Word, access the columns feature again in the **Format menu,** change the number of columns to 1, and select the option to have the changes take effect from this point forward. In WordPerfect, select **Format (Layout), Columns, Off.**

2. Parallel Columns

To practice setting up parallel columns in WordPerfect, we will use an example of a deposition summary. Deposition summaries can be drafted using parallel columns or the table feature that will be discussed in Section E. Word relies on the table feature for creating parallel columns. Follow the steps below in a blank document to set up a deposition summary using parallel columns.

a) Type in the specifics about the deposition at the top of the document as shown below.

SUMMARY OF THE DEPOSITION OF

HUBERT M. SMITH

Taken November 9, 1997

b) Press the **[Enter]** key to move down a few lines.

c) Select **Format (Layout), Columns, Define** to access the Define Columns dialog box.

d) In the **Number of Columns** box, type **2.**

e) In the **Type** box, click on **Parallel.**

f) Define your margins in the **Margins** box by clicking on the boxes with margins that need to be changed, deleting the existing entry, and then typing in the new entry. The margins are shown below.

	Left	Right
1:	1"	2.5"
2:	3"	7.5"

g) Click on the **OK** button to return to your document. The column number will be displayed in the lower right-hand corner of the screen.

h) Type Page:Line in column 1 at the left margin and move to column 2 by pressing **[Ctrl] + [Enter]**. Under normal circumstances this would create a hard page break. If you do get a hard page break (= = = = = = = = = = = =), then your columns are not turned on. Check your Reveal Codes to make sure that you are typing after the **(Col On)** code. If you do not see a **(Col On)** code, then you need to turn the columns on under **Format (Layout), Columns.**

i) At the second column, type Summary and press **[Ctrl] + [Enter]** to get back to column 1 and begin your summary.

Try entering the summary in Figure 2.12 into your document. To change columns, use **[Ctrl] + [Enter]**. **[Alt] + [Left Arrow]** and **[Alt] + [Right Arrow]** will move you quickly back and forth between your columns when you need to edit the column text. When you have finished using Columns in your document, turn them off with **Format (Layout), Columns, Off.**

E.   TABLES

The Table feature in word processors is very similar to an electronic spreadsheet. A table contains columns and rows, the intersection of which forms cells. A cell is identified by its column letter followed by the row number. Text, numbers, or characters are then entered into the cells. Tables can be used in place of parallel or tabbed columns. For example, the deposition summary created using parallel columns in Section D could also be created using a table. The heading would remain the same, and then a table would be created with two columns and four rows (new rows can be added as needed). The result would look exactly like Figure 2.12. The benefit of using a table over parallel columns is the ease of making corrections. When editing text in parallel columns, you can really mess up the document if your cursor is not within the **(Col On)** and **(Col Off)** codes. With a table, each section of the text is in a box. You do not need to worry about whether you are within the proper codes. If the cursor is in the box, you are there.

Another benefit of the Table feature is that you can perform mathematical equations similar to those used in electronic spreadsheets. For example, a billing statement can be created that automatically computes the totals for you. An example is shown in Figure 2.14.

SAMUEL J. COUNSEL
Attorney at Law
43 Main Street
Anywhere, Texas 32008
(909) 555-2945

December 31, 1996

Haley Corporation
35200 Oil Road
Anywhere, Texas 32008

    Re: <u>Haley v. Reaves</u>

LEGAL SERVICES RENDERED:

Date	Description	Time	Amount
12/19/96	Review motion to strike and demurrer. Legal research re statute of limitations on disputed causes of action. Legal research re relation back to original cause of action. Review original complaint. Begin drafting opposition to demurrer.	7.1	$994.00
12/20/96	Draft opposition to demurrer. Begin drafting opposition to motion to strike.	2.9	$406.00
12/21/96	Pull file at courthouse to obtain copy of minute order. Complete motion to strike. Cite check all cases. Prepare table of authorities for opposition to demurrer. Finalize documents.	3.3	$462.00
	TOTAL HOURS AND AMOUNT DUE:	13.3	$1,862.00

Figure 2.14   A billing statement created using a table

1.   Preparing a Table

    To set up a table, you need to look at how many columns and approximately how many rows you will need. As an example, we will walk through the creation of the table portion of the billing statement in Figure 2.14. Select **Create** or **Insert Table** from the **Table menu.** In the dialog box that appears, specify the number of columns and the number of rows that you need. Clicking on the **OK** button will place the table into your document.

2. Adjusting the Column Size

To adjust the column size, use the mouse to drag the column borders. When you move the mouse pointer over the center line between the two columns, you will see it change into a double arrow symbol. Clicking and holding when you see this symbol will allow you to drag the column divider. The first column should be approximately 1 inch wide. The third and fourth columns should be approximately 3/4 of an inch wide. The second column will be the largest. You will need to move back and forth between the columns making adjustments until you are satisfied with their appearance. The **[Arrow]** keys will move you from cell to cell.

3. Entering Data into the Table

To enter data into the table, you move to the desired cell and type the entry. To move to the next cell, you can use the **[Tab]** key. To move to the left, you can use **[Shift] + [Tab].** Each cell is like a separate document, so any formatting such as boldfacing or centering must be performed in each cell. For our first row, each of the headings needs to be centered and boldfaced. Move to cell A1, select a centering option for your word processor, select boldfacing from the Toolbar, and type the heading. Then move to B1, C1, and D1 and repeat the process with these headings.

In rows 2, 3, and 4, enter the dates, descriptions, and times. Do not enter the amounts. We will have the table compute them. When you are entering the descriptions, let the text word wrap within the cell. In the last row, row 5, move to cell B5 and select right justification in the Format menu or from a button on the Toolbar, and then type the cell entry.

4. Using the Table Math Features

To use the table math features to compute our billing statement, move the cursor to the amount cell for the 12/19/96 billing item.

a. *Performing Calculations in WordPerfect*

In WordPerfect, you will select the **Formula Bar** from the **Table menu.** With this bar open, you can enter all of the formulas needed. For row 2, the formula should be C2*140. Move the cursor to the Amount column for row 3 and enter C3*140. Move the cursor to the Amount column to rows 4 and 5 and repeat the formula, changing the row number in the formula each time. The final formula will be used to add the times in column C. Place the cursor in the cell, and click on the **Sum** or **QuickSum** button on the Formula Bar. Click on the **Close** button to close the Formula Bar. You will need to have the table calculated any time you change numbers within the table. To do this, select **Table,**

Calculate, and select **Calculate Table** from the dialog box that appears. In the Calculate dialog box, there is an option to turn on automatic calculation so that you do not have to keep selecting Calculate Table.

b. *Performing Calculations and Formatting Numbers in Word*

In Word, you will select **Formula** from the **Table menu** to enable you to enter the formulas needed in the table. Move the cursor to cell D2 and select **Table, Formula.** In the dialog box that appears, type the formula C2*140. Also in the dialog box is a place to select the number format. Select the format for dollar signs and two decimal places. Clicking on the **OK** button places the entry in the cell. Repeat this process for the remaining cells in column D remembering to change the row number in the formula each time. For the total time in cell C5, put the cursor in that cell and select **Table, Formula.** The formula that appears automatically in the dialog box should be similar to =SUM(ABOVE) or =SUM(C2:C4). Do not select any formatting for this cell. After the formula has been entered, click on the **OK** button. The table does not recalculate automatically when numbers are added or changed. To perform a recalculation, place the cursor in the cell that needs to be recalculated and press **[F9].**

5. Formatting Numbers in WordPerfect

In WordPerfect, there is a separate menu item for formatting the numbers in the table. Our numbers need dollar signs and a uniform number of decimal places, and need to be aligned vertically by their decimal points. Place the cursor in column D. Then, select **Table, Numeric Format (Number Type).** Click on the option for acting upon the entire column, click on currency, and click on the **OK** button. To align the numbers in columns C and D, place the cursor within the column and select **Table, Format,** select the column option, and change the justification to Decimal Align.

6. Lines Within a Table

Tables may or may not contain lines when you create them. Most word processors contain automatic formatting options to choose from. They can be found in the Table menu under the option Expert, Speed Format, or AutoFormat. To manually change the lines in a table, you need to highlight the cells that you want to make changes to and select a menu item. In WordPerfect, you will select **Table, Lines/Fill.** In Word, you will select **Format, Borders and Shading.** To remove lines, highlight the cells and select "none" from the line options. Try to change the lines within the table to resemble the bill in Figure 2.14.

F. AUTOMATIC SORTING

Automatic Sort features allow you to reorder your text and numbers in many different ways. Sort can be used to sort a list of items or names to be shown alphabetically, or to place a list of documents in chronological order.

1. Sorting Basics

The Sort feature can be used to sort single lines of information, paragraphs, information within a table, and several other types of data. Word processors will sort according to the keys that you provide. A **key** is the criterion for the sort. It identifies the type of data to be sorted and where it is located within the line, paragraph, table, or secondary merge file. More than one key may be needed to sort the data within a document. For example, if you were sorting a list of names and two people had the same last name, you might need two keys. The first key would sort by last name. The second key would sort by first name.

2. Sorting by Line

Line sorts are the most common type of sort. The information within the document is entered on a single line, with fields of information separated by tabs. An example is shown below.

Smith, John	123 Main Street	555-1212
Keefer, Karen	156 Vine Road	555-3040
Smith, Alfred	7686 Apple Lane	555-9030
Armor, Peter	23 Mill Road	555-3219

You may find that you need to adjust your tab settings to get your tabbed columns to align. If you use more than one tab to make your data line up, the lines might not have the information in the correct field. Make sure that your cursor is at the beginning of the list when you change the tab settings.

A key in a line sort will ask whether the data is alphanumeric (text, words, addresses, and telephone numbers) or numeric (numbers and dates, although date may be a separate type of data), the field number, and in WordPerfect, the word number. The fields are normally separated by the tabs. Word allows you to choose if you want the fields to be separated by other indications such as commas. WordPerfect considers spaces between words or the slashes in a date to indicate separate words for its searches. In the example above, there are three main fields. To practice a line sort, enter the example shown above into a blank document. Use the **[Tab]** key once between the name and address, and between the address and telephone number. The columns may not align unless you move the cursor to the top of the document and change the tab settings on the Ruler Bar. Save your document prior to performing the sort. You can undo a sort by selecting **Edit, Undo.** The sort will be explained separately for WordPerfect and for Word.

a. *Sorting in WordPerfect*

In WordPerfect, field number one in the above example is the field containing the names; word number one would be the last name and word number two would be the first name.

To perform the sort, highlight the list to be sorted, and select **Tools, Sort.** The Sort dialog box will appear as shown in Figure 2.15. The input and output files are set up to use the current document. They should be left as is unless you are sorting from or to someplace other than the current document. Next, you should click on the **Options** button and make sure that the option to undo the sort is clicked.

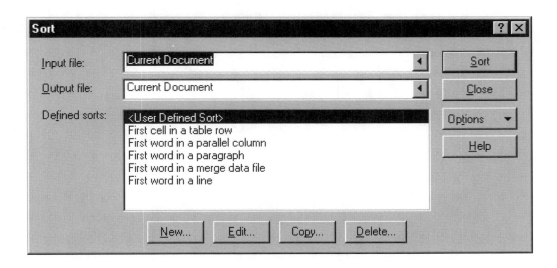

Figure 2.15   The Sort Dialog Box in WordPerfect

The Sort dialog box gives some common sorts to choose from or allows you to create a user-defined sort. The first sort that we will perform will be a sort by the last name. We could choose the option for sorting the first word in a line, but to demonstrate this feature fully, we will create a new user-defined sort. To do this, click on the **New** button at the bottom of the dialog box. The New Sort dialog box will appear as shown in Figure 2.16. In this dialog box, you will select the type of sort, and define the keys for the sort. Make sure that a Line sort is selected. The default key in the New Sort dialog box is set up to sort an alphanumeric in field number 1, and will sort on word number 1. The order of the sort will be ascending, and it will be a line sort. Click on the **OK** button and then on the **Sort** button in the Sort dialog box to perform the sort. In older versions of WordPerfect, the entries will now appear as shown below. In WordPerfect versions 7 and later, this sort will also place the two Smiths in the correct order.

Armor, Peter	23 Mill Road	555-3219
Keefer, Karen	156 Vine Road	555-3040
Smith, John	123 Main Street	555-1212
Smith, Alfred	7686 Apple Lane	555-9030

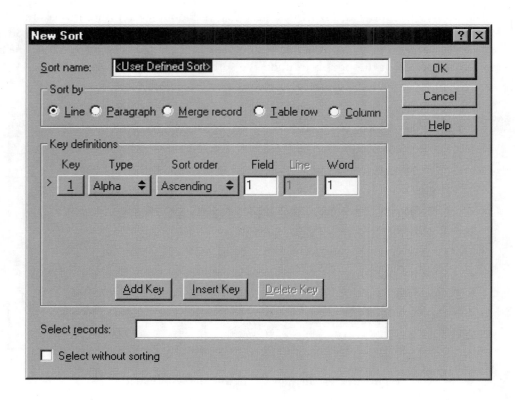

Figure 2.16   The New Sort Dialog Box in WordPerfect

In WordPerfect versions prior to version 7, you must provide a second key so that people with the same last name alphabetically will be sorted by first name. To do this, highlight the list to be sorted, select **Tools, Sort,** and click on the **New** button to get to the New Sort dialog box. Make sure that a Line sort is selected, then add a new key by clicking on one of the buttons at the bottom of the dialog box. For this second key, the field number will remain 1, but the word number should be changed to 2. Click on the **OK** button, and then on the **Sort** button in the Sort dialog box to complete the sort. The data should now appear as shown below.

Armor, Peter	23 Mill Road	555-3219
Keefer, Karen	156 Vine Road	555-3040
Smith, Alfred	7686 Apple Lane	555-9030
Smith, John	123 Main Street	555-1212

b. *Sorting in Word*

In Word, field number one can be the field containing the names or you can choose to have your fields separated by commas, in which case the first field would be the last name, and the second field would be the first name.

To perform the sort, highlight the list to be sorted, and select **Table, Sort Text.** The Sort Text dialog box will appear as shown in Figure 2.17. Change the Sort By option from "Paragraph" to "Field 1." Clicking on the **Options** button will allow you to choose how the fields will be separated. Word will treat the last name and first name as one field if you select "Separate Fields at Tabs." Clicking on the **OK** button and again on the **OK** button in the Sort Text dialog box will complete the sort.

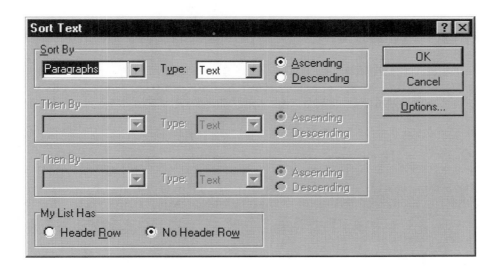

Figure 2.17   The Sort Dialog Box in Word

If the sort does not place the Smiths in the correct order, a second key will need to be added. Highlight the list to be sorted and select **Table, Sort Text.** Click on the **Options** button in the Sort Text dialog box and select to have the fields separated by commas. Click the **OK** button, and in the Sort Text dialog box add a second key by clicking on the pull down arrow in the "Then by" box and select "Field 2." Clicking on the **OK** button will complete the sort.

3.   Sorting a Line by Date

To practice sorting items by date, enter the following dates and descriptions. You may need to change the tab settings again to make the columns line up. Make sure that your cursor is at the top of the list when you change the tab settings. In Word, you may need to highlight the entire list before making the tab changes.

2/23/97	Letter to insurance company.
1/2/97	Witness statement.
12/31/96	Police accident report.
1/1/97	Hospital bill.
12/31/96	Ambulance bill.

a. *Sorting in WordPerfect*

For this sort, we will need to set up three keys, one for each portion of the date. The slashes in the date are treated as spaces, so field number 1 contains three words. Date sorts are also considered numeric sorts.

To begin the sort, highlight the list, select **Tools, Sort,** and click on the **New** button. We will need three keys. The first key will sort by the year, the third word. The second key will sort by the month, and the third key will sort by the day. In the first key, change the Type to Numeric and change the Word to 3. Add a second key with the Type as Numeric, the Field as 1, and the Word as 1. Add a third key with the Type as Numeric, the Field as 1, and the Word as 2. Click on the **OK** button and then click on the **Sort** button in the Sort dialog box to complete the sort. Your data should be sorted in chronological order.

b. *Sorting in Word*

Sorting this list in Word is a bit easier. Highlight the list and select **Table, Sort Text.** If there is anything listed in the "Then by" box, change it to "none." In the "Sort by" box, make sure that the Field is Field 1 and that the Type is Date. Clicking on the **OK** button will complete the sort.

4. Sorting by Paragraph

Sorting by paragraph is not really a valuable feature unless you have set up a structure similar to the one shown below.

2/23/97	Letter from Plaintiff to his insurance company explaining the nature of the accident and the extent of his injuries.
1/2/97	Statement of Alice Jones. She was driving next to the plaintiff and witnessed the accident.
12/31/96	Police report detailing the circumstances of the accident and noting that both the plaintiff and our client were given citations.

When setting up this kind of list, you must use an indent option to indent the paragraph. You may need to adjust your tab settings to align the information. In Word, you will need to create a hanging indent under **Format, Paragraph, Indents and Spacing, Special,** and then use a regular tab after the date. The paragraph will then word wrap to the tab stop. In Word, do not leave a blank line between the paragraphs. In WordPerfect, you will need a hard return at the end of each paragraph and before the next item so that the word processor can recognize the end of a record. Therefore, you need to press **[Enter]** at the end of each paragraph and again before typing the next item. To practice sorting by paragraph, type the example into a blank document. Follow the instructions below to sort the items by date.

a. *Sorting in WordPerfect*

Highlight the paragraph list and select **Tools, Sort.** Click on the **New** button and make sure that **Paragraph** is selected in the Sort By box. You will notice that the keys have added a new option, **Line,** to the paragraph sort. You will need three keys for this sort. The keys should all be Numeric, Line 1, Field 1. The Word number for the first key should be 3. The Word number for the second key should be 1, and the Word number for the third key should be 2. Clicking on the **OK** button and then the **Sort** button in the Sort dialog box will complete the sort.

b. *Sorting in Word*

Highlight the paragraph list and select **Table, Sort Text.** In the Sort By box, make sure that the entry is **Paragraphs.** In the Type box, make sure that the entry is **Date.** Click on the **OK** button to process the search.

5. Sorting Information in a Table

A table is set up in columns, which makes it a natural for sorting. To sort data in a table, you identify the column number, the type of data, and in WordPerfect, the word number. The sorting procedures are similar to line sorts. Enter the table below into a document and practice sorting the information by name. Make sure that your cursor is within the table when you make the menu selections. Also, notice in Word that the menu selection for sorting within a table is **Table, Sort.** You may find after you have completed a table sort that lines that existed within the table have changed. This can be fixed in WordPerfect by selecting **Table, Lines/Fill,** and in Word by selecting **Format, Borders and Shading.**

Peters, Susan	123 Main Street Constance, GA 10239	(404) 555-1212
Fields, William	2783 Silver Court La Jolla, CA 92810	(619) 555-2345
Fields, John	23 State Street Los Angeles, CA 92009	(213) 555-6849
Hooper, Karen	1920 Poplar Place Phoenix, AZ 83456	(808) 555-1200

If the table contained a row of headings, you would need to highlight the area to be sorted prior to sorting so that the headings would not be sorted along with the data.

G. DOCUMENT MERGING

Mass mailings and frequently used forms can be produced quickly using WordPerfect's merge features.

In a large litigation case, there may be 25 or more opposing counsel. Creating a separate letter for each counsel can be very time consuming. It is much easier to create a merge letter and address list than to type each individual letter. The address list can then be used for future mailings. By merging the merge letter with the address list, a personalized letter will be created for each individual.

1. Primary and Secondary Files

Merging documents involves the use of primary and secondary files. The primary file is the main document or form into which information will be merged. The secondary file is the data to be merged into the primary file document.

To practice using merge, we will create a simple letter acknowledging an extension of time to respond to a complaint. This letter will be the primary file. The list of addresses for each of the plaintiffs' counsel (in this case, there are four separate law firms representing the plaintiffs) will be the secondary file.

2. The Merged Document

A merge will combine the information from the primary and secondary files creating a copy of the primary file for each of the records in the secondary file. After our merge is completed, the merged document will contain a letter for each counsel with a hard page break created between each letter. Sending the merged document to the printer will print all of the letters.

3. Drafting the Primary File

For our example, we will create a letter and make it our primary file. We will then create a second document containing the names and addresses of counsel and make it our secondary file. Type the letter shown in Figure 2.18 into a blank screen. Use the centering, underline, and bold features where applicable. The closing and signature line should not be centered. Use the **[Tab]** key to move the cursor to the middle of the screen to begin typing these. Use your own name at the signature line.

SMITH AND SMITH
Attorneys at Law
1234 Hampton Avenue
La Jolla, California 99999
(619) 555-1212

January 17, 1997

Opposing Counsel, Esq.
22 Court Boulevard
San Diego, California 99999

Re: <u>Potter, et al. vs. Polluter Co.; Case No. 85549</u>

Dear Mr. Counsel:

  Pursuant to a telephone conference of this date, Mr. Johnson of Pote & Tate, on behalf of all plaintiffs in this action, has granted our client, Polluter Co., an extension until May 15, 1997, in which to answer or otherwise respond to the complaint on file in this matter.

Sincerely,

JAMES SMITH
SMITH AND SMITH

Figure 2.18 A letter like this one can be turned into a primary document
for use in a mail merge

Before we continue, use **File, Save As** to save the letter. Remember to specify where you wish to save it (i.e., A: or C:) and any folder you wish to place it in, and give the letter the name **EXTEND.** Check the spelling in the letter using the Spell Check feature in the Tools menu.

4. Preparing the Secondary File and Merging in Word

In Word, the secondary file is called the Data file. To prepare the Data file, you need to look at the data that will be in the file. The Data file for our letter will contain the names, addresses, and salutations for each of the persons who will be receiving a letter. The data we will use is as follows:

Marvin Pearce, Esq.
Fenner & Pearce
64 Honor Avenue, 14th Floor
San Diego, California 99999
Mr. Pearce

James Franklin, Esq.
22 Windship Lane, Suite 3
San Diego, California 99999
Mr. Franklin

John Simpson, Esq.
Sampson, Newberry & Simpson
34 Rome Avenue, Suite B
La Jolla, California 99999
Mr. Simpson

Marsha Mendleson, Esq.
Mendleson, Teedlebaum & Mason
6552 Main Street, Suite 2003
San Diego, California 99999
Ms. Mendleson

To set up the merge, select **Tools, Mail Merge** while still in the Extend document. The dialog box shown in Figure 2.19 will appear. In the Main Document box, click on **Create** and select **Form Letters.** When you receive a prompt for the location of the letter, select the option for the document in the active window. At this point, you will be able to set up the Data file. Click on the button to Get Data, and select **Create Data Source.** You then will see a dialog box with several default field names. Remove all of these fields from the box. There are five fields that will be needed to be created in Word. They will be:

Name

Firmname

Address1

Address2

Salutation

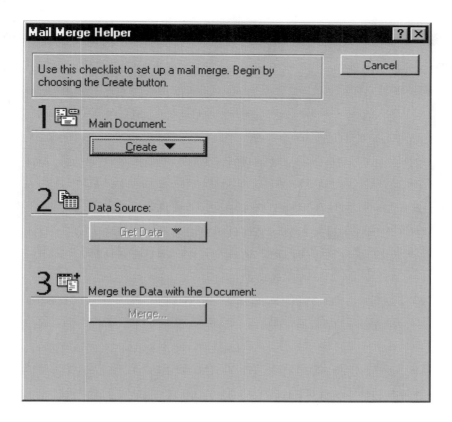

Figure 2.19 The Merge dialog box in Word

Word does not allow spaces in the field names. After they have been entered, click on the **OK** button and give the data file the name **ADDRESS.** You will then select the option to Edit the Data Source. Select this option and enter the information for the four people in our example. If a person does not have information for a specific field (such as Firmname), simply skip that field as shown in Figure 2.20. At the end of each person's record, click on the **Add New** button. After you have entered all four records, click on the **OK** button. This will return you to the primary file document.

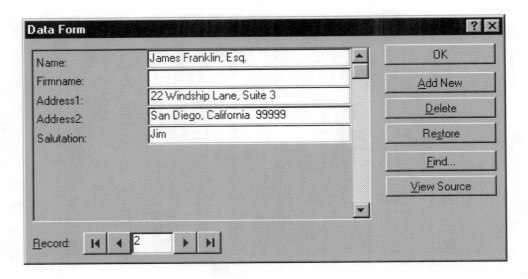

Figure 2.20 The secondary file information is entered into a Data Form for merging into the primary document

Now, the fields must be placed into the document. Delete the name "Opposing Counsel Esq." and replace it with the field name "Name" by clicking on the **Insert Merge Field** button and selecting "Name." Next, press the **[Enter]** key to create a blank line and insert the merge field "Firmname." Next, replace each of the two lines of the address with the merge fields "Address1" and "Address2." Finally, replace Mr. Counsel's name in the salutation (making sure to leave a space after "Dear" and before the colon) with the field "Salutation." Your completed main document should look like the one in Figure 2.21.

To complete the merge you will merge to a new document through a button on the button bar, or by selecting **Tools, Mail Merge,** and selecting **Merge.** The merged letters will be prepared as multiple pages of a single document. They will appear similar to those in Figure 2.22.

5.   Preparing the Secondary and Primary Merge Files in WordPerfect

To prepare the secondary merge file containing the data, select **Tools, Merge,** and click on the **Data** button. Select the option to create a new document window from the small dialog box that appears. You will then be prompted with a dialog box, similar to the one in Figure 2.23, in which to enter the field names. The field names that should be entered are listed below.

Name

Firm Name

Address1

Address2

Salutation

SMITH AND SMITH
Attorneys at Law
1234 Hampton Avenue
La Jolla, California 99999
(619) 555-1212

January 17, 1997

«Name»
«Firmname»
«Address1»
«Address2»

Re: <u>Potter, et al. vs. Polluter Co.; Case No. 85549</u>

Dear «Salutation»:

Pursuant to a telephone conference of this date, Mr. Johnson of Pote & Tate, on behalf of all plaintiffs in this action, has granted our client, Polluter Co., an extension until May 15, 1997, in which to answer or otherwise respond to the complaint on file in this matter.

Sincerely,

JAMES SMITH
SMITH AND SMITH

Figure 2.21   The completed primary file document contains the fields where information from the secondary file will be placed

SMITH AND SMITH
Attorneys at Law
1234 Hampton Avenue
La Jolla, California 99999
(619) 555-1212

January 17, 1997

Marvin Pearce, Esq.
Fenner & Pearce
64 Honor Avenue, 14th Floor
San Diego, California 99999

Re: <u>Potter, et al. vs. Polluter Co.; Case No. 85549</u>

Dear Mr. Pearce:

Pursuant to a telephone conference of this date, Mr. Johnson of Pote & Tate, on behalf of all plaintiffs in this action, has granted our client, Polluter Co., an extension until May 15, 1997, in which to answer or otherwise respond to the complaint on file in this matter.

Sincerely,

JAMES SMITH
SMITH AND SMITH

SMITH AND SMITH
Attorneys at Law
1234 Hampton Avenue
La Jolla, California 99999
(619) 555-1212

January 17, 1997

James Franklin, Esq.
22 Windship Lane, Suite 3
San Diego, California 99999

Re: <u>Potter, et al. vs. Polluter Co.; Case No. 85549</u>

Dear Mr. Franklin:

Pursuant to a telephone conference of this date, Mr. Johnson of Pote & Tate, on behalf of all plaintiffs in this action, has granted our client, Polluter Co., an extension until May 15, 1997, in which to answer or otherwise respond to the complaint on file in this matter.

Sincerely,

JAMES SMITH
SMITH AND SMITH

SMITH AND SMITH
Attorneys at Law
1234 Hampton Avenue
La Jolla, California 99999
(619) 555-1212

January 17, 1997

John Simpson, Esq.
Sampson, Newberry & Simpson
34 Rome Avenue, Suite B
La Jolla, California 99999

Re: <u>Potter, et al. vs. Polluter Co.; Case No. 85549</u>

Dear Mr. Simpson:

Pursuant to a telephone conference of this date, Mr. Johnson of Pote & Tate, on behalf of all plaintiffs in this action, has granted our client, Polluter Co., an extension until May 15, 1997, in which to answer or otherwise respond to the complaint on file in this matter.

Sincerely,

JAMES SMITH
SMITH AND SMITH

SMITH AND SMITH
Attorneys at Law
1234 Hampton Avenue
La Jolla, California 99999
(619) 555-1212

January 17, 1997

Marsha Mendleson, Esq.
Mendleson, Teedlebaum & Mason
6552 Main Street, Suite 2003
San Diego, California 99999

Re: <u>Potter, et al. vs. Polluter Co.; Case No. 85549</u>

Dear Ms. Mendleson:

Pursuant to a telephone conference of this date, Mr. Johnson of Pote & Tate, on behalf of all plaintiffs in this action, has granted our client, Polluter Co., an extension until May 15, 1997, in which to answer or otherwise respond to the complaint on file in this matter.

Sincerely,

JAMES SMITH
SMITH AND SMITH

Figure 2.22 The Merged Documents

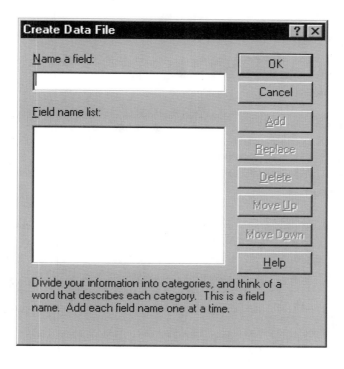

Figure 2.23   The field names are entered into this dialog box in WordPerfect

When you have finished entering these, click on the **OK** button. WordPerfect will then present a dialog box in which to enter the four records listed below. If one of the records does not contain one of the fields (e.g., James Franklin does not have a firm name), then leave that field blank. Enter the records shown below, clicking on the **New Record** button after completing each record except the last. After the last record, click on the **Close** button.

Marvin Pearce, Esq.
Fenner & Pearce
64 Honor Avenue, 14th Floor
San Diego, California 99999
Mr. Pearce

James Franklin, Esq.
22 Windship Lane, Suite 3
San Diego, California 99999
Mr. Franklin

John Simpson, Esq.
Sampson, Newberry & Simpson
34 Rome Avenue, Suite B
La Jolla, California 99999
Mr. Simpson

Marsha Mendleson, Esq.
Mendleson, Teedlebaum & Mason
6552 Main Street, Suite 2003
San Diego, California 99999
Ms. Mendleson

You will then be prompted to save the file. Give it the name **ADDRESS.**

To place the fields into the primary document, the form letter, switch to the file "**EXTEND**" using the Window menu. Then, select **Tools, Merge,** click on the **Form** button, and select the option to use the document in the active window. You will then be prompted for the name of the Data file. Click on the folder button to see the available files, and select the ADDRESS file, and click on the **OK** button. This will put you back into the form letter and give you a Merge button bar.

Now, the fields must be placed into the document. Delete the name "Opposing Counsel, Esq." and replace it with the field name "Name" by clicking on the **Insert Field** button and selecting "Name." Next, press the **[Enter]** key to create a blank line and insert the merge field "Firm Name." Next, replace each of the two lines of the address with the merge fields "Address1" and "Address2." Finally, replace Mr. Counsel's name in the salutation (making sure to leave a space after "Dear" and before the colon) with the field "Salutation." Your completed main document should look like the one in Figure 2.24.

```
┌─────────────────────────────────────────────────────────────────┐
│                                                                   │
│                      SMITH AND SMITH                              │
│                       Attorneys at Law                            │
│                      1234 Hampton Avenue                          │
│                    La Jolla, California  99999                    │
│                        (619) 555-1212                             │
│                                                                   │
│                                                                   │
│                      January 17, 1997                             │
│                                                                   │
│                                                                   │
│       FIELD(Name)                                                 │
│       FIELD(Firm Name)                                            │
│       FIELD(Address1)                                             │
│       FIELD(Address2)                                             │
│                                                                   │
│              Re:  Potter, et al. vs. Polluter Co.; Case No. 85549 │
│                                                                   │
│       Dear FIELD(Salutation):                                     │
│                                                                   │
│           Pursuant to a telephone conference of this date, Mr.    │
│       Johnson of Pote & Tate, on behalf                           │
│       of all plaintiffs in this action, has granted our client,  │
│       Polluter Co., an extension until May 15,                    │
│       1997, in which to answer or otherwise respond to the        │
│       complaint on file in this matter.                           │
│                                                                   │
│                              Sincerely,                           │
│                                                                   │
│                                                                   │
│                                                                   │
│                              JAMES SMITH                          │
│                              SMITH AND SMITH                      │
│                                                                   │
└─────────────────────────────────────────────────────────────────┘
```

Figure 2.24 The Completed Primary File in WordPerfect

Close the Field Name dialog box and click on the **Merge** button on the button bar. In the Merge dialog box, click on the **Merge** button. You will be prompted for the file names of the Form, Data, and Output files. The default selections should be correct, so you can click on the **OK** button to complete the merge. The merged letters will be prepared as multiple pages of a single document. They will appear similar to those in Figure 2.22.

H.   CREATING A PLEADING CAPTION

There are several ways to create a pleading caption in Windows word processors. Word outshines WordPerfect here by including a pleading wizard that creates the pleading paper and prompts for the information to be included within the caption. Word also allows you to create the document as a template. This is valuable if you will be using the caption repeatedly for a case. The template can then be accessed each time you draft a pleading for that case.

1. Creating a Pleading Caption in Word

The **Pleading Wizard** is accessed by selecting **File, New** and clicking on the folder for **"Other Documents."** The Pleading Wizard prompts you for the style and information needed for the pleading. The only problem with the Pleading Wizard is that it does not prompt for the font size and usually creates a caption in a very small font. To remedy this, highlight the text of the document and change the font to the size required in the court rules. Also, you may need to highlight the title of the pleading and change it to single spacing. Lastly, move the cursor down to the actual text of the pleading and change the justification to full justification (termed "Justify" by Word) by selecting **Format, Paragraph, Alignment, Justify,** or the button on the Toolbar.

If you create the caption as a template, when you save the document you will be prompted to include it in one of the template folders. Choose one of the folders and give the template a name. Then, close the template document and select **File, New,** and choose your template. You may get an error message at this time stating that the Pleading Wizard cannot be run with this document. If this occurs, click on the **OK** button of the error message and just continue with your document.

2. Creating a Pleading Caption in WordPerfect

WordPerfect has several ways to create a pleading caption on pleading paper depending on the version of the program that you are using. The Pleading Style or Macro is used in versions prior to version 6.1. Versions 6.1 and later of WordPerfect for Windows contain a Pleading Template. Instructions for each method are outlined below. If you are printing on preprinted pleading bond, you can skip to section d below on changing the bottom margin.

a. *Selecting the Pleading Template (Versions 6.1 and Later)*

The newest versions of WordPerfect contain the Pleading template. The Pleading template is accessed by selecting **File, New,** clicking on the **Legal Group,** and selecting the **Pleading Paper** option. If you are using version 6.1 of WordPerfect for Windows, you will need to change your line spacing to 1 and proceed to section d below. If you are using WordPerfect for Windows version 7.0 or later, you will be prompted with a dialog box similar to the one shown in Figure 2.25. In this dialog box, the margins should normally be set so that the left margin is 1″, the right margin is .5″, the top margin is 1″, and the bottom margin is .5″. The font that should be selected will be the one delineated in the court rules. The page numbering should also be selected. The line spacing should be set at 1, and the justification should be "Left." Once all the settings have been made, click on the **OK** button. You may then skip down to section f below to complete the pleading.

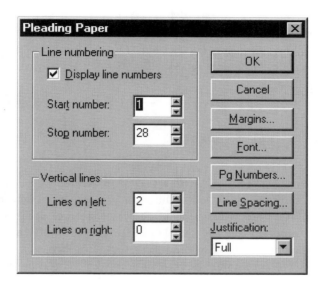

Figure 2.25   A Pleading Paper Dialog Box in WordPerfect

b.   *The Pleading Style (Versions 6.0a and Prior)*

The Pleading Style in WordPerfect is an option that numbers the lines on your paper from 1 to 28 and places a double vertical line on the left side next to the numbers. The problem with the Pleading Style is that it is set up with margins that can be difficult to change if you are a novice WordPerfect user.

Before you begin creating the pleading, *it is essential* that Auto Code Placement is turned off. It is necessary to do this in all WordPerfect for Windows versions prior to 6.1. To check this, select **File, Preferences, Environment.** In the Settings box you will see a selection for Auto Code Placement. If there is an X in the box next to Auto Code Placement, it is turned on. If it is on, click on the box to remove the X. Then, click on the **OK** button to complete the change.

To begin the pleading, make sure you are at the very top of the first page of your document by pressing **[Home], [Home], [Home], [Up Arrow],** and follow the instructions below.

To choose the Pleading Style for your document, select **Format (Layout), Styles.** The **Styles** dialog box will appear. Highlight **Pleading** and click on the **On** button. The appearance of your document will not change. If you Reveal Codes, you will see that you have selected the pleading style. Your document is now set up for pleading paper. Skip down to section d to continue.

> *If you open the **Styles** dialog box and no styles are listed on the screen, it may be that the style library has not been set up on your computer. To set up your styles, select **File, Preferences, Location of Files.** You will need to type in where your Style Files are located (usually where your WordPerfect files are located, e.g. C:\WPWIN). Then you will need to type in the Library filename: **LIBRARY.STY.** When you exit out of this menu, you will then find that your styles are listed in the **Styles** dialog box.*

c. *The Pleading Macro (All Versions)*

The Pleading Macro is a way to set up your pleading paper that allows you to create your own style and margins. The Pleading Macro is played by selecting **Macro, Play.** This will be found under the **Tools** menu in newer versions of the program. The **Play Macro** dialog box will appear. Click on the **Pleading** macro in the **Files** box (pleading.wcm) and click on the **Play** button to play the macro. A dialog box will appear prompting for the specific margins and appearance of your pleading style. In some versions, you will need to provide a style name. If so, name the style "Pleading1".

In versions 6.1 and later, the left margin should be set at 1″, the right margin should be set at .5″, the top margin should be set at 1″, and the bottom margin should be set at .5″. The appropriate font and page numbering should be selected. Line spacing should be set to 1, and the justifications should be set to Left. You can then click on the **OK** button and move on to section f below.

In versions prior to 6.1, the left margin should be set at 1.5″, the right margin should be set at .5″. Leave the Left Line as a double line, and change the Right Line to a single line by typing 1 in the Right Line box. Click on the **Create** button to create the Pleading1 style. The appearance of your document will not change. If you reveal codes you will see that you have selected the Pleading1 style. You can now move on to section d below.

d. *Changing the Bottom Margin*

In order to accommodate page numbers at the bottom of each page, the bottom margin must be changed to .5″ for all pleadings except those created in WordPerfect 7.0 and later. If we had made this change in the Pleading macro, line 28 would have been placed .5″ from the bottom. We want line 28 to remain 1″ from the bottom and the page number to be placed .5″ from the bottom.

To change the bottom margin, make sure that your insertion point is after the Pleading Style code in the document using Reveal Codes. Select **Format (Layout), Margins,** and change the bottom margin to .5″. Click on the **OK** button to complete the change.

e. *Page Numbering*

Before you select page numbering, make sure that your insertion point is after the margin code using Reveal Codes. To page number your pleading, select **Format (Layout), Page, Numbering.** Select Bottom Center. This will place the page number at the bottom center of your pleading.

f. *Attorney Address*

Starting on line 1 of the pleading paper, type the attorney's name, state bar number, address, telephone number, and representation designation as shown below. This should be single spaced.

Attorney Name
Attorney at Law
State Bar Number
Address
Telephone Number

Attorney for (Plaintiff, Defendant, etc.)

g. *Court Designation*

Different jurisdictions will have different ways that they wish their pleadings to be created. In many jurisdictions, the court designation should begin at line 8 on pleading paper. If you are unable to see the line numbers, this is line 3.33″ if you are using WordPerfect's Pleading Style. If you created a pleading style using the Pleading Macro, line 8 of the pleading paper is located at line 3.29″. The line inches are displayed in the lower right-hand corner of the WordPerfect screen.

The court designation should be centered, capitalized, and double spaced (do not change your spacing to double spacing; just press the **[Enter]** key between the lines). For example:

SUPERIOR COURT OF THE STATE OF CALIFORNIA

IN AND FOR THE COUNTY OF SAN DIEGO

h. *Creating the Caption Columns*

Move three lines down from the Court Designation to begin the caption. We will need to set the line justification to Left at this point so that the caption and pleading title do not spread to the right margin of their columns. To do so, use the **Justification** button on the **Toolbar** to select Left.

Now prepare the three parallel columns of the caption following these steps.

a) Select **Format (Layout), Columns, Define.**

b) Change the number of columns to **3,** and change the type of columns to **Parallel.**

c) In the **Margins** box, enter the margins shown below for the pleading style or pleading macro. If there is an option to turn the columns on, make sure that this is selected and then click on the **OK** button.

WordPerfect Pleading Style and Pleading Macro with Margins L–1.0, R–.5

Column 1	1″	4.5″
Column 2	4.5″	4.6″
Column 3	5″	7.5″

Pleading Macro with Margins L–1.5″, R–.5″

Column 1	1.5″	4.7″
Column 2	4.7″	4.8″
Column 3	5.3″	8.0″

For versions that contain the **Pleading Template** the dialog box for setting up columns is a little different. In the **Column Widths** portion of this dialog box, click the **Fixed** boxes on the first four widths so that they all contain x's. Then, place your cursor in the width measurement for column 1 and delete the current entry and replace it with **3.2.**

Press the **[Tab]** key to move to the next space and enter **0.** Tab to the width for column 2 and enter **.1.** Press the **[Tab]** key to move to the next space.

You may now close the dialog box by clicking on the **OK** button.

i. *Entering the Caption*

In the first column of the caption, type the plaintiff and defendant names in a similar manner to the example shown below.

JOHN SMITH and MARY SMITH,

   Plaintiffs,

vs.

**ABCD CORPORATION, and DOES 1
through 100, Inclusive,**

   Defendants.

After typing "Defendants.", return to the left margin by pressing the **[Enter]** key and use the underline character "_", to create an underline from the left margin to the right margin of Column 1. If you word wrap back to the left margin, use the backspace key to back up.

Press **[Ctrl] + [Enter]** to move to the second column and insert ")" characters until they are even with the underline in the first column. Your caption should now appear similar to the one shown below.

JOHN SMITH and MARY SMITH,   )
)
      Plaintiffs,   )
)
vs.   )
)
ABCD CORPORATION, and DOES 1   )
through 100, Inclusive,   )
)
      Defendants.   )
_____)

When the second column is completed, press **[Ctrl] + [Enter]** to move to the third column and enter the case number and pleading name. Your caption should now look like the one below.

JOHN SMITH and MARY SMITH,   )   CASE NO. 567320
)
      Plaintiffs,   )   **TITLE OF PLEADING AND**
)   **HEARING INFORMATION IF**
vs.   )   **NECESSARY**
)
ABCD CORPORATION, and DOES 1   )
through 100, Inclusive,   )
)
      Defendants.   )
_____)

When the third column is completed, turn the columns off by selecting **Format (Layout), Columns, Off.** This will return you back to the left margin. Turn the full justification back on by clicking on the Justification button to select Full.

j.   *Entering the Text of the Pleading*

The text of the pleading should follow the caption and should be double spaced. To make sure that the text will line up with the pleading line numbers on the left-hand side, you must begin the text on the correct line. This is easy with the Pleading Template and in versions 6.0 and later because you can see the line numbers.

In older versions of WordPerfect for Windows, you can tell if you are aligned with a line number by looking at the line position at the bottom of the screen or by selecting **File, Print Preview.** For the WordPerfect pleading style, your first line of text must begin on a line inch ending in .00, .33, or .67. For the pleading style created with the Pleading macro, move down one line and type a few characters. Then, use **File, Print Preview** to check to see if the text is aligned. If it is not, return to your document and insert another line above the characters that you typed. Then, use **File, Print Preview** again to check to see if you are now aligned. When you are at a numbered line, make sure that the insertion point is at the beginning of the line and change to double spacing.

You may now begin typing the text of the pleading.

I. PARAGRAPH NUMBERING WITH OUTLINE

Paragraph numbering is a part of the Outline feature that will sequentially number items in a document. This feature is beneficial in the creation of discovery requests and contracts. Not only does the feature provide sublevel numbers and letters, but it also will renumber all paragraphs when others are added or removed. The Outline feature automatically generates a new level number each time you press **[Enter]** or **[Tab].**

1.   Activating the Outline Feature

To activate the Outline feature in WordPerfect, select **Tools, Outline.** A button bar will appear that allows you to select the type of paragraph numbering and to create your own numbering styles. For example, an option will allow you to create an automatic numbering outline that places "Interrogatory No.:" in front of each number. To activate the Outline feature in Word, select **Format, Bullets and Numbering, Multilevel.** A dialog box will appear giving you options for numbering and the ability to place text in front of the numbers.

To demonstrate the Outline feature, we will enter the discovery requests shown below.

1.   **Plaintiff requests that Defendant produce all records evidencing the existence of a contract between Plaintiff and Defendant including, but not limited to, the following:**

   a. **The written contract between the parties.**
   b. **Any correspondence between the parties regarding the contract.**
   c. **All invoices, internal memoranda, or other documents generated as a result of the contract.**
   d. **All documents, spreadsheets, or databases existing in electronic format that evidence the existence of a contract.**

2. Plaintiff requests that Defendant produce all accounting records of Defendant corporation for the years 1995, 1996, and 1997.

Activate the Outline feature in your word processor and select the option for this type of numbering. In WordPerfect, this is the Paragraph style. In Word, you will click on the appropriate picture. Word automatically inserts an indent after the paragraph number, so click on the Modify button and deselect the Hanging Indent option so that the text will wrap back to the margin. The text in the subparts of the outline will remain indented. To get a **[Tab]** after the paragraph number in WordPerfect, you will need to press **[Home], [Tab]** or **[Ctrl] + [Tab].** If you were typing a very long list of numbered items, you could set up a style that would insert the **[Tab]** for you.

Type the first part of discovery request number 1 and press the **[Enter]** key to return to the left margin. You will be given a number 2 at the left margin. To move this in a level in the outline, press the **[Tab]** key. Word will already have the item indented for you. In WordPerfect, you will need to select **Format (Layout), Paragraph, Indent,** or press a function key to indent the item. When you press the **[Enter]** key, the cursor will create the next subpart. When you press the **[Enter]** key after the last subpart, you will be given another subpart letter. Use the **[Shift] + [Tab]** key combination to move one level to the left and type request number 2.

2. Inserting and Deleting Paragraphs

To insert a new paragraph or level, move the cursor to the end of the paragraph above where you wish to place the inserted paragraph, press the **[Enter]** key, and then tab in to the desired level. To insert a blank line between paragraphs, follow the same procedure, but instead of tabbing in to a level, use the **[Backspace]** key to remove the paragraph number.

To delete a paragraph, move to the left document margin in front of the paragraph number if possible, highlight the paragraph, and press **[Delete].**

J. Preparing a Table of Authorities

A table of authorities is similar to a table of contents and is included at the beginning of legal briefs and points and authorities to list the statutes, cases, and other materials referenced within the pleading. An example of a table of authorities is shown in Figure 2.26.

There are four steps to creating a table of authorities:

1. **Identify the categories of materials** contained within the pleading and the order in which you wish them to appear in the table. The usual order of these materials is
   - Cases
   - Constitutional Provisions
   - Statutes
   - Regulations
   - Court Rules
   - Miscellaneous

TABLE OF AUTHORITIES

CASES

City of Los Angeles v. Gleneagle Development Co.
    62 Cal. App. 3d 543, 133 Cal. Rptr. 212 (1976) 5, 6

Denham v. Superior Court
    2 Cal. 3d 557, 564, 86 Cal. Rptr. 65 (1970) 3, 4, 6

Dunsmuir Masonic Temple v. Superior Court
    12 Cal. App. 3d 17, 22, 90 Cal. Rptr. 405, 408 (1970) 4, 5

Farrar v. McCormick
    25 Cal. App. 3d 701, 705, 102 Cal. Rptr. 190 (1972) 5

Ordway v. Arata
    150 Cal. App. 2d 71, 79, 309 P.2d 919 (1957) 3, 6

Tannatt v. Joblin
    130 Cal. App. 3d 1063, 1070, 182 Cal. Rptr. 112 (1982) 3, 4

STATUTES

Cal. Code Civ. Proc. §583.410 2-5

Cal. Code Civ. Proc. §583.410(a) 2

Cal. Code Civ. Proc. §583.410(b) 2

COURT RULES

Cal. Rules of Court, Rule 373 2

Cal. Rules of Court, Rule 373(a) 5

      Figure 2.26   A table of authorities can be quickly generated by marking
              the authorities within the text of the document and then
              allowing the word processor to generate the table

2. **Mark each authority** within the document.
3. **Prepare the table of authorities,** identifying where the categories of materials should be listed.
4. **Generate the table.**

The most time-consuming aspect of this process is the actual marking of each authority. However, when you have completed the marking, you may regenerate the table after making any corrections to the text and have the old table replaced with a new table.

The pleading used in this example is included in Appendix A to Chapter 1. In order to practice preparing the table of authorities, you will need to type it yourself, or your instructor will provide it to you on a disk. We will follow the four steps for creating a table of authorities using this pleading.

1. Identifying the Categories of Materials

In reviewing the pleading, we see that it contains cases, statutes, and court rules. Therefore, the sections of our table of authorities will be labeled Cases, Statutes, and Rules.

2. Marking the Authorities

Now that we have defined the sections of the table, we must mark the occurrence of each authority. Each authority will be marked in full form at its first occurrence. A short form name, like a nickname, will also be given. Subsequent occurrences of the authority will be marked with the short form name.

If you are using WordPerfect for Windows version 5.2 or later, there is a Toolbar that performs the table of authorities functions. Point at the Toolbar with the mouse pointer and press the right mouse button. A list of the available Toolbars will be displayed. Select the **Generate** *Button Bar. In the newest versions, you will need to also click on a button containing the "scales of justice" to get the Toolbar.*

The first authority within the text, in Part II, is California Code of Civil Procedure, Section 583.410(a). Mark this authority with the following steps.

a. *Full Form Marking*

a) Highlight the entire authority, from "California" to the section number.

b) In **Word,** press **[Alt] + [Shift] + I.** Edit the full form in the text box so that it reads as you would like it to read in the final table of authorities. The authority should appear as shown below.

Cal. Code Civ. Proc. §583.410(a)

Use **[Alt] + 21** on the number keypad to get the section symbol (you may need to turn on the [Num Lock] key). Choose the **Statutes** category. In the **Short Citation** box delete all but the section number. The dialog box will look similar to the one in Figure 2.27. Click on the **Mark All** button to mark all occurrences of this authority. You will notice that all of the formatting codes are placed within your document. This is so you can see when an authority has been marked. To hide the codes when you are finished, click on the button containing the paragraph symbol on the Toolbar.

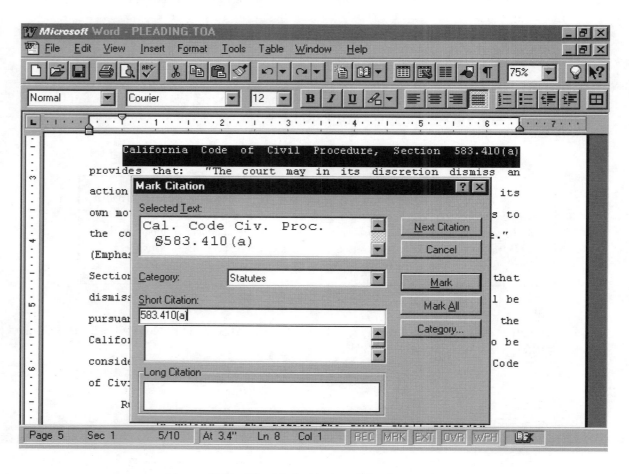

Figure 2.27 The Mark Citation dialog box in Word

c) In **WordPerfect,** use the Toolbar and click on the **Create Full Form** button. You will first be prompted for the Section Name and the Short Form of the citation. Enter the Section Name "Statutes" and delete everything in the Short Form box except for the section number. Click on the OK button to move to the Full Form Edit screen. In this screen, you will set up how the full form will look in the final table. For this authority, we would like the full form to appear as follows:

Cal. Code Civ. Proc. §583.410(a)

Insert the section symbol with **[Alt] + 21** (your [Num Lock] key may need to be turned on). Click on the **Close** button when you are done and proceed to the next authority.

The next authority is found within the same paragraph. Repeat the steps we used for the previous authority, giving it the short form name "583.410(b)" and the full form name "Cal. Code Civ. Proc. §583.410(b)."

Mark the next authority using the short form name "583.410" and the full form name "Cal. Code Civ. Proc. §583.410."

The next authority is a citation to California Rules of Court, Rule 373. This authority will be in the Rules section of the table. Mark this authority with the short form name "Rule 373" and the full form name "Cal. Rule of Court, Rule 373."

b. *Short Form Marking*

The next authority is another reference to California Code of Civil Procedure, Section 583.410. Since we have already identified the full form of this authority, we need only mark this authority and identify its short form name. In Word, this citation may already be marked. If it is, you may proceed to the next citation. When you find a repeat reference that has not been marked, follow the steps below.

a) Highlight the text to be marked.

b) In **Word,** press **[Alt] + [Shift] + I.** Select the short form name for this cite and click on the **Mark** button.

c) In **WordPerfect,** select the short form name for this cite from the drop-down list and click on the **Mark** button. In older versions of the program, you may need to click on a short form button.

Mark the next reference to Rule 373 using the short form method.

After identifying the short form of the next reference to CCP 583.410, you will come to the first case authority.

c. *Marking Cases*

     The first case authority is <u>Ordway v. Arata</u>. To mark a case authority, highlight the case name, citation(s), and date. Mark the first reference to this case using the full form method. It will be in the Cases section. Give it the short form name "Ordway."

     a) In **Word,** you do not need to alter the format of the full form. When the table is generated, you will have a number of styles to choose from.

     b) In **WordPerfect,** the full form of the authority needs to be edited so that it appears as you would like it to appear in the table. A common method is to place the case name on the first line at the left margin, and the citation(s) on the second line one tab stop in. An example using <u>Ordway</u> is shown below.

> **Ordway v. Arata**
> **150 Cal. App. 2d 71, 79, 309 P.2d 919 (1957)**

     You will need to decide if you want your case name underlined in the table of authorities. If you do, underline it in the full form edit screen. If you do not, reveal your codes in the full form edit screen and delete any underline codes.

     Mark the next two cases, <u>Denham</u> and <u>Tannatt</u>, using the full form method. When you come to the next case authority, you will see that it is another reference to <u>Denham</u>. In Word, it will probably have been marked already. If it has not, or if you are using WordPerfect, mark this reference with the short form method.

     Continue on through the pleading, marking new authorities with the full form method, and identifying repeated authorities with the short form method.

3. Preparing the Sections of the Table

     After you have marked all of the authorities, you need to prepare the table. Note: This step is not necessary if you are using Word, and you may proceed to Section 4 below. If you are using WordPerfect, move to the page of the pleading where the table is to appear. Space down two or three lines from the heading to where you would like the first section of the table to appear. Type in the heading at the left margin as follows:

<u>CASES</u>

Press **[Enter]** twice to double space down. At this point, you will identify where the cases will begin to appear in the table. (Make sure that you have turned off the bold and underline that you used in the section title.)

     a) Click on the **Define** button on the Toolbar. The Define Table of Authorities dialog box will appear.

     b) In the Define Table of Authorities dialog box, select or enter the section name ("Cases"). Then, make selections in the Edit or Numbering Format box. The common format is to have the Dot Leaders and Blank Line Between Authorities options selected. Click on the **Insert** or **OK** button when you are finished. To mark the second section, press the **[Enter]** key twice to double space down from where we entered the definition for the Cases section, and type **<u>STATUTES</u>** at the left margin. Double space down and access the Define feature again and type in or select the section name ("Statutes"). Double space down again and type **<u>COURT RULES</u>** at the left margin. Double space down and define the section as "Rules." When you have finished, you are ready to generate the table.

4. Generating the Table

Before you generate the table, you should adjust the page numbering of your document so that the beginning of the text (the page with the Introduction section) begins on page 1. You will then generate the table.

a. *Using Word*

In Word, you need to create a section break to get the document to start renumbering. Move to the page that contains the table of authorities heading and reveal your formatting codes by clicking on the Toolbar button that contains the paragraph symbol. Move the cursor in front of the code for the page break and use the **[Delete]** key to remove it. Next, select **Insert, Break** and under the options for a Section Break, select **Next Page** and click on the **OK** button. This type of section break inserts a hard page break and starts the text as a new section. To change the page numbering, select **Insert, Page Numbers,** click on the **Format button,** click on the **Start At** option, and make sure that it reads that it will start at page 1. Click on the **OK** buttons to return to the document. If you would like the beginning of the document to be numbered with i, ii, iii, etc., move to the top of the document and select **Insert, Page Numbers.** Click on the **Format** button, select the appropriate numbering option, and click on the **OK** button.

To generate the table in Word, move down a couple of lines from the Table of Authorities heading and select **Insert, Index and Tables,** select the options for table of authorities, choose from the styles that are available (such as "Formal"), make sure that the Category selection is All, and click on the **OK** button to prepare the table of authorities. You will find that Word mismarked Rule 373(a) in Section IV of the pleading as "Rule 373." To fix this error, go to the reference to 373(a) and remove the marking code. Then highlight the reference and mark it using the full form method. To regenerate the table, move back up to the table of authorities page, place the cursor above the Cases section, select **Insert, Index and Tables,** change the Category to All so that all of the categories will be adjusted, and click on the **OK** button.

b. *Using WordPerfect*

In WordPerfect, move to the first page of the text and select **Format (Layout), Page, Numbering.** In the Page Numbering dialog box, select Bottom Center and make sure that the Numbering Type is **1,2,3,4.** In older versions of the program, change the New Page Number to **1.** In newer versions of the program, click on the Value button and change the New Page Number to **1.** Frequently, the first pages of a brief containing the table of contents and table of authorities will be numbered i, ii, iii, iv. You may move to the top of your pleading document and change the page numbering option to this if you like. If you do, make sure that you choose a position for the page numbering. In newer versions of the program, you will need to click on the **Options** button and change the Page options to Lowercase Roman.

To generate the table in WordPerfect, select **Tools, Generate** (or press the **Generate** button on the Toolbar). Your table of authorities should appear similar to the one in Figure 2.26. If you have authorities that are listed with an asterisk, they were marked with a short form that did not match the one used when the first reference to the authority was identified. Use Reveal Codes to see how that reference is marked. Then, either delete the old code and remark the authority using the correct short form, or go back to the reference for the full form, place your cursor after the authority, and access Mark Text Full Form. Since no text has been selected, WordPerfect will assume that you want to edit the last table reference. You can edit either the full form or press the appropriate button to edit the short form.

The benefit of all the work that went into creating this table of authorities occurs when changes are made to the pleading resulting in authorities moving to different pages or being eliminated entirely. If this happens, all that needs to be done is to follow the steps again for generating a table. Word users need to make sure that the category selected is All. The new table will write over the existing table. If new authorities are added to the pleading, they should be marked and the table should be generated again.

Summary

Windows word processors are programs that allow you to create and edit documents. WordPerfect and Word are the two word processors that are primarily used by legal professionals. The features that they offer are almost identical. Most of the features in these word processors are accessed through pull-down menus or from the Toolbars at the top of the screen. As these programs progress and new versions are created, the features tend to remain the same but may be found under a different menu name or may have a new dialog box.

There are two typing modes in a word processor, insert and typeover. Insert inserts new text at the point of the cursor, pushing existing text to the right. Typeover types over the extisting text. You may switch between these two typing modes by pressing the **[Insert]** key.

Deleting text can be accomplished with the **[Delete]** or **[Backspace]** key. You can also highlight a portion of text and press the **[Delete]** key. Highlighting text is an important feature in word processors. In Word, the mouse or **[Shift] + [Arrow]** keys can be used to highlight text. In WordPerfect, the mouse, a function key, or **[Shift] + [Arrow]** keys can be used to highlight text. Once text has been highlighted, features can be activated that will act only on that text.

Spell checking and thesaurus features will help you in finalizing a document. Columns and tables add style to a document. Features like automatic sorting and paragraph numbering enhance the preparation of a document. Pleading templates and wizards help to create a pleading caption on lined and ruled pleading paper. All of these features make creating a document interesting and offer powerful tools to assist the user.

Appendix A

The deposition transcript contained in this appendix is to be used with Exercise 3 at the end of Chapter 2.

```
 1                Frontera, California, July 10, 1993

 2

 3                        10:45 a.m.

 4

 5

 6                     MARY ALICE KIPPER,

 7  produced as a witness by and on behalf of the Defendants, and having

 8  been first sworn, was examined and testified as follows:

 9

10                        EXAMINATION

11  BY MR. BROWN:

12      Q     Could you state your name and spell your last name for the

13  record.

14      A     Mary Alice Kipper, M-a-r-y A-l-i-c-e K-i-p-p-e-r.

15      Q     Ms. Kipper, have you ever had your deposition taken before?

16      A     No.

17      Q     What I'd like to do is to go over some things and explain

18  to you what this is all about to make you feel comfortable and make

19  sure you understand what we're going to be doing here today.

20      A     Great.

21      Q     First of all, even though we're sitting here in a room and

22  you've been placed under oath by the court reporter, it's the same as

23  if you were in a court of law or before a judge or jury.  Do you

24  understand that?

25      A     Yes.

26      Q     I'm going to go through some basic things I go through with

27  everyone that we take a deposition of, and I want you to know I'm not

28  trying to pry into your personal background at all.  I'm going to ask

                                1
```

1 a few questions about you, but I have to ask a few basic ones, okay?

2 A Okay.

3 Q In order to make a clear record so that the court reporter

4 can sit and take down my questions and your answers, what I'm going

5 to do is try to let you finish your answer before I ask you my next

6 question. I tend not to do that sometimes. At the same time, I'm

7 going to ask that you try to wait until I finish my question and then

8 you can give me your answer, and that way we'll be able to figure it

9 out later when we look at it in the book.

10 It's going to be typed into a booklet form. It will have

11 my questions and your answers and you'll be able to take a look at

12 that. I'll send you a copy of that and you'll be able to review it

13 and make any changes you like. I'll ask you to sign and date it at

14 the end under penalty of perjury. And even though you have the

15 opportunity to make changes and things, I'd ask that you give us your

16 best and truthful testimony today so you don't have to change it later

17 on, okay? But you'll have the opportunity to do so if you want.

18 I'm going to be asking you mostly about an accident which

19 happened in May of 1992. That was a few years ago.

20 A I know.

21 Q But I'm going to ask for you to give me your best

22 recollection of the events that happened around May of 1992, okay?

23 A Okay.

24 Q In order for the court reporter to understand what you're

25 saying, I'm going to ask that you give me an audible response. You

26 and I in everyday conversation might look at each other and shake

27 heads, and that doesn't come out on the record. So I'll ask you to

28 say yes, and you may catch me saying, is that a yes or no, and you'll

2

1 know why I'm doing it. I'm going to ask you to give me an audible
2 response so that if you say uh-huh, I may ask you, is that a yes,
3 okay?

4   A   Okay.

5   Q   What I'm going to assume, that if I ask you a question, if
6 you give me an answer, I'll assume that you've understood my question.
7 If you don't understand my question, you can just say, "I don't
8 understand that question, what you're talking about there," and I'll
9 rephrase it for you or try to make it make more sense. Sometimes I
10 don't ask the clearest questions in the world, but we'll try.

11   I might as well go ahead and introduce everyone that is
12 here.

13   I'm Peter Brown. I represent John Fredricks, who owned the
14 truck that was involved in the automobile accident.

15   To my right is James Mallon. He represents Susan Reynolds
16 who is the plaintiff in this action.

17   And then the court reporter is also present.

18   Could you give your date of birth?

19   A   December 18, 1957.

20   Q   Do you have a residence in Chula Vista?

21   A   I live with my parents.

22   Q   Could you give me that address?

23   A   14445 Highcliff Road, Chula Vista.

24   Q   In case we needed to get ahold of you in the San Diego area,
25 is there a phone number that we could leave a message at?

26   A   My parents, 555-4441.

27   Q   When do you expect to be returning back to San Diego?

28   A   I get out of here the 20th of August, so I'll be home then.

3

1   Q   There's an outside chance that the trial in this matter
2 might still be going on at the time, so we may need to get in touch
3 with you to see if you'll be available to assist us.
4   A   That's where I'm paroling to. I won't necessarily be there.
5 As soon as I can make arrangements to live there, I will. They'll
6 know where I am.
7   Q   Super. The trial in the case is now scheduled for July
8 17th, coming up next week. We don't know whether it'll actually get
9 out, whether a courtroom will be available or what. In case it does,
10 it may go that long, so we may contact you.
11   A   Okay.
12   Q   Are you a high school graduate?
13   A   I got my high school diploma at Las Colinas Womens Jail.
14   Q   When was that?
15   A   1991.
16   Q   Are you aware or do you have any knowledge of a person by
17 the name of Monica Olsen?
18   A   Yes.
19   Q   Could you tell me when you first met Monica Olsen?
20   A   I don't remember. Probably 1990 -- last part of 1990 or
21 first part of 1991, I think.
22   Q   Do you remember where you first met her?
23   A   At Bob Wilson's.
24   Q   Is that a friend of yours?
25   A   Yeah.
26   Q   Did you have occasion to socialize with Monica Olsen in
27 1991?
28   A   When I first met her was back in '90 or '91, and I met her

4

1 as a result of knowing her husband, I had known her husband. And then

2 she and I were introduced just through some friends somewhere. And

3 I never connected the fact that the two of them were husband and wife

4 until I met her at Bob's house.

5   Q   Did you have occasion to spend some time or visit with

6 Monica in 1991 at all?

7   A   No, 'cause I was in jail most of 1991. The first part of

8 that year I saw her a few times, you know, just here and there but

9 never really socialized with her much.

10   Q   What about 1992?

11   A   The first part of 1992 she was in jail at Las Colinas. And

12 she called where I was living at and I answered the phone. And when

13 she got out of jail she came over to see me. And that's how she and

14 I got started socializing again.

15   Q   When you say the first part of 1992, would that have been

16 in January of '92?

17   A   I don't remember. I really don't remember.

18   Q   If the accident occurred on May 29th of '92, was it at least

19 a couple of months before that time that she had given you a call when

20 you first got back together socializing again?

21   A   Probably, yes. I didn't see her on a regular basis like we

22 lived about three or four blocks from each other. And I lived in an

23 apartment complex that was right next to the parking lot at the liquor

24 store. Whenever Monica came down to get cigarettes or buy beer, she

25 would drive by and honk her horn. And sometimes she would pull in and

26 say hi and come over and have a beer, whatever.

27   Q   In May of 1992 did you see her at all during that month, if

28 you recall?

5

```
 1     A     Uh-huh, yeah.  The week before the accident on Friday she
 2   and I had driven up to -- actually Thursday night, we had driven up
 3   to Soledad to pick up my brother when he was released.  I don't
 4   remember what the date was, but it was the Friday right before the
 5   accident.
 6     Q     When you say that you and Monica drove up, would that have
 7   been in her car?
 8     A     Yes.
 9     Q     Do you know if that was the same car that she was driving
10   on the --
11     A     Yes.
12     Q     Let me finish.
13           -Was that the same car that she was driving on the day of
14   the accident?
15     A     Yes.
16     Q     Could you describe it at all to me?
17     A     I just remember it was an older car, turquoise in color,
18   four doors.  No, it was like a silver, a gray-blue.
19     Q     But you're sure that it was the same car?
20     A     Yes, I'm positive.
21     Q     When you drove up to pick up your brother, did Monica drive?
22     A     I drove when we left Chula Vista.  We left about 10 minutes
23   after 8:00 that night and I drove up to Gorman.  We stopped in Gorman
24   to get gas.  Monica said she'd drive.
25     Q     What time of night was that?
26     A     However long it takes, if you leave at 8:00 to get to
27   Gorman.  I have no idea.
28     Q     Was it dark out?
```

6

1   A   Yeah, it was real dark.

2   Q   Monica told you that she was going to drive?

3   A   She just said, "I'll drive 'cause you've been driving all

4 the way up here." So I said "okay."

5   Q   Could you tell me what happened when Monica got into the car

6 and started to drive?

7   A   She scared me to death. She was driving in the middle lane

8 and she was weaving over to the outside lane and then over to the

9 inside lane and all the way across the three lanes of traffic.

10   So I asked her if she was all right to drive 'cause we'd

11 been drinking a few beers on the way up. And she said, "Well yeah,

12 I'm okay to drive. I'm not drunk, but I'm having a hard time seeing."

13   And I asked her why and she said, "I have night-blindness."

14   And I told her to pull the car over and let me drive.

15   Q   Did she pull the car over?

16   A   That was the extent of her driving that night.

17   Q   Did she tell you that she had a hard time seeing cars on the

18 road at night?

19   A   She told me she had a hard time seeing everything.

20   Q   Did she tell you she had a hard time seeing vehicles parked

21 on the road or driving on the road?

22   A   I don't remember. All that she told me was that she had a

23 hard time seeing, period.

24   Q   When she was weaving in and out on the road, were you

25 nervous and upset about being in the same car with her?

26   A   Yes. It took about 30 seconds for me to realize that she

27 wasn't going to be driving while I was riding.

28   Q   When you said that she was weaving in and out, did that mean

7

1 across from one lane to the next lane?

2   A   You know, we were in the center lane, and then we'd be over,

3 going over the line and back in the lane, and pretty soon we'd be over

4 the line and back in the lane again.

5   Q   As far as you know, was she drunk at all, would you say?

6   A   It's hard to say because I hadn't seen her earlier that day.

7 But from the time she came and picked me up that night, we were

8 drinking, not heavy, we were drinking beers. And we took a 12-pack

9 with us when we left.

10   Q   When she told you that she didn't think that she had any

11 problem because of the alcohol, was it at that time that she also told

12 you that it was because she was night-blind and she was having a hard

13 time?

14   A   Yeah, because you know, I told her, "Maybe you ought to pull

15 over and let me drive."

16   Q   Do you know if Monica was wearing glasses that evening?

17   A   I couldn't tell you, I really couldn't.

18   Q   Do you know if she had a prescription to wear glasses at

19 all?

20   A   Yes, she did. But whether she wore them or not -- sometimes

21 she had them with her and sometimes she didn't.

22   Q   Do you happen to know whether or not her driver's license

23 was restricted for eyesight?

24   A   I have no idea.

25   Q   While you were traveling in the car while Monica was

26 driving, did she keep her eyes on the road or did she turn to look at

27 where you were sitting?

28   A   I don't know. It's hard to say 'cause it was late at night.

8

1　It was real dark. We were traveling up the grapevine road and there
2　wasn't any traffic. So I couldn't tell you if she was looking at me
3　when she was talking or not.
4　　　Q　What about the speed of her car when she drove, did she tend
5　to drive fast?
6　　　A　Yeah.
7　　　Q　Had you been driving with Monica at any time prior to this
8　occasion?
9　　　A　A few times, but not any distance, just maybe to the store
10　and back. You know, just a few blocks.
11　　　Q　Did she explain to you what night-blindness meant at all?
12　　　A　No, because knowing what my definition of night-blindness
13　is or what I perceive night-blindness to be.
14　　　Q　What would that be?
15　　　A　That you have a real hard time seeing at night.
16　　　Q　And the way that she was driving on the occasion that you
17　were driving with her the week before the accident would indicate that
18　she was having a hard time seeing at night?
19　　　A　Real hard. I was tired when we got to Gorman, but I
20　preferred driving being tired as to riding in a panic all the way up
21　there.
22　　　Q　Did you actually tell her to stop the car and say, "You are
23　not driving anymore," or something to this effect?
24　　　A　Yes.
25　　　Q　Did you refuse to let her drive the car?
26　　　A　No, I just told her to pull over and let me drive.
27　　　　She said, "Are you okay? I'm okay."
28　　　　And I said, "No you're not, Monica."

9

```
 1              And she said, "Okay."
 2       Q    Do you know if anyone else was aware that Monica had night-
 3  blindness at all?
 4       A    I couldn't tell you.
 5       Q    When was the last time that you spoke to Monica?
 6       A    It was a little while after the accident, but I couldn't say
 7  how long.  Maybe a couple of weeks, three weeks or so.  And then I saw
 8  her probably about a year later.
 9       Q    The first time that you saw her after the accident would
10  have been when?
11       A    Sometime in June.
12       Q    Do you recall whether or not you saw her personally or just
13  spoke to her on the telephone?
14       A    No, I saw her in person.
15       Q    Do you recall when that was or where that was?
16       A    At my house.
17       Q    Did you talk about the accident at all?
18       A    Yes.  Monica was real drunk and she was crying.
19       Q    Was Monica drunk at your house at the time you saw her after
20  the accident?
21       A    Yes.
22       Q    Can you tell me in substance what the conversation was that
23  you had with Monica about the accident?
24       A    She just felt bad because she hurt Susan so bad and said it
25  should have been her in the hospital instead of Susan.
26       Q    Did she talk about whether or not she had anything to drink
27  that night?
28       A    Which night?
```

10

1   Q   I'm sorry. Let me clarify that.

2   On the night that she was at your house after the accident,

3   the first time that you had a conversation with her, did she talk

4   about the night of the accident and whether or not on that night she

5   had had anything to drink?

6   A   I know she'd been drinking 'cause she and Susan and I had

7   been together off and on that whole day, not together the whole day,

8   but you know, at different times during the day.

9   Monica came by herself at one time. She had stopped at the

10   store and bought a couple of six-packs of beer and we drank a six-

11   pack. And we took a beer over to Susan.

12   Susan walked over to the store later when she was expecting

13   her husband. She stopped and picked up some beer and stopped to have

14   a beer with me and went home.

15   Monica came back over later. We sat out in the backyard and

16   drank some more beers, so I know she was drinking.

17   Q   Getting back to the conversation that you had with her after

18   the accident, do you recall anything else she would have said about

19   the accident other than the fact that she felt bad because she had

20   hurt Susan and wished that she would have been the one in the

21   hospital?

22   A   She said she didn't see the trailer.

23   Q   Do you recall anything else she might have said about the

24   accident?

25   A   Huh-uh.

26   Q   Is that a no?

27   A   No.

28   Q   Did she talk to you at all about the reason why she and

11

1 Susan had left on the evening of the accident in her automobile?

2 A Yeah. They'd gone to buy some drugs, or they were looking

3 for some drugs.

4 Q After the first time that you talked to her after the

5 accident, when was the next time you would have talked to Monica after

6 the accident?

7 A It was quite awhile. It was after she had her next baby.

8 Q Do you recall where that conversation took place?

9 A No. Probably in a bar. Seems to me that's where I saw her.

10 Q Do you recall what the substance of that conversation was?

11 A It had nothing at all to do with Susan. Monica was just --

12 she was real belligerent and real drunk. I think she was arguing with

13 her boyfriend. It seems to me that was what was going on.

14 Q In May of 1992 how would you describe Monica personally as

15 you knew her?

16 A She was mostly just into partying a lot then. Having a good

17 time. She and her husband had split up. She was renting a room from

18 my friend, and she was just all about partying and having a good time.

19 Q Do you know if she used to drink alcohol in May of 1992 on

20 a daily basis?

21 A Pretty much so, I think.

22 Q Would you say she would have consumed mostly beer at that

23 time?

24 A Yeah.

25 Q When you were with her, would she usually drink more than

26 a six-pack?

27 A I don't know. Most of the time Monica would -- She would

28 get her share of however much there was there.

12

```
 1      Q    Other than the conversation at the bar that you might have
 2  had with her a year after the accident, have you talked to her or seen
 3  Monica since that time?
 4      A    I saw her a few times in that period of time after I saw her
 5  at the bar, but it was usually at a bar and she was usually arguing
 6  with her boyfriend.  And other than that, no.
 7      Q    Did you know Monica to have a temper?
 8      A    When she was drinking, yeah.
 9      Q    How would you describe the type of temper she might have
10  when she was drinking?
11      A    Just real explosive.  She'd just go off, just right now, I
12  mean, you know.  And it would sometimes be nothing, just something
13  someone had said or -- who knows.  Just whatever.
14      Q    So you would describe her as having an explosive temper if
15  she got mad at the same time she would have been drinking?
16      A    Uh-huh.
17      Q    Is that a yes?
18      A    Yes.
19      Q    Would you say that you had observed this type of behavior
20  before the accident?
21      A    Yes.
22      Q    How many occasions would you have observed Monica's
23  explosive behavior?
24      A    Quite a few.
25      Q    When you say "quite a few," would that be more than 20
26  times?
27      A    Oh, probably not.  But 20 is a good safe number.  Usually
28  when she was drinking, she ends up getting mad at something because
```

13

```
 1  she was drinking because she was mad to begin with.  She was always
 2  mad about something.
 3       Q    Again, this would have been in 1992?
 4       A    Uh-huh.
 5       Q    Is that correct?
 6       A    Yes.
 7       Q    Let's take a break now.  We'll resume the deposition after
 8  lunch.
 9
10
11
12
13
14
15
16
17
18
19
20
21
22
23
24
25
26
27
28
```

14

WORD PROCESSING EXERCISES

Exercise 1

You work for The Law Offices of Peter Baer. Mr. Baer has asked you to telephone opposing counsel in the *Friend v. Foe* case, Lance Wilson, to request a ten-day extension of time to respond to the complaint filed by Mr. Wilson's client John Friend. Our firm represents Tim Foe. Mr. Wilson granted the extension of time when you telephoned him. Now you must prepare a letter to confirm the extension. Prepare this letter to Mr. Wilson for your own signature. You may make up your own addresses for The Law Offices of Peter Baer and for Lance Wilson. This letter should be short and to the point. Use the spell check feature to check your spelling.

Exercise 2

Use a memorandum template or Wizard to create a memorandum to your boss, Peter Baer, letting him know that you sent the confirmation letter referred to in Exercise 1. If you are using WordPerfect for DOS, create a memorandum with a heading similar to the one on page 45 of Chapter 1. Memoranda are not signed, so do not include a signature line. It is customary, however, for authors of memoranda to handwrite their initials next to their name in the heading of a memorandum.

Exercise 3

Use the table feature to summarize the deposition transcript in Appendix A to Chapter 2.
The case you are working on involves an automobile accident. You are a paralegal working with attorney Peter Brown. Your firm's client, John Fredricks, is being sued by Susan Reynolds for personal injuries resulting from an automobile accident.
On May 29, 1992, at approximately 10:00 p.m., Susan Reynolds was a passenger in a car driven by Monica Olsen. They were southbound on Interstate 805 in the right lane when their car struck a truck and trailer rig owned and operated by Mr. Fredricks. Mr. Fredricks' rig had broken down and he had pulled over to the right shoulder. The rig was large and part of the left side remained in the right traffic lane. Monica's vehicle struck the rig and caused severe injuries to Reynolds. Susan Reynolds states that she and Monica were arguing at the time of

the accident, but at no time was Monica distracted from operating the vehicle. Mr. Fredricks states that his hazard flashers were on and that he was preparing to light flares when the accident occurred.

While Mr. Fredricks does have some liability for leaving the truck in the traffic lane, Mr. Brown's strategy is to show that Monica Olsen's driving ability was impaired on the night of the accident and that Susan Reynolds knew, or should have known, about this impairment. It is his contention that this impairment caused Monica Olsen to hit the truck, which she could easily have avoided had she not been so impaired.

Mr. Brown sent a notice of deposition to Mary Kipper, a friend of both Monica and Susan. She is expected to testify to Monica's character and driving ability. Mr. Brown traveled to Frontera State Prison to take Ms. Kipper's deposition. The court reporter has prepared the transcript and delivered it to your offices. Mr. Brown has asked you to summarize it.

To begin a deposition summary, you type the summary heading at the top of the page. A sample heading is shown below.

SUMMARY OF THE DEPOSITION OF

HUBERT M. SMITH

Taken November 9, 1997

Press the **[Enter]** key to move down a few lines to set up your table. Your table will need two columns and eight rows to begin with. More rows can be added as they are needed. Adjust the columns so that the left column is approximately 1.5 inches and the right column extends to the right margin. In the first row of the table, place the column headings, "PAGE:LINE" and "SUMMARY" as shown below.

PAGE:LINE	SUMMARY

The first entry that you make into your deposition summary table is the name of the person asking the questions of the witness. This may change during a deposition and should be noted similarly when someone new begins questioning.

PAGE:LINE	SUMMARY
	EXAMINATION BY MR. ATKINS

As you begin your summarization of the deposition, you will read the transcript noting where a line of questioning begins and where the questioning then shifts to another subject. A deposition transcript normally begins with opening statements to the witness about the deposition process. The page and line numbers where these statements begin are noted in the first column, and the phrase "Opening statements" is entered in the Summary column.

After the opening statements, you will probably find questions regarding the witness' name, address, education, and occupation. These can be grouped as a single line of questioning. In the summary you will note the page and line number where the questioning begins and then summarize the responses to the questioning. As you type in the Summary column, the text will word wrap and the row height will increase. You will continue through the transcript noting in the summary where a new line of questioning begins, and then summarizing the responses to those questions. Not all questioning in a deposition is organized, so you may find it difficult at times to define the beginning and end of a line of questioning. You may also wonder if some fact should be included within the summary as it may not seem important to the case. Use your judgment from what you know of the case, and do your best. An example of a deposition summary is shown below.

SUMMARY OF THE DEPOSITION OF

HUBERT M. SMITH

Taken November 9, 1997

PAGE:LINE	SUMMARY
	EXAMINATION BY MR. ATKINS
1:3	Opening statements
2:26	Mr. Smith was born in Walla Walla, Washington on December 12, 1945. He currently resides at 345 Main Street, Seattle, Washington 00990. Mr. Smith obtained a Bachelor of Science degree in Economics from the University of Washington in 1967. He is presently employed by the State of Washington as an Economist.
5:15	Mr. Smith has prepared a report of the economic damages suffered by XYZ Corporation as a result of the breach of contract by User Industries. He prepared this report by reviewing sales figures of XYZ for the previous 10 years and anticipating the growth in the market for the 1990's.

When you are finished with your deposition summary, you may want to erase the lines in the table. Some people prefer to leave them in. The decision is up to you.

Exercise 4

Prepare the following fee contract using the Outline feature to automatically insert paragraph numbers.

ATTORNEY-CLIENT FEE CONTRACT

This ATTORNEY-CLIENT FEE CONTRACT ("Contract") is entered into by and between _____ ("Client") and _____("Attorney").

1. CONDITIONS. This Contract will not take effect, and Attorney will have no obligation to provide legal services, until Client returns a signed copy of this Contract and pays the deposit called for under paragraph 3.

2. SCOPE AND DUTIES. Client hires Attorney to provide legal services in connection with _____. Attorney shall provide those legal services reasonably required to represent Client, and shall take reasonable steps to keep Client informed of progress and to respond to Client's inquiries. Client shall be truthful with Attorney, cooperate with Attorney, keep Attorney informed of developments, abide by this Contract, pay Attorney's bills on time and keep Attorney advised of Client's address, telephone number, and whereabouts.

3. DEPOSIT. Client shall deposit $_____ by _____. The sum will be deposited in a trust account, to be used to pay:

_____ Costs and expenses only.
_____ Costs and expenses and fees for legal services.

Client hereby authorizes Attorney to withdraw sums from the trust account to pay the costs and/or fees Client incurs. Any unused deposit at the conclusion of Attorney's services will be refunded.

4. LEGAL FEES. Client agrees to pay for legal services at the following rates:
   a. Partners: _____/hour
   b. Associates: _____/hour
   c. Paralegals: _____/hour
   d. Law Clerks: _____/hour
   e. Other Personnel as follows: _____
Attorney charges in minimum units of _____ hours.

5. COSTS AND EXPENSES. In addition to paying legal fees, Client shall reimburse Attorney for all costs and expenses incurred by Attorney, including, but not limited to, process servers' fees, fees fixed by law or assessed by courts or other agencies, court reporter's fees, long distance telephone calls, messenger and other delivery fees, postage, in-office photocopying at $_____ per page, parking, mileage at $_____ per mile, investigation expenses, consultants' investigators, consultants' fees or expert witnesses' fees reasonably necessary in Attorney's judgment, unless one or both of the clauses below are initialed by Client and Attorney.

_____ Attorney shall obtain Client's consent before incurring any cost in excess of $_____.

_____ Attorney shall obtain Client's consent before retaining outside investigators, consultants, or expert witnesses.

6.   STATEMENTS. Attorney shall send Client periodic statements for fees and costs incurred. Client shall pay Attorney's statements within _____ days after each statement's date. Client may request a statement at intervals of no less than 30 days. Upon Client's request Attorney will provide a statement within 10 days.

7.   DISCHARGE AND WITHDRAWAL. Client may discharge Attorney at any time. Attorney may withdraw with Client's consent or for good cause. Good cause includes Client's breach of this Contract, Client's refusal to cooperate with Attorney or to follow Attorney's advice on a material matter, or any other fact or circumstance that would render Attorney's continuing representations unlawful or unethical.

8.   CONCLUSION OF SERVICES. When Attorney's services conclude, all unpaid charges shall become immediately due and payable. After Attorney's services conclude, Attorney will, upon Client's request, deliver Client's file to Client, along with any Client funds or property in Attorney's possession.

9.   DISCLAIMER OF GUARANTEE. Nothing in this Contract and nothing in Attorney's statements to Client will be construed as a promise or guarantee about the outcome of Client's matter. Attorney makes no such promises or guarantees. Attorney's comments about the outcome of Client's matter are expressions of opinion only.

10.   EFFECTIVE DATE. This Contract will take effect when Client has performed the conditions stated in paragraph 1, but its effective date will be retroactive to the date Attorney first provided services. The date at the beginning of this Contract is for reference only. Even if this Contract does not take effect, Client will be obligated to pay Attorney the reasonable value of any services Attorney may have performed for Client.

"Attorney"

By: _____

Address: _____   "Client"
_____
Telephone: _____   _____

To complete the exercise, insert the following paragraph that was accidentally omitted. It should be placed after the paragraph entitled "STATEMENTS."

LIEN. Client hereby grants Attorney a lien on any and all claims or causes of action that are the subject of Attorney's representations under this Contract. Attorney's lien will be for any sums due and owing to Attorney at the conclusion of Attorney's services. The lien will attach to any recovery Client may obtain, whether by arbitration award, judgment, settlement, or otherwise.

Spell check and print the document.

Exercise 5

Using the instructions for drafting a pleading caption, draft a complaint with one cause of action for breach of contract. You can make up the parties and the facts of the case. Spell check and print the document.

Chapter Index

Electronic Spreadsheets

CHAPTER 3

LOTUS® 1-2-3®

Chapter Preface

Lotus 1-2-3 for DOS is an electronic spreadsheet program. Electronic spreadsheets are similar to an accountant's pad but much more flexible. There is little difference between electronic spreadsheets, so learning Lotus 1-2-3 will make you proficient in almost any other spreadsheet program.

An electronic spreadsheet can be used to create any type of spreadsheet that can be created on paper. The advantages of the electronic spreadsheet are that you can manipulate the columns and rows, and that the computer calculates the totals for you, eliminating mistakes in calculations (as long as you write the formula correctly). Graphs may be created from the data for visual effects, and database functions may be performed upon data in a spreadsheet.

This chapter will introduce you to the Lotus 1-2-3 for DOS environment and commands. These commands will be used to act upon sample spreadsheets within the chapter. Chapter 4 covers Windows-based electronic spreadsheets. At the end of Chapter 4 are several electronic spreadsheet exercises for use with Chapter 3 or Chapter 4. At the end of this chapter is a Lotus 1-2-3 Command List. The Command List provides a quick reference for the most common Lotus 1-2-3 for DOS commands.

A.   ENTERING THE PROGRAM

To enter Lotus 1-2-3 for DOS, type: **lotus [Enter]**

OR select the Lotus 1-2-3 option or icon from a menu screen.

Upon entering the program, you will be greeted by the Lotus 1-2-3 Access menu, shown in Figure 3.1, which displays the Lotus 1-2-3 options.

```
 Create worksheets, graphs, and databases
 1-2-3        PrintGraph        Translate        Install        Exit
```

```
                            Lotus
                       1-2-3 Access Menu
                         Release 2.4

        Copyright 1990, 1991, 1992 Lotus Development Corporation
                       All Rights Reserved.


To select a program to start, do one of the following:

    *  Use  →, HOME, or END to move the menu pointer
       to the program you want and then press ENTER.

    *  Type the first character of the program's name.

Press F1 (HELP) for more information.
```

Figure 3.1   The Lotus 1-2-3 Access Screen

The options available in the Access menu are:

1-2-3   The Lotus 1-2-3 Worksheet.

PrintGraph   The utility that prints graphs from your worksheet information.

Translate   The utility that translates files created in other software programs (dBASE, Symphony, etc.) so that they may be used in Lotus 1-2-3.

Install   The utility used to install the Lotus 1-2-3 program onto your computer system. You will not need to access this utility unless you are installing the program for the first time or are changing a material part of your computer system, such as the printer.

Exit   Leave the program.

To reach the Lotus 1-2-3 worksheet, highlight **1-2-3** and press **[Enter]**.

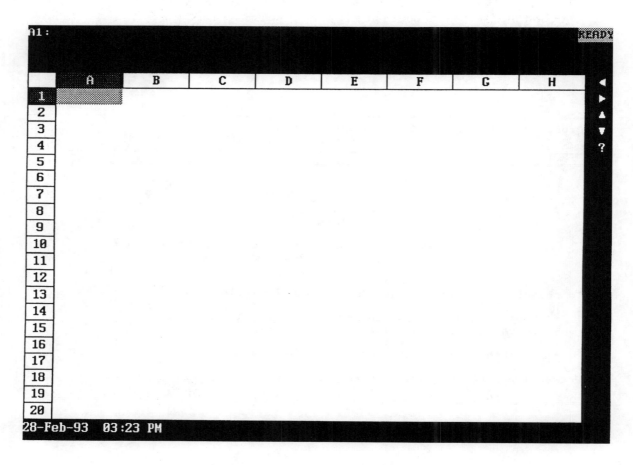

Figure 3.2   The Lotus 1-2-3 Worksheet

B. THE LOTUS 1-2-3 WORKSHEET

The Lotus 1-2-3 worksheet, shown in Figure 3.2, is the screen in which you create your spreadsheets. The worksheet is made up of columns and rows. The columns are labeled with letters, the rows with numbers.

Lotus 1-2-3 versions 2.4 and later will have icons to the right of the worksheet that are accessed with a mouse. These icons allow you to move left, right, up, or down, and access help. If your version of Lotus 1-2-3 has the WYSIWYG ("wi-see-wig" or What You See Is What You Get) add-in attached, you will also see icons that can add, copy, move, and perform many other actions upon the worksheet.

In the Lotus 1-2-3 worksheet, the intersection of a column and a row forms a cell where data is entered. The cells are identified by their cell address, the letter of the column followed by the number of the row. Cell B2 is highlighted in Figure 3.3.

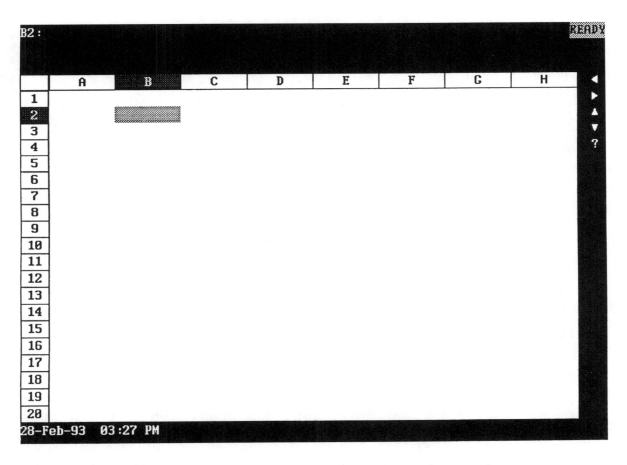

Figure 3.3   Cells are identified by their column letter and row number. Cell B2 is highlighted.

1. Worksheet Components

The main components of the Lotus 1-2-3 worksheet are explained below.

Rows The horizontal divisions of the worksheet. The rows of the Lotus 1-2-3 worksheet are numbered from 1 to 8,192.

Columns The vertical divisions of the worksheet. The columns of the Lotus 1-2-3 worksheet are labeled A through IV. After Z, the columns begin with AA, AB, AC, continuing to AZ and then beginning BA, BB, BC. There are 230 columns in Lotus 1-2-3.

Cells The intersection of a column and a row.

Cell Address The column letter of the cell followed by the row number. The cell at the top left-hand corner of the worksheet is A1.

Cell Pointer The reverse video bar that is moved around the worksheet using the **[Arrow]** keys. The cell pointer points to the cell where data will be entered.

Control Panel The portion of the screen above the column labels. This is where the menu selections will be displayed when the menu is accessed.

Mode Indicator The mode indicator is located at the upper right corner of the worksheet screen. The mode indicator displays the current mode of the worksheet. For example, when the worksheet is ready to receive information, the mode indicator will display READY. When the worksheet is busy, the mode indicator will display WAIT.

2. Movement Within the Worksheet

The keys that are used to move the cell pointer around within the Lotus 1-2-3 worksheet are explained below.

Arrow Keys The **[Arrow]** keys, located to the right of the keyboard, allow you to move the cell pointer around the worksheet one cell at a time. When preceded by the **[End]** key, they allow you to move in the direction of the **[Arrow]** key to the boundary of an empty and filled space. For example, in an empty worksheet, press the **[End]** key, release it, and press the **[Right Arrow]** key. In a blank worksheet this will take you to column IV. **[End], [Down Arrow]** will take you to row 8,192.

Home The **[Home]** key will always return the cell pointer to cell A1.

Page Up	The **[Page Up]** key moves the cell pointer up one screen.
Page Down	The **[Page Down]** key moves the cell pointer down one screen.
Tab	The **[Tab]** key moves the cell pointer right one screen.
Shifted Tab	Holding down the **[Shift]** key and pressing the **[Tab]** key (**[Shift] + [Tab]**) moves the cell pointer left one screen.
GoTo [F5]	The **GoTo** function key, **[F5]**, allows you to move to a specific cell address. After pressing **[F5],** Lotus 1-2-3 will prompt you to enter the destination cell address.

3. The Function Keys

In Lotus 1-2-3, the function keys F1 through F10, excepting F6, each have two functions. The function keys perform one function when pressed alone, and another when pressed while holding down the **[Alt]** or **[Shift]** key.

Alone, the function keys perform the following functions.

F1	Help	Accesses the Help facility.
F2	Edit	Shifts Lotus 1-2-3 into the Edit mode to allow you to alter the contents of a cell without having to retype the entire entry.
F3	Name	Displays a list of the range names in the current worksheet.
F4	ABS	Used while creating or editing a cell entry; will change a relative cell address to an absolute or mixed address.
F5	GoTo	Allows you to move to a specified cell address.
F6	Window	Moves the cursor to the other side of a split screen. You may divide the worksheet screen into two windows with a menu selection.
F7	Query	Repeats the most recent data query operation.
F8	Table	Repeats the most recent data table operation.
F9	Calc	Recalculates the worksheet formulas and functions when in the READY mode. When creating or editing a cell entry, converts the formula or function to its value.
F10	Graph	Draws a graph defined by the current graph settings.

When combined with the **[Alt]** or **[Shift]** key, the function keys perform advanced program functions. The beginning to intermediate Lotus 1-2-3 user will not be using most of these functions. If you wish to learn about them, they are explained in the Lotus 1-2-3 Manual and in the Lotus 1-2-3 Help menu.

4. The Help Menu

The Lotus 1-2-3 Help menu provides information regarding most of the worksheet features. The Help menu is accessed by pressing the **[F1]** (Help) key. Whenever you press the Help key, Lotus 1-2-3 temporarily suspends the worksheet session and takes you to the Help menu shown in Figure 3.4.

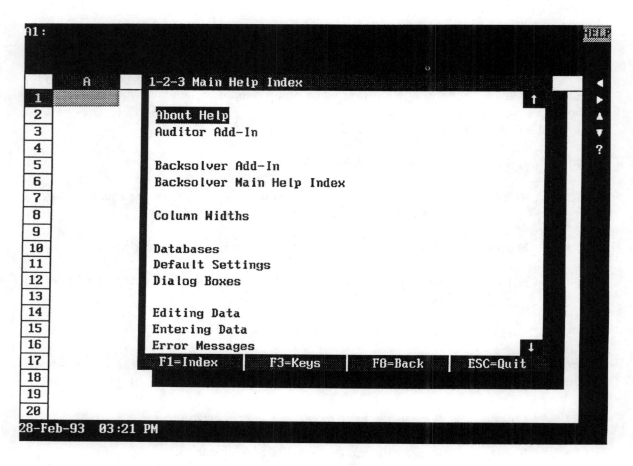

Figure 3.4   The Help Menu

To review a Help topic, highlight the item and press the **[Enter]** key. To exit Help, press the **[Esc]** key. To return to the Help topic you were last reviewing, use **[Ctrl] + [F1]** (Bookmark) to access Help from the worksheet.

Lotus® 1-2-3®

5. The Command Menu

Lotus 1-2-3 is traditionally a menu-driven program. This means that commands are selected from a menu. With later versions of the program, you may also access commands with a mouse.

The Lotus 1-2-3 Command menu is accessed by pressing the forward slash **[/]** key. When the **[/]** key is pressed, two lines of commands are displayed above the column letters of the worksheet as shown in Figure 3.5.

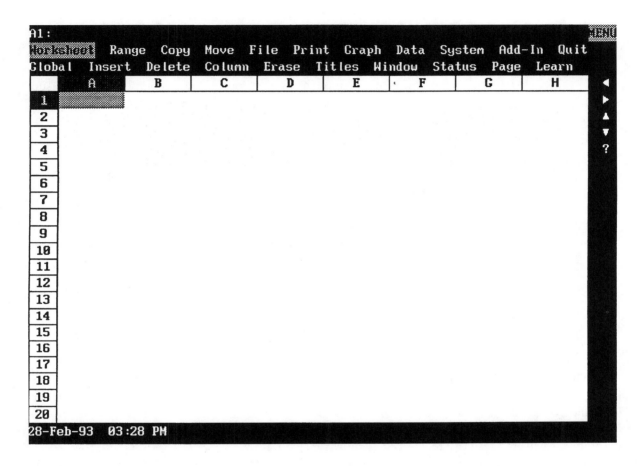

Figure 3.5 Lotus 1-2-3 command options are displayed above the column letters when the [/] is pressed

The top line of the menu indicates the available selections. A highlight bar is moved along the top row with the **[Left Arrow]** and **[Right Arrow]** keys. As you highlight an item in the top row of the menu, the options available under that item are shown on the bottom line.

a. *Selecting a Command*

To select a command from the menu, either highlight the command and press **[Enter]**, or type the first character of the command name. Commands will be referred to within this workbook beginning with a "/" and followed by the command selections. For example, to save a file, you access the menu with the forward slash key **[/]** and select **File** and then **Save.** This will be referred to as **/File Save.**

b. *The Worksheet and Range Commands*

The first two selections in the Lotus 1-2-3 menu are Worksheet and Range. Selecting **Worksheet** will take you to commands that are performed upon complete columns and rows of the worksheet. Selecting **Range** will take you to commands that are performed upon a single cell, or a group of cells. Under the Worksheet command is a Global selection. Selecting **Global** will take you to commands that will act upon the entire worksheet.

c. *Exiting the Command Menu*

To leave the Command menu, you can either complete a command or back out with the **[Esc]** key. The **[Esc]** key will always take you one step backward in a Lotus 1-2-3 command.

C.   CELL ENTRIES

The entering of data into a Lotus 1-2-3 cell involves moving the cell pointer to the cell and typing the entry. As you are typing a cell entry, the characters being typed are displayed in the upper left-hand corner of the screen as shown in Figure 3.6.

Pressing the **[Enter]** key or moving the cell pointer with one of the **[Arrow]** keys places the entry, or a calculated result, into the cell as shown in Figure 3.7.

There are two types of cell entries in Lotus 1-2-3, Labels and Values.

1.   Labels

A Label cell entry begins with a letter or a justification character. Examples of Label cell entries are:

= = = = = =
John Smith
TOTAL

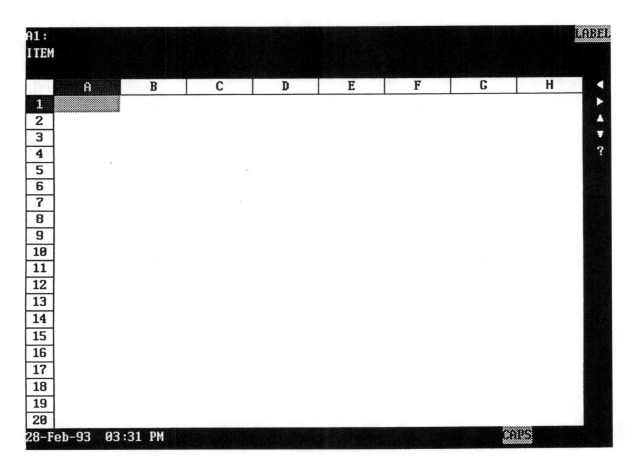

Figure 3.6 As the word "ITEM" is typed into cell A1, the characters are displayed in the upper left-hand corner of the screen

a. *Justification Characters*

Justification characters are used to position a Label entry within a cell. The three Lotus 1-2-3 justification characters are:

> '   **Left justifies the entry**
> "   **Right justifies the entry**
> ^   **Centers the entry**

Left	Right	Center
TOTAL	TOTAL	TOTAL

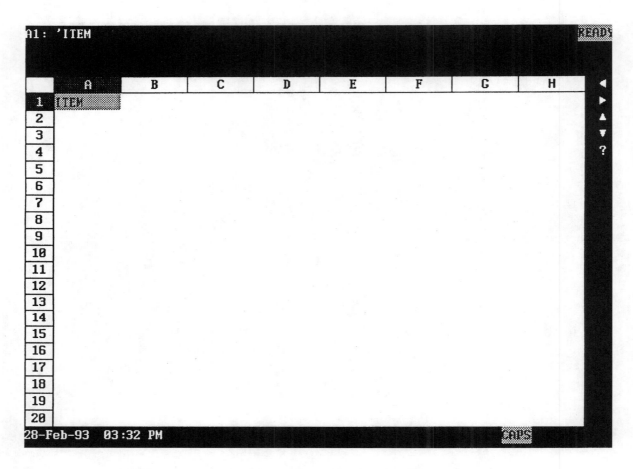

Figure 3.7 The entry is placed within the cell when the [Enter] key or an [Arrow] key is pressed

Lotus 1-2-3 automatically left justifies Label cell entries. Right or center justifying requires that you type the justification character before you type the entry.

To **left justify** "TOTAL," you type: **TOTAL**

To **right justify** "TOTAL," you type: **"TOTAL**

To **center** "TOTAL," you type: **^TOTAL**

> *Justification characters may only be used with Label cell entries. If they are used with a Value cell entry, Lotus 1-2-3 will read the value as a Label, and treat it as such.*

These justification characters are also useful when entering an alphanumeric such as a telephone number or address. Beginning with a justification character lets 1-2-3 know that the entry is a label and prevents telephone numbers from subtracting and addresses from creating error messages.

b. *Underlining*

A cell can contain only one entry. Therefore, in order to underline a cell entry, you must, in most cases, put the underline in the cell below as shown in Figure 3.8.

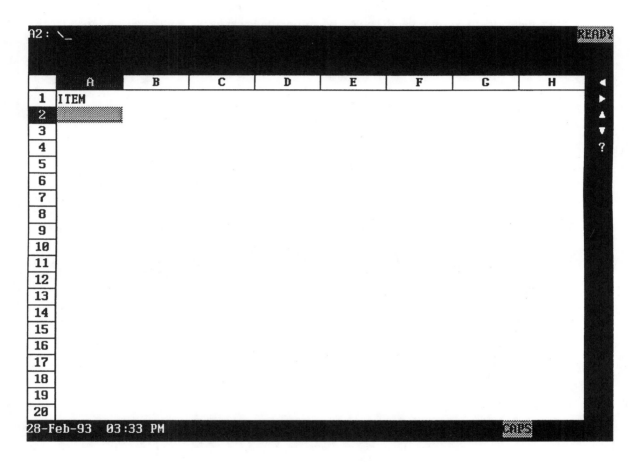

Figure 3.8 To underline a cell entry, the underline characters are placed in the cell below

c. *The Repeater*

Underlining is made simple with the Repeater. To make a cell entry full of the underline character "___", you do not need to hold down the underline key. The Repeater, [\], followed by one underline character, will repeat the underline character throughout the cell. Any character(s) that follow the Repeater will be repeated throughout a cell. Below are examples of cell entries using the Repeater and their results.

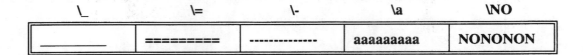

_	\\=	\\-	\\a	\\NO
_____	========	-------------	aaaaaaaaa	NONONON

The advantage of using the Repeater is that the repeated characters will adjust to increases or decreases in column width. If you type underline characters to fill a cell, and then change the width of that cell, you will need to edit your cell entry to increase or decrease the number of underline characters.

2. Values

A Value cell entry is a number to be used for math, a formula, or a Lotus 1-2-3 function.

a. *Numbers*

Numbers are Value cell entries that begin with a number, a plus or minus sign, a period, a parenthesis, or a dollar sign, and are intended to be used for calculation purposes. Numbers such as addresses and telephone numbers are not considered Values; they are Labels. Lotus 1-2-3 will interpret an address or a telephone number *as a Value* unless a justification character is placed in front of them.

Examples of Number cell entries are:

126
199000
10E+30

> *You may not type commas in your numbers as you enter them into a cell. Later, you will learn about the */Range Format* command, which allows you to add commas and other symbols such as dollar signs and percent symbols.*

---

b. *Formulas*

A Formula is a Value cell entry that performs a calculation upon one or several cells. In Figure 3.9, the formula +B3+C3+D3+E3 has been entered in cell **F3.** As you can

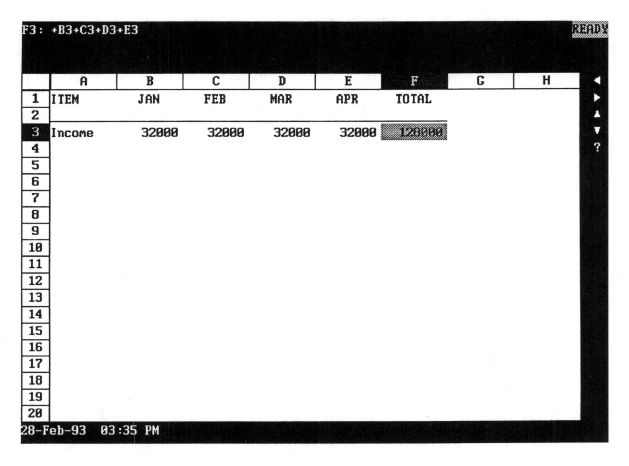

Figure 3.9 The formula entered into cell F3 is displayed at the top of the screen

see, the formula is displayed in the upper left-hand corner of the screen. The calculated results are displayed in the cell.

Examples of Formula cell entries are:

+B2 + B3 + B4
123*B6
(-C14/C15) + C16

Formulas that begin with a cell address must be preceded by a plus or minus sign, or a parenthesis. If they are not, Lotus 1-2-3 will receive the letter of the cell address and interpret the entry as a Label instead of a Value.

When a cell address is placed within a formula, the electronic spreadsheet finds the cell by its position relative to the cell containing the formula, not by its address. For example, in Figure 3.9, the formula in cell F3 contains relative cell addresses. In reading the formula, +B3 + C3 + D3 + E3, the electronic spreadsheet does not look at the actual cell addresses.

It reads the formula as "Take the cell that is four cells to the left of the formula, and add it to the cells that are three, two, and one to the left of the formula." Relative cell addresses give you the ability to copy the formula in cell F3 to other cells in column F. When you perform the copy, the electronic spreadsheet places the appropriate relative addresses within the other formulas.

In some instances, you want the formula to always use a figure found in one particular column, row, or cell, even when you copy the cell. In these instances, you can use the dollar sign "$" to "absolute" part or all of the cell address. If you place the dollar sign in front of the column letter, the column letter becomes absolute and the row number remains relative and can change. The row number within the formula can be absoluted by placing the dollar sign in front of the row number in the cell address. To completely absolute a cell address within a formula, you place a dollar sign before the column letter and the row number. This will make the formula always reference the same cell.

ENTERING FORMULAS AND NUMBERS

When you enter a number or a formula, there are certain rules that must be followed.

1. *It must begin with 0-9, a plus or minus sign, a period, a parenthesis, or a dollar sign.*

2. *A number may end with a %, which has the same effect as if you entered the number /100.*

3. *Numbers may not contain commas or spaces and may have only one decimal point. (Commas may be added later.)*

4. *"@NA" may be entered into a cell when the information for that cell is not yet available. This will make any calculation that is dependent on this cell display "NA". This will save you from using a total that does not contain all necessary information.*

5. *If a Value cell displays asterisks, this means that the cell is not wide enough to hold the entry. Use /Worksheet Column Set-Width to increase the width of the column.*

---

c. *Functions*

A function is a pre-programmed Lotus 1-2-3 formula. Lotus 1-2-3 functions are sometimes called "at functions" because they begin with the @ symbol.

Examples of Function cell entries are:

@SUM(B3..E3)
@AVG(B3..E3)

The three characters after the @ symbol indicate the function type. The addition and average functions are shown as examples above. Within the parentheses is the cell range to be acted upon. "B3..E3" is interpreted as "cell B3 through E3." An @SUM Function could be entered in cell F3 in Figure 3.10 in place of the formula that was entered in Figure 3.9.

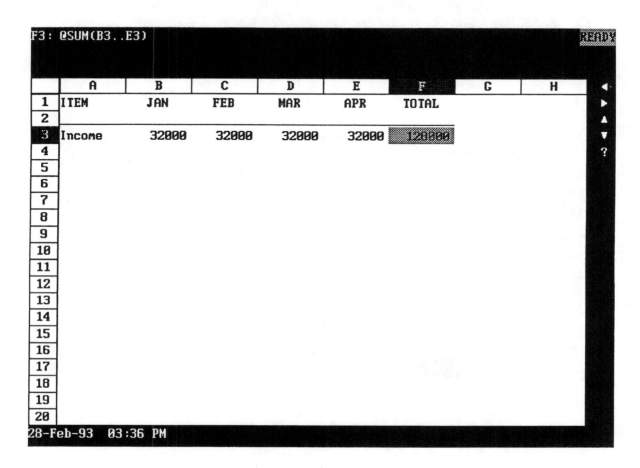

Figure 3.10 An @SUM Function entered in cell F3 produces the same result as the formula previously entered in Figure 3.9

The question often arises, "When should I use @SUM(B3..E3) as opposed to +B3+C3+D3+E3?" Well, in this example you could use either one. However, when you are adding cells B3 through Z3, you can see that the @SUM Function is a better choice.

3.   Ranges of Cells

A Range is a cell or a group of cells identified by the cell address in the upper left-hand corner of the range and the cell address in the lower right-hand corner of the range. In identifying the two corners of the range, Lotus 1-2-3 uses two periods to indicate "through." Some range examples will be explained using the spreadsheet in Figure 3.11.

```
E1:                                                                    READY

          A           B         C         D        E        F        G      ◄
    1    ITEM        JAN       FEB       MAR                                 ►
    2   ─────────────────────────────────────────                          ▲
    3  INCOME                                                               ▼
    4    Wages       2023      2023      2023                               ?
    5    Interest      54        54        54
    6
    7  TOTAL INCOME  2077      2077      2077
    8
    9
   10  EXPENSES
   11    Mortgage    1025      1025      1025
   12    Car          250       250       250
   13    Food         325       325       325
   14   ─────────────────────────────────────────
   15  TOTAL EXPENSES 1600     1600      1600
   16   ─────────────────────────────────────────
   17  NET INCOME     477       477       477
   18  ═════════════════════════════════════════
   19
   20
13-Apr-93  11:50 PM
```

Figure 3.11   A Sample Worksheet

The headings "ITEM," "JAN," "FEB," and "MAR," are shown in cells A1 through D1. This range would be identified as:

A1..D1

The Expense Item amounts for January through March are shown in columns B, C, and D, and in rows **11** through **13.** This range would be identified as:

B11..D13

The **entire** spreadsheet range shown here would be identified as:

A1..D18

The phrase "NET INCOME" is in the single cell identified as:

A17..A17

4. Editing a Cell Entry

Changing the contents of a cell can be accomplished in two ways. With the cell pointer in the cell to be changed, either:

a) Type a new entry into the cell and press **[Enter]**; or

b) Press the **[F2]** (Edit) key. This places your cursor in the upper left corner of the screen where the contents of the cell are displayed. After any changes have been made, pressing the **[Enter]** key will place the new entry into the cell.

5. Erasing a Cell Entry

Lotus 1-2-3 versions 2.3 and later allow you to erase the contents of a single cell by moving the cell pointer to the desired cell and pressing the **[Delete]** key. To erase a range of cells, or to erase a single cell in versions before 2.3, you must use **/Range Erase** and specify the range of cells to be erased.

D. USING LOTUS 1-2-3 COMMANDS

Lotus 1-2-3 commands are accessed through the Lotus 1-2-3 Command menu with the **[/]** key. To illustrate how commands are executed, we will walk through the **/Move** command with the spreadsheet shown in Figure 3.11. Take a few minutes and enter this spreadsheet into Lotus 1-2-3 if you would like to follow along.

1. The Command Process (Using /Move)

The **/Move** command will be used with the spreadsheet in Figure 3.11 to illustrate a typical command process. For this example, all of the Expense and Net Income items will be moved up one row so that they will begin in row 9.

a. *Accessing the Menu*

Accessing the menu with the **[/]** key displays the menu options as shown in Figure 3.12. Remember that the first line lists the options available. The second line lists the options available under the highlighted option on the first line.

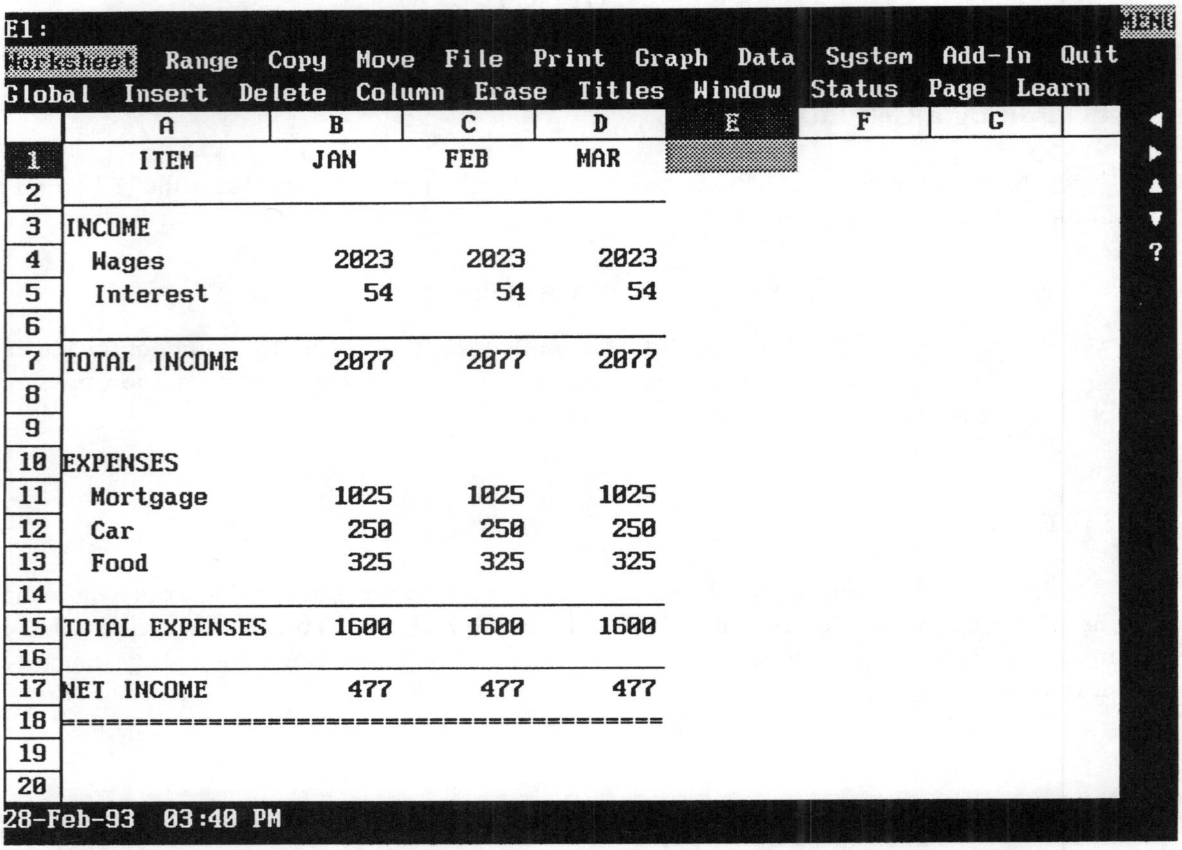

```
E1:                                                                        MENU
Worksheet  Range  Copy   Move   File   Print  Graph  Data   System  Add-In  Quit
Global     Insert Delete Column Erase  Titles Window Status Page    Learn
           A           B         C         D         E        F        G        ◄
 1         ITEM        JAN       FEB       MAR                                   ►
 2      ─────────────────────────────────────                                   ▲
 3     INCOME                                                                    ▼
 4        Wages        2023      2023      2023                                  ?
 5        Interest       54        54        54
 6      ─────────────────────────────────────
 7     TOTAL INCOME    2077      2077      2077
 8
 9
10     EXPENSES
11        Mortgage     1025      1025      1025
12        Car           250       250       250
13        Food          325       325       325
14      ─────────────────────────────────────
15     TOTAL EXPENSES  1600      1600      1600
16      ─────────────────────────────────────
17     NET INCOME       477       477       477
18     ═══════════════════════════════════════
19
20
28-Feb-93   03:40 PM
```

Figure 3.12   The menu options are displayed when the [/] key is pressed

Moving the highlight bar to "Move," we see in Figure 3.13 that the second line displays a description of the **/Move** command.

b. *Selecting a Command*

A command is selected by highlighting it and pressing the **[Enter]** key, or by typing the first character of the command name. Selecting **Move** by highlighting it and pressing

```
E1:                                                                    MENU
Worksheet  Range  Copy  Move  File  Print  Graph  Data  System  Add-In  Quit
Move a cell or range of cells
        A            B         C         D      E          F         G
  1      ITEM        JAN       FEB       MAR
  2  _____
  3  INCOME
  4    Wages         2023      2023      2023
  5    Interest        54        54        54
  6
  7  TOTAL INCOME    2077      2077      2077
  8
  9
 10  EXPENSES
 11    Mortgage      1025      1025      1025
 12    Car            250       250       250
 13    Food           325       325       325
 14  _____
 15  TOTAL EXPENSES  1600      1600      1600
 16  _____
 17  NET INCOME       477       477       477
 18  ==================================================
 19
 20
28-Feb-93  03:44 PM
```

Figure 3.13   Highlighting the Move item displays a description of the
/Move command

the **[Enter]** key brings up either of the following two messages depending on your Lotus
1-2-3 version.

> **Enter range to move FROM:**

or

> **Move what?**

```
E1:                                                                    POINT
Move what? E1..E1
```

	A	B	C	D	E	F	G
1	ITEM	JAN	FEB	MAR			
2							
3	INCOME						
4	Wages	2023	2023	2023			
5	Interest	54	54	54			
6							
7	TOTAL INCOME	2077	2077	2077			
8							
9							
10	EXPENSES						
11	Mortgage	1025	1025	1025			
12	Car	250	250	250			
13	Food	325	325	325			
14							
15	TOTAL EXPENSES	1600	1600	1600			
16							
17	NET INCOME	477	477	477			
18	===						
19							
20							

```
28-Feb-93  08:24 PM
```

Figure 3.14   Upon selecting the /Move command, Lotus 1-2-3 prompts
you for the range that you wish to move

The range of the cell containing the cell pointer at the time the /Move command is accessed
is specified in the command message as shown in Figure 3.14.

At this point, you can either type in the range to be moved, A10..D18, or point at
the range with the cell pointer. Pointing involves anchoring the cell pointer and spreading
it to highlight the range. Anchoring will be explained in the next section. For this example,
type in the range:

A10..D18

Pressing the **[Enter]** key displays one of the following two messages.

Enter range to move TO:

or

To where?

Lotus® 1-2-3®

```
E1:                                                                        POINT
Move what? a10..d18                          To where? E1

           A          B        C        D        E        F        G          ◄
   1      ITEM       JAN      FEB      MAR                                     ►
   2                                                                          ▲
   3   INCOME                                                                 ▼
   4     Wages      2023     2023     2023                                    ?
   5     Interest     54       54       54
   6
   7   TOTAL INCOME 2077     2077     2077
   8
   9
  10   EXPENSES
  11     Mortgage   1025     1025     1025
  12     Car         250      250      250
  13     Food        325      325      325
  14
  15   TOTAL EXPENSES 1600   1600     1600
  16
  17   NET INCOME    477      477      477
  18   ======================================
  19
  20
28-Feb-93  08:27 PM
```

Figure 3.15 After entering the range to be moved, Lotus 1-2-3 prompts
for the new location

The address of the cell in which the cell pointer was located at the time the command was accessed is displayed in the command as shown in Figure 3.15.

To move the entire range up one row, only the upper left-hand corner of the new range needs to be specified. So, we type **A9.** Pressing the **[Enter]** key completes the command and moves the range as shown in Figure 3.16.

---

*When using the **/Move** command, be careful that you do not move your range over other cells containing data. If you do, those cell entries will be lost.*

```
E1:                                                              READY
        ┌──────┬──────┬──────┬──────┬──────┬──────┬──────┐   ◄
        │   A  │   B  │   C  │   D  │  E   │  F   │  G   │   ►
   ┌──┐ │ ITEM │ JAN  │ FEB  │ MAR  ▓▓▓▓▓▓▓│      │      │   ▲
   │ 1│                                                         ▼
   │ 2│                                                         ?
   │ 3│ INCOME  ─────────────────────────────
   │ 4│   Wages      2023    2023    2023
   │ 5│   Interest     54      54      54
   │ 6│
   │ 7│ TOTAL INCOME 2077    2077    2077
   │ 8│
   │ 9│ EXPENSES
   │10│   Mortgage   1025    1025    1025
   │11│   Car         250     250     250
   │12│   Food        325     325     325
   │13│
   │14│ TOTAL EXPENSES 1600   1600    1600
   │15│
   │16│ NET INCOME    477     477     477
   │17│ ========================================
   │18│
   │19│
   │20│
   28-Feb-93  08:28 PM
```

Figure 3.16   The Worksheet After the Move

2. Pointing and Anchoring

As an alternative to typing ranges, you may point to the range to be acted upon by anchoring the cell pointer and then highlighting the cells with the **[Arrow]** keys. The anchor is what holds the cell pointer in one place and allows you to spread the pointer to highlight other cells.

In commands like the **/Move** command, the cell pointer is anchored at the cell containing the cell pointer at the time the command is selected. You can tell it is anchored, because the "through" periods ".." are present. See Figure 3.14.

To demonstrate pointing and anchoring, we will move the range of cells used in the previous example back down to row 10. To begin the command, access the Menu and select **Move.** The prompt for the range to move will appear, followed by the range of the cell that contained the cell pointer at the time the command was accessed. Moving the cell pointer around the worksheet with the **[Arrow]** keys will expand the cell pointer.

We want to move the range A9..D17. To point to this range, we need to release the anchor so that we may re-anchor at cell A9. The **[Esc]** key will release the anchor. When the **[Esc]** key is pressed, the "through" periods and ending cell address are removed from the prompt as shown in Figure 3.17.

```
E1:                                                                    POINT
Move what? E1

         │      A       │   B    │   C    │   D    │    E    │    F    │    G    │        │ ◄
    1    │    ITEM      │  JAN   │  FEB   │  MAR   │░░░░░░░░░│         │         │        │ ►
    2    │              │        │        │        │         │         │         │        │ ▲
    3    │INCOME        │        │        │        │         │         │         │        │ ▼
    4    │   Wages      │  2023  │  2023  │  2023  │         │         │         │        │ ?
    5    │   Interest   │    54  │    54  │    54  │         │         │         │        │
    6    │              │        │        │        │         │         │         │        │
    7    │TOTAL INCOME  │  2077  │  2077  │  2077  │         │         │         │        │
    8    │              │        │        │        │         │         │         │        │
    9    │EXPENSES      │        │        │        │         │         │         │        │
   10    │   Mortgage   │  1025  │  1025  │  1025  │         │         │         │        │
   11    │   Car        │   250  │   250  │   250  │         │         │         │        │
   12    │   Food       │   325  │   325  │   325  │         │         │         │        │
   13    │              │        │        │        │         │         │         │        │
   14    │TOTAL EXPENSES│  1600  │  1600  │  1600  │         │         │         │        │
   15    │              │        │        │        │         │         │         │        │
   16    │NET INCOME    │   477  │   477  │   477  │         │         │         │        │
   17    │==============│========│========│========│=========│         │         │        │
   18    │              │        │        │        │         │         │         │        │
   19    │              │        │        │        │         │         │         │        │
   20    │              │        │        │        │         │         │         │        │
28-Feb-93   08:30 PM
```

Figure 3.17 Pressing the [Esc] key removes the anchor

The cell pointer is moved to cell A9 and re-anchored by pressing the period key once. This will display the newly anchored range A9..A9 as shown in Figure 3.18.

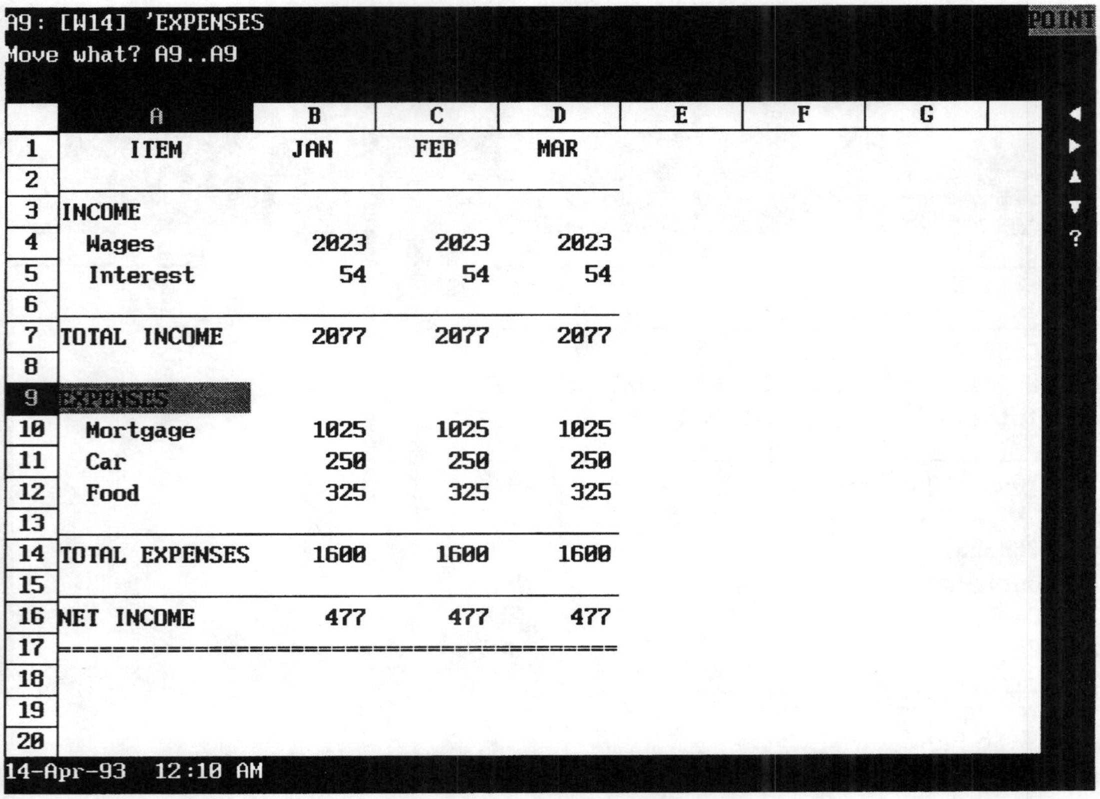

```
A9: [W14] 'EXPENSES                                                    POINT
Move what? A9..A9

          A            B         C         D       E        F        G
   1     ITEM         JAN       FEB       MAR
   2   ─────────────────────────────────────────────────
   3  INCOME
   4     Wages       2023      2023      2023
   5     Interest      54        54        54
   6
   7  TOTAL INCOME   2077      2077      2077
   8
   9  EXPENSES
  10     Mortgage    1025      1025      1025
  11     Car          250       250       250
  12     Food         325       325       325
  13
  14  TOTAL EXPENSES 1600      1600      1600
  15
  16  NET INCOME      477       477       477
  17  =================================================
  18
  19
  20
14-Apr-93  12:10 AM
```

Figure 3.18   Re-anchoring is accomplished by pressing the period key one time

The cell pointer may now be moved to highlight the range of cells to be moved, A9..D17, as shown in Figure 3.19.

```
D17: \=                                                        POINT
Move what? A9..D17

          A        B       C       D      E       F       G      ◄
  1     ITEM      JAN     FEB     MAR                              ►
  2    ─────────────────────────────────────                      ▲
  3   INCOME                                                       ▼
  4     Wages    2023    2023    2023                              ?
  5     Interest   54      54      54
  6    ─────────────────────────────────────
  7   TOTAL INCOME 2077   2077    2077
  8
  9   EXPENSES
 10     Mortgage 1025    1025    1025
 11     Car       250     250     250
 12     Food      325     325     325
 13
 14   TOTAL EXPENSES 1600 1600    1600
 15
 16   NET INCOME  477     477     477
 17
 18
 19
 20
28-Feb-93  08:32 PM
```

Figure 3.19 Highlighting the Range of Cells

Pressing the **[Enter]** key displays the prompt for the new location of the range. To point to this new location, move the cell pointer to cell A10 with the **[Arrow]** keys. To complete the move, press the **[Enter]** key.

EXAMPLE 1

Using what you have learned so far, try entering the spreadsheet below into Lotus 1-2-3. If you need a clean worksheet screen, select **/Worksheet Erase.** The formulas and functions are displayed to assist you. When you enter the formulas and functions, the calculated totals will appear in the "Total Amount" column and "Totals" row.

Begin the heading "JANUARY REVENUE" in column B, and leave row 2 blank. You will notice that this heading will overlap into cell C1. This will not create a problem unless there is an entry in C1.

	A	B	C	D
1		JANUARY REVENUE		
2				
3	BILLER	HOURS	RATE	TOTAL AMT
4				
5	JLD	160	250	+B5*C5
6	STR	176	245	+B6*C6
7	MMD	125	245	+B7*C7
8				
9	Totals	@sum(B5..B7)		+D5+D6+D7

When you are finished, your worksheet should look like the one shown in Figure 3.20.

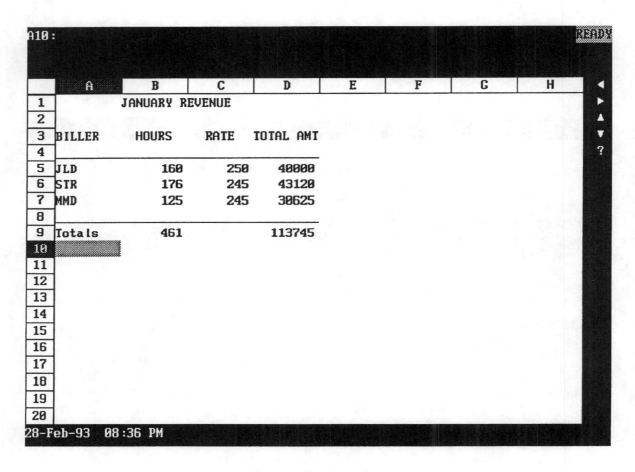

Figure 3.20 Example 1

1. Formatting a Range [/Range Format]

To improve the appearance of our worksheet, we need to add commas and dollar signs to the numbers in columns C and D. The **/Range Format** command allows you to format a range of values in a variety of ways. Accessing the **/Range Format** command displays the options shown in Figure 3.21.

The three types of formats most often used by legal professionals are the Fixed, Currency, and Comma (,) formats. These three formats are explained below using the number "12345." We will assume that we want two decimal places in this number.

> *The Comma format is represented by the comma character (**[,]**) because "currency" and "comma" both begin with a "c". This way, the Currency format may be selected by pressing the letter **[c]**, and the Comma format may be selected by pressing **[,]**.*

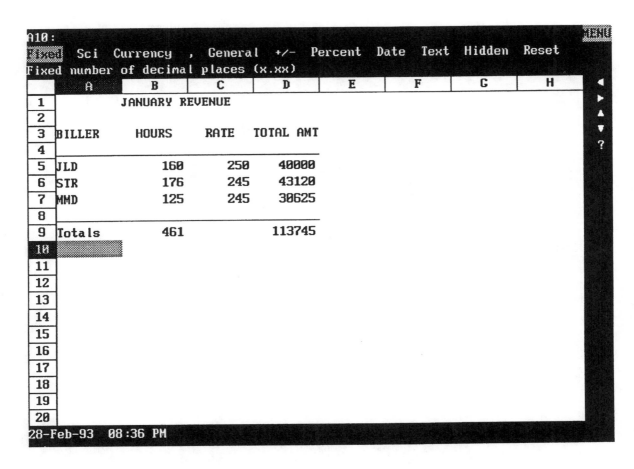

Figure 3.21 /Range Format Options

| Fixed | Displays a number *without commas,* and lets you set the number of decimal places. |

12345.00

| Currency | Displays a number preceded by a dollar sign ($), *with commas,* and lets you set the number of decimal places. |

$12,345.00

| , | Displays a number *with commas,* and lets you set the number of decimal places. |

12,345.00

For our example, we will select the **Currency** format. After **Currency** has been selected, Lotus 1-2-3 prompts for the number of decimal places for the numbers. For this example, type **0** and press the **[Enter]** key. Lotus 1-2-3 will then prompt for the range to be formatted. At this point, you can either type **C5..D9,** or point to the range to be formatted with the cell pointer. If you have trouble with pointing to the range, refer to Section D2, regarding pointing and anchoring. Your spreadsheet should now look like the one in Figure 3.22.

```
A10:                                                                    READY

          A        B        C        D        E        F        G        H     ◄
  1             JANUARY REVENUE                                                 ►
  2                                                                             ▲
  3   BILLER    HOURS     RATE    TOTAL AMT                                     ▼
  4                                                                             ?
  5   JLD        160      $250     $40,000
  6   STR        176      $245     $43,120
  7   MMD        125      $245     $30,625
  8
  9   Totals     461               $113,745
 10
 11
 12
 13
 14
 15
 16
 17
 18
 19
 20
28-Feb-93  08:38 PM
```

Figure 3.22 The Formatted Spreadsheet

Lotus® 1-2-3®

2.   Saving the Worksheet [/File Save]

The **/File Save** command is used to save a worksheet. Upon accessing the command, Lotus 1-2-3 prompts for the name of the file:

Enter name of file to save:

To name the file, specify the disk drive, directory, and a 1- to 8-character name for the file. Lotus 1-2-3 will provide the file with an extension.

Lotus 1-2-3 often displays a pre-set drive and directory where files will be saved:

Enter name of file to save: C:\LOTUS

If this is not where you wish to save your files, press the **[Esc]** key to remove the directory and the disk drive designation before typing your selection. Type the location and name of the file and press the **[Enter]** key.

3.   Clearing the Lotus 1-2-3 Worksheet Screen [/Worksheet Erase]

When you have finished using a worksheet and want to begin another, you need to clear the worksheet screen. To do this, you use the **/Worksheet Erase** command. You will be prompted with a **No Yes** to confirm that you wish to erase the worksheet. Highlight **Yes** and press the **[Enter]** key. This will erase the worksheet. If you have not saved the worksheet, a warning message will appear asking if you really wish to erase the worksheet.

EXAMPLE 2

The spreadsheet in Figure 3.23 is a law firm's income forecast for the first quarter of the year. Since this is a forecast, the amount of revenue from each legal professional is an estimate. This section will follow the creation of this worksheet. Lotus 1-2-3 commands that help in creating the worksheet will be explained as they are needed.

a) To create the Income Forecast worksheet, begin by entering the **title** of the spreadsheet in cell **B1.**

b) In row **3,** center the headings in their respective columns. Remember that typing the [^] character before you type the heading will center it within the cell.

c) In cell **A4,** use the Repeater to place an underline throughout the cell (_).

Lotus® 1-2-3®   *221*

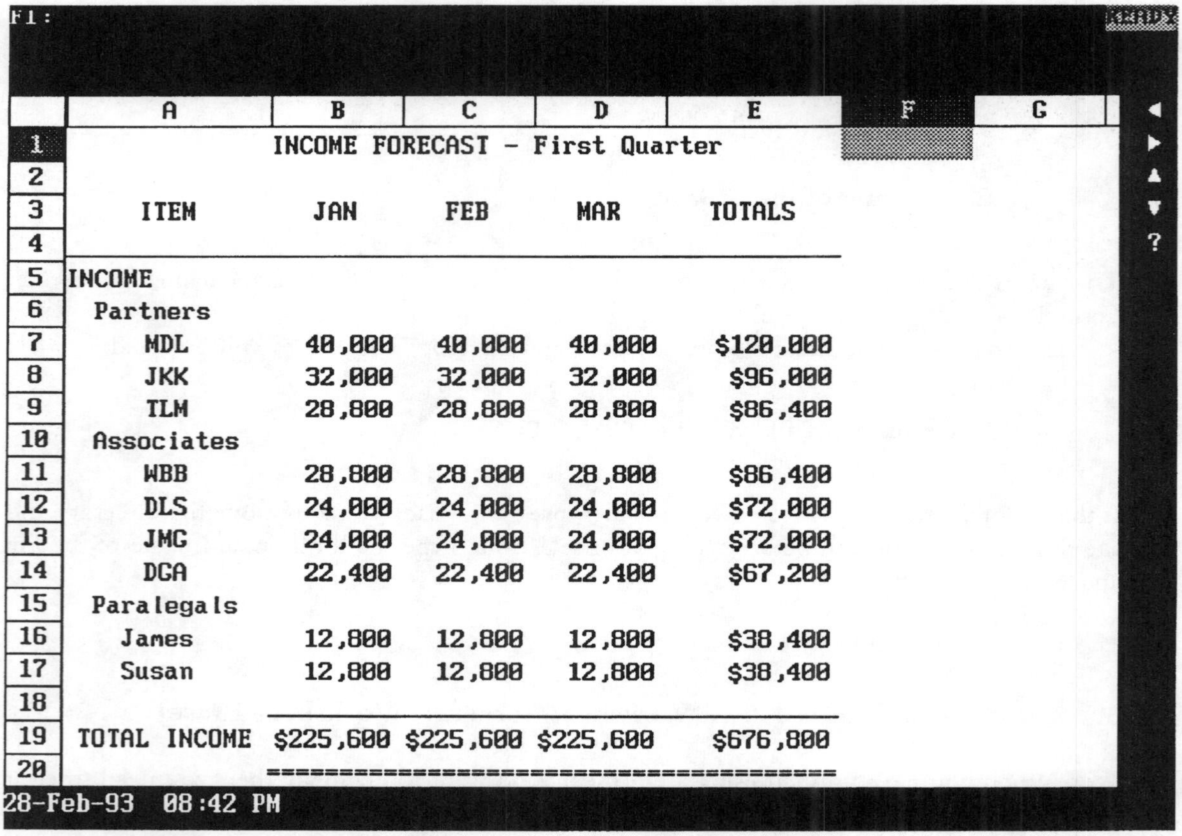

```
F1:                                                                    READY

         A         B         C         D         E         F      G

 1              INCOME FORECAST - First Quarter
 2
 3       ITEM      JAN       FEB       MAR      TOTALS
 4       ─────────────────────────────────────────────
 5  INCOME
 6    Partners
 7      MDL      40,000    40,000    40,000    $120,000
 8      JKK      32,000    32,000    32,000     $96,000
 9      TLM      28,800    28,800    28,800     $86,400
10  Associates
11      WBB      28,800    28,800    28,800     $86,400
12      DLS      24,000    24,000    24,000     $72,000
13      JMC      24,000    24,000    24,000     $72,000
14      DCA      22,400    22,400    22,400     $67,200
15  Paralegals
16    James      12,800    12,800    12,800     $38,400
17    Susan      12,800    12,800    12,800     $38,400
18             ─────────────────────────────────────────
19  TOTAL INCOME $225,600 $225,600 $225,600    $676,800
20             ==========================================
28-Feb-93  08:42 PM
```

Figure 3.23 The Income Forecast Worksheet

At this point, your worksheet should look like Figure 3.24. To proceed to the next step in the worksheet creation, you need to learn about the **/Copy** command.

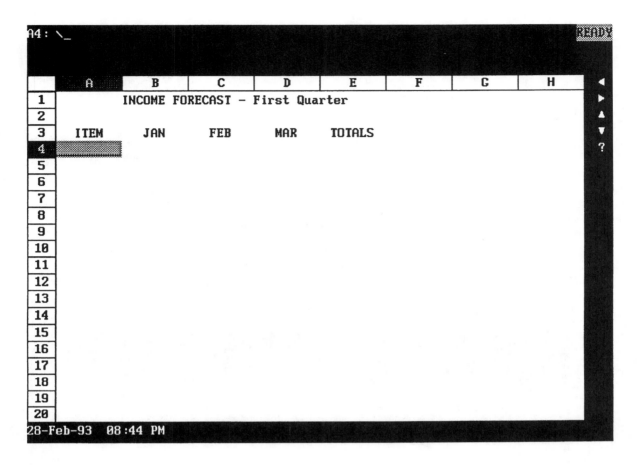

Figure 3.24   The Income Forecast Worksheet with Titles and Headings

1.   Copying a Cell Entry [/Copy]

Copying a cell entry is accomplished with the **/Copy** command. Instead of entering a repeating underline in cells B4, C4, D4, and E4, we can copy the entry in **A4** to the range **B4..E4.** The following steps make up the **/Copy** command.

a) Access the menu with the **[/]** key and select **Copy.** Lotus 1-2-3 will display one of the following messages:

> **Enter range to copy FROM:**

or

> **Copy what?**

b) Type the range of the cell to be copied, **A4..A4,** or highlight the range with the cell pointer (if you need to release the anchor, press **[Esc]**). Pressing the **[Enter]** key completes this portion of the command.

c) After entering the range to copy, a prompt will appear asking where to copy the range:

Enter range to copy TO:

or

To where?

d) Type the range of cells you wish to copy this entry to, **B4..E4,** or highlight the range with the cell pointer. Pressing the **[Enter]** key completes the copy as shown in Figure 3.25.

Hint: Move the cell pointer to the cell you wish to copy before accessing the menu to begin the copy. This will make it easier to enter the range to be copied.

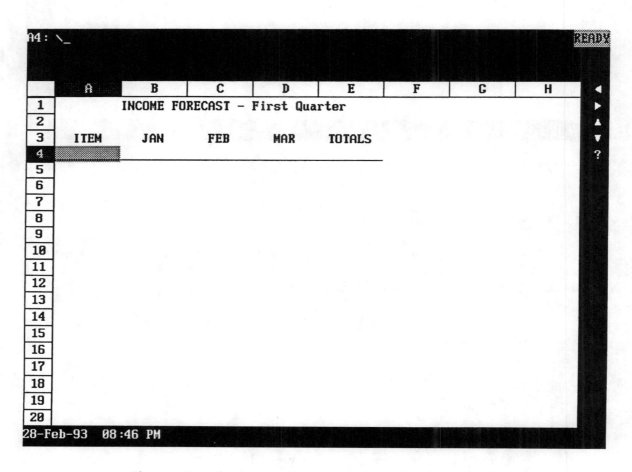

Figure 3.25   The entry in cell A4 is copied to cells B4 through E4

2. Changing the Width of a Column [/Worksheet Column Set-Width]

The items in column A will be the next part of the worksheet we will enter. Lotus 1-2-3 pre-sets the width of all worksheet columns at nine spaces. We will need to increase the width of column A to accommodate the item names.

To increase or decrease the width of a column, the **/Worksheet Column Set-Width** command is used. To use this command, the cell pointer must be within the desired column before accessing the menu. To increase the width of column A in our worksheet, follow the steps below.

a) Place the cell pointer in **column A,** access the menu with the **[/]** key, and select **Worksheet.**

b) Select **Column,** and then **Set-Width.** A prompt for the new width of the column will be displayed.

Enter column width (1..240): 9

The number 9 is present because this is the default width. You may alter the width using the **[Left Arrow]** and **[Right Arrow]** keys, or type in a number for the new width.

c) Change the width of **column A** to **14.** Press the **[Enter]** key to complete the command.

Now that you have changed the width of column A, enter the items in **column A, rows 5** through **19.** You will use the **[Space Bar]** to indent "Partners," "Associates," and "Paralegals." The initials, names, and "Total Income" will be centered. Leave row 18 blank. Your worksheet should now look like the one in Figure 3.26.

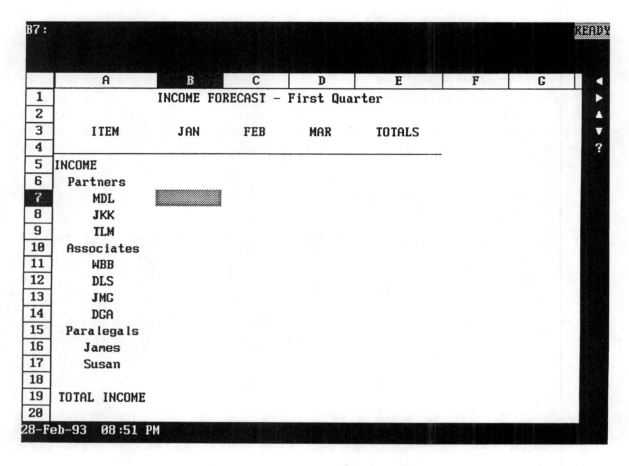

	A	B	C	D	E	F	G
1	INCOME FORECAST – First Quarter						
2							
3	ITEM	JAN	FEB	MAR	TOTALS		
4							
5	INCOME						
6	Partners						
7	MDL						
8	JKK						
9	TLM						
10	Associates						
11	WBB						
12	DLS						
13	JMC						
14	DGA						
15	Paralegals						
16	James						
17	Susan						
18							
19	TOTAL INCOME						
20							

28-Feb-93 08:51 PM

Figure 3.26 The Income Forecast Worksheet with the items entered in column A

3.   Copying a Group of Cells

The next step in the creation of our worksheet will demonstrate the value of the **/Copy** command. First, enter the income amounts for each attorney and paralegal in the January column. (Remember that you may not use commas when entering a number. We will format these numbers later.) Your worksheet should now look like the one in Figure 3.27.

	A	B	C	D	E	F	G
1		INCOME FORECAST – First Quarter					
2							
3	ITEM	JAN	FEB	MAR	TOTALS		
4							
5	INCOME						
6	Partners						
7	MDL	40000					
8	JKK	32000					
9	TLM	28800					
10	Associates						
11	WBB	28800					
12	DLS	24000					
13	JMG	24000					
14	DCA	22400					
15	Paralegals						
16	James	12800					
17	Susan	12800					
18							
19	TOTAL INCOME						
20							

28-Feb-93   08:52 PM

Figure 3.27   The Income Forecast Worksheet with the amounts for January entered

Instead of entering the same amounts in the February and March columns, use the **/Copy** command to copy the numbers in January to February and March. When the command prompts you to enter the range to copy, type or highlight **B7..B17** and press **[Enter].** When the command prompts you to enter where to copy, type or highlight **C7..D7** and press **[Enter].** Your worksheet should now look like the one in Figure 3.28.

	A	B	C	D	E	F	G
1		INCOME FORECAST - First Quarter					
2							
3	ITEM	JAN	FEB	MAR	TOTALS		
4							
5	INCOME						
6	Partners						
7	MDL	40000	40000	40000			
8	JKK	32000	32000	32000			
9	TLM	28800	28800	28800			
10	Associates						
11	WBB	28800	28800	28800			
12	DLS	24000	24000	24000			
13	JMG	24000	24000	24000			
14	DGA	22400	22400	22400			
15	Paralegals						
16	James	12800	12800	12800			
17	Susan	12800	12800	12800			
18							
19	TOTAL INCOME						
20							

28-Feb-93 08:54 PM

Figure 3.28　The Income Forecast Worksheet after the amounts in the January column have been copied to the February and March columns

4.　Entering and Copying Formulas

Entering the formulas in column E is the next step in the creation of the spreadsheet. Enter a *formula* in **cell E7** that will add **cells B7, C7,** and **D7.** Then, use the **/Copy** command to copy the entry in **cell E7** to the range **E8..E9.**

Lotus 1-2-3 will automatically change the row numbers or column letters in your formulas as you copy them to create the correct formula for each cell.

After you have copied the formula to the range **E8..E9,** execute another **/Copy** command to copy the formula to the range **E11..E14.** Then, execute the **/Copy** command again to copy the formula to the range **E16..E17.** Your worksheet should now look like the one in Figure 3.29.

	A	B	C	D	E	F	G
1	INCOME FORECAST – First Quarter						
2							
3	ITEM	JAN	FEB	MAR	TOTALS		
4							
5	INCOME						
6	Partners						
7	MDL	40000	40000	40000	120000		
8	JKK	32000	32000	32000	96000		
9	TLM	28800	28800	28800	86400		
10	Associates						
11	WBB	28800	28800	28800	86400		
12	DLS	24000	24000	24000	72000		
13	JMC	24000	24000	24000	72000		
14	DCA	22400	22400	22400	67200		
15	Paralegals						
16	James	12800	12800	12800	38400		
17	Susan	12800	12800	12800	38400		
18							
19	TOTAL INCOME						
20							

28-Feb-93 08:55 PM

Figure 3.29   The Income Forecast Worksheet with the Row Totals entered

You could also have copied the entry in **cell E7** to **E8..E17. Cells E10** and **E15** would have displayed zeros, but they can be removed with the **[Delete]** key or **/Range Erase.**

5.   Entering the Column Totals

The next step in the creation of our spreadsheet is to enter the underlines and column totals. First, enter a repeating underline (_) in **cell B18.** Then, copy **cell B18** to the range **C18..E18.**

For the totals of **columns B** through **E,** we will use an **@SUM** Function. In **cell B19,** type an **@SUM** Function to add the range **B7..B17.** Then, copy **cell B19** to the range **C19..E19.**

The last step in creating the spreadsheet is to place a double underline in the range **B20..E20.** A double underline can be created with a repeating equals sign (\=). Enter the repeating equals sign in **cell B20,** and then copy the entry to the range **C20..E20.**

6. Formatting the Spreadsheet

To complete our spreadsheet, we will format the income numbers in the **Comma** format and the totals in the **Currency** format. We will use **0** decimal places.

First, format the range **B7..D17** in the **Comma** format with **0** decimal places using **/Range Format , (Comma) 0.** Then, format the range **E7..E19** in the **Currency** format with **0** decimal places using **/Range Format Currency 0.** The format will not affect cell **E18.** Repeat this format with range **B19..D19.**

> *If a value cell entry becomes too large for its cell, it will appear in exponential form or asterisks will fill the cell. When you increase the width of the cell sufficiently, the value will appear.*

7. Inserting a Column or Row [/Worksheet Insert]

To demonstrate how to insert a column or row into a worksheet, *you* will be added as an attorney or paralegal in our spreadsheet. Inserting a row is accomplished with the **/Worksheet Insert Row** command. To insert a column, you would use **/Worksheet Insert Column.** Rows are inserted directly above the position of the cell pointer when the menu is accessed. Columns are inserted to the left of the cell pointer. To insert a row, follow the steps below.

a) Move the cell pointer to the row of the spreadsheet directly below the place where you would like your row to appear.

b) Access the Menu with the **[/]** key and select **Worksheet.** Select **Insert,** and then **Row.** Lotus 1-2-3 will prompt you to

Enter row insert range:

If you wish to insert only one row above the cell pointer, press **[Enter]** to complete the command. If you wish to insert more than one row, move the pointer up or down the number of rows that you desire to insert, and then press the **[Enter]** key to complete the command.

Enter your initials or name and the income amount you would expect to bring into the firm each month. Remember that very large numbers will appear exponentially or be replaced with asterisks until you increase the column width.

Copy a row total formula to your row in column E. You may need to edit (**[F2]**) your "Total Income" functions to include the addition of another row. Sometimes the program will automatically adjust the functions to include the new row, but you should always check to make sure that it is accurate. Your monthly income numbers will need to be formatted with **/Range Format , (Comma) 0.** Your final worksheet should appear similar to the one in Figure 3.30.

```
A16: {H13} [W14] ^Kris                                                    READY

        A            B        C        D        E        F        G      ◄
  1          INCOME FORECAST - First Quarter                             ►
  2                                                                      ▲
  3     ITEM        JAN      FEB      MAR      TOTALS                     ▼
  4  ──────────────────────────────────────────────────────────        ?
  5  INCOME
  6    Partners
  7      MDL       40,000   40,000   40,000   $120,000
  8      JKK       32,000   32,000   32,000    $96,000
  9      TLM       28,800   28,800   28,800    $86,400
 10    Associates
 11      WBB       28,800   28,800   28,800    $86,400
 12      DLS       24,000   24,000   24,000    $72,000
 13      JMG       24,000   24,000   24,000    $72,000
 14      DGA       22,400   22,400   22,400    $67,200
 15    Paralegals
 16      Kris      30,000   30,000   30,000    $90,000
 17      James     12,800   12,800   12,800    $38,400
 18      Susan     12,800   12,800   12,800    $38,400
 19  ──────────────────────────────────────────────────────────
 20  TOTAL INCOME $255,600 $255,600 $255,600   $766,800
 21  =============================================================
28-Feb-93   09:01 PM
```

Figure 3.30 The New Income Forecast Worksheet

E. USING A LOTUS 1-2-3 WINDOW [/WORKSHEET WINDOW]

A Lotus 1-2-3 **Window** splits the worksheet screen into two windows. This feature becomes useful when your worksheet becomes so large that you can no longer see the headings at the top or left side while you are working. If the worksheet in Figure 3.30 had several more rows of data, you would reach a point in entering data at the bottom of the worksheet where you could no longer see the headings at the top of the screen. To keep the headings at the top of the worksheet screen, we can place a Window above row 5.

A Window can be horizontal or vertical. Placing a Window in the worksheet is accomplished with the **/Worksheet Window** command. The following steps will create a horizontal Window above row 5.

a) With the cell pointer in row 5, access the menu with the **[/]** key.

b) Select **Worksheet,** and then select **Window.**

c) Select **Horizontal.**

A horizontal Window will be placed above row 5. To move from one side of the Window to the other, use the **[F6]** key. Move to the lower half of the screen and use the **[Down Arrow]** key to scroll down in the spreadsheet to see how the headings remain intact.

To clear the Window, select **/Worksheet Window Clear.**

F. PRINTING A WORKSHEET [/PRINT PRINTER]

Printing a worksheet is accomplished with the **/Print Printer** command. Before you execute this command, however, save your worksheet with the **/File Save** command. In the event that the print job causes your computer to freeze, this will prevent you from losing your worksheet. Follow the steps below to print the worksheet.

a) Access the menu with the **[/]** key and select **Print.** Select **Printer.**

b) Select **Range** to specify the range of the spreadsheet to be printed. You may type the range, **A1..E21,** or move to **cell A1** with the **[Home]** key, anchor the cell pointer with the period, and highlight the range. Pressing **[Enter]** returns you to the Print menu.

c) Selecting **Go** will send your spreadsheet to the printer. Lotus 1-2-3 does not always automatically send a command to the printer to eject the page after a range has been printed. This is so that you may print other ranges on the same page. To eject your worksheet from the printer, select **Page** after selecting **Go.**

> *With some network versions of Lotus 1-2-3, you must select Quit, after selecting Page, in order to print the spreadsheet.*

d) Selecting **Quit** will return you to the worksheet.

G. DATABASE FEATURES

Lotus 1-2-3 is equipped with database features that will allow you to sort, query, and perform other actions upon a worksheet. The most helpful database feature is Sort. Enter the worksheet in Figure 3.31 to practice the Sort feature. You will need to increase the width of column A to 14. The expense items are each indented with two spaces.

	A	B	C	D	E	F	G
1	EXPENSES	JAN	FEB	MARCH	APRIL		
2							
3	Utilities	45	45	45	45		
4	Car Payments	700	700	700	700		
5	Medical	100	100	100	100		
6	Car Repairs		300				
7	Telephone	35	35	35	35		
8	Clothing	200	200	200	200		
9	Property Tax			795			
10	Gardener	38	38	38	38		
11	Car Registr.	78					
12	Gasoline	175	175	175	175		
13	Food	400	400	400	400		
14	Cable	21	21	21	21		
15	Mortgage	1,124	1,124	1,124	1,124		
16	City Fees	33	33	33	33		
17	Insurance			433			
18	==						
19	TOTAL EXPENSES	2,949	3,171	4,099	2,871		
20	==						

02-Apr-93   02:53 PM

Figure 3.31   The Expense Worksheet

To sort the expense items follow the instructions below.

a) Access the menu with the **[/]** key.

b) Select **Data,** select **Sort.**

c) Select **Data-Range** to specify the entire body of information to be sorted. This range will include each of the expense items and their monthly amounts. Type in, or highlight, the range **A3..E17,** and press **[Enter].**

d) Select **Primary-Key.** The Primary-Key is the range you wish to sort upon. We will sort by expense item name. Type in, or highlight, the range **A3..A17,** and press **[Enter].**

e) When you are prompted for the sort order, select **A** for ascending, and press **[Enter].**

f) Select **Go** to perform the sort. The completed sort should look like Figure 3.32.

	A	B	C	D	E	F	G
1	EXPENSES	JAN	FEB	MARCH	APRIL		
2							
3	Cable	21	21	21	21		
4	Car Payments	700	700	700	700		
5	Car Registr.	78					
6	Car Repairs		300				
7	City Fees	33	33	33	33		
8	Clothing	200	200	200	200		
9	Food	400	400	400	400		
10	Gardener	38	38	38	38		
11	Gasoline	175	175	175	175		
12	Insurance			433			
13	Medical	100	100	100	100		
14	Mortgage	1,124	1,124	1,124	1,124		
15	Property Tax			795			
16	Telephone	35	35	35	35		
17	Utilities	45	45	45	45		
18	===						
19	TOTAL EXPENSES	2,949	3,171	4,099	2,871		
20	===						

14-Apr-93 01:27 AM

Figure 3.32   The Sorted Expense Items

H.   GRAPHING

Using the Expense worksheet, we will graph the total expenses for January through April.

a) Access the menu with the **[/]** key.

b) Select **Graph,** select **Type.** There are several types of graphs available. We will select **Bar.**

c) You must specify the **X** axis (the bottom of the graph) and at least one data range **A—F** (the left side of the graph). Select **X** and type, or highlight, the range **B1..E1,** then press **[Enter].** Select **A** and type, or highlight, the range **B19..E19,** then press **[Enter].**

d) To view the graph, select **View.** The graph is shown in Figure 3.33. Press the **[Space Bar]** to return to the menu. Select **Quit** to return to the worksheet.

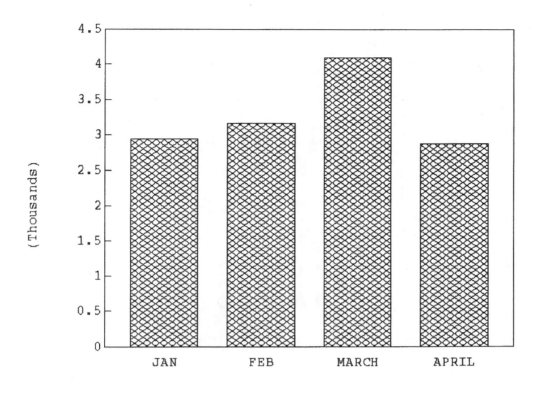

Figure 3.33   A bar graph created from the totals in the Expense worksheet

If you wish to print the graph, you must select **Save** from the **/Graph** Menu, give the file a name, press **[Enter],** and select **Quit.** Then, exit the Lotus 1-2-3 worksheet to the Lotus 1-2-3 Access menu where **PrintGraph** is located.

I.   RETRIEVING A FILE [/FILE RETRIEVE]

To retrieve a file into a blank worksheet, follow the instructions below.

a) Access the menu with the **[/]** key.

b) Select **File,** select **Retrieve.** The Lotus 1-2-3 worksheet files in the selected default directory will be displayed along with the message:

Name of file to retrieve:

This message will be followed by the name of the default directory. You may retrieve one of the listed files by highlighting its name and pressing the **[Enter]** key. (You may change the default directory with **/File Directory**.)

c) If you would like to view files in a different directory, or on a different disk, press the **[Esc]** key to remove the default drive and directory from the retrieve message. Then, type in the new file location such as **A:**. If you specify a directory, follow the directory name with another backslash, **C:\TEMP**. Pressing **[Enter]** will bring up Lotus 1-2-3 files located in the drive and/or directory. Highlight the desired file name and press the **[Enter]** key.

J.   EXITING LOTUS 1-2-3

To exit from Lotus 1-2-3, use the **/Quit** command.

a) Access the menu with the **[/]** key and select **Quit.** Lotus 1-2-3 will ask you if you wish to quit. Highlighting **Yes** and pressing the **[Enter]** key will take you to the Lotus 1-2-3 Access menu, or beep you with a warning message if you have not saved your spreadsheet.

b) From the Lotus 1-2-3 Access menu, select **Exit** to leave the program.

Summary

Lotus 1-2-3 for DOS can be used to create many types of spreadsheets. The Lotus 1-2-3 worksheet uses the function keys, mouse, and menus to execute commands. The Command menus are accessed with the forward slash key **[/]**. Items from the menu are selected by highlighting them and pressing **[Enter]** or by pressing the first character within their name.

There are two types of cell entries in Lotus 1-2-3, Labels and Values. Labels are character entries and numbers that are not intended to be used for mathematical computations (e.g., a telephone number). Labels may be centered or left or right justified within a cell by preceding the Label with a justification character. All Labels are automatically left justified unless they are preceded with a justification character.

Values are numeric cell entries. These entries consist of numbers, formulas, and functions. A formula is any equation placed within a cell. A function is a formula that has been pre-programmed into Lotus 1-2-3. Value cell entries may not be justified. If a Value is preceded by a justification character, Lotus 1-2-3 will think that the entry is a Label and will not perform computations with the entry.

Cell entries may be copied or moved within the Lotus 1-2-3 worksheet. Column widths may be increased or decreased, and columns or rows may be inserted or deleted. Database actions may be performed within the worksheet, and graphs may be created from the worksheet data. In total, the Lotus 1-2-3 worksheet is a flexible tool for helping to plan and analyze past and future events.

Lotus 1-2-3 Command List

This command list provides a quick reference for the Lotus 1-2-3 commands.

Copying Cells

The copy command allows you to copy a cell entry from one or more cells to one or more other cells. It is accomplished by the following steps:

/
COPY
Type or highlight the range of cells you wish to copy and press [Enter].
Type or highlight the range of cells where you wish to copy and press [Enter].

Deleting a Column or Row

This command is similar to the command to insert a column or row. Before you begin this command, place the cell pointer within the column or row to be deleted.

/
WORKSHEET
DELETE
COLUMN or ROW
Highlight the column(s) or row(s) to be deleted and press [Enter].

Erasing a Range

To erase a single cell, or a group of cells, use the **[Delete]** key or the command to erase a range.

/
RANGE
ERASE
Specify the range to be erased and press [Enter].

Erasing the Worksheet

To clear the worksheet so that you may begin a new one, the worksheet must be erased.

/
WORKSHEET
ERASE
Respond Yes to the prompt.

Exiting Lotus 1-2-3

To exit the program, make sure that you have saved your spreadsheet and follow the steps below.

/
QUIT
Respond Yes to the prompt.
At the Lotus 1-2-3 Access menu, select EXIT.

Formatting Cells

The Format command allows you to create a uniform appearance for a range of numbers.

/
RANGE
FORMAT
Select the desired format type.
Type or highlight the range to be formatted and press [Enter].

Increasing or Decreasing the Width of a Column

To increase or decrease the width of a column, move the cell pointer to that column and follow these steps:

/
WORKSHEET
COLUMN
SET-WIDTH
Use the [Arrow] keys or type the width (number of characters) you desire for this column and press [Enter].

Inserting a Column or Row

This command allows you to insert a new column or row within the worksheet. Before you begin this command, you must place the cell pointer in the column to the right of where you want the new column to be placed, or in the row below where you want the new row to be placed.

/
WORKSHEET
INSERT
COLUMN or ROW
Move the highlight bar to highlight the number of columns or rows to be inserted and press [Enter].

Moving Cells

To move a range of cells, use the command below.

/
MOVE
Type or highlight the range of cells to be moved and press [Enter].
Move the cell pointer to the row and column where you would like to move the cells and press [Enter].

Printing a Worksheet

Follow the commands below to print a worksheet.

/
PRINT
PRINTER
RANGE
Type or highlight the range of cells and press [Enter].
GO
PAGE   **This command sends a blank page after your worksheet to flush the worksheet out of the printer. Lotus 1-2-3 may not automatically send a page feed to the printer. This enables you to print more than one range on a single page.**

Retrieving a Worksheet

To retrieve a worksheet, you need to tell Lotus 1-2-3 where the worksheet is located and its name.

> /
> **FILE**
> **RETRIEVE**
> **Specify the location and name of the file and press [Enter].**
> **Use the [Esc] key to remove any unwanted directory or drive designations.**

Saving a Spreadsheet

To save a spreadsheet, you need to access the Save command and specify a location and name for the file.

> /
> **FILE**
> **SAVE**
> **Specify the location and name for the file and press [Enter]. If the file has previously been saved, press [Enter] and respond to the prompts.**

Windows

A Window can be created within the worksheet screen to split the screen into two windows. You can move back and forth between the windows with the **[F6]** key. Begin the command with the cell pointer in the row below where you wish the Window to appear.

> /
> **WORKSHEET**
> **WINDOW**
> **Select HORIZONTAL, VERTICAL, or CLEAR (to remove the Window)**

Chapter Index

CHAPTER 4

WINDOWS ELECTRONIC SPREADSHEETS

Chapter Preface

Windows-based electronic spreadsheets are used to create any type of spreadsheet that can be created on paper. These programs all utilize menus, buttons, and key combinations in a graphical environment. This chapter will cover the basics of using a Windows-based electronic spreadsheet and many of the advanced features that take advantage of the power of these applications. The figures chosen to illustrate the features of these programs are shown in the Microsoft® Windows® 95 operating system. The instructions in this chapter will apply to programs in Microsoft Windows or Windows 95. The primary Windows electronic spreadsheets demonstrating these features will be Microsoft® Excel® and Corel® Quattro® Pro. However, electronic spreadsheet programs are so similar that the features demonstrated will be found in Lotus® 1-2-3® and many other electronic spreadsheet programs. There are many versions of all of these programs in use. The steps in this chapter are geared toward the newest versions, but the steps are usually very similar in the older versions. The only difference may be in the button or menu selected to activate a feature.

A. THE SPREADSHEET PROGRAM ENVIRONMENT

An electronic spreadsheet consists of columns and rows, the intersection of which forms a cell. The cell is where data is entered. The advantages to using an electronic spreadsheet as opposed to a paper spreadsheet are that you can manipulate the columns and rows, and the computer calculates the totals for you, eliminating mistakes in calculations (as long as you write the formula correctly). Graphs can be created from the spreadsheet data for visual effects, and database functions may be performed upon data in the spreadsheet. This section will discuss the environment of the electronic spreadsheet and how you move around within it and utilize its features.

1. Entering the Application

To enter an application in Windows, double-click on the application's icon. To enter a Windows 95 application, either double-click on its icon on the desktop or click the Start button, point to Programs, point to the spreadsheet's program group, and click on the program name. Upon entering the program, you will see the main window of the electronic spreadsheet. The main windows of Microsoft Excel and Quattro Pro are shown in Figures 4.1 and 4.2.

2. The Electronic Spreadsheet Window

The main screen of a Windows-based electronic spreadsheet is a window. A window has a Title Bar, a Control menu button, Minimize and Maximize buttons (and a Close button in Windows 95), Menus, and Scroll Bars.

- The **Title Bar** is at the top of the window and will display the application name and the name of the document that you are working on.
- The **Control menu** button, in the upper left-hand corner of the window, will give you options to minimize, maximize, or close the window. In Windows this button will look like a file drawer. In Windows 95, this button is represented by the application's icon.

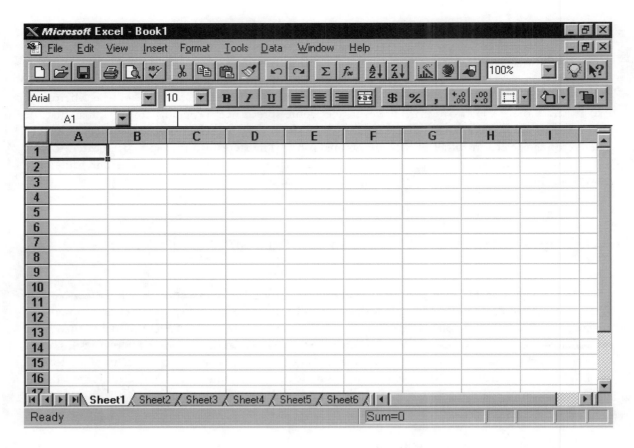

Figure 4.1 The Main Window of Microsoft® Excel®

- The **Minimize** and **Maximize** buttons, in the upper right-hand corner of the window, will change the size of the application's window. The Minimize button will take the window down to an icon. The Maximize button will take the window to the full screen. When a window is maximized, the maximize button will turn into a button that will take the window to a mid-size window. In Windows, these buttons are represented by up and down arrows. In Windows 95, they are represented by icons that look like windows. Also in Windows 95 you will find a button with an "X" that will close the application.
- **Menus** under the Title Bar activate the options available in the window.
- **Scroll Bars** are found in some windows at the right and/or bottom of the windows. Clicking on the up or down arrows, or dragging the scroll box, will move the contents of the window up, down, or from side to side.

3. Toolbars and Status Bar

Windows-based electronic spreadsheets have **Toolbars** at the top of the window and **Status Bars** at the bottom of the window. Toolbars consist of buttons that activate frequently used

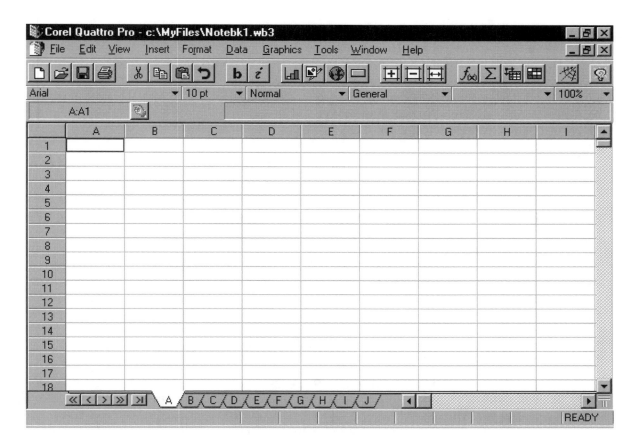

Figure 4.2 The Main Window of Corel® Quattro Pro®

features. These features are also available through the menus. Different electronic spreadsheet programs may have different names for these bars, but they will all have them. The Toolbars can be removed from, or added to, the electronic spreadsheet window, usually through selections in the View menu. Alternatives to the standard Toolbar can also be chosen from a list that is activated by pointing at a Toolbar and clicking the right mouse button.

The Status Bar at the bottom of the screen displays information about the status of your spreadsheet. It will show that the spreadsheet is ready to receive information or that you are entering a certain type of information.

4. Pull-Down Menus

The pull-down menus at the top of the electronic spreadsheet window can be accessed with a mouse or the keyboard. These menus contain the many features available within the electronic spreadsheet. To access a menu with the mouse, click on the menu name and then click on the desired option. To use the keyboard to access a menu, hold down the **[Alt]** key and press the underlined letter in the menu name and the letter for a menu option. For example, to print you can access the File menu with **[Alt] + [F],** and then select print by pressing the **[P]** key. You can also press the **[Alt]** key and then use the gray **[Arrow]** keys on the keyboard to move among the menu options. A menu can be closed by clicking the mouse outside of the menu or by pressing the **[Alt]** key or the **[Esc]** key.

The menus available within the electronic spreadsheet will vary between programs. The menus commonly found in Microsoft Excel and in Quattro Pro are File, Edit, View, Insert, Format, Tools, Window, Data, and Help.

- The **File menu** contains the options that open, close, save, preview a spreadsheet to be printed, and print your spreadsheets. It also contains the option to exit the program. You will notice that there are two save options, Save and Save As. The Save As option will prompt you for a file name. The Save option is used after your file has a name to quickly save the file.
- The **Edit menu** contains options to undo mistakes that you have made, to cut or copy and paste, to find and replace text, and to go to a specific page of the document.
- The **View menu** changes the appearance of your spreadsheet screen. Within this menu are options to add or remove the Toolbars, and to zoom in to view a portion of the spreadsheet or out to see the entire page. Some programs also include the option to split the spreadsheet within this menu.
- The **Insert menu** gives you the options to insert rows, columns, and page breaks into your spreadsheet.
- The **Format menu** will allow you to change the format of your spreadsheet by giving you options to change the structure of the spreadsheet's columns and rows or the data within the cells.
- The **Tools menu** contains options for spell checking, creating macros, and many other features.
- The **Window menu** lists the spreadsheets that you currently have open in the program and allows you to set up ways to view them simultaneously on the screen. You can switch between your spreadsheets by clicking on the desired spreadsheet name in this menu. A check is placed next to the current spreadsheet on the screen. Switching between spreadsheets becomes useful when you are copying data from one to another. Microsoft Excel also includes the feature to split a window within this menu.
- The **Data menu** contains database features, such as Sort, to enable you to organize the data within a spreadsheet.
- The **Help menu** can contain tutorials, experts, and Wizards. Each of these features will teach you how to perform different functions. You can also search for a specific topic or look through a list of contents. If you cannot find the appropriate information in the Help menu, check the software manual or contact the company's technical support department by telephone or on-line.

5. The Input Line

Below or above the Toolbar is the Input Line. This is the place where the contents of a cell are displayed as you enter them into a cell. With newer electronic spreadsheet programs, the contents will also be displayed in the cell as you are entering them. The Input Line is especially important when you have entered a formula or function into a cell. The calculated total will be visible within the cell, and the formula or function will be visible in the Input Line. Editing a cell entry can be accomplished by clicking within the Input Line and making the change. Pressing the **[Enter]** key completes the change.

6.   Function Keys

The Function keys are the keys at the top or left-hand side of the keyboard labeled F1 through F10 or F12. A Function key can be pressed by itself or in combination with the **[Alt]**, **[Shift]**, or **[Ctrl]** keys. The features activated by the Function keys can be found in the Help menu. Function keys are not frequently used with Windows-based electronic spreadsheets, but the F5 key may be the exception. Pressing **[F5]** activates the Go To feature in almost every electronic spreadsheet program.

7.   Highlighting Cells

You will use highlighting to select a group of cells to act upon. This can be done with the mouse by dragging the cell pointer over the desired cells, or with the **[Shift]** key in combination with the **[Arrow]** keys. You may find that highlighting with the mouse is difficult. In Quattro Pro, if you do not begin the highlight fast enough, a hand will appear, indicating that you want to move the cell. If you need to highlight past the edge of the screen, the highlighting speeds up and you can get lost. There are some remedies for this. Quattro Pro gives you an option in the preference setting to change the amount of time it takes for the hand to appear. Slowing this time down will enable you to highlight without accidentally moving a cell. If you do accidently perform a move while you are trying to highlight cells, select **Edit, Undo** to move the cells back. The **[Shift]** key in combination with the **[Arrow]** keys is an easy way to highlight cells. Hold down the **[Shift]** key, move the cell pointer with the **[Arrow]** keys, and then release the **[Shift]** key when the area is highlighted. To remove a highlight, click outside of it.

8.   The Spreadsheet

The spreadsheet itself is made up of columns and rows. The columns are labeled with letters; the rows are numbered. There are normally 256 columns and 8,192 rows in an electronic spreadsheet. Microsoft Excel's latest versions have 16,384 rows. The columns are labeled A to Z. After Z, they continue AA through AZ, then BA through BZ, and so on. A cell is identified by its column letter followed by its row number. Cell B2 is highlighted in Figure 4.3. A cell pointer is the dark rectangle that appears in one cell in the spreadsheet. Some programs call the cell pointer the "selector" or the "selected cell." Data is entered in the cell containing the cell pointer. The cell pointer can be moved using the keys on the keyboard or with the mouse.

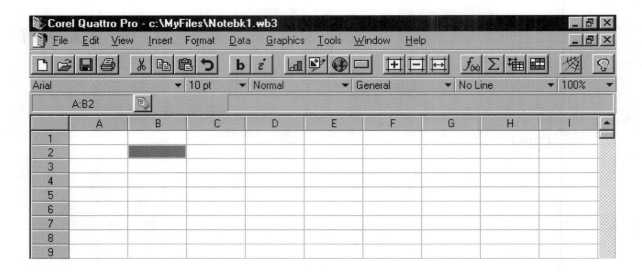

Figure 4.3   Cell B2 is highlighted

Ranges are groups of cells within a spreadsheet. A range of cells is identified with the address of the cell in the upper left-hand corner and the address of the cell in the lower right-hand corner. In Figure 4.4, the cells **B2 through D5** are highlighted. In Microsoft Excel this range would be identified as **B2:D5.** In Quattro Pro and Lotus 1-2-3 this range would be identified as **B2..D5.** Ranges will be used when acting upon a group of cells simultaneously.

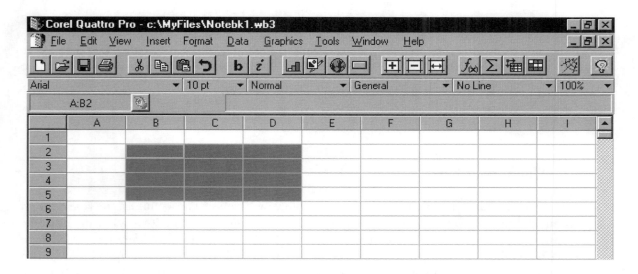

Figure 4.4   The range of cells B2 through D5 is highlighted

The newest spreadsheet programs contain multiple sheet pages within the spreadsheet file. This allows you to save several spreadsheets under one file name. The sheet pages are indicated with tabs. Clicking the mouse on a tab will take you to a different sheet page. In most programs, clicking the right mouse button within the tab will allow you to change its name.

9.   Movement Within the Spreadsheet

Many people use the mouse to move around within Windows. In electronic spreadsheets, the keyboard is also an important tool for movement. The keys that are used to move the cell pointer around within electronic spreadsheets are explained below.

Arrow Keys   The **[Arrow]** keys, located to the right of the keyboard, allow you to move the cell pointer around the worksheet one cell at a time. When preceded by the **[End]** key, they allow you to move in the direction of the **[Arrow]** key to the boundary of an empty and filled space. For example, in an empty worksheet, press the **[End]** key, release it, and then press the **[Right Arrow]** key. **[End], [Right Arrow]** in a blank worksheet will take you to column IV. **[End], [Down Arrow]** will take you to the bottom row.

Home   The **[Home]** key in Quattro Pro and Lotus 1-2-3 will always return the cell pointer to cell A1.

Ctrl + Home   The **[Ctrl] + [Home]** key combination in Microsoft Excel will always return the cell pointer to cell A1.

Page Up   The **[Page Up]** key moves the cell pointer up one screen.

Page Down   The **[Page Down]** key moves the cell pointer down one screen.

Tab   The **[Tab]** key in Quattro Pro and Lotus 1-2-3 moves the cell pointer right one screen.

Shifted Tab   Holding down the **[Shift]** key and pressing the **[Tab]** key (**[Shift] + [Tab]**) moves the cell pointer left one screen in Quattro Pro and Lotus 1-2-3.

GoTo [F5]   The **GoTo** function key, **[F5]**, allows you to move to a specific cell address. After pressing **[F5]**, you will be prompted to enter the destination cell address.

10.   Inserting and Deleting Columns and Rows

There will be many times when you need to insert or delete columns or rows in a spreadsheet. Columns are inserted to the left of the cell pointer. Rows are inserted above the cell pointer. To insert a column or row, position the cell pointer and select **Insert** and the appropriate option within the menu. In Quattro Pro, the options for inserting columns and rows are found under **Insert, Block.** To delete a column or row, select **Edit, Delete.** Inserting and deleting options often can also be accessed from the Toolbar or by right-clicking the mouse in the column or row.

B.   CELL ENTRIES

The entering of data into a cell involves moving the cell pointer to the cell and typing the entry. As you are typing a cell entry, the characters being typed are displayed in the Input Line. Pressing the **[Enter]** key, or moving the cell selector with one of the **[Arrow]** keys, places the entry, or a calculated result, into the cell. Some programs will move one cell down after the **[Enter]** key is pressed. Others remain in the same cell and require that you move to the next cell with the **[Arrow]** keys. This option can usually be changed in the program preferences.

There are two types of cell entries in electronic spreadsheets, Text and Values.

1.   Text Entries in Quattro Pro and Lotus 1-2-3

Text entries are called "Labels" in Quattro Pro and Lotus 1-2-3. A **Text** cell entry in these programs begins with a letter or a justification character. A justification character (sometimes referred to as a "label-prefix" character) is used to position a text entry within a cell. The three justification characters are

     '   **Left justifies the entry**
     "   **Right justifies the entry**
     ^   **Centers the entry**

Left	Right	Center
TOTAL	TOTAL	TOTAL

These programs automatically left justify Text cell entries. Right or center justifying requires that you type the justification character before you type the entry.

To **left justify** "TOTAL," you type: **TOTAL**

To **right justify** "TOTAL," you type: **"TOTAL**

To **center** "TOTAL," you type: **^TOTAL**

> *Justification characters may only be used with Text cell entries. If they are used with a Value cell entry, the program will read the Value as Text and will treat it as such.*

Examples of text entries in Quattro Pro and Lotus 1-2-3 include:

John Smith
January 3, 1997
TOTAL
555-1212
54 Comstock Hill Road

The last two examples above begin with numbers. All but the latest versions of Quattro Pro and Lotus 1-2-3 will believe that these entries are numbers unless you begin your entry with a justification character. So, if you are going to type a telephone number, an address, or any other entry that begins with a number but is a text entry, begin the entry with one of the justification characters.

To wrap text within a cell, click on the Wrap Text option in the **Alignment** section of the **Format** menu. In Quattro Pro, alignment options can be found by selecting **Format, Block.**

2. Text Entries in Microsoft Excel

In Microsoft Excel, a text entry is any combination of numbers, spaces, and nonnumeric characters. Some examples of text entries in Microsoft Excel include:

John Smith
January 3, 1997
TOTAL
555-1212
54 Comstock Hill Road
477 92 6574
344ABC

You do not need to use any special justification character in front of an entry that begins with a number. All text entries are left-aligned in a cell. To change the alignment, select **Format, Cells,** and choose the **Alignment** option, or use the alignment buttons on the Toolbar.

To wrap text within a cell, select **Format, Cells,** choose the **Alignment** option, and click on **Wrap Text.** You can also enter a hard carriage return within a cell using **[Alt] + [Enter].**

3. Values

A **Value** cell entry is a number to be used for math, a formula, or a function. Values will appear right-aligned in a cell. In newer programs, you can change the alignment of a value entry by selecting an alignment in the Format menu or an alignment option from the Toolbar. Do not use a justification character with a value or it will turn it into a text entry. If value entries get too large, they will not extend into the next cell. Instead, the cell will be filled with asterisks or number symbols (#). Increasing the width of the cell will bring the number back.

a. *Numbers*

In most electronic spreadsheets, a number entry can contain only numerals (0 to 9), a negative ($-$) sign, a positive ($+$) sign, a single decimal point, a trailing percent sign (%), or an E (if you are using scientific notation). Microsoft Excel will also accept the following characters:

( ) , / $ e

While Microsoft Excel allows commas in its numbers, most programs will not allow them when the numbers are being entered. Numbers are formatted with options found on the Toolbar or in the Format menu. You can highlight cells and choose a formatting option before or after entering the numbers.

b. *Formulas*

A **formula** is a Value cell entry that performs some type of calculation upon one or more cells. In Quattro Pro and Lotus 1-2-3, a formula should begin with a plus ($+$) sign or a parenthesis. In Microsoft Excel, a formula must begin with an equals ($=$) sign. An example of a formula to be placed in cell D1 that will add cells A1, B1, and C1 is shown below.

Quattro Pro and Lotus 1-2-3	$+A1+B1+C1$
Microsoft Excel	$=A1+B1+C1$

The example is shown using Microsoft Excel in Figure 4.5. The formula will be displayed on the Input Line. The calculated results will be displayed in the cell as soon as the **[Enter]** key is pressed or an **[Arrow]** key or the mouse is used to move to another cell.

To reference a cell from a different sheet page of the spreadsheet, you need to identify the sheet name (shown on the tab for the sheet) followed by a colon in Quattro Pro and Lotus 1-2-3, or an exclamation point in Microsoft Excel, and then identify the cell address. For example, to insert the contents of cell A5 from the sheet page identified as tab "B," the formula would be:

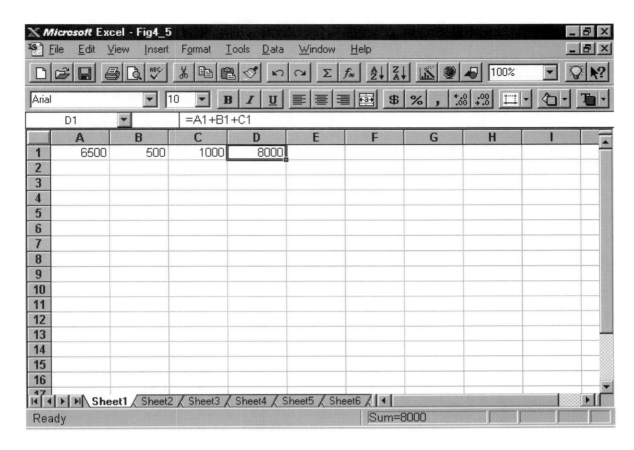

Figure 4.5 A formula in Microsoft Excel begins with an equals symbol. The formula will remain on the Input Line. The result of the calculation will be placed in the cell.

Quattro Pro and 1-2-3	Microsoft Excel
+B:A5	=B!A5

Examples of other formula cell entries are:

Quattro Pro and 1-2-3	Microsoft Excel
+B2+B3+B4	=B2+B3+B4
+23*B6	=23*B6
(-C14/C15)+C16	=(-C14/C15)+C16
+A25-Expenses:B30	=A25-Expenses!B30

In the last example above, "Expenses" is the name of one of the sheet pages.

c. *Functions*

A **function** is a pre-programmed formula that is part of the electronic spreadsheet program. In Quattro Pro and Lotus 1-2-3, functions begin with the **@** symbol and are followed by the name for the function type, such as SUM. In Microsoft Excel, functions begin with the = symbol and are followed by the name of the function. The names and syntax of functions can be found in the Help menu of an electronic spreadsheet. There are functions that will perform almost any calculation. The most commonly used function is the SUM function. Its most commonly used syntax is as follows:

Quattro Pro and 1-2-3   @SUM(Range of numbers to be summed)
                              @SUM(A1..A20)

Microsoft Excel   =SUM(Range of numbers to be summed)
                              =SUM(A1:A20)

A SUM function could have been used in cell D1 of Figure 4.5 to add cells A1, B1, and C1. That function would have been written as @SUM(A1..C1) or =SUM(A1:C1). Other forms of the SUM function are shown below.

Quattro Pro and 1-2-3	Microsoft Excel
@SUM(A6..C6,500)	=SUM(A6:C6,500)
@SUM(A5,650)	=SUM(A5,650)
@SUM(B1..B5,D1..D5)	=SUM(B1:B5,D1:D5)
@SUM(B1..D5)	=SUM(B1:D5)

Another way to perform a SUM function is to highlight the cells that you want to add and click on the SUM button on the Toolbar. This button usually contains a Σ symbol. It is important when you do this that the cell that will contain the SUM function is empty, and that you begin your highlight in that cell and then extend it to the cells to be summed.

4. Relative and Absolute Cell Addresses

When a cell address is placed within a formula, the electronic spreadsheet finds the cell by its position relative to the cell containing the formula, not by its address. For example, in Figure 4.5, the formula in cell D1 contains relative cell addresses. In reading the formula, =A1+B1+C1, the electronic spreadsheet does not look at the actual cell addresses. It reads the formula as "Take the cell that is three cells to the left of the formula, and add it to the cells that are two and one cell(s) to the left of the formula." Relative cell addresses give you the ability to copy the formula in cell D1 to other cells. Given the spreadsheet shown in Figure 4.6, the formula in cell D1 can be copied to cells D2 through D5. When you perform the copy, the electronic spreadsheet places the appropriate relative addresses within the other formulas.

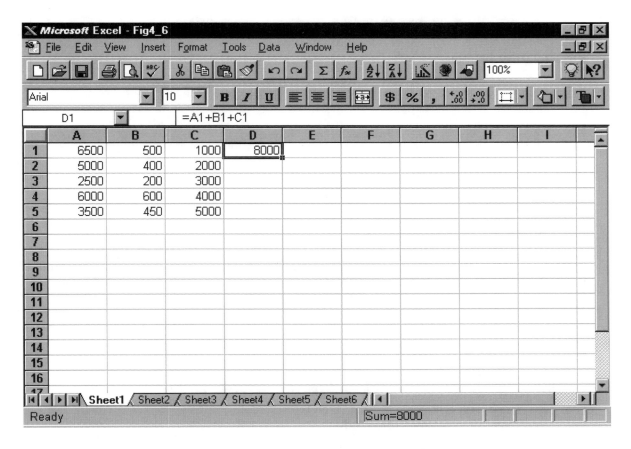

Figure 4.6   The formula in cell D1 contains relative cell addresses. This formula can be copied to cells D2 through D5, and the electronic spreadsheet will automatically adjust the rows in the formula accordingly.

In some instances, you want the formula to always use a figure found in one particular column, row, or cell, even when you copy the cell. In these instances, you can use the dollar sign "$" to "absolute" part or all of the cell address. If you place the dollar sign in front of the column letter, the column letter becomes absolute and the row number remains relative. The row number within the formula can be absoluted by placing the dollar sign in front of the row number in the cell address. To completely absolute a cell address within a formula, you place a dollar sign before the column letter and the row number. This will make the formula always reference the same cell. The function key F4 can be used to place the dollar signs within a cell address in a formula. While entering or editing the formula, press **[F4]** until the cell address displays the dollar sign(s) in the correct location.

5.   Adding Emphasis with Bold, Italics, and Underlining

Emphasis can be added within a spreadsheet by **boldfacing,** *italicizing,* or underlining the contents of cells. You may also use a combination of these styles. To add this emphasis to your spreadsheet, you turn on the feature prior to typing the cell entry or highlight existing cell entries and activate the feature. These features are activated by clicking on the appropriate button on the Toolbar or by using the following keystroke combinations:

Bold   **[Ctrl] + [B]**

Italics   **[Ctrl] + [I]**

Underline   **[Ctrl] + [U]**

6. Editing a Cell Entry

A cell entry can be changed or edited by typing a new entry into the cell, clicking inside the Input Line to make changes to the entry, or double-clicking on the cell. When editing changes have been made, pressing the **[Enter]** key will place the new contents into the cell.

7. Deleting Cell Entries

To delete the contents of a cell or group of cells, move the cell pointer to the cell or highlight the group of cells, and press the **[Delete]** key. Cells that have been accidentally deleted can be undeleted by selecting **Edit, Undo.**

C. MOVING AND COPYING CELLS

Moving and copying cells involve highlighting the cells to be acted upon, selecting the option to cut or copy the cells, and then pasting them in a new location. Moving and copying can also be accomplished by dragging the highlighted cells to a new location.

1. Moving Cells

A move is called a "cut and paste." To move one or more cells, place the cell pointer on the cell or highlight the group of cells and select **Edit, Cut.** Then, move the cell pointer to the cell where you want the cut cells placed and select **Edit, Paste.** The cut and paste options can also be found on the Toolbar. If you paste a cut upon cells that already contain data, you will write over those cells.

To move a cell or group of cells with the mouse, place the cell pointer on the cell or highlight the group of cells.

- In **Quattro Pro,** point the mouse pointer within the highlight and click and hold the left mouse button. You will see the mouse arrow turn into a hand. When the hand appears, you can drag the cells to the new location.
- In **Microsoft Excel** and **Lotus 1-2-3,** move the mouse pointer to the edge of the cell or highlighted group of cells. In Microsoft Excel, the mouse pointer will turn into an arrow. In 1-2-3, the mouse pointer will turn into a hand. Then click and hold the left mouse button and drag the cells to the new location.

2. Copying Cells

A copy is called a "copy and paste." To copy one or more cells, place the cell pointer on the cell or highlight the group of cells and select **Edit, Copy.** Then, move the cell pointer to the cell you want the cut cells copied to and select **Edit, Paste.** The copy and paste options can also be found on the Toolbar. If you paste a copy upon cells that already contain data, you will write over those cells.

To copy a cell or group of cells with the mouse, place the cell pointer on the cell or highlight the group of cells.

- In **Quattro Pro,** point the mouse pointer within the highlight, hold down the **[Ctrl]** key, and click and hold the left mouse button. You will see the mouse arrow turn into a hand. When the hand appears, you can drag the cells to the new location. Do not release the **[Ctrl]** key until you have dropped the cells in the new location.
- In **Microsoft Excel** move the mouse pointer to the edge of the cell or highlighted group of cells. The mouse pointer will turn into an arrow. Click and hold the left mouse button and drag the cells to the new location. Before you drop the cells, hold down the **[Ctrl]** key.
- In **1-2-3,** move the mouse pointer to the edge of the cell or highlighted group of cells. The mouse pointer will turn into a hand. Then hold down the **[Ctrl]** key and click and hold the left mouse button and drag the cells to the new location.

EXAMPLE 1

Using what you have learned so far, try entering the following spreadsheet into an electronic spreadsheet. The formulas and functions are displayed to assist you. Microsoft Excel users should begin the formulas in column D with an equals symbol, and write the SUM function as =SUM(B5:B7). When you enter the formulas and functions, numbers will appear in the "Total Amount" column and "Totals" row.

Begin the heading "JANUARY REVENUE" in column B, and leave row 2 blank. You will notice that this heading will overlap into cell C1. This will not create a problem unless there is an entry in C1.

	A	B	C	D
1		JANUARY REVENUE		
2				
3	BILLER	HOURS	RATE	TOTAL AMT
4				
5	JLD	160	250	+B5*C5
6	STR	176	245	+B6*C6
7	MMD	125	245	+B7*C7
8				
9	Totals	@sum(B5..B7)		+D5+D6+D7

1. Changing the Width of a Column or the Height of a Row

To change the width of a column or the height of a row, simply move the mouse pointer between the column letters at the top of the spreadsheet window, or between the row numbers at the left of the spreadsheet, until a double arrow appears. You may then drag the column width or row height to where you desire.

2. Formatting Values

To improve the appearance of our spreadsheet, we need to add commas and dollar signs to the numbers in columns C and D. To do this, you will highlight the cells containing the numbers with the mouse. Then select **Format, Cells** (Microsoft Excel) or **Format, Block** (Quattro Pro). Select a numeric style and the number of decimal places, and then click on the OK button. The three most common formats are explained below.

Fixed   Displays a number *without commas,* and lets you set the number of decimal places.

12345.00

Currency   Displays a number preceded by a *$, with commas,* and lets you set the number of decimal places.

$12,345.00

Comma   Displays a number *with commas,* and lets you set the number of decimal places.

12,345.00

For our example, we will select the **Currency** format. In this example, use no decimal places. Most electronic spreadsheets also have common numeric formats available on the Toolbar.

D.   SAVING AND OPENING SPREADSHEETS

To save a spreadsheet, you must store it on a magnetic disk, optical disk, or magnetic tape by identifying the storage location and giving it a name. There are three menu options found in the **File menu** that will save your spreadsheets: **Save As, Save,** and **Close.**

To open a spreadsheet, you must identify its location and its name. There are two menu options in the **File menu** that will open spreadsheets. The **New** option will open a new spreadsheet. The **Open** option will open an existing spreadsheet from a disk or tape.

1.   Save As

The **Save As** option opens a dialog box that prompts you for a location and name for your spreadsheet. An example of this type of Save As dialog box is shown in Figure 4.7.

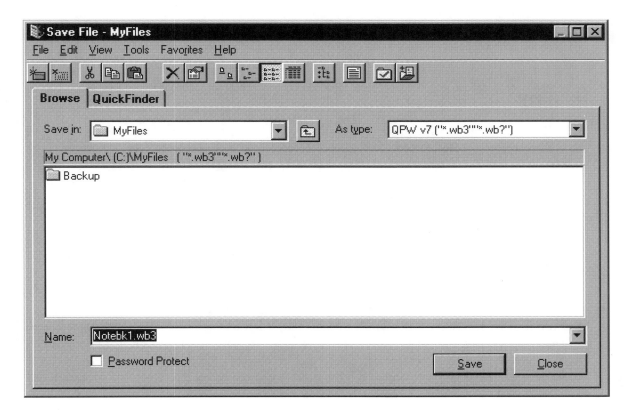

Figure 4.7   When you select File, Save As, a dialog box will appear for
you to enter the file location, name, and type if necessary

In this dialog box, you can type the drive letter, folder, and file name in the space indicated for the file name. You can also change the default directory to the drive letter and folder in which you want to save the spreadsheet by clicking on drive and folder icons. Then, you can place just the file name in the space indicated. Note that electronic spreadsheets attach their own three-character extension to a file name. So, if you are using a DOS and Windows environment, you are limited to eight characters for your file name. If you are using Windows 95, and the electronic spreadsheet is written for Windows 95, you can use a long file name. If you would like to save the file in a spreadsheet format that is different from the electronic spreadsheet that you are using, you can also make this change in the dialog box. Pressing the **[Enter]** key or clicking on a **Save** or **OK** button will complete the process of saving the spreadsheet.

2. Save

The **Save** option stores changes in a spreadsheet without opening a dialog box or otherwise prompting you. This option is used after you have given the spreadsheet a file name. If the spreadsheet does not yet have a name, you will be prompted with the Save As dialog box. You should use this option often when creating a spreadsheet. This will prevent you from losing most of your spreadsheet in the event of a power loss to your computer.

3. Close

The **Close** option is used to exit from the spreadsheet you are working on and leave you in the electronic spreadsheet program. If all changes in the spreadsheet have been saved, this option will close the spreadsheet. If all changes have not yet been saved, you will be prompted to save the changes. Responding **Yes** to the prompt will save the changes and close the spreadsheet. If the spreadsheet has not yet been given a name, the Save As dialog box will appear.

4. Opening a New Spreadsheet

The **New** option in the **File menu** will open a new spreadsheet on the screen. You can also use the **New** button on the Toolbar. When you first enter the electronic spreadsheet, you will have a new spreadsheet on your screen. It is usually part of a spreadsheet notebook with many pages. If you want to create a new spreadsheet within the same notebook, you can use another notebook page by clicking on a page tab. It is only when you want a new spreadsheet notebook, or when you have closed the spreadsheet on the screen, that you will need to use this option. When the New option has been selected, you will be prompted in many electronic spreadsheet programs to select a spreadsheet template. The default template is a blank spreadsheet, but you can choose from preformatted spreadsheets to create many standard formats.

5. Opening a Spreadsheet from a Disk or Tape

The **Open** option in the **File menu** allows you to open a spreadsheet file that has been saved to a disk or to a tape. When this option is selected, the Open dialog box will appear on the screen and prompt you for the name of the file. You can type the drive, folder (directory), and file name in the space for the file name, or you can open drives and folders to find the file by clicking on their icons. When you have found the file, you click on the file name and click on the **Open** or **OK** button to complete the process.

Most electronic spreadsheet programs now have the ability to open spreadsheets created in other programs. If your electronic spreadsheet program does not recognize the spreadsheet as one of its own, you will be prompted to select the type of program it was created in and the spreadsheet will be converted.

EXAMPLE 2

The spreadsheet below is a law firm's income forecast for the first quarter of the year. Since this is a forecast, the amount of revenue from each legal professional is an estimate. This section will follow the creation of this spreadsheet. Commands that help in creating the spreadsheet will be explained as they are needed.

INCOME FORECAST - First Quarter

ITEM	JAN	FEB	MAR	TOTALS
INCOME				
Partners				
MDL	40,000	40,000	40,000	$120,000
JKK	32,000	32,000	32,000	$96,000
TLM	28,800	28,800	28,800	$86,400
Associates				
WBB	28,800	28,800	28,800	$86,400
DLS	24,000	24,000	24,000	$72,000
DGA	22,400	22,400	22,400	$67,200
Paralegals				
James	12,800	12,800	12,800	$38,400
Susan	12,800	12,800	12,800	$38,400
TOTAL INCOME	$ 201,600	$ 201,600	$ 201,600	$ 604,800

- To create the Income Forecast spreadsheet, begin by entering the title of the spreadsheet in cell B1. Activate the bold feature to boldface the title. The title will spread into cells C1, D1, and E1. Many new spreadsheet programs have an option to center a title across the spreadsheet. This option will be explained below.

1. Centering Titles Across the Spreadsheet

Many new spreadsheets include an option that allows you to center titles across the columns of a spreadsheet. In Microsoft Excel, the feature is called "Center across columns." In Quattro Pro, it is called "Center across block." To use this feature, first determine how many columns the spreadsheet will have. Then, type the heading in the leftmost cell of the title row. Press the **[Enter]** key to place it in the cell. To perform the centering, highlight from the cell containing the title, in this case A1, to the cell in the rightmost column of the spreadsheet, in this case E1, as shown in Figure 4.8. Then, select the feature from the Toolbar or within the Format menu.

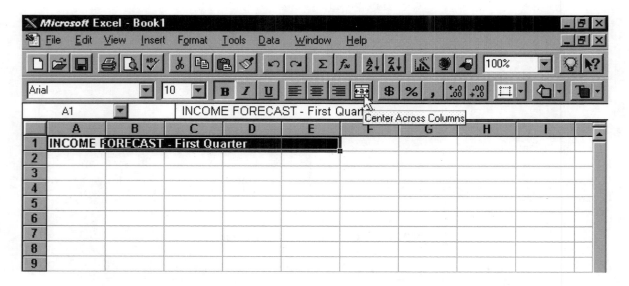

Figure 4.8   To center a title over the spreadsheet, type the entry in the first column, highlight from the first to the last column, and select the Center Across Columns option

After entering the title, move down to row 3 and continue entering the spreadsheet, following the instructions below.

- In row 3, center and boldface the headings in their respective cells. To place a line beneath the headings, follow the instructions below.

2. Creating Lines Within the Spreadsheet

Prior to the Windows versions of electronic spreadsheets, lines were created in a blank row by filling the cells with underline characters from the keyboard. In Windows-based electronic spreadsheets, lines are created on the borders of the cells through the Format menu, a right mouse button menu, and most recently an option on the Toolbar. To place lines on the top, bottom, left, or right edge of a cell or cells, you place the cell pointer on the cell, or highlight the group of cells, and select the **Border** (Microsoft Excel) or **Line Drawing** (Quattro Pro) feature.

To create lines under the headings in row 3, highlight the headings from A3 to E3. If you have a **Border** or **Line** option on the Toolbar, this is the easiest way to get the line across the bottom of these cells. The button on the Toolbar will provide several line thicknesses to choose from. Choose the thin line. Microsoft Excel's button is split. The left side will place the displayed line option immediately on the cells; the right side gives the drop-down list of lines. If you do not have a button on the Toolbar, or want a different type of line, move the cell pointer within the highlighted heading row and click the right mouse button. A drop-down menu will appear. In Microsoft Excel, select **Format Cells;** in Quattro Pro, select **Block Properties.** You then will see options similar to those you would receive if you had made your selection from the **Format** menu. Choose the **Border** or **Line** option, select the thin line, click on the bottom line of the displayed graphic or the selection for **Bottom,** and click on the **OK** button. When you remove the highlight from the heading row by clicking outside of it, you will see the line.

To remove a line, move the cell pointer to the cell, or highlight the cells containing the line, and select a Line option for "no line."

Your spreadsheet should now look similar to the one shown in Figure 4.9. Continue with the instructions below to create the spreadsheet.

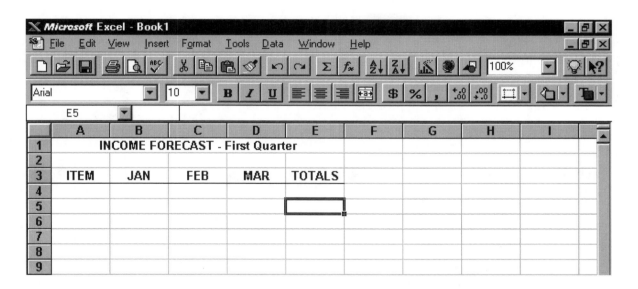

Figure 4.9 Column headings are each placed within their own cells

- Increase the width of column A so that it will be able to hold the entries that will be placed in this column. To do this, place the mouse pointer in between the column letters A and B at the top of the spreadsheet. When the mouse pointer turns into a double arrow, click and hold the left mouse button, and drag the border of column A to the right about an inch.

• Enter the items in column A, rows 4 through 16. Use the **[Space Bar]** to indent "Partners," "Associates," and "Paralegals" two spaces. The initials, names, and "TOTAL INCOME" will be centered. If you forget a row or need to remove a row, click the right mouse button in the row below where you want a new row inserted, or in the row you want to delete, and select **Insert** or **Delete.** Your spreadsheet should now look like the one in Figure 4.10.

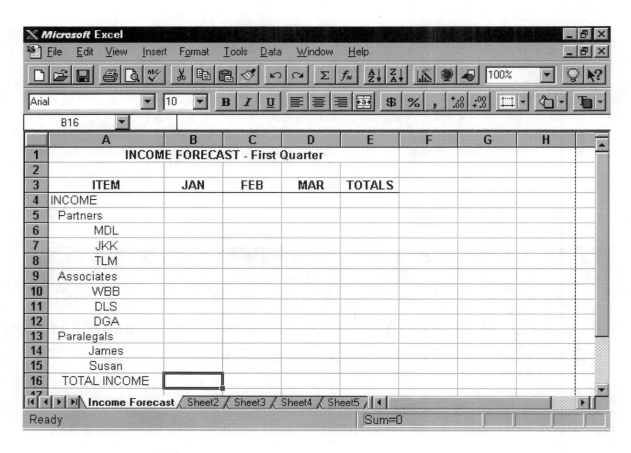

Figure 4.10   Column A needs to be widened to hold its entries

• Enter each person's January income. Quattro Pro and Microsoft Excel users must remember that commas are not normally permitted when entering numbers in these programs. After entering the January incomes, the spreadsheet should look similar to the one in Figure 4.11.

Windows Electronic Spreadsheets

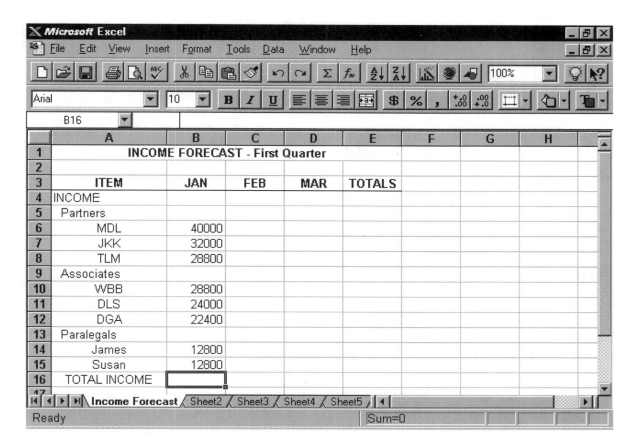

Figure 4.11 In most electronic spreadsheet programs, commas and dollar signs may not be used as the numbers are being entered. They are added later with a formatting option.

- Use the copy and paste feature to copy the numbers in the January column to February and March. To do this, highlight the cells containing the numbers (B6 through B15) and select Copy. Then, highlight the top cell for the February and March numbers (C6 and D6) and select Paste. Your spreadsheet should now look like the one in Figure 4.12.

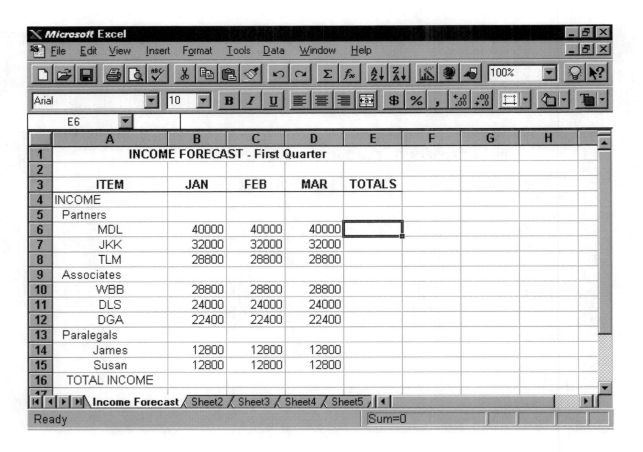

Figure 4.12   Time can be saved by copying the numbers in the January column to February and March

- In cell E6, enter a formula that will total the January, February, and March income amounts for MLD. In Microsoft Excel, the formula will begin with an equals symbol. In Quattro Pro or 1-2-3, the formula will begin with a plus symbol.

- Copy the formula in cell E6 and paste it into cells E7 through E15. Cells E9 and E13 will contain zeros after the paste. Move to those cells and delete the entry with the **[Delete]** key.

- In the TOTAL INCOME row, use a SUM function in Cell B16 to total the January numbers. Then, copy the function in B16 and paste it into cells C16 through E16. Your spreadsheet should now appear similar to the one in Figure 4.13.

Windows Electronic Spreadsheets

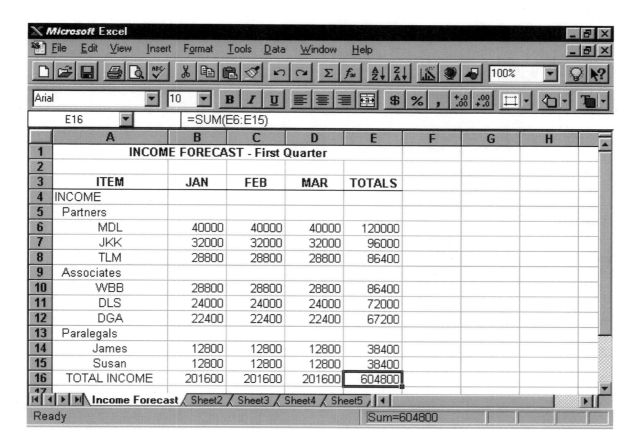

Figure 4.13   The formula in cell E6 can be copied to E7 through E15. The function in B16 can be copied to C16 through E16.

- Format the income numbers (not the totals in column E or row 16) by highlighting them and selecting the **Comma** format with no decimal places from the **Format** menu or the Toolbar.

- Highlight the numbers in row 16 and select the **Currency** format with no decimal places. You will find that the numbers no longer fit within their cells, and you will see entries similar to those in Figure 4.14. The columns will need to be widened by dragging the column borders or by clicking on a **Fit** button on the Toolbar.

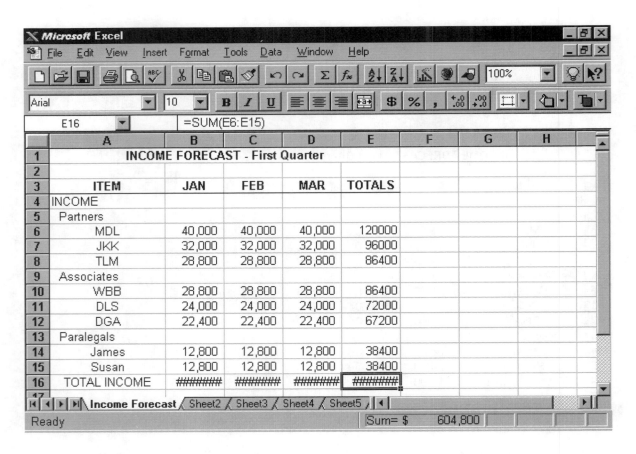

Figure 4.14 When numbers become too wide to fit within a cell, the cell will display number symbols (asterisks in Quattro Pro and Lotus 1-2-3). Widening the columns will make the numbers reappear.

- Highlight the numbers in column E and format them in the **Currency** format with no decimal places.

- To complete the spreadsheet, we need a single line along the top of Row 16 and a double line along its bottom. Highlight cells A16 through E16. Place the cell pointer back within the highlight and press the right mouse button. Select **Format Cells** or **Block Properties** and set up the **Borders** or **Lines** so that the single line is displayed at the top and the double line is at the bottom. The completed spreadsheet should now look like Figure 4.15.

- Save the spreadsheet with **File, Save As.**

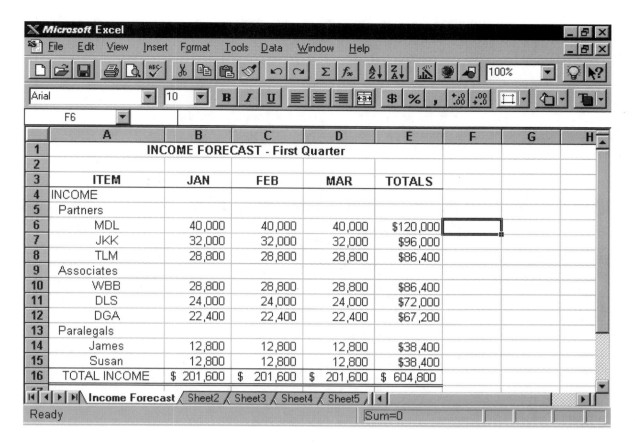

Figure 4.15 The Completed Spreadsheet

E. PRINTING A SPREADSHEET

To print a spreadsheet, you need to highlight the cells to be printed and select printing options.

- **To print in Microsoft Excel,** you will need to set the print area prior to selecting print options. To do this, with the area to be printed highlighted, select **File, Print Area, Set Print Area.** You then can go straight to **File, Print,** or set up the page with **File, Page Setup.** At any time, you can also preview your printed document with **File, Print Preview.**
- **To print in Quattro Pro,** make sure that the cells to be printed are highlighted and select **File, Print.** In the Print dialog box, you will find page setup options to customize your printed spreadsheet. Print Preview can be selected from the Print dialog box or by selecting **File, Print Preview.**

F. SPLITTING THE SPREADSHEET WINDOW

As a spreadsheet becomes larger, you can reach a point as you are entering data when you can no longer see the headings at the top or left side of the spreadsheet. For these instances, the spreadsheet window can be split horizontally or vertically to keep the headings on the screen as you continue to move down or right in the spreadsheet. In the spreadsheet shown in Figure 4.16, a horizontal split has been placed in the spreadsheet just below the headings.

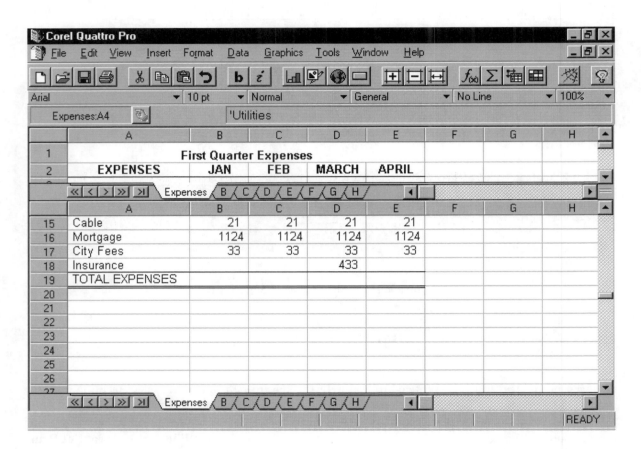

Figure 4.16   A spreadsheet window can be split horizontally or vertically so that headings can remain in view as you move down or right in the spreadsheet

Options to split a spreadsheet window can usually be found in the **Window menu,** although recent versions of Quattro Pro have moved it to the **View menu.** You can choose one of these menu options or use the drag buttons available at the right of the screen. In Microsoft Excel, the drag buttons are seen at the top of the right scroll bar and to the right of the bottom scroll bar. In Quattro Pro, both split options are seen in the bottom right-hand corner. As you run your mouse over these buttons, the mouse pointer will turn into a graphic representing a horizontal or vertical split. To place the split within the spreadsheet window, drag the graphic to where you would like the split to be placed and drop it. You can move back and forth between the two windows by clicking with the mouse.

To remove the window split, select the option to remove it in the **Window** or **View menu.** Another way to remove the split is to drag it off the screen. In Microsoft Excel, click on the border of the split and drag it. In Quattro Pro, click the button at the bottom or right of the split border and drag it.

G. DATABASE FEATURES

Electronic spreadsheets are equipped with database features that will allow you to sort, query, and perform other database actions upon the data in a spreadsheet. The most helpful database feature is Sort. Enter the spreadsheet shown in Figure 4.17 into an electronic spreadsheet program to practice the Sort feature. You will need to increase the width of column A. The height of row 1 has also been increased.

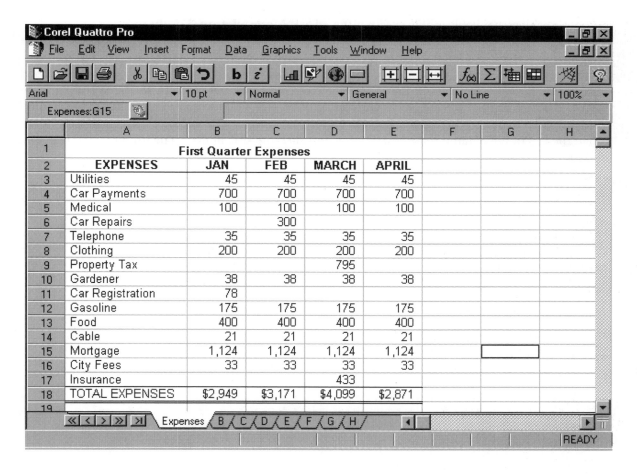

Figure 4.17   An Expense Spreadsheet Prior to Sorting

a) Use a SUM function to add up the TOTAL EXPENSES for each of the months.

b) Use the line options to place the lines within the spreadsheet. The single line at the bottom of the spreadsheet should be attached to the top of the TOTAL EXPENSES row. Do not attach it to the bottom of the insurance row or it will move when the sort is activated.

c) Format the numbers in the TOTAL EXPENSES row in the **Currency** format with no decimal places. Format the numbers within the spreadsheet in the **Comma** format with no decimal places.

d) Save the spreadsheet prior to performing the sort. **Edit, Undo** will undo a sort if you make a mistake, but have it saved as a backup.

To perform the sort, you need to highlight the spreadsheet from A3 to E17. If you only highlighted the entries in column A, the numbers associated with them would not accompany them in the sort. The highlight needs to begin from column A because that is how the spreadsheet determines which column the sort is to act upon. If you began the highlight from column E, the information would be sorted by the numbers present there.

The Sort feature can be activated by a button on the Toolbar, or by selecting **Data, Sort.** The button on the Toolbar will offer A-Z or Z-A sorting. In Quattro Pro version 7, this button is found by right-clicking the Toolbar and selecting the **Block Manipulation Toolbar.**

If you use **Data, Sort,** a Sort dialog box will appear. Here, you will need to identify the column on which to sort by. Additional columns can be specified if more sort keys are needed. For example, if the first column contained last names, an additional sort key could be added to sort on the second column containing first names in the event that there were two people with the same last name. In Microsoft Excel, the Sort dialog box is fairly straightforward. You identify the heading of the column that you want to sort and click on the **OK** button. In Quattro Pro, identify the cell address of the cell at the top of the column to be sorted upon and click the **OK** button. The sorted spreadsheet will look similar to the one in Figure 4.18.

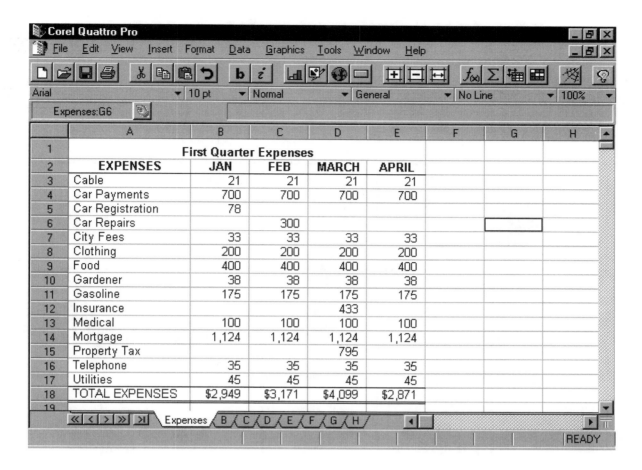

Figure 4.18 The Sort Results

H. GRAPHS AND CHARTS

Graphs and charts are an important part of an electronic spreadsheet and are beneficial in presenting the spreadsheet data. Using the expense spreadsheet from Figure 4.18, we will chart the total expenses for January through April. Charts can be placed on the spreadsheet page or on a separate page for charts. If you choose to create the chart on a separate page, Microsoft Excel will create a tab for the chart at the bottom of the spreadsheet window. In Quattro Pro, you can move between the chart page and the spreadsheet page using the **Window menu.**

1. Chart Basics

When creating a chart, you will often need to identify the type of chart to be used, its title, a legend, and the series of information to be charted. When using line and bar charts, you will need to identify the information for the X-axis, the Y-axis, and the Z-axis (in three-dimensional charts). Some examples of charts are shown in Figure 4.19. Electronic spreadsheets offer many types of charts; the most common are the pie, line, and bar charts. A title is the title you want to assign to the chart. A legend is the part of the chart that identifies what each color or line represents. When you are using line and bar charts, the bottom axis is the X-axis. The left-side axis is the Y-axis. In three-dimensional charts, the third axis is the Z-axis. A series is a collection of data to be charted. For example, in a line or bar chart you may want to compare data using two or more lines or bars at each X-axis point. Each separate section of data would be identified as a series. Because creating charts can be difficult, experiment with different settings to get the feel of how charting works.

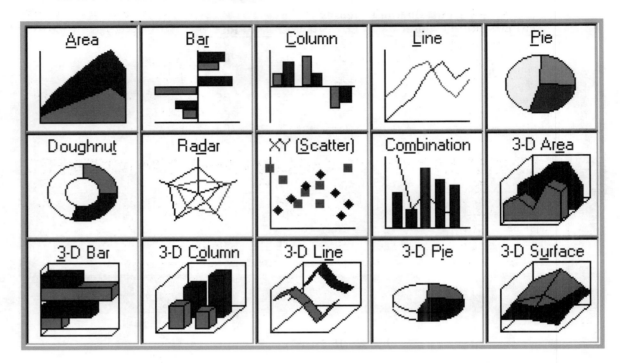

Figure 4.19   There are many different types of charts to choose from

2.   Creating a Quick Chart Using the Toolbar

When you use the Toolbar to create a chart, the chart will be placed on the spreadsheet page. To create a quick chart using the Toolbar, you need to highlight the data to be charted. How you highlight the data will often determine how your chart will appear. For example, if the data to be charted is in the cells adjacent to its headings, you can highlight the headings along with the data, and the Chart feature will place those headings into the chart. In the example that we will use, Figure 4.18, the month headings are not adjacent to the total amounts at the bottom of the spreadsheet. In Quattro Pro, you will need to separately identify the X-axis headings in a menu. In Microsoft Excel, you can highlight the totals at the bottom of the spreadsheet, and then hold down the **[Ctrl]** key and also highlight the month headings at the top of the spreadsheet. This will associate the headings with the numbers when you create the chart. Follow the instructions below to create a line chart for the total monthly expenses. A chart can be deleted from the spreadsheet page by clicking on it, and then pressing the **[Delete]** key.

Windows Electronic Spreadsheets

- In **Microsoft Excel,** highlight the totals in cells B18 through E18. Then, hold down the **[Ctrl]** key, use the mouse on the right Scroll Bar to scroll up, and highlight the month headings in B2 through E2. Both highlights should be visible. Next, click on the charting button on the Toolbar. Your mouse pointer will have a graphic attached to it. Move to the place in the spreadsheet page where you would like to place the chart, and drag a square to create the size of the chart. If you just click within the spreadsheet, the program will determine the size for you. Microsoft Excel will then prompt you for information about the chart. Choose a Line chart, and add titles if you like. You must add any information at this point in the creation as it is difficult to add to the chart once it has been placed into the spreadsheet.

    Once you have finished, you can edit the structure of the chart by double-clicking inside the chart, clicking the right mouse button on an object, and making selections from the menu that appears. You can also change the size of the chart by clicking and dragging the boxes on the border of the chart. The completed chart is shown in Figure 4.20.

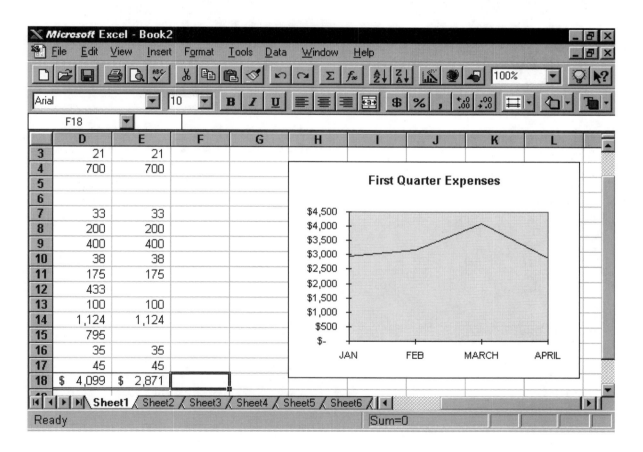

Figure 4.20 A Line Chart in Microsoft Excel

- In **Quattro Pro,** highlight the totals in cells B18 through E18. Next, click on the charting button on the Toolbar. Your mouse pointer will have a graphic attached to it. Move to the place in the spreadsheet page where you would like to place the chart, and drag a square to create the size of the chart. If you just click within the spreadsheet, the program will determine the size for you. Quattro Pro will then create the chart for you. The chart that Quattro Pro selects will likely be a pie chart. To make any changes, click the right mouse button within the chart.

To change to a line chart, click the right mouse button and select **Type/Layout** from the menu. Then select a type of line chart. To change the size of the chart, you can click and drag the boxes on the border of the chart. To add the month headings across the bottom of the chart, select **Series** from the right click menu. A dialog box will appear. Identify the X-axis as **B2..E2** and click on the **OK** button. A legend can also be added from the Series menu, and titles can be added from the Titles menu. A completed chart is shown in Figure 4.21.

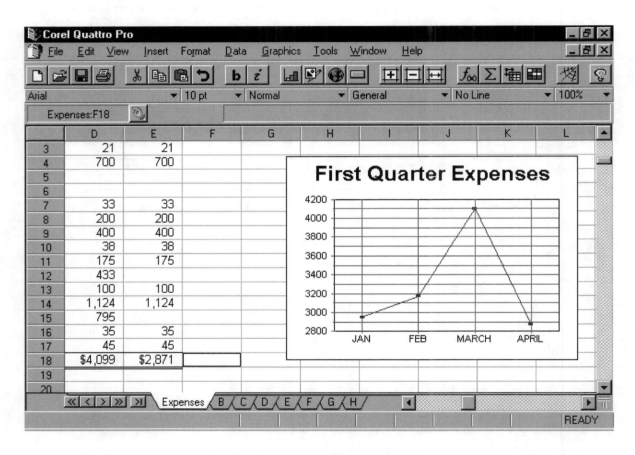

Figure 4.21   A Line Chart in Quattro Pro

3. Creating a Chart on a Separate Page

Charts can be created on a separate page using chart options from the spreadsheet menus. In Microsoft Excel, you can also create a chart on a separate page using **[F11].** When you have created a chart on a separate page, Microsoft Excel will give you a new tab displaying the name of the chart page. Quattro Pro will put the chart on the last page, called the "Objects" page. You can get to this page in Quattro Pro by clicking on the first button to the left of the tabs at the bottom of the screen. You can return to the spreadsheet page in the same manner. To create the chart on a separate page, follow the instructions below.

- In **Microsoft Excel,** highlight the totals in cells B18 through E18. Then hold down the **[Ctrl]** key, use the mouse on the right Scroll Bar to scroll up, and highlight the month headings in B2 through E2. Both highlights should be visible. Next, select **Insert, Chart, As New Sheet,** and proceed through the selections in the ChartWizard. Create a line chart. Add a title for the chart when the selection for this appears. You must add any information at this point in the creation as it is difficult to add to the chart once it has been placed into the spreadsheet.

  Once you have finished, you can edit the structure of the chart by clicking inside the chart, clicking the right mouse button, and making selections from the menu that appears. You can also change the size of the chart by clicking and dragging the boxes on the border of the chart. You can move back to the spreadsheet page by clicking on the appropriate tab at the bottom of the screen.

  Microsoft Excel also contains a chart feature that will automatically create a chart for you when you press the **[F11]** key. Simply highlight the totals and the month headings as in the previous example and press **[F11].** You can change the type of chart or other features by clicking on the chart and clicking the right mouse button.

- In **Quattro Pro,** highlight the totals in cells B18 through E18, and select **Graphics, New Chart.** In the New Chart dialog box, enter the range **B2..E2** in the X-axis box. Next, select a chart type, add titles and a name for the chart (it must have a name), and click on the **OK** button. A chart page in Quattro Pro contains special menus and a Toolbar that will assist in making changes and adding features to a chart. When you are finished, you will return to the spreadsheet by selecting the spreadsheet page from the Window menu.

Summary

Electronic spreadsheets can be used to create many different types of spreadsheets. These programs utilize pull-down menus, Toolbars, and function keys to access a multitude of features. Many new Windows-based electronic spreadsheets contain multiple spreadsheet pages that are all stored under the same file name. These pages are represented by tabs. The tab name can usually be changed by clicking the right mouse button upon it.

There are two types of cell entries in an electronic spreadsheet, Text and Values. Text entries contain words, numbers that are not intended for math (e.g., telephone numbers), and word and number combinations (e.g., addresses). Value entries contain numbers, formulas, or functions. Formulas are equations that include the cell addresses to be acted upon. Functions are preprogrammed formulas that accompany the electronic spreadsheet. The most common function is the SUM function. Formulas and functions can include cell addresses from different spreadsheet pages to link information from one page to another. Entries can be positioned within a cell using buttons on the Toolbar. Quattro Pro and Lotus 1-2-3 include justification characters that can be used to position text entries.

The entries within cells can be highlighted and moved or copied to other parts of a spreadsheet or other spreadsheet pages. Most formulas and functions contain relative addresses that enable them to be easily copied to other cells. All or part of a cell address can be absoluted within a formula or function by placing a dollar sign before the column letter and/or row number.

Columns and rows may be inserted or deleted when necessary. Their widths and heights can also be changed by dragging their borders with the mouse. Database actions may be performed upon a spreadsheet, and charts may be created from the data within a spreadsheet. In total, electronic spreadsheets are flexible tools for helping to plan and analyze past and future events.

ELECTRONIC SPREADSHEET EXERCISES

Exercise 1

Part 1

You have been asked to prepare a federal tax computation spreadsheet for the Talbot family. An example of the spreadsheet, with figures supplied by the Talbots, is shown below.

TAX COMPUTATION (Fed.)—THE TALBOT FAMILY

DESCRIPTION	AMOUNT
INCOME	
Wages, Salaries, Tips, Etc.	45612
Taxable Interest Income	756
Dividend Income	175
Tax Refunds	632
Other Gains (Losses)	500
TOTAL INCOME	
Less Adjustments	135
ADJUSTED GROSS INCOME	
ITEMIZED DEDUCTIONS	
Paid Taxes	
State and Local Taxes	1010
Other Taxes	135
Total Paid Taxes	
Personal Interest	56
Total Paid Interest	
Total Misc. Contributions	545
TOTAL ITEMIZED DEDUCTIONS	
EXEMPTIONS	6000
TAXABLE INCOME	
TAXES OWED BEFORE CREDITS (20% of Taxable Income)	

Enter this spreadsheet into an electronic spreadsheet program. The totals of certain items have been left blank for you to enter formulas or functions. Most of these totals are self-explanatory. Taxable income is adjusted gross income less itemized deductions and exemptions. After all values have been entered, format the numbers in the **Comma** format with **0** decimal places.

Enter your name in column A, below the last line of your spreadsheet. Save and print the spreadsheet.

Part 2

The Talbots would like to see what effect the purchase of a home would have on their taxes. Purchasing a home adds a deduction for paid real estate taxes and mortgage interest. The Talbots estimate the following amounts for these items:

Real Estate Taxes	1,500
Mortgage Interest	10,400

Add these two items to the Itemized Deductions portion of the spreadsheet, adjusting your formulas and functions accordingly.

Save this spreadsheet under a new file name. Print the spreadsheet.

Exercise 2

Our firm represents 156 plaintiffs in an action against Big Builders, PolyPipe Corporation, KLL Chemical Company, and Yoom Oil Company. Each of the plaintiffs owns a house in the Sunrise housing tract built by Big Builders in 1987. Big Builders installed a plastic pipe plumbing system in all of the houses in the Sunrise tract. This pipe was manufactured by PolyPipe Corporation. PolyPipe Corporation used resins to manufacture the pipe that were purchased from KLL Chemical Company and Yoom Oil Company.

Many of the homeowners within the Sunrise tract have experienced leaks, some catastrophic, in their plumbing. One homeowner returned from a vacation to find his home flooded. Many articles have appeared in newspapers and magazines regarding the failure of this type of plumbing system. The Sunrise tract homeowners association contacted our firm to represent the 156 plaintiffs.

Using an electronic spreadsheet program, create a spreadsheet that will show the itemized damages suffered by each of the plaintiffs. The first column should contain the individual damage items. These items are pipe repairs, furniture damage, wallpaper replacement, painting, drywall repair, lodging, other costs, and cost of replacement. Each subsequent column will represent the damages for one plaintiff. The damages for four of the plaintiffs are given below.

- Plaintiff Abbott has paid $250 for pipe repairs, has incurred $0 in furniture damage, has paid $125 to replace wallpaper, has paid $75 for painting, has paid $50 for drywall repair, has incurred $0 for lodging during repairs, and has incurred $0 in other costs. It will cost $5,000 to replace the plumbing system in this house.

- Plaintiff Barnes has paid $1,500 for pipe repairs, has incurred $3,000 in furniture damage, has paid $500 to replace wallpaper, has paid $1,000 for painting, has paid $400 for drywall repair, has incurred $275 for lodging during repairs, and has incurred $350 in other costs. It will cost $6,500 to replace the plumbing system in this house.
- Plaintiff Draper has paid $100 for pipe repairs, has incurred $0 in furniture damage, has paid $0 to replace wallpaper, has paid $50 for painting, has paid $50 for drywall repair, has incurred $0 for lodging during repairs, and has incurred $0 in other costs. It will cost $3,500 to replace the plumbing system in this house.
- Plaintiff Dunne has paid $300 for pipe repairs, has incurred $100 in furniture damage, has paid $140 to replace wallpaper, has paid $250 for painting, has paid $150 for drywall repair, has incurred $0 for lodging during repairs, and has incurred $0 in other costs. It will cost $6,500 to replace the plumbing system in this house.

Prepare this spreadsheet and provide a row that totals the damages for each plaintiff. Big Builders has offered to settle its portion of the litigation by paying 40 percent of each plaintiff's damages. In a new row, calculate the settlement offer for each plaintiff.

Place your name under the last row of the spreadsheet. Format the Value cells in the Currency format with no decimal places. Print the spreadsheet.

Exercise 3

You have been asked to set up a spreadsheet for the Brown conservatorship. Mr. Brown was deemed incompetent to handle his own finances, and a conservator was appointed to deposit his social security checks and to write checks for expenses. The conservator of Mr. Brown is a client of our firm. The conservator is required to keep a detailed accounting of all monies that come in to Mr. Brown and all monies that are paid out. The court has determined the amounts that can be spent on the following items during this calendar year.

Clothing	$500
Furniture and Furnishings	$1000
Groceries	$3600
Entertainment	$1200

Any other expenses will be placed in the category of "Miscellaneous Expenses."

Create a spreadsheet with **columns** labeled as follows:

Date

Payee

S.S. Income

Misc. Income

Clothing

Furniture & Furnishings

Groceries

Entertainment

Misc. Expenses

The following income has been accrued, and expenses have been incurred, so far this year for Mr. Brown. Each should be entered into a row in the spreadsheet with the amount placed in the appropriate column.

1/3/97	Social Security Check	$600
1/5/97	Thorpe Department Store (underwear and shirts)	$80
1/6/97	Hamburger Place (entertainment)	$10
1/9/97	Cable Company	$35
1/9/97	Telephone Company	$40
1/10/97	Water Company	$30
1/10/97	Electric Company	$100
1/16/97	Birthday Check from Susie	$500
1/17/97	The Furniture Place (rocking chair)	$250
1/20/97	Grocery Store	$80
1/23/97	T.V. Heaven (large-screen television—furniture)	$750
1/25/97	Grocery Store	$40
1/30/97	Cash	$100

Below the last row of the spreadsheet, total each of the columns. Your boss is a little worried that Mr. Brown's conservator may be spending too much if he is going to stay within the court's guidelines. He wants you to show, underneath the totals row, the percentage that has been spent in each of the four categories that the court set limits on. To do this, set up a row for each and enter a formula to determine the percentage. Format the values in the spreadsheet in the **Currency** format with no decimal places. Place your name under the bottom row of the spreadsheet. When you print the spreadsheet, use the Landscape option. You may need to alter the size of your columns so that they will fit on the page.

Exercise 4

Enter the list of payments shown in Exercise 3 into a new spreadsheet with columns for the date, the payee, and the amount. Format the values in the **Currency** format with two decimal places. Place your name under the last row of the spreadsheet and print it.

For the second part of this exercise, use **Data, Sort** to sort these items alphabetically by payee. Print the spreadsheet again and turn in both sheets.

Exercise 5

Enter the spreadsheet shown below into an electronic spreadsheet program.

PARKER ESTATE

Cash	250000
Real Estate	2600000
Stocks and Mutual Funds	750000
Personal Property	1500000

Format the values in the **Currency** format with no decimal places. Then, use a **Chart** (Graph) feature to create a pie chart displaying the makeup of the Parker estate. Print the pie chart.

Chapter Index

Summary Databases

CHAPTER 5

DBASE IV® FOR DOS

Chapter Preface

dBASE IV is a database management system (DBMS) that allows you to organize documents or items of information for easy retrieval. Databases can be set up in this program for case evidence, in-house forms, client and case records, calendars, library updates, and many other pieces of information.

In this chapter, we will create a database for a law firm's list of current cases. We will enter records and perform searches on the database. At the end of Chapter 6 are several database exercises that can be used with either Chapter 5 or Chapter 6.

A.   THE dBASE IV DATABASE

dBASE is a summary database program. Summary databases contain pieces of information about each document or item within the database. They do not contain the full text of documents.

Summary databases are made up of files, fields, and records. The example we will be using in this chapter is a law firm's case list database. This database will contain items of information about every case currently handled by the firm.

1.   Files

A database file is a collection of related information. The file name for our case list database will be:

CASELIST

2. Fields

Fields are the structure of a database. They are items of information that will commonly be found in each of the entries in the database. The fields for the law firm case list database will be information that we want to store about each of the cases.

Case Name
Case Number
Client
Subject
Date Case Filed
Responsible Attorney
Date File Opened
Date File Closed

3. Records

The records of the database are the group of field entries for each case to be contained within the case list database file. A record for the *Smith v. Berry* case is shown below.

Case Name	**Smith v. Berry**
Case Number	**80023**
Client	**Berry, Simon Jr.**
Subject	**Breach of contract**
Date Case Filed	**06/24/92**
Responsible Attorney	**EMD**
Date File Opened	**04/19/92**
Date File Closed	

B. DBASE IV FILE NAMES, FIELD NAMES, AND FIELD TYPES

There are certain rules that must be followed in creating files and fields in dBASE IV. These rules are explained in this section.

1. File Names

In order to save your database file, you will need to give it a name. In dBASE, file names may be one to eight characters in length. They must begin with a letter and may not contain spaces. You do not give your file name a three-character extension. dBASE automatically assigns a .DBF extension to all database files. The name for our firm's case list database is:

CASELIST

2. Field Names

When you construct your database, you will give each field a name. Field names may be ten characters or fewer. They must begin with a letter and may not contain spaces or periods. After the first letter, you can use letters, numbers, or the underline character. The field names that we have developed for this database have been changed below to meet the dBASE field name requirements.

> **CASE_NAME**
> **CASE_NUMBR**
> **CLIENT**
> **SUBJECT**
> **DATE_FILED**
> **RESP_ATTY**
> **DATE_OPEN**
> **DATE_CLOSE**

3. Field Types

There are six types of fields in dBASE IV. They are:

Character Anything you can type from your keyboard. Numbers such as telephone numbers or addresses are character fields, not numerics, because they are not used for math.

> **JANUARY 22   Post Road   = = = = = = =**

Numeric Any number used in a mathematical computation. These numbers will have a fixed number of decimal places and may contain a + or −.

> **8.13   9.20   10.36   11.21   12.00**

Float Float is a numeric field that allows you to vary the number of places after the decimal point.

> **8.13   9.2   10.356   11.20943**

Date Dates in the form: mm/dd/yy. The forward slashes are entered for you.

> **08/25/92   01/01/45**

Logical Used for data that will be (T)rue or (F)alse, (Y)es or (N)o, or some other either/or combination.

> **T F   Y N**

Memo	For lengthy descriptions, dBASE creates a separate memo file where you can store memos up to 64K characters in length. When entering data in the memo field, you need to get to the memo screen with **[Ctrl] + [Home]** or **[F9] (Zoom).** When you are finished with your entry, you return to the database edit screen through the **Exit menu** or by pressing **[Ctrl] + [End].**

Our case list database consists of the following field types:

CASE_NAME	**Character**
CASE_NUMBR	**Character**
CLIENT	**Character**
SUBJECT	**Memo**
DATE_FILED	**Date**
RESP_ATTY	**Character**
DATE_OPEN	**Date**
DATE_CLOSE	**Date**

The CASE_NUMBR field is a character field because the number will not be used in mathematical computations.

C.   ENTERING THE PROGRAM

To enter dBASE type **dBASE [Enter]** OR select the program name or icon from a menu screen.

When you enter dBASE, you will be greeted by a dBASE program graphic and a license explanation. After the user assents to the license agreement, the dBASE IV Control Center will be displayed.

D.   WORKING WITH dBASE IV

dBASE IV offers two ways to work with the program, the Control Center and the Dot Prompt.
The Control Center is a menu panel that helps the user formulate commands. It is shown in Figure 5.1.
The Dot Prompt is a blank screen displaying only a period at the lower left-hand corner. This is the original way that dBASE was operated, and requires knowledge of the dBASE command structure. Many advanced users continue to prefer this method. The Dot Prompt screen is shown in Figure 5.2.

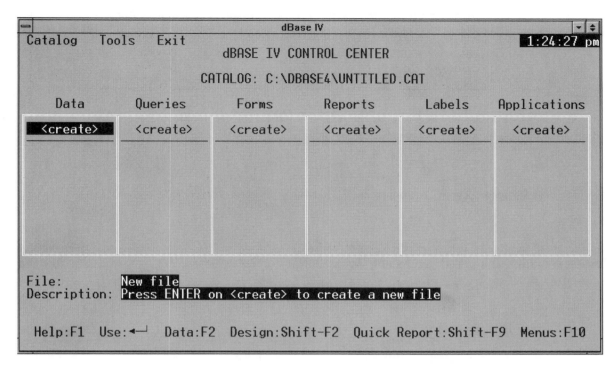

Figure 5.1 The dBASE IV Control Center

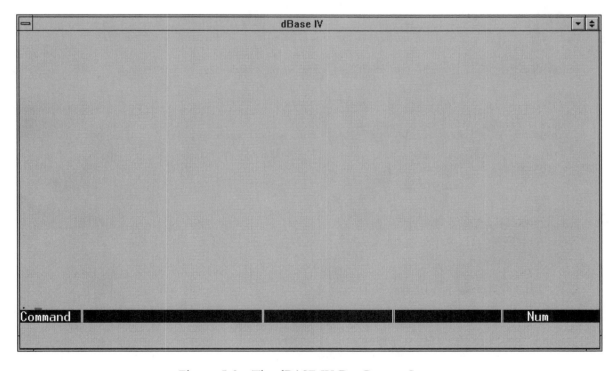

Figure 5.2 The dBASE IV Dot Prompt Screen

In this workbook, we will operate dBASE from the Control Center. Use of the Dot Prompt commands is explained later in this chapter in Section O.

E. THE CONTROL CENTER

Figure 5.1 shows the dBASE IV Control Center. The Control Center contains file panels, a catalog identifier, and pull-down menus. At the bottom of the screen is a list of special keys that can be used with the program.

1. The File Panels

The Control Center contains six file panels. Each file panel will contain the names of files created in that panel. The file panels are as follows:

Data	Lists the names of your database files.
Queries	Lists the names of the query files that perform of database searches.
Forms	Lists the names of files containing customized input forms.
Reports	Lists the names of files containing report formats you have designed.
Labels	Lists all files containing label formats for mailing and other types of labels.
Applications	Lists the names of all files that contain custom dBASE programs and applications.

To create a new file in any one of the six file panels, highlight **<create>** in the desired panel and press **[Enter].**

2. The Catalog Identifier

Catalogs are where dBASE IV stores its database files. The dBASE catalogs function in a manner similar to directories. When a file is created, it will be put into the current catalog. The catalog identifier displays the current catalog.

3. The Pull-Down Menus

The Control Center contains pull-down menus at the top of the screen that will assist you in performing many dBASE functions. You may access these menus by pressing the **[F10]** key or by holding down the **[Alt]** key and pressing the first letter of the menu option name. For example, **[Alt] + [E]** will open the **Exit menu** as shown in Figure 5.3. The **[Esc]** key will back you out of a menu selection.

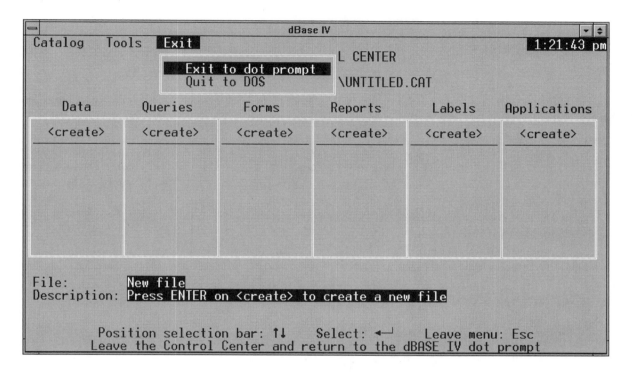

Figure 5.3   The **Exit menu** is opened using the **[F10]** key or **[Alt] + [E]**

4. The Special Keys

dBASE's special keys are found on the **navigation line** at the bottom of the screen. Some of these special keys are listed below.

F1   **Help.**

F2   **Data.** This key takes you to your database Edit and Browse screens.

Shift-F2   **Design.** From the Control Center, this key takes you to the Database Design screen. The Database Design screen is used to create and alter your field structure.

From the Browse and Edit screens, this key will take you to the Query Design screen.

Shift-F9   **Quick Report.** This key allows you to print a quick report of your database.

F10   **Menus.** This key takes you to the Menu Bar at the top of the screen.

ESC   **Escape.** This key allows you to move back one database screen.

F. CATALOGS

Catalogs are where your database files will be stored. dBASE lets you create separate catalogs for storing different types of databases. Personal databases, databases for a single client, in-house databases, and so forth can all be stored in separate catalogs.

The catalog identifier at the Control Center displays the disk drive, directory location, and name of the current catalog in use. This is where your files will be stored unless you change catalogs. The common default catalog is the UNTITLED catalog. You may save your database files in this catalog if you wish.

If you wish to store your database files on a diskette, you will want to create a catalog on the diskette in which to store the files.

If you have your database files in a catalog other than the current catalog, or in a catalog present on a diskette, you will need to change the current catalog in order to use the database files present there.

To create a new catalog, or to change the current catalog, follow the steps below.

a) Open the **Catalog menu** using **[F10]** or **[Alt] + [C].**

b) Select **Use a different catalog.** A **create** option and a list of the catalog selections are displayed at the right side of the screen. If your catalog is listed, highlight the name and press the **[Enter]** key.

c) To create a new catalog, or to change to an existing catalog on a disk in a drive other than the one listed in the catalog identifier, you will need to select **<create>.** After you have selected **<create>** you will be prompted for a catalog name. Type the appropriate disk drive letter followed by a catalog file name. Catalog names may be one to eight characters and may not contain spaces or punctuation. The underline character is acceptable. An example of a catalog created on a diskette in the A: drive would be **A:DBFILES.** If you have a catalog present on the diskette and are using **<create>** to change to that catalog, you will type the drive letter followed by the catalog name as shown in the previous example. This does not damage your database files stored in the catalog.

Occasionally, a database file will have been stored to a disk without being placed in a catalog. To add such a file to the current catalog:

a) Open the **Catalog menu** and select **Add file to catalog.**

b) If you need to change the drive letter for the file location, highlight the displayed drive letter and press **[Enter].** Possible drive selections will be displayed. Highlight the appropriate drive letter and press **[Enter].**

c) Highlight the file name and press **[Enter].**

As you create files, they will automatically be saved into the current catalog.

G. CREATING A DATABASE FILE

To create the CASELIST database select **<create>** in the **data panel.** dBASE will take you to the Database Design screen where you will create your database structure. The Database Design screen is shown in Figure 5.4.

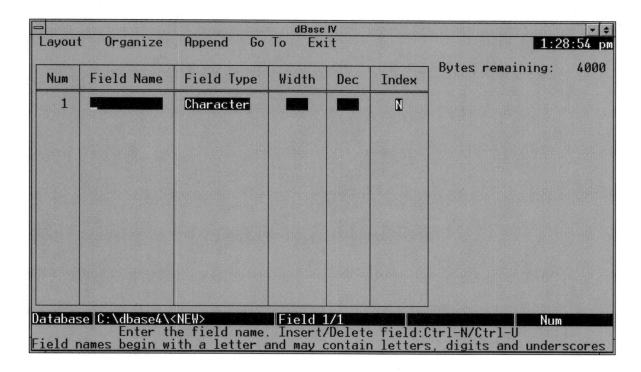

Figure 5.4 The Database Design Screen

In addition to supplying the names for the database fields, you must identify the field types, their widths, the number of decimal places for numeric fields, and indicate whether you wish to create an index upon individual fields.

1. Fields

The fields that we will create for this database are:

CASE_NAME
CASE_NUMBR
CLIENT
SUBJECT
DATE_FILED
RESP_ATTY
DATE_OPEN
DATE_CLOSE

Type the name of the first field and press the **[Enter]** key. You will then be prompted for the field type.

2. Field Type

For each field, the type of field must be specified so that dBASE knows what type of data is to be stored within the field. The field types for our fields are:

CASE_NAME	**Character**
CASE_NUMBR	**Character**
CLIENT	**Character**
SUBJECT	**Memo**
DATE_FILED	**Date**
RESP_ATTY	**Character**
DATE_OPEN	**Date**
DATE_CLOSE	**Date**

"Character" is already entered in the field type column as shown in Figure 5.5. Press the **[Enter]** key if this is the type of field you want. To switch to another field type, type the first letter of the field type or toggle through the field types with the **[Space Bar]** and press **[Enter]** when the desired field type is displayed.

3. Field Width

The field width column is where you tell dBASE the maximum amount of characters you will be entering into the field. For example, in the CASE_NAME field, we will be entering

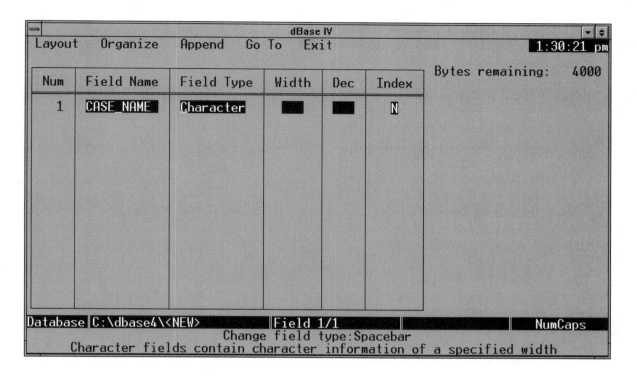

Layout   Organize   Append   Go To   Exit   1:30:21 pm

Bytes remaining: 4000

Num	Field Name	Field Type	Width	Dec	Index
1	CASE_NAME	Character	■	■	N

Database C:\dbase4\<NEW>   Field 1/1   NumCaps

Change field type:Spacebar

Character fields contain character information of a specified width

Figure 5.5   The field type may be selected by pressing the first letter of the field type or by using the **[Space Bar]** to toggle to the desired type and pressing **[Enter]**

names like "SDF Corporation v. Terra, Inc." For this name we will need 30 spaces. To be on the safe side, we will make this field 40 spaces long. In the event that we need to enter a longer case name, we can come back to this screen and increase the field width. Type **40** and press the **[Enter]** key.

The widths of our fields will be:

CASE_NAME	Character	40
CASE_NUMBR	Character	10
CLIENT	Character	25
SUBJECT	Memo	10
DATE_FILED	Date	8
RESP_ATTY	Character	4
DATE_OPEN	Date	8
DATE_CLOSE	Date	8

There are some fields that have a pre-set width that is automatically entered when that field type is selected. These fields are:

Logical Fields:	Automatic width of 1
Date Fields:	Automatic width of 8
Memo Fields:	Automatic width of 10

> *The width of 10, which is set for Memo Fields, does not mean that there are only 10 spaces available for your memos. You still have 64K of space.*

4. Number of Decimal Places

The decimal column requires an entry only when the field type selected is Numeric. In this column, you will specify the number of decimal places that the numbers in the field will contain.

5. Index Creation

dBASE IV offers the option of creating an index upon a field at the time the field is created. An index is a file that will sort your database upon that field. For example, an index on the CASE_NAME field will order the records alphabetically by case name. We will respond **Y** for yes in the CASE_NAME field to create an index sorting by the names of the cases. Indexes may be created on more than one field. You may also create indexes later through a menu selection.

Enter the fields for the CASELIST database into the Database Design screen.

CASE_NAME	**Character**	**40**	**Y**
CASE_NUMBR	**Character**	**10**	**N**
CLIENT	**Character**	**25**	**N**
SUBJECT	**Memo**	**10**	**N**
DATE_FILED	**Date**	**8**	**N**
RESP_ATTY	**Character**	**4**	**N**
DATE_OPEN	**Date**	**8**	**N**
DATE_CLOSE	**Date**	**8**	**N**

The completed structure should look like Figure 5.6.

6. Saving the Database Structure

To save the Database Structure, press **[Ctrl] + [End],** or with the highlight bar on the blank row beneath your last field, press the **[Enter]** key. You will be prompted for the location and name of the file as shown in Figure 5.7. Type the appropriate drive letter and the file name **CASELIST** and press **[Enter]** (e.g., A:CASELIST).

The file will be placed in the current catalog, and you will be asked if you wish to enter records at this time. Select **No** at this time to return to the Control Center.

As you can see in Figure 5.8, the name of your database file is placed above the line in the Data panel. This means that the file is in use. To close the file, you can highlight its name and press the **[Enter]** key. Select **Close file** from the menu that appears. A closed file is placed below the line as shown in Figure 5.9.

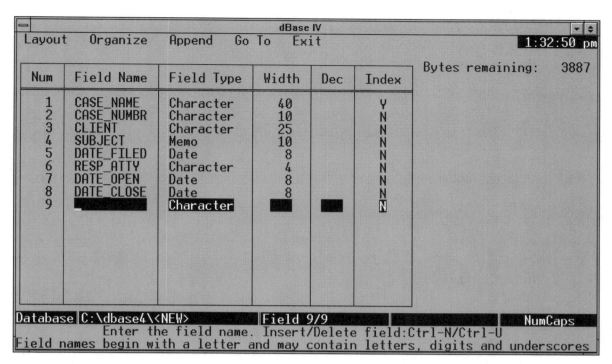

Figure 5.6 The Completed Database Structure

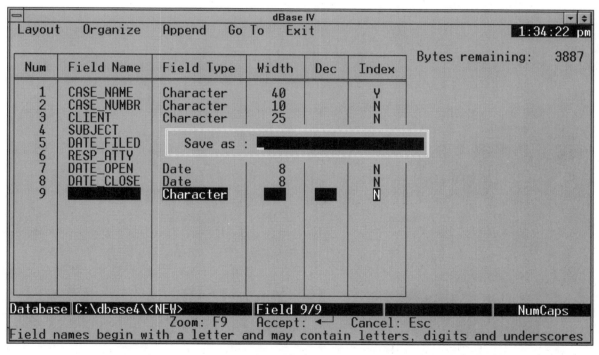

Figure 5.7 Pressing the **[Enter]** key at the blank row prompts you for
the name of the file

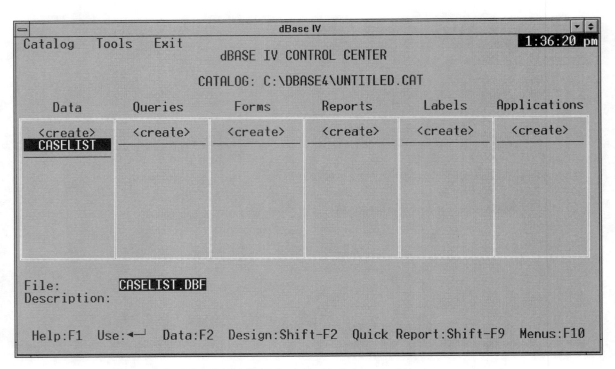

Figure 5.8 The CASELIST database file is in use when its name appears above the line in the Data panel

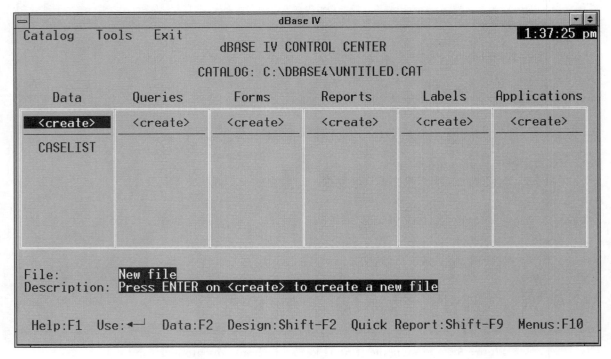

Figure 5.9 A file is closed when its name appears below the line within a panel

To place the file in use again, highlight the file name and press **[Enter].** A screen similar to the Close File screen appears. Select **Use file** to place the file name above the line in the Data panel.

> *When you exit dBASE correctly through the **Exit menu**, or by typing **quit** at the Dot Prompt, dBASE automatically saves your databases. It is not necessary to close your files before you exit.*

H. ENTERING RECORDS

Records may be entered into a database from the **Database Edit screen** or the **Browse screen.**

1. The Database Edit Screen

To enter the first records into your database, make sure that the database file is in use and move to the Edit screen by pressing the **[F2]** (Data) key. The Edit screen displays one record at a time as shown in Figure 5.10.

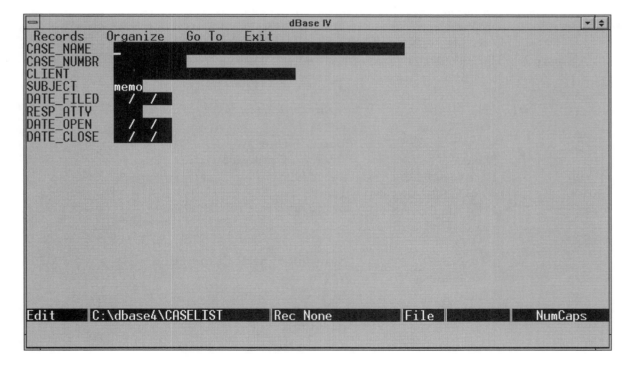

Figure 5.10 The Database Edit Screen

2. Entering the Records

At the Edit screen enter the five records listed below. You can move between fields with the **[Enter]** key and the **[Arrow]** keys. You can move between records with **[Page Up]** and **[Page Down]**.

In the memo field SUBJECT, type a short memo beginning with the words shown for the SUBJECT fields. Entering data into memo fields requires that you move to a screen that will allow you to type up to 64K of data. As you can see in Figure 5.10, when you look at where you enter your records, the SUBJECT field contains the word *memo*. To create the SUBJECT field for each record, follow the steps below.

a) With the highlight bar in the memo field, press the **[F9] (Zoom)** key or **[Ctrl] + [Home]** to get to the Memo Creation screen.

b) Enter a sentence or short paragraph describing the record.

c) Return to the Edit screen by pressing **[Ctrl] + [End],** or leave through the **Exit menu.**

After data has been entered into a memo field, the word *MEMO* will appear in capital letters. This lets you know that there is an entry in the memo field. After data has been entered into a memo field, you may look at the data again at any time with the **[F9]** key, and then leave the memo by again pressing the **[F9]** key. However, if you make any changes, you will want to leave with **[Ctrl] + [End]** or through the **Exit Menu.**

The responsible attorneys in each record are identified by their initials. This is a customary practice in the law office.

The Case Number in Record 4 indicates that this is the first patent we have filed for this corporation. This record is not a court case and will not have a case number.

A completed record is shown in Figure 5.11.

#1	Case Name	**Smith v. Berry**
	Case Number	**80023**
	Client	**Berry, Simon Jr.**
	Subject	**Breach of contract . . .**
	Date Case Filed	**06/24/92**
	Responsible Attorney	**EMD**
	Date File Opened	**04/19/92**
	Date File Closed	

#2	Case Name	**Simpson v. SDF Corporation**
	Case Number	**71176**
	Client	**SDF Corporation**
	Subject	**Wrongful termination . . .**
	Date Case Filed	**04/01/91**
	Responsible Attorney	**DGL**
	Date File Opened	**08/25/90**
	Date File Closed	

#3	Case Name	SDF Corporation v. Terra, Inc.
	Case Number	72587
	Client	SDF Corporation
	Subject	Patent infringement . . .
	Date Case Filed	06/11/91
	Responsible Attorney	DGL
	Date File Opened	11/08/90
	Date File Closed	

#4	Case Name	SDF Corporation—Earth Grinder Patent
	Case Number	1
	Client	SDF Corporation
	Subject	Patent filing . . .
	Date Case Filed	01/23/92
	Responsible Attorney	DGL
	Date File Opened	10/12/91
	Date File Closed	01/01/93

#5	Case Name	Barker v. South Landfill
	Case Number	76645
	Client	South Landfill
	Subject	Injunctive relief . . .
	Date Case Filed	12/15/91
	Responsible Attorney	BBK
	Date File Opened	11/30/91
	Date File Closed	06/20/92

3. The Browse Screen

An alternative to the Edit screen is the Browse screen shown in Figure 5.12. This screen displays multiple records in column form. You may move to the Browse screen from the Edit screen (after you have entered at least one record) by pressing the **[F2]** key.

The **[Tab]** and **[Shift]** + **[Tab]** keys will move the highlight bar between the fields. The **[F2]** key will toggle you back and forth between the Edit and Browse screens. You may enter and edit records in either screen.

4. Saving the Records

To save the database records, press **[Ctrl]** + **[End]** or return to the Control Center through the **Exit menu,** (**[Alt]** + **[E]**), and select **Exit.**

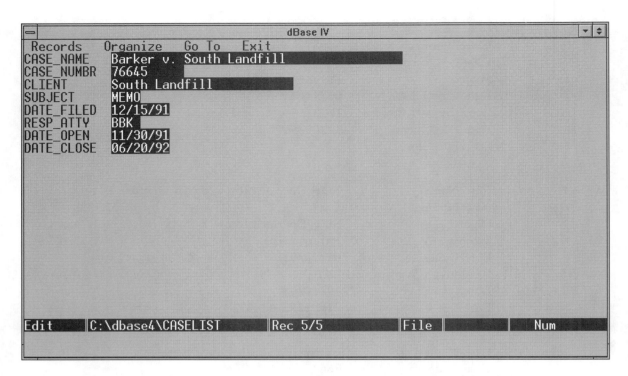

Figure 5.11   A record displayed in the Edit screen

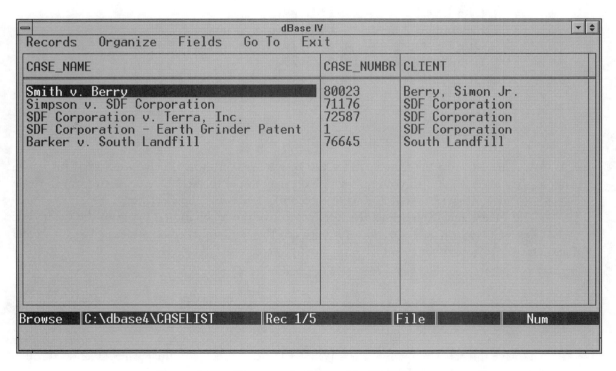

Figure 5.12   The records displayed in the Browse screen

5. Looking at the Records

From the Control Center the records of a database may be viewed at any time by highlighting the database name and pressing the **[F2]** key. Once in the Edit or Browse screens, the **[F2]** key will toggle back and forth between them. To return to the **Control Center,** you may press the **[Esc]** key if you have not altered any records. If you have altered the records, exit through the **Exit menu.**

I. DELETING RECORDS

Deleting records is a two-step process. First, you must mark the record for deletion, and then you must delete it. The two steps act as a safety measure to prevent accidental deletions.

It is easiest to delete records from the Browse screen. To get to the Browse screen from the Control Center, press the **[F2]** key once or twice.

1. Marking a Record

To mark a record for deletion, highlight the record to be deleted in the Browse screen, and follow the steps below.

a) Access the **Records menu** using the **[F10]** key or **[ALT] + [R].**

b) Select **Mark the record for deletion.** The Status Bar will indicate that this record is marked for deletion.

> *You can also remove the deletion mark in the Records Menu.*

2. Deleting the Record

Permanently removing the marked record(s) from your database is called packing. You pack (erase) the marked records by following the steps below.

a) Access the **Organize menu.**

b) Select **Erase Marked Records.** dBASE will ask you if you are sure you wish to delete this record. Normally you will say "yes," but if you are following along with this chapter, say "no" so that you may keep all of the records.

To remove the deletion mark from the marked record, open the **Records Menu** and select **Clear deletion mark.**

Return to the **Control Center** through the **Exit Menu.**

J. CHANGING THE DATABASE DESIGN

If you find that you need to add or alter a field in your database, you need to change the database design. To change the database design, you must return to the Database Design screen where we entered the field specifics of the database.

From the Control Center, move to the database design screen by pressing **[Shift] + [F2]** (Design). The **Organize menu** is automatically opened. You do not need to use this menu, so press the **[Esc]** key to back out of it. We will change the width of the CASE_NAME field to **45.**

Using the **[Arrow]** keys and the **[Tab]** and **[Shift] + [Tab],** you can move around in this screen and make any necessary changes. Move to the width column of the CASE_NAME field, type in the new width, and press **[Enter].**

Save this change by exiting through the **Exit menu** and selecting **Save Changes and Exit.** Answer **Yes** at the prompt.

To insert a new field, use **[Ctrl] + [N].** To delete a field, use **[Ctrl] + [U].**

K. SEARCHING THE DATABASE

A search within a database is called a query. Queries are instructions to dBASE requesting records that fit certain criteria. For example, we could request a list of all cases in our CASELIST database where DGL is the responsible attorney.

dBASE IV uses a query design method called QBE or "Query by Example."

To develop a query, the database file you are querying must be in use (above the line) in the Data panel. With the database in use, move the highlight bar to the **Queries panel** and select **<create>.** dBASE will take you to the **Query Design screen** shown in Figure 5.13.

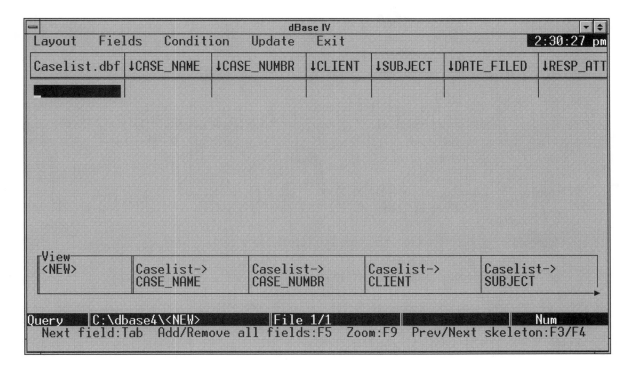

Figure 5.13 The Query Design Screen

1. The File Skeleton and View Skeleton

The top of the **Query Design screen** is called the **file skeleton.** The bottom of the screen is called the **view skeleton.**

The **file skeleton** is where you request particular items from the database. The **view skeleton** is where you can limit the fields that are displayed in the query results. For example, if you wanted to see a list of case names and the dates they were filed, you could select only these two fields for viewing by eliminating the other fields from the view skeleton.

The **[F3]** and **[F4]** keys will move you back and forth between the file and view skeletons.

2. Query By Example (QBE)

The file skeleton is used to search for items within your database. Each of the database fields is displayed in the file skeleton. To perform a query, use the **[Tab]** and **[Shift] + [Tab]** keys to move to the field column (field box) in which you desire to search.

The **field box** is where you enter a search condition for a particular field. There are different rules for how you enter a query into a field box depending on the type of field you are querying.

Character	Items to be searched for within a Character field must be enclosed within quotation marks.

"DGL"

dBASE will search for an entry in the queried field exactly as it is typed within the quotation marks. For example, **"dgl"** will not find **"DGL".** This is why it is important that the persons entering records into the database enter them in a uniform manner (e.g., all caps, no caps, or initial caps).

Numeric	Numbers to be searched for within a Numeric field do not require quotation marks or any other qualification.

153

Float	Float fields are searched in the same manner as Numeric fields.

176.453

Date	When searching a Date field, the date must be enclosed within curly braces "{ }."

{12/05/78}

Logical	Logical fields may only contain **T** or **F, Y** or **N,** or some other either/or combination. Searches for any one of these letters within a Logical field requires that the letter appear between two periods.

.T.

Memo	Searches may be performed on Memo fields using a **condition box** and the **$** (containing) operator.

$ "Construction defect"

The following search will demonstrate a search within a Character field. Perform the search on the CASELIST database.

SEARCH #1:   All cases where DGL is the responsible attorney.

To search for **DGL** in the **Responsible Attorney** field:

• Tab to the **RESP_ATTY** field box.

• Type **"DGL"** and press **[Enter].** The entry will look like the one in Figure 5.14.

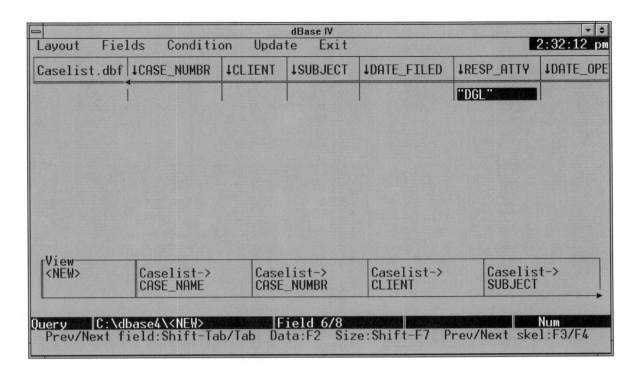

Figure 5.14 Entering a query in the RESP_ATTY field

- Press the **[F2]** (Data) key to process the query.

The results of your query will appear in the Edit or Browse screen depending on the screen in which you last viewed your records. The **[F2]** key will take you to the Browse screen if you are in the Edit screen. The **[Tab]** and **[Shift]** + **[Tab]** keys will move you between the field columns. The results viewed in the Browse screen should look like Figure 5.15. When you are finished viewing the records, return to the query design screen by pressing **[Shift]** + **[F2]** (Design).

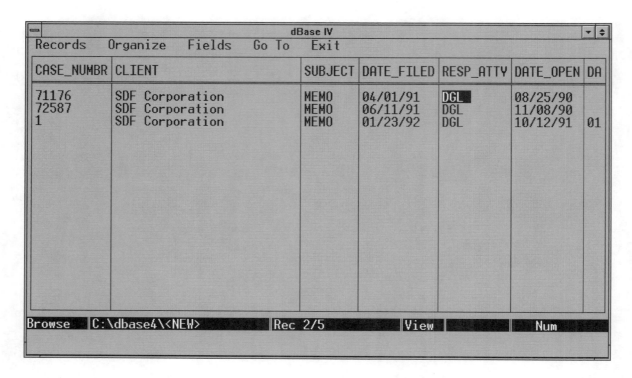

Figure 5.15 The results of the query search for DGL with the RESP_ATTY field

3. Using Relational Operators

The relational operators used in dBASE IV are:

=	**Equals**
>	**Greater than**
<	**Less than**
>=	**Greater than or equal to**
<=	**Less than or equal to**
<> or #	**Not equal to**
$	**Containing**
Like	**Word search using wildcard characters**
Sounds Like	**Search for words with similar sounds**

We will perform the following search using a relational operator.

SEARCH #2: All cases filed on or after January 1, 1992.

To look within our database for all of the cases that have been filed since the beginning of 1992, we will use the greater than or equal to operator (**>=**) in the **DATE_FILED** field box.

- Remove "**DGL**" from the **RESP_ATTY** field box by pressing **[Ctrl] + [Y]**.

- Use **[Shift] + [Tab]** to move back to the **DATE_FILED** field.

- In the **DATE_FILED** field type **>= {01/01/92}** and press the **[Enter]** key. Your entry should look like the one shown in Figure 5.16.

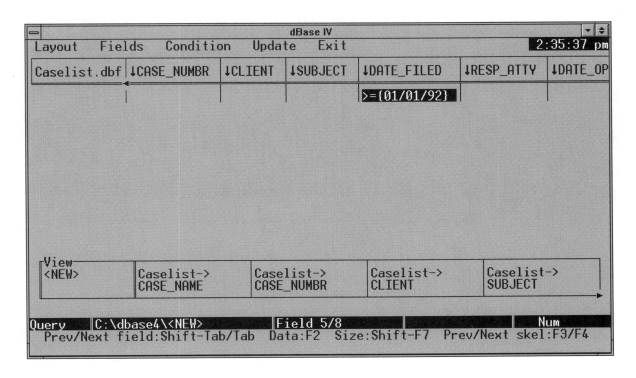

Figure 5.16   A Date Search

- Press the **[F2]** (Data) key to process the query. The query results are shown in Figure 5.17.

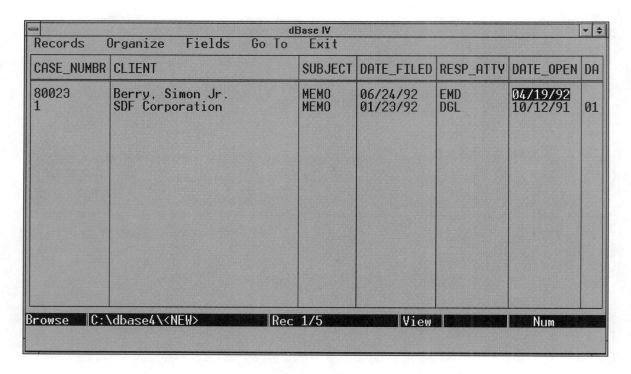

Figure 5.17 The query results in the Browse screen

- Return to the Query Design screen by pressing **[Shift] + [F2].**

4. Combining Searches Using Connectors

The **AND** and **OR** connectors are represented in Query By Example by constructing AND queries along the same row, and placing OR queries in separate rows. When AND queries are within the same field box, the entries are separated by commas.

> **SEARCH #3:** **All cases filed on or after January 1, 1992, where the responsible attorney is DGL.**

To search for all cases filed after 01/01/92 where the Responsible Attorney is DGL, we would construct an **AND** query as follows:

- Leave the previous query as constructed in the **DATE_FILED** field.

- Tab to the **RESP_ATTY** field, and in the first row type **"DGL"** and press the **[Enter]** key. Your query should look like the one in Figure 5.18.

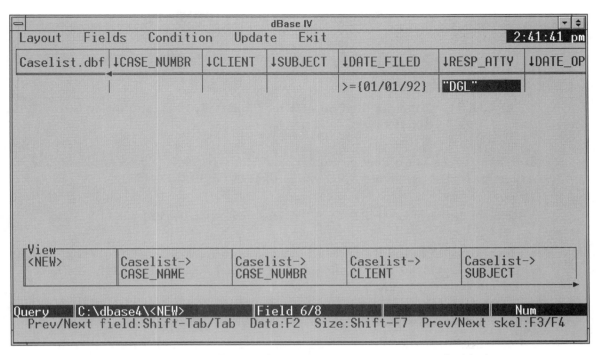

Figure 5.18 A search using the AND connector is constructed with the conditions in the same row

- Press the **[F2] (Data)** key to process the query. The query results are shown in Figure 5.19.

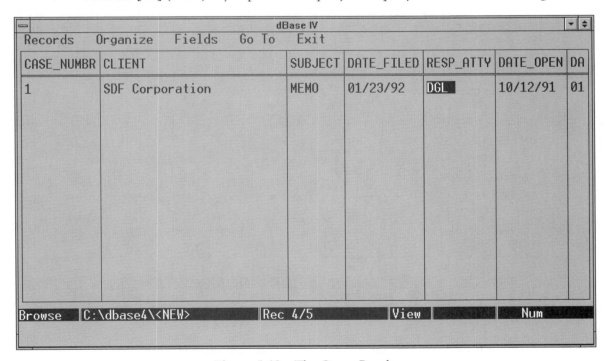

Figure 5.19 The Query Results

• Return to the Query Design screen with **[Shift] + [F2]** (Design).

Constructing a query with the AND connector in the same field box is demonstrated in Search #4.

SEARCH #4: All cases filed on or after January 1, 1992, and on or before June 30, 1992.

If we wish to see all the cases filed on or after January 1, 1992, and on or before June 30, 1992, a comma is used to indicate **AND** within the **DATE_FILED** field box.

• Remove the entry in the **RESP_ATTY** field with **[Ctrl] + [Y].**

• Move to the **DATE_FILED** field and add a **comma** after **> = {01/01/92}.** Without spacing, add **< = {06/30/92}** and press the **[Enter]** key. Your query should look like the one shown in Figure 5.20.

• Press the **[F2]** (Data) key to process the query. The query results are shown in Figure 5.21.

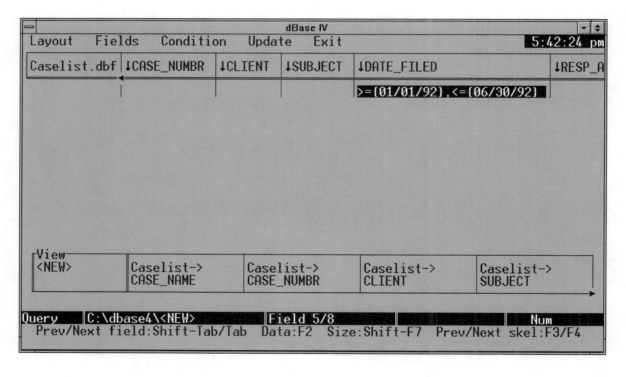

Figure 5.20 To use the AND connector within a field box, the query conditions are separated with a comma

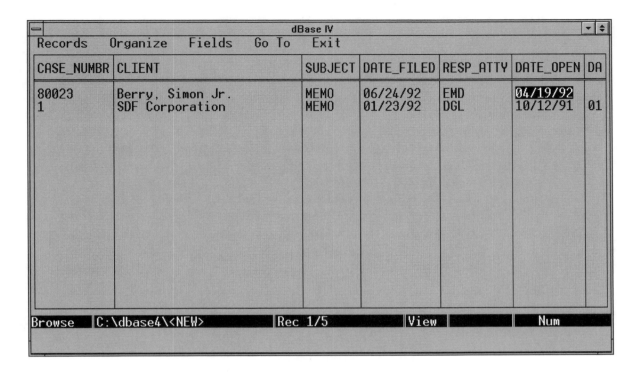

Figure 5.21 The Query Results

- Return to the Query Design screen with **[Shift] + [F2]** (Design).

A query using the OR connector is demonstrated in Search #5.

SEARCH #5: **All cases where the responsible attorney is DGL OR EMD.**

To construct a query using OR, the entries are placed in separate rows. For example, if we wish to see all cases where the responsible attorney is **DGL** or **EMD** we follow the steps below.

- Remove the entry in the **DATE_FILED** field box with **[Ctrl] + [Y].**

- Move to the **RESP_ATTY** field and type **"EMD"**; press the **[Down Arrow]** key and type **"DGL"** in the row below **"EMD"**; then, press the **[Enter]** key. The query should look like the one in Figure 5.22.

- Press the **[F2]** (Data) key to process the query. The query results are shown in Figure 5.23.

- Return to the Query Design screen with **[Shift] + [F2]** (Design).

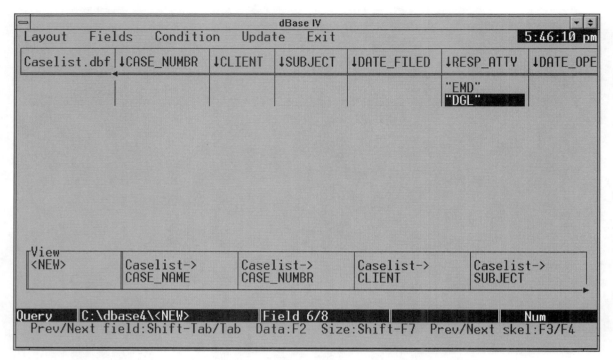

Figure 5.22 The OR connector is used by placing query conditions in separate rows

```
━━━━━━━━━━━━━━━━━━━━━━━━━━━━━━━━━━ dBase IV ━━━━━━━━━━━━━━━━━━━━━━━━━ ▼ ◆
 Records    Organize    Fields    Go To   Exit
┌──────────┬───────────────────────────┬─────────┬───────────┬──────────┬──────────┬────┐
│CASE_NUMBR│CLIENT                     │SUBJECT  │DATE_FILED │RESP_ATTY │DATE_OPEN │DA  │
├──────────┼───────────────────────────┼─────────┼───────────┼──────────┼──────────┼────┤
│80023     │Berry, Simon Jr.          │MEMO     │06/24/92   │ EMD      │04/19/92  │    │
│71176     │SDF Corporation           │MEMO     │04/01/91   │DGL       │08/25/90  │    │
│72587     │SDF Corporation           │MEMO     │06/11/91   │DGL       │11/08/90  │    │
│1         │SDF Corporation           │MEMO     │01/23/92   │DGL       │10/12/91  │01  │
│          │                          │         │           │          │          │    │


 Browse    C:\dbase4\<NEW>        Rec 1/5          View            Num
```

Figure 5.23 The Query Results

5. Querying a Memo Field

Since a Memo field may contain up to 64K of data, a query is performed using a condition box and the $ (containing) operator.

SEARCH #6:   All records that contain the words "Breach of contract" within the SUBJECT field.

Follow the steps below to create a query searching for the words **"Breach of contract"** within the **SUBJECT field.**

- Remove the entries from the **RESP_ATTY** field box with **[Ctrl] + [Y].**

- Access the **Condition menu** with **[Alt] + [C]** and select **Add condition box.** A condition box will appear in the lower right-hand corner of the screen as shown in Figure 5.24.

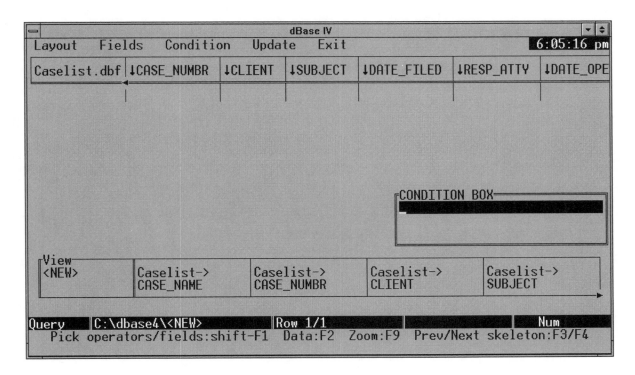

Figure 5.24   A Condition Box

- In the condition box, the query of the **SUBJECT** field is formulated by typing the text to be located, followed by the **$** (containing) operator, and then the name of the field ("Breach of contract"$SUBJECT). Press **[Enter]** to check the syntax of the query. The query entered in the condition box is shown in Figure 5.25.

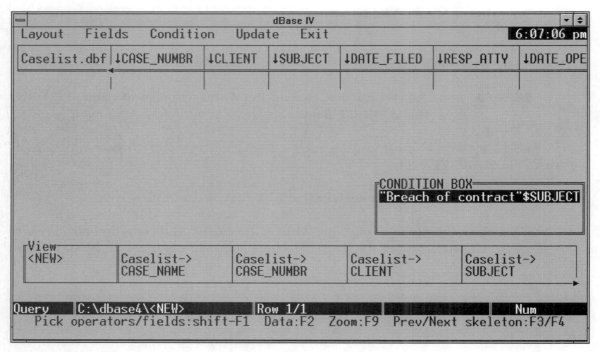

Figure 5.25 A query of the memo field, SUBJECT, using a condition box and the containing operator ($)

• Press **[F2]** to process the query. The query results are shown in Figure 5.26.

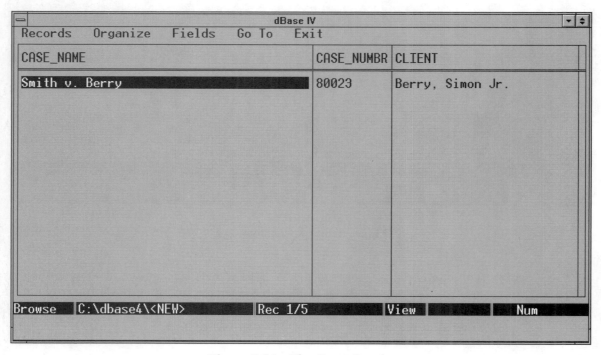

Figure 5.26 The Query Results

- Tabbing to the memo field (SUBJECT) in the search results and pressing **[F9]** will display the contents of the memo as shown in Figure 5.27. You may leave the memo by pressing **[F9]** again.

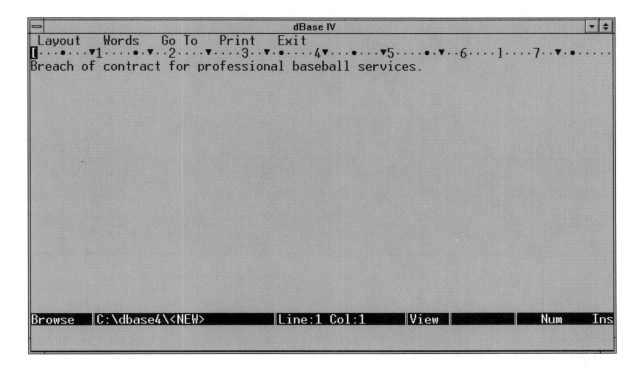

Figure 5.27   The memo containing the words *breach of contract*

- Return to the Query Design screen with **[Shift] + [F2]** (Design).

- Remove the condition box by accessing the **Condition menu** and selecting **Delete condition box.**

The containing operator may also be used within a field box.

SEARCH #7:   Locate all cases where SDF Corporation is a party.

We will conduct this search using the containing operator ($) to search for **"SDF"** within the **CASE_NAME** field.

- In the **CASE_NAME** field box, enter **$"SDF"** as shown in Figure 5.28 and press **[Enter].**

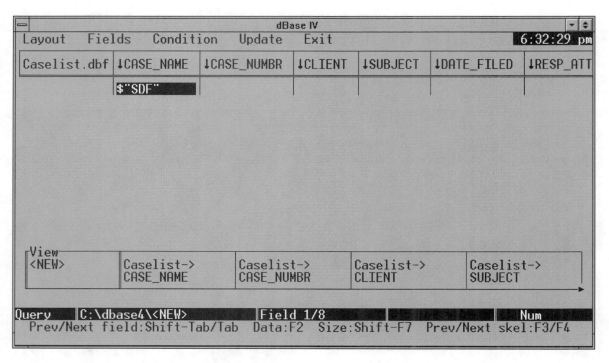

Figure 5.28   A search using the containing operator within a field box

• Press **[F2]** to process the query. The query results are shown in Figure 5.29.

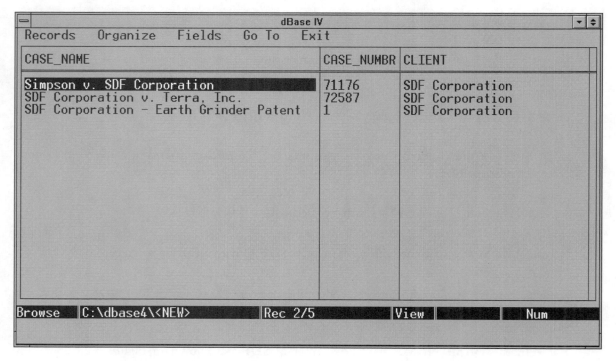

Figure 5.29   The results containing SDF in the CASE_NAME field

dBASE IV® for DOS

- Press **[Shift] + [F2]** to return to the Query Design screen and use **[Ctrl] + [Y]** to erase the field entry in the **CASE_NAME** field.

6. View Queries

The lower half of the Query Design screen, the view skeleton, is used to limit the fields that will be displayed in the query results. For example, we might want to see a list of all of the firm's cases and their responsible attorneys. For this query, we will want to view all of the records, but only the **CASE_NAME** and **RESP_ATTY** fields.

To remove unwanted fields from the view skeleton, use the **[Tab]** and **[Shift] + [Tab]** keys *in the file skeleton* to move to the field names to be removed. Press the **[F5]** key to remove them from the view skeleton. If you remove the wrong field, highlight the field name again and press **[F5].** This will put the field back. You may remove or replace all of the fields by moving to the Caselist.dbf box and pressing **[F5].**

For our view query example, follow the steps below.

- Move to the **Caselist.dbf** box and press **[F5].** This will remove all of the fields from the view skeleton.

- Move to the **CASE_NAME** field and press **[F5].**

- Move to the **RESP_ATTY** field and press **[F5].**

Your view skeleton should now contain only the **CASE_NAME** and **RESP_ATTY** fields as shown in Figure 5.30.

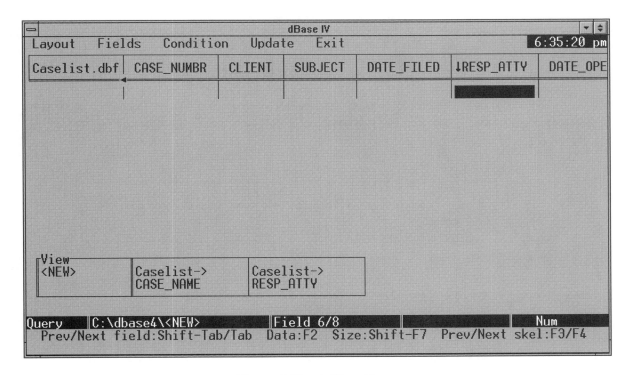

Figure 5.30 A View Query

• Process the query by pressing the **[F2]** key. The query results are shown in Figure 5.31.

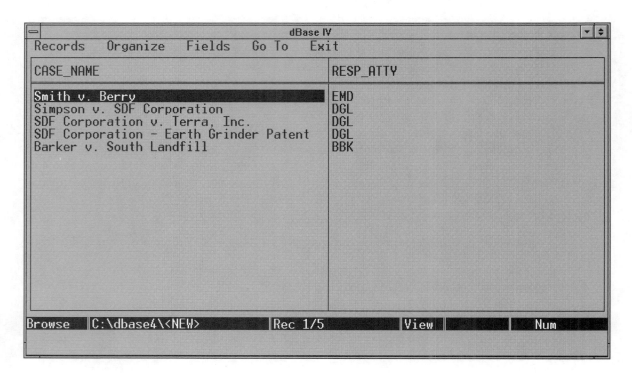

Figure 5.31   The Query Results

• Return to the Query Design screen using **[Shift] + [F2]** (Design).

Exit the Query Design screen through the **Exit menu** using **[Alt] + [E]**, select **Abandon changes and exit,** and respond **yes** when asked if you are sure. You will return to the Control Center.

> *If you wanted to save a query file, you would select* ***Save changes and exit*** *from this* ***Exit menu.***

L.   SORTING AND INDEXING

Most records within a database file have not been entered in any particular order. There are two ways to reorder your records, **Sorting** and **Indexing.**

Sorting creates a *new database file* with the records rearranged in the order you have specified. Therefore, you will have a database file with your records in the order in which they were entered, and another with the records in the sorted order.

Indexing is the fastest and most efficient way to reorder. Indexing creates an index file that tells dBASE how to order the data in your database file. The original database remains intact. You may have up to 47 different indexes for each database.

1.   Sorting

To Sort a file, highlight the file name in the Data panel of the Control Center and press **[Shift] + [F2]** (Design). At the **Database Design** screen, the **Organize menu** will automatically be opened for you. Select **Sort Database on Field List** and you will reach the **Sort** box shown in Figure 5.32.

To create a new database, with the CASELIST records ordered alphabetically by the name of the case, we will sort the database on the **CASE_NAME** field. The steps below will accomplish the sort and save our new sorted database as **CASES**.

- Enter the field name to sort upon, **CASE_NAME,** in the field order column and press **[Enter].**

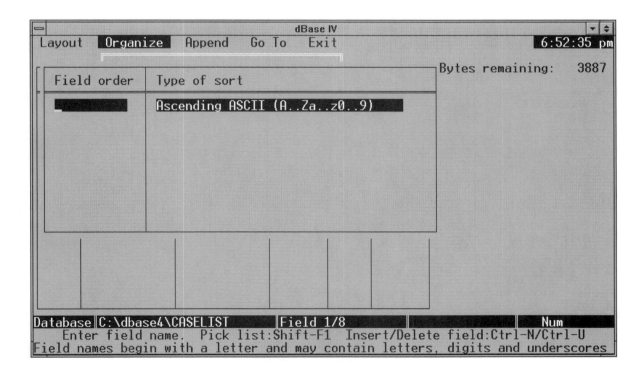

Figure 5.32   The Sort Box

> *If you cannot remember the exact name of your field, [Shift] + [F1] will give you a list of your fields and allow you to highlight your field name and select it with the [Enter] key.*

- In the **Type of Sort Box,** toggle the four available ordering options with the **[Space Bar]** until you reach **Ascending Dictionary,** and press **[Enter].** Your screen should now look like the one in Figure 5.33.

- If you wanted to sort on further criteria (e.g., if you had a LAST_NAME field and a FIRST_NAME field), you could add another field name on the next line.

  We do not wish to sort on any other fields, so press the **[Enter]** key at the blank second line and you will be prompted for a database name for the sorted file. Save the sorted file as **CASES** (or A:CASES or B:CASES). dBASE will then prompt for a description of the file. You can enter one if you wish and/or press **[Enter]** to return to the database design screen.

- **Exit** to the **Control Center** through the **Exit menu** selecting **Save changes and exit.** Press **[Enter]** to confirm the exit.

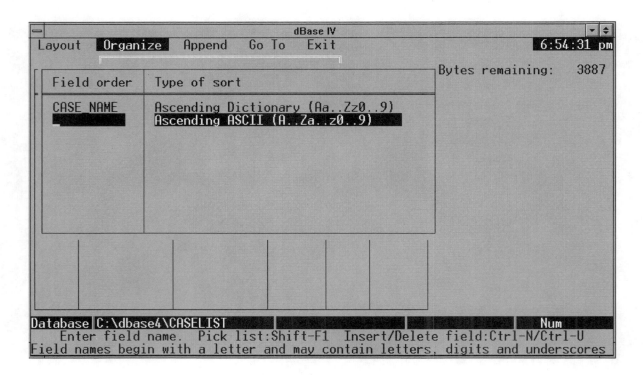

Figure 5.33 A sort on the CASE_NAME field

The new database file is placed in the Data panel as shown in Figure 5.34. The CASELIST database has the records in the original order. The CASES database has the records ordered by the name of the case.

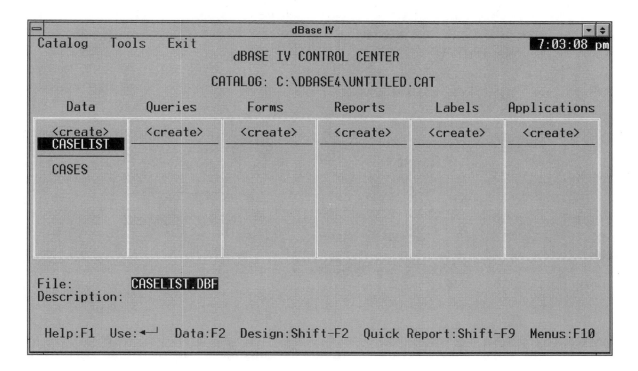

Figure 5.34 The new database, CASES, is placed below the line in the Data panel

To see the sorted records in the CASES database, highlight **CASES,** press the **[Enter]** key twice to place it in use, and press **[F2].** The records will be displayed in the Browse or Edit screen. To toggle between the screens use **[F2].** The records in the Browse screen are shown in Figure 5.35.

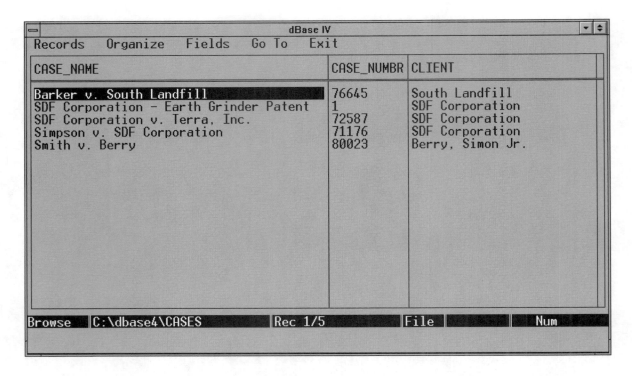

Figure 5.35 The records within the sorted database, CASES

Exit to the **Control Center** through the **Exit menu** and place the CASELIST database back in use by highlighting it and pressing the **[Enter]** key twice.

2. Indexing

Indexing is the fastest and most efficient way to reorder your records. You use the original database file and create indexes according to ways you desire to see your records. The selected index file temporarily reorders your records. The records retain their original record number.

You can create indexes at the time you design the database by typing a **Y** in the Index Column, or you can create an index manually. You may create up to 47 indexes on a single database, and you can index query files as well as database files.

The main advantage of an index over a sort is that when you add new records to your database, and it is indexed, the records will automatically be placed in the proper order. If we added a new record to the sorted CASES database, we would have to resort it and create an entirely new database to place the record in the correct order.

We created an automatic index on the **CASE_NAME** field when we created the CASELIST database. The steps below will create a new index that can order the records by the date filed.

- From the **Control Center,** highlight the database name (**CASELIST**) and press **[Shift] + [F2]** (Design).

- In the **Organize menu, Create new index** is highlighted. Press **[Enter]** to select this option. The **Index box** shown in Figure 5.36 will appear. To make entries into the items in the Index box, you need to move to an item and press **[Enter]** to open it to receive the entry.

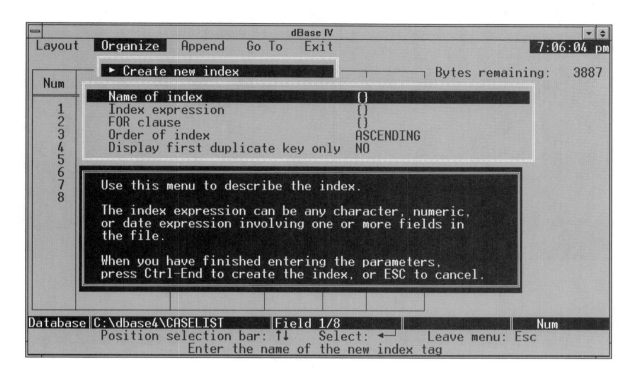

Figure 5.36   The Index Box

- With the **Name of index** box highlighted, press **[Enter]** to open it to receive data. We will name this Index file **BYDATE** since we will be ordering the records on the Date field. Type **BYDATE** and press **[Enter].**

- Open the **Index expression** box by highlighting it and pressing **[Enter].** This is where you place the name of the field you wish to index on. Assuming that we cannot remember the name of our Date field, press **[Shift] + [F1]** (Pick) to see a list of the fields as shown in Figure 5.37.

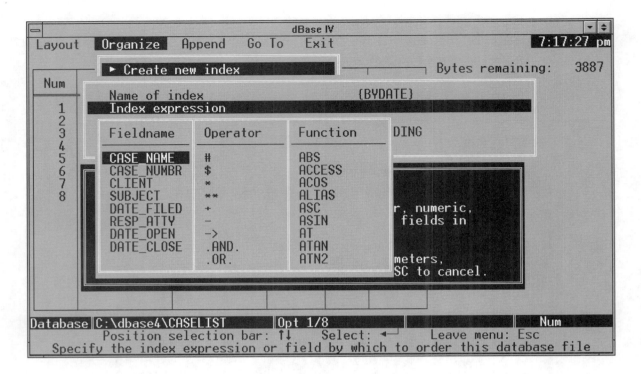

Figure 5.37 The Pick List of Field Names

- Highlight the name of the Date Filed field in the pick list, **DATE_FILED,** and press **[Enter].** Press **[Enter]** again to complete the entry.

We are creating a simple index, so we have entered all that is needed. The screen should look like the one in Figure 5.38.

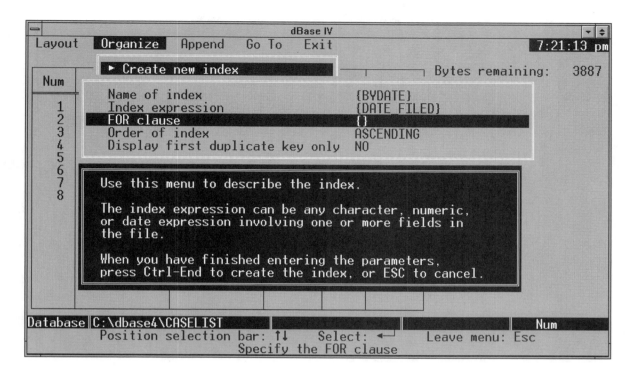

Figure 5.38 The creation of an index on the DATE_FILED field

- To complete the index creation, press **[Ctrl] + [End].** You will be returned to the Database Design screen.

- Exit to the Control Center through the **Exit menu** with **[Alt] + [E].** Select **Save changes and exit,** and press the **[Enter]** key to confirm.

To see the records as they are now indexed by date, make sure the CASELIST database name is highlighted and press **[F2].** Look at the DATE_FILED field and you will see that the cases are now ordered by the date filed. After looking at your records, press the **[Esc]** key to return to the Control Center.

To change to another index, move to the Database Design screen from the Control Center by pressing **[Shift] + [F2].** The **Organize menu** is automatically opened. Select **Order records by index.** The indexes that have been created for this database will appear at the right of the screen. Natural Order is the order in which the records were entered. Any index may be selected by highlighting its name and pressing **[Enter].** Highlight the **CASE_NAME** index as shown in Figure 5.39 and press **[Enter].** You will be returned to the Database Design screen. You may press **[F2]** at the Database Design screen to see the new order of your database.

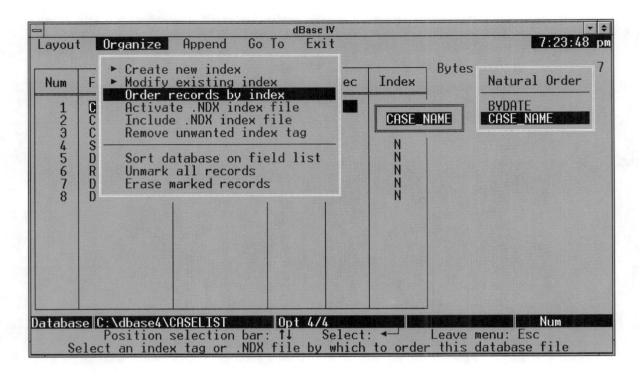

Figure 5.39 The indexes for the CASELIST database

Return to the Control Center through the **Exit menu,** selecting **Exit.**

M. PRINTING A DATABASE

You may print the contents of a database file or a query file using a Quick Report option or by creating a Report.

1. Quick Report

To receive a quick printout of your database, or the results of a query, you can use **[Shift] + [F9]** (Quick Report). The results of a Quick Report may be unformatted and difficult to read.

To perform a Quick Report from the Control Center, highlight the database or query file name, press **[Shift] + [F9]** and select **Begin printing.** Be patient; it can take more than a few moments for dBASE to process the report.

2. Creating a Report

For a simple report that will display your data in a readable fashion, create a report in the **Reports panel** of the Control Center using the **Quick Layouts** option. To create a Report on a database file, the database file name must be above the line in the Data panel. For a Report on a query, the query file name must be above the line in the Query panel.

The following steps will create the Report.

a) From the **Control Center,** move the highlight bar to the **Reports panel,** highlight **<create>,** and press **[Enter].**

b) The **Layout menu** is automatically opened and **Quick layouts** is highlighted. Select **Quick layouts.**

c) At the sub-menu of **Quick layouts,** select **Form layout.** The screen shown in Figure 5.40 will appear. Each field name is accompanied by a field length containing an indication of the type of data contained within the field. As you get more experienced with dBASE IV, you can try altering the field names and lengths, and adding headings, in the Report.

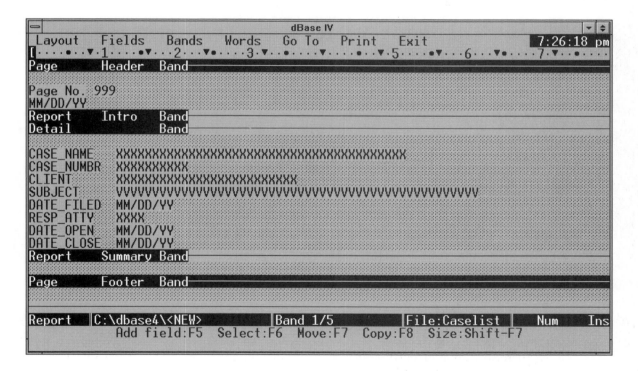

Figure 5.40   The Form Layout Design

d) To print the Report, access the **Print menu** with **[Alt] + [P]** and select **Begin printing.** Your Report will appear similar to the one shown in Figure 5.41.

e) Exit to the Control Center through the **Exit menu** with **[Alt] + [E].** You may save the Report form and give it a name or select **Abandon changes and exit** and confirm with a **Y** for yes.

N. EXITING dBASE

To leave the dBASE program, access the **Exit Menu** with **[Alt] + [E]** and select **Quit to DOS.** If you accidentally exit to the Dot Prompt, type **quit** to exit.

O. THE DOT PROMPT COMMANDS

The same tasks that are performed in the Control Center can be performed using the Dot Prompt. In fact, when you become more familiar with dBASE, you may prefer the Dot Prompt. Go to the Dot Prompt from the Control Center through the Exit menu. The Dot Prompt commands are listed here for reference purposes. You can move from the Control Center to the Dot Prompt at any time when you are working with a database to try some of these commands. To return to the Control Center from the Dot Prompt, press **[F2].**

1. Creating a Database File

To create the database file CASELIST: **CREATE C:CASELIST.**

The same Create screen that you see in the Control Center will be displayed. Fields are entered in the same manner and saved with **[Ctrl] + [End].**

2. Using a Database File

To place the CASELIST file in use: **USE C:CASELIST.**

3. Entering Records

Enter records by typing **APPEND.**

Save the records with **[Ctrl] + [End].** View the records with **LIST.**

```
Page No.     1
05/20/97

CASE_NAME    Barker v. South Landfill
CASE_NUMBR   76645
CLIENT       South Landfill
SUBJECT      Injunctive relief sought by our client against
             Barker Builders.
DATE_FILED   12/15/91
RESP_ATTY    BBK
DATE_OPEN    11/30/91
DATE_CLOSE   06/20/92

CASE_NAME    SDF Corporation - Earth Grinder Patent
CASE_NUMBR   1
CLIENT       SDF Corporation
SUBJECT      Patent filing for the Earth Grinder automatic
             rototilling machine.
DATE_FILED   01/23/92
RESP_ATTY    DGL
DATE_OPEN    10/12/91
DATE_CLOSE   01/01/93

CASE_NAME    SDF Corporation v. Terra, Inc.
CASE_NUMBR   72587
CLIENT       SDF Corporation
SUBJECT      Patent infringement on the soil digger patent.
DATE_FILED   06/11/91
RESP_ATTY    DGL
DATE_OPEN    11/08/90
DATE_CLOSE     /  /

CASE_NAME    Simpson v. SDF Corporation
CASE_NUMBR   71176
CLIENT       SDF Corporation
SUBJECT      Wrongfull termination brought by former employee.
DATE_FILED   04/01/91
RESP_ATTY    DGL
DATE_OPEN    08/25/90
DATE_CLOSE     /  /

CASE_NAME    Smith v. Berry
CASE_NUMBR   80023
CLIENT       Berry, Simon Jr.
SUBJECT      Breach of contract for professional baseball
             services.
DATE_FILED   06/24/92
RESP_ATTY    EMD
DATE_OPEN    04/19/92
DATE_CLOSE     /  /
```

Figure 5.41   A Report created with the Form Layout

4. Editing Records

You can edit records by typing **APPEND, EDIT,** or **BROWSE. [Ctrl] + [End]** will save the changes.

5. Deleting Records

As in the Assistant, deleting records is a two-step process. You must first mark the record for deletion and then pack the database. To mark a record for deletion, type **DELETE RECORD n** (where **n** is the number of the record). Typing **LIST** will list the records and display the deletion mark (*). if you have many records, use **DISPLAY ALL.** To complete the deletion, type **PACK.** Type **LIST** again to view the results.

6. Changing the Database Structure

You may change the structure of your database by typing:

MODIFY STRUCTURE

[Ctrl] + [End] will save the changes.

You may list the structure of your database by typing:

LIST STRUCTURE

You may print a list of the structure by typing:

LIST STRUCTURE TO PRINTER

7. Listing Records

You may list your records in the following ways:

LIST	Lists all records
LIST RECORD n	Lists a specific record number
LIST NEXT n	Lists the next **n** number of records
LIST REST	List the remaining records
LIST CASE_NAME, CLIENT	Lists specific fields

LIST FOR RESP_ATTY = "DGL"   Lists records that meet specific criteria

LIST FOR DATE_FILED >= CTOD("01/01/92")

Lists for specific criteria in a date field. The required elements are **CTOD("MM/DD/YY")**.

LIST FOR DATE_FILED >= CTOD("01/01/92") .AND. RESP_ATTY = "DGL"

Lists for specific criteria using the AND connector. Note that the connector must be contained in periods.

8. Displaying Records

Display is performed in much the same manner as List. However, the display will pause with each full screen of records. Some examples of its use are:

> **DISPLAY ALL**
> **DISPLAY RECORD n**
> **DISPLAY NEXT n**
> **DISPLAY REST**

9. Sorting

To perform a sort and create the new sorted file, you use the following command demonstrated with the CASE_NAME field creating a new file named BYCASE:

> **SORT ON CASE_NAME TO C:BYCASE**

If you were sorting on more than one field, the field names would be separated by commas.

> **SORT ON RESP_ATTY, CASE_NAME TO C:BYATTY**

10. Indexing

To index a file, the following command is used:

> **INDEX ON CASE_NAME TO C:BYCASE**

If indexing on more than one field, the field names are separated with the + symbol.

> **INDEX ON RESP_ATTY + CASE_NAME TO C:BYATTY**

To place a the CASELIST database file in use with the BYATTY index, type:

USE C:CASELIST INDEX BYATTY

11. Printing

To route lists and other displays to the printer, add the following to the end of the command:

TO PRINTER

To create a customized report named CASEREP, you can get to the screen where reports are created by typing:

CREATE REPORT C:CASEREP

12. Exiting dBASE

To exit dBASE from the Dot Prompt, type **QUIT**.

Summary

dBASE is a summary database program that keeps records of data within a file. There are two ways to work with dBASE, from the Control Center and from the Dot Prompt. The beginning user should use the Control Center.

The Control Center consists of a menu bar, a catalog identifier, a list of special keys, and six data panels. The data panels display the files that have been created. A file can be put in use by highlighting the file name and pressing the **[Enter]** key twice to place it above the line in the panel. The data within the file can be viewed by pressing the **[F2]** key.

There are two screens in which you may view your data, the Edit screen and the Browse screen. The Edit screen displays one record at a time. The Browse screen displays multiple records at once. The **[F2]** key toggles between these two screens. To return to the Control Center, press the **[Esc]** key or exit through the menu if you have made changes.

When creating a new database, you must designate the fields, the field types, their widths, the number of decimal places (numeric fields only), and whether you would like an index created on the field. After you have created the database, you may enter your records.

Databases may be ordered by sorting or indexing. Sorting creates a new database file with the records sorted in the requested order. Indexing creates an index file that may be used at any time on your database. You may have up to 47 separate index files for a single database.

To search for records within a database, you develop a query in the Query Design screen. The Query Design screen is divided into two parts, the file skeleton and the view skeleton. The file skeleton is where you place your search conditions. The view skeleton lets you select particular fields to be displayed in your query results.

A database or query may be printed using the **[Shift] + [F9]** (Quick Report) keys, or by creating a Report in the Reports Panel of the Control Center.

Dot Prompt Command List

This is just a partial list of the Dot Prompt commands available in dBASE. A full list of commands can be found by typing **help.**

APPEND	To add records to the database file.
ASSIST	To go back to the Control Center from the dot prompt.
AVERAGE	Computes the average of specified numeric fields.
BROWSE	Allows full screen menu editing of several records.
CLEAR	Erases the screen.
CLEAR ALL	Closes all open database files.
COUNT	Counts the number of records in a database file that meet a specific condition.
CREATE	Lets you establish a new database.
DELETE	Marks a record for removal from a file.
DELETE FILE	Removes a specific database file from the directory.
DIR	Displays the disk directory.
DISPLAY	Lists the current record.
EDIT	Full-screen editor to change contents of fields and records.
ERASE	Deletes a specified file from the directory and catalog.
GO/GOTO	Followed by a record number, this command moves you to a specific record.

GO BOTTOM	Moves to the last record in the file.
GO TOP	Moves to the first record in the file.
INDEX	Creates an index file that causes the contents of the database file to be displayed as if rearranged based on the specified field, although the data remains in the original record number order of the file.
LIST	Displays the contents of a database file.
LOCATE	Searches the database file for the first record that meets specified criteria.
PACK	Permanently removes records marked for deletion.
QUIT	Closes all open files and exits dBASE.
RECALL	Allows records that are marked for deletion to be reinstated.
p RENAME	Changes the name of a file. An open file cannot be renamed.
REPLACE	Replaces the contents of the named field with the desired new contents. Used when the change affects all the records in the database.
REPORT FORM	Displays a tabular report form generated with CREATE/MODIFY REPORT.
SEEK	Conducts a very rapid record search by seeking the first record in an indexed database file with a key that matches the value of the specified expression.
SKIP	Moves the record pointer in an active database file forward or backward a specified number of records.
SORT	Physically reorders records in a database.
SUM	Totals expressions involving numeric fields in the active database file.
USE	Opens a database file. Also simultaneously closes any active database file currently in use.

Chapter Index

CHAPTER 6

WINDOWS SUMMARY DATABASES

Chapter Preface

Summary database programs, sometimes referred to as database management systems (DBMS), allow you to organize documents or items of information for easy retrieval. Windows-based versions of these programs provide an interface that is graphical, colorful, and easy to use. Databases can be set up in these programs to keep track of case evidence, in-house forms, client and case records, calendars, library updates, and many other pieces of information.

In this chapter, we will create a database to keep track of case evidence—an activity often delegated to the paralegal. We will create the database's structure, enter records, perform searches upon the database, and create a report of the results. Corel® Paradox® and Microsoft® Access® will be used to illustrate the features of Windows-based summary databases. At the end of this chapter are several exercises that can be used to practice creating databases.

A. THE DATABASE PROGRAM ENVIRONMENT

A summary database program consists of database files, often called "tables," that contain the records of the database. Each record contains fields of information that the person who created the database determined were the important pieces of information to gather from each item in the database.

The program also contains options to create query files, report files, and form files, and often options to create new software programs using a database programming language. Query files will be created when you want to perform a search on the database table. Report files will be created to see a printout of the database file or a query. Form files will be created if you would like to customize the input screen for the records of the database. Some basics regarding Windows-based summary database programs are explained below.

1. Entering the Application

To enter an application in Windows, double-click on the application's icon. To enter a Windows 95 application, either double-click on its icon on the desktop or click the Start button, point to Programs, point to the database's program group, and click on the program name. Upon entering the program, you may be greeted with options to assist you in creating the database. In this chapter, we will close these quick help options and use the File menu to create our databases. The main windows of Paradox and Microsoft Access are shown in Figures 6.1 and 6.2.

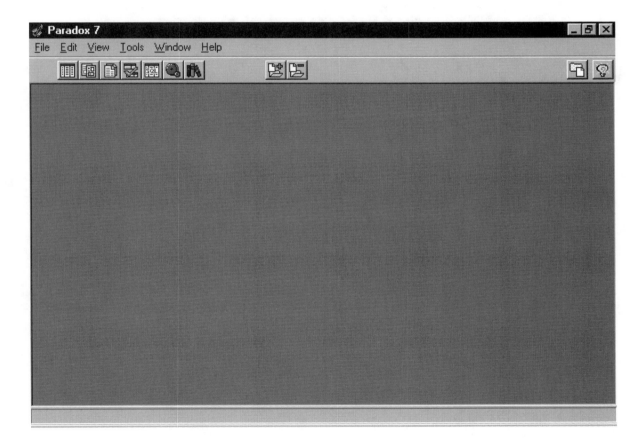

Figure 6.1   The Main Window of Corel® Paradox®

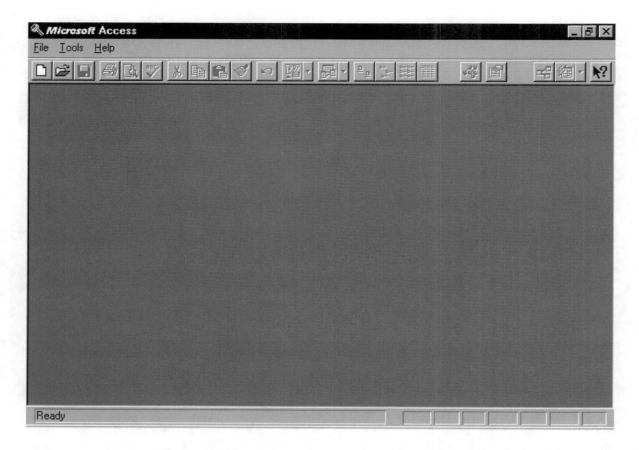

Figure 6.2 The Main Window of Microsoft® Access®

2. The Summary Database Window

The main screen of a Windows-based summary database is a window. A window has a Title Bar, a Control menu button, Minimize and Maximize buttons (and a Close button in Windows 95), menus, and occasionally Scroll Bars.

- The **Title Bar** is at the top of the window and will display the application name and the name of the document that you are working on.
- The **Control menu** button, in the upper left-hand corner of the window, will give you options to minimize, maximize, or close the window. In Windows this button will look like a file drawer. In Windows 95 this button is represented by the application's icon.
- The **Minimize and Maximize** buttons, in the upper right-hand corner of the window, will change the size of the application's window. The Minimize button will take the window down to an icon. The Maximize button will take the window to the full screen. When a window is maximized, the Maximize button will turn into a button that will take the window to a mid-size window. In Windows these buttons are represented by

up and down arrows. In Windows 95 they are represented by icons that look like windows. In Windows 95 you also will find a button with an "X" that will close the application.

- **Menus** under the Title Bar activate the options available in the window.
- **Scroll Bars** are found in some windows at the right and/or bottom of the windows. Clicking on the up or down arrows, or dragging the scroll box, will move the contents of the window up, down, or from side to side.

When you use different features of the database, windows will open for the features. To close these windows, either select **File, Close,** double-click on the **Control menu** button, or click on the X button in the upper right-hand corner of its window (Windows 95 only).

3. Toolbars and Status Bars

Windows-based summary databases have **Toolbars** at the top of the window and **Status Bars** at the bottom of the window. Toolbars consist of buttons that activate frequently used features. These features are also available through the menus. Different summary database programs may have different names for these bars, but most will have them. The Toolbars can be removed from, or added to, the summary database window, usually through selections in a View menu. Alternatives to the standard Toolbar can also be chosen from a list that is activated by pointing at a Toolbar and clicking the right mouse button.

The Status Bar at the bottom of the screen displays information about the status of your database.

4. Pull-Down Menus

The **Pull-down menus** at the top of the summary database window can be accessed with a mouse or the keyboard. These menus contain the many features available within the summary database. To access a menu with the mouse, click on the menu name and then click on the desired option. To use the keyboard to access a menu, hold down the **[Alt]** key and press the underlined letter in the menu name, and then press the letter for a menu option. For example, to create a new database table, you can access the **File menu** with **[Alt] + [F],** and then select "new" by pressing the **[N]** key. You can also press the **[Alt]** key and then use the gray arrow keys on the keyboard to move among the menu options. A menu can be closed by clicking the mouse outside of the menu or by pressing the **[Alt]** key or the **[Esc]** key.

The menus available within the summary database will vary between programs. The menus commonly found in Paradox and Microsoft Access are File, Edit, View, Tools, Window, and Help.

- The **File menu** contains the options that open, close, save, and print your databases. It also contains the option to exit the program. You will notice that some **File menus** have two save options, **Save** and **Save As.** The Save As option will prompt you for a file name. The Save option is used after your file has a name to quickly save the file.
- The **Edit menu** contains options to cut, copy, and paste text and provides other editing features.

- The **View menu** changes the appearance of your program screen. The option to add or remove the Toolbars often appears within this menu.
- The **Tools menu** contains database utilities and other options for fine-tuning the database.
- The **Window menu** lists the files that you currently have open in the program and allows you to set up ways to view them simultaneously on the screen. You can switch between open files by clicking on the desired file name in this menu. A check is placed next to the current file on the screen.
- The **Help menu** can contain tutorials, experts, and wizards. Each of these features will teach you how to perform different functions. You can also search for a specific topic or look through a list of contents. If you cannot find the appropriate information in the **Help menu,** check the software manual or contact the company's technical support department by telephone or on-line.

5. Exiting the Application

Exiting Windows summary databases is accomplished by selecting **File, Exit.** If any tables, queries, reports, or forms are currently open, you will be asked if you would like to save them.

B. CREATING THE DATABASE STRUCTURE

The structure of a summary database is the fields that are selected to keep track of the data. To determine the fields that are necessary, you must look at the data that the database is keeping track of and decide which pieces of information are important. For example, if you were keeping track of the books in a library, your fields would include Title, Author, Subject, Card Catalog Number, and a Bar Code. A rolodex database would include fields for Last Name, First Name, Street Address, E-Mail Address, Home Telephone Number, Work Telephone Number, and Fax Number.

The data that we will be keeping track of in this chapter is evidentiary documents in the hypothetical case of the Grove Dumpsite. Some background of the case is provided below.

1. The Grove Dumpsite Case

In 1941 the Department of Defense ordered major oil and gas companies in southern California to convert their refineries from the production of gasoline for automobiles to the production of high octane aviation fuel for the aircraft being used in World War II. A by-product of this high octane fuel was a form of hazardous sludge. The oil companies, faced with having to dispose of tons of this sludge, asked the Department of Defense where they should dump it. The Government ordered the oil companies to dispose of the sludge at the Grove Dumpsite, located some 30 miles south of Los Angeles in a rural, undeveloped area. At the end of World War II, the dumpsite was covered over with dirt and forgotten.

In 1980 the once rural area containing the dumpsite had become the affluent neighborhood of Oak Grove in Casper County, California. A developer purchased the land around the dumpsite and built several tracts of luxury homes. Prospective purchasers who inquired about the vacant lot adjacent to the homes were told that the next phase of homes would be built there.

In 1982, while playing at the "vacant lot," some children found a mud puddle of oil that appeared to be bubbling up from underground. They told their parents, and the parents started asking questions about the lot. After making inquiries at the city manager's office, homeowners learned that the vacant lot was actually the Grove Dumpsite.

The homeowners soon began to wonder what effect the dumpsite was having on their health. The dumpsite became the suspected cause of every cold, allergy, disease, miscarriage, and birth defect. In 1983 the homeowners filed a class action lawsuit in Casper County Superior Court naming each of the dumping oil companies, the developer, and the city and county as defendants.

2. The Evidentiary Documents

Some of the evidence in this case is shown on the following pages. You will notice that each document has a number stamped in the upper right-hand corner. This is often called "Bates stamping" due to the common use of the Bates Numbering Machine to stamp the numbers on the documents. To keep track of every page of the evidence as it comes into the firm, each page receives a number. You may use a numbering machine to stamp on these numbers or stickers that can be affixed to the pages. The numbering machine is similar to a price stamper that is used in a grocery store, except as each page is stamped, the numbering machine increases the number by one. A set of the evidentiary documents is often kept in numerical order, and other sets of the documents may be placed in chronological order or in some other order. No matter what the order, each page retains its original number. When referring to a document that has been number stamped, you may identify it by the number on its first page or by all of its inclusive numbers (e.g., "3-7").

We need to look at these documents to determine the fields that we should create for our database. The fields for this database could be as follows:

Document Number
Number of Pages
Date
Document Type
To
To Company
From
From Company
Summary

Attorneys will often want to include fields for certain issues in the case so that they can search for documents that are related to a specific issue. The fields shown above are a basic structure for an evidentiary database.

1

OAK FIELD HOMEOWNERS ASSOCIATION
21 Yarrow Drive
Oak Grove, California 92000

June 6, 1982

Jim Dodd
City Manager
City of Oak Grove
100 Main Street
Oak Grove, California 92000

Dear Mr. Dodd:

Our planned community is located just south of the intersection of Yarrow Drive and Beacon Avenue. Adjacent to the property is a vacant lot that the association may be interested in purchasing for a common area. Could you please let me know the status of this property and whether it is available for our purchase and development.

Thank you,

Clayton Hicks
President, Oak Field Homeowners Association

2

UNITED STATES OF AMERICA
Department of Defense

December 8, 1941

Harry Thompson, President
Oyster Oil Company
500 Oyster Plaza
Los Angeles, California 91320

Dear Mr. Thompson:

It is hereby ordered by the President of the United States and the Department of Defense that your Wilmington Refinery cease its production of gasoline and immediately begin production of high octane aviation fuel for the war effort. This is not a request. It is expected that your company will comply by January 1, 1942.

Sincerely,

James Petrie
Secretary of Defense

3

Oyster Oil Company
500 Oyster Plaza
Los Angeles, California 91320

December 20, 1941

James Petrie
Secretary of Defense
Department of Defense
1 Capitol Plaza
Washington, D.C. 00334

Dear Mr. Petrie:

I am in receipt of your letter dated December 8, 1941. Oyster Oil Company is proud to comply with your order and to support this great nation in the time of war. In order to complete our conversion to the production of high octane aviation fuel at our Wilmington Refinery, we must have a site suitable for depositing the sludge waste by-product of the aviation fuel production. Could your department please supply me with a recommended site for the sludge. The expected monthly amounts of sludge are compiled in the attached four-page report.

I will await your reply.

Very truly yours,

Harry Thompson
President

8

UNITED STATES OF AMERICA
Department of Defense

December 30, 1941

Harry Thompson, President
Oyster Oil Company
500 Oyster Plaza
Los Angeles, California 91320

Dear Mr. Thompson:

Oyster Oil Company is hereby directed to place all waste by-products from the production of aviation fuel at the Wilmington Refinery in the Grove Dumpsite. The Grove Dumpsite is located in an unincorporated area of Casper County. Mr. Donald Rewald, the manager of the site, will be contacting you to make arrangements for the deposits.

Sincerely,

James Petrie
Secretary of Defense

9

FIELD DEVELOPERS

Present

Oak Field
A residential community for the selective home buyer

This brochure includes a map of the Oak Field Development and future plans for the adjacent properties

---

35

FIELD DEVELOPERS
Developers of the Finest Homes
33 Harper Avenue, Suite 100
Newport Beach, California 90022

February 3, 1979

Jim Dodd
City Manager
City of Oak Grove
100 Main Street
Oak Grove, California 92000

Dear Jim:

We are interested in developing the piece of property adjacent to our Oak Field residential development. Could you please forward to me all information concerning ownership of the property and any soils reports that have been conducted there. I understand that it may once have been a dumpsite for oil waste.

Sincerely,

John Field
President, Field Developers

36

SOIL AND PLANT LABS
200 Washington Avenue
San Diego, California 92101

January 15, 1955

Tom Osborne
City Engineer
City of Oak Grove
100 Main Street
Oak Grove, California 92000

Dear Mr. Osborne:

After a careful review of the materials and samples taken from the Grove Dumpsite, it is the opinion of this company that the materials contained therein are extremely hazardous to humans. We would therefore recommend that the site be immediately excavated and transported to an ocean barge for disposal a few miles offshore. We have done this for many other clients and can send you an estimate of our fees if your city is interested.

Thank you for your business.

Sincerely,

E. Dusunt Gedit
Vice President
Soil and Plant Labs

37

CITY OF OAK GROVE
Department of Engineering

Report Date: March 23, 1955
Prepared By: Tom Osborne, City Engineer

Re: Grove Dumpsite

It has recently come to the attention of the City of Oak Grove that the abandoned property known as the Grove Dumpsite contains a by-product of high octane aviation fuel. This by-product is a sludge that should be considered as a hazardous substance. The owner of the property has covered the sludge with approximately three feet of earth. It is the opinion of the Department of Engineering that the sludge should be left in place at this time. The opinion received from Soil and Plants Labs has been considered and rejected as too costly to the city. The area surrounding the subject site is undeveloped and several miles from paved roadways. It is our opinion that the impact to the population is minimal.

---

3. Creating the Database Structure

To create the database structure in the summary database program, you will select **File, New** and the option for a new database or table. After going through a few prompts, you will see a dialog box similar to the one shown in Figure 6.3. In the newest versions of Microsoft Access, you will need to give the database a name, select a new table, and select Design View.

Most database structures require the field name, the type of data that will be stored in the field, and the size (in number of characters) of the field. Many also give you the option to "key" a field in the structure. When a field is keyed, the database will not allow a duplicate entry within that field when records are entered. It would be advantageous for us to key the Document Number field in our database because we would not want anyone to make the mistake of entering two separate documents with the same document number. **Paradox** requires that the keyed fields be the top fields in the field list. The **[Tab]** key and **[Shift] + [Tab]** are used to move between the entry spaces in the database structure.

Enter the name of the first field, **Document Number,** and tab to the field type column. The field types available can usually be seen by pressing the **[Space Bar],** clicking on a drop-down list, or pressing a function key. The different types of fields are explained below.

- An **Alpha, Character,** or **Text** field will contain information that includes letters, numbers, or a combination of both. Numbers in this field type will be those numbers

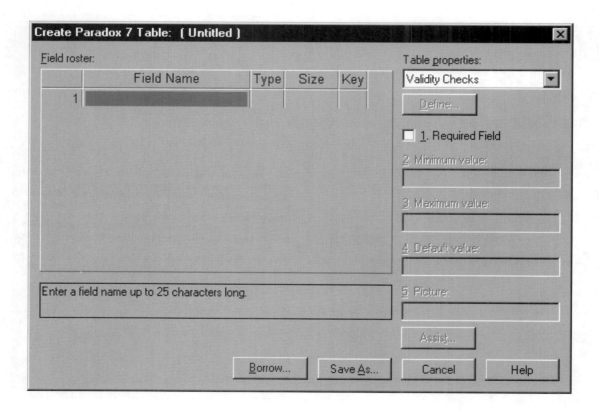

Figure 6.3   A dialog box for creating the structure of the database

that are not used for mathematical computations, such as telephone and social security numbers.

- A **Number** or **Numeric** field will contain positive or negative numbers that may be used in mathematical calculations.
- A **Currency** field will contain money amounts that are intended to be used in mathematical calculations.
- A **Date** field will contain dates.
- A **Time** field will contain times.
- A **Memo** field will contain text entries that are too long to be contained in an Alpha, Character, or Text field. This type of field will contain words, sentences, paragraphs, or pages of information about the document or item to be included in the database.
- A **Logical** field will contain an either/or combination of Yes/No, True/False, On/Off, or the like.
- An **OLE** (Object Linking and Embedding) field will link to information in a spreadsheet or document from another program and can include sound and images.

Database programs may offer additional field types. The definitions for these can be found in the program's Help feature.

The field type for the **Document Number** field will be **Number.** Although we will not be using this field for mathematical calculations, it must remain a Number field type to keep the documents properly sorted sequentially by document number. You can often type the first letter of the field type or click on a selection from a drop-down list to place the entry in the field type box. After selecting the field type, you will tab to the field size or enter the field size in the appropriate place.

When you enter certain field types, a field size may not be necessary, so the program may skip to the next entry. A Number field is one of these field types. Most databases will jump over the field size for a Number field, but if they do not, the field size for the **Document Number** field should be **5.** We will assume that there will not be more than 99,999 pages of evidence in this case. The next step will be to key the Document Number field.

To key a field in Paradox, you tab to the Key column and double-click in the Key box, or press any key. An asterisk will appear in the Key box to let you know that the field is keyed. **To key a field in Microsoft Access,** while entering the field, click on the **Key** button on the **Toolbar.**

To move on to the next field, press the **[Tab]** key. You will also notice several other selections that you may make for each field, such as validation checks and minimum and maximum values. These selections are there so that you can restrict the data that is entered or make sure that the data conforms to certain criteria. We will not be using these other selections in our example. Enter the remaining fields as shown below. You do not need to key any of these fields.

Field Name	Type	Size
Number of Pages	Number	(If necessary, 3)
Date	Date	(If necessary, 8)
Document Type	Alpha (Text)	20
To	Alpha (Text)	35
To Company	Alpha (Text)	30
From	Alpha (Text)	35
From Company	Alpha (Text)	30
Summary	Memo	(In Paradox, type 100)

A Memo field in Paradox will prompt you for the number of characters that will be stored in the database file itself. To save file space, Paradox stores the remainder of the Memo field in a separate linked file. The files work together, so you will not notice that they are being stored separately.

When you have finished entering the fields, your table structure will look similar to the one in Figure 6.4.

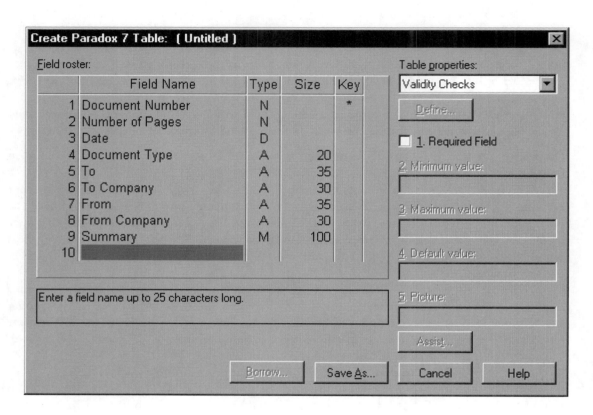

Figure 6.4   The completed field structure using Paradox

Save the table by clicking on the **Save As** button or selecting **File, Save As.** You will be prompted for a table name. If you have the choice to save to a disk drive or folder other than the default, click on the appropriate disk drive and folder, or precede the file name with the drive letter and any folder names. Give the file the name **Grove.** After the file is saved, Paradox will take you to a blank screen. In Microsoft Access, you may need to select **File, Close.** Microsoft Access will leave the Grove database's window open on the screen as shown in Figure 6.5.

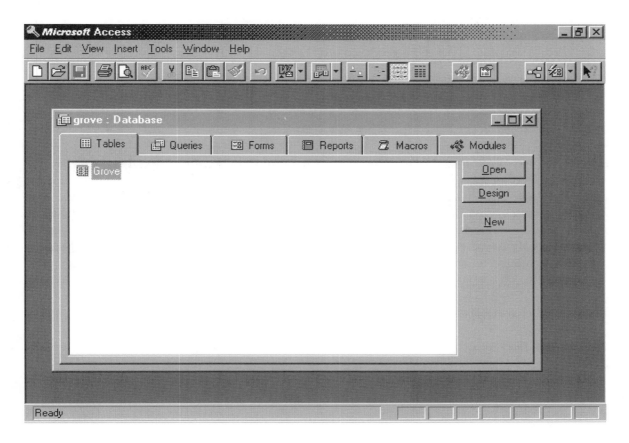

Figure 6.5 In Microsoft Access, the Grove database window remains open on the desktop

4. Inserting or Deleting Fields

You can insert or delete a field while you are creating the database structure or after you have saved the database structure. To get back to the database structure once you have finished it, choose **Table, Restructure** while in the Record Entry screen **in Paradox. In Microsoft Access,** select the table name and click on the **Design** button. If you need to insert a field, place the cursor in the row below which you would like the new field, and press the **[Insert]** key. **To delete a field in Paradox,** place the cursor on the row and press **[Ctrl] + [Delete].** **To delete a field in Microsoft Access,** click on the row selector at the left of the field row and press the **[Delete]** key.

C. ENTERING RECORDS

Records are entered into the database from the document itself or a code sheet.

1. Code Sheets

A code sheet is set up with the name of the case and the field names. It is usually created using a word processor and may be designed by the attorney in charge of the case or by someone else. Sample code sheets for this database are shown on the following pages. The first code sheet has been completed for you. Complete the remainder of the code sheets for the Grove evidentiary documents. Note that the Document Number will be the number on the first page of the document, and the Number of Pages can be determined by looking at the Document Number and the number of the next document. For example, Document 3 contains five pages.

CODE SHEET
Grove Dumpsite Case

Document Number: __1___

Number of Pages: ___1___

Date of the Document: **6 / 6 / 82**

Type of Document: _**Letter**_____
    (Letter, Report, Memorandum, Brochure, etc.)

To: _**Dodd, Jim**_____
    (Last Name, First Name. Leave blank if not applicable.)

To Company: _**City of Oak Grove**_____
    (Who does "To" work for? Leave blank if not applicable.)

From: _**Hicks, Clayton**_____
    (Last Name, First Name. Leave blank if not applicable.)

From Company: _**OFHA**_____
    (Who does "From" work for? Leave blank if not applicable.)

Summary (Write a short summary of the evidence contents):

Letter to the City Manager of Oak Grove expressing an interest on behalf of the Oak Field Homeowner's Association in purchasing the vacant lot adjacent to the community for a common area. Requests status and availability of property.

CODE SHEET
Grove Dumpsite Case

Document Number: _____

Number of Pages: _____

Date of the Document: / /

Type of Document: _____
    (Letter, Report, Memorandum, Brochure, etc.)

To: _____
    (Last Name, First Name. Leave blank if not applicable.)

To Company: _____
    (Who does "To" work for? Leave blank if not applicable.)

From: _____
    (Last Name, First Name. Leave blank if not applicable.)

From Company: _____
    (Who does "From" work for? Leave blank if not applicable.)

Summary (Write a short summary of the evidence contents):

_____
_____
_____
_____
_____
_____
_____

CODE SHEET
Grove Dumpsite Case

Document Number: _____

Number of Pages: _____

Date of the Document: / /

Type of Document: _____
    (Letter, Report, Memorandum, Brochure, etc.)

To: _____
    (Last Name, First Name. Leave blank if not applicable.)

To Company: _____
    (Who does "To" work for? Leave blank if not applicable.)

From: _____
    (Last Name, First Name. Leave blank if not applicable.)

From Company: _____
    (Who does "From" work for? Leave blank if not applicable.)

Summary (Write a short summary of the evidence contents):

_____
_____
_____
_____
_____
_____

CODE SHEET
Grove Dumpsite Case

Document Number: _____

Number of Pages: _____

Date of the Document: / /

Type of Document: _____
    (Letter, Report, Memorandum, Brochure, etc.)

To: _____
    (Last Name, First Name. Leave blank if not applicable.)

To Company: _____
    (Who does "To" work for? Leave blank if not applicable.)

From: _____
    (Last Name, First Name. Leave blank if not applicable.)

From Company: _____
    (Who does "From" work for? Leave blank if not applicable.)

Summary (Write a short summary of the evidence contents):

_____
_____
_____
_____
_____
_____

CODE SHEET
Grove Dumpsite Case

Document Number: _____

Number of Pages: _____

Date of the Document: / /

Type of Document: _____
    (Letter, Report, Memorandum, Brochure, etc.)

To: _____
    (Last Name, First Name. Leave blank if not applicable.)

To Company: _____
    (Who does "To" work for? Leave blank if not applicable.)

From: _____
    (Last Name, First Name. Leave blank if not applicable.)

From Company: _____
    (Who does "From" work for? Leave blank if not applicable.)

Summary (Write a short summary of the evidence contents):

_____
_____
_____
_____
_____
_____
_____

CODE SHEET
Grove Dumpsite Case

Document Number: _____

Number of Pages: _____

Date of the Document: / /

Type of Document: _____
    (Letter, Report, Memorandum, Brochure, etc.)

To: _____
    (Last Name, First Name. Leave blank if not applicable.)

To Company: _____
    (Who does "To" work for? Leave blank if not applicable.)

From: _____
    (Last Name, First Name. Leave blank if not applicable.)

From Company: _____
    (Who does "From" work for? Leave blank if not applicable.)

Summary (Write a short summary of the evidence contents):

_____
_____
_____
_____
_____
_____

CODE SHEET
Grove Dumpsite Case

Document Number: _____

Number of Pages: _____

Date of the Document: / /

Type of Document: _____
    (Letter, Report, Memorandum, Brochure, etc.)

To: _____
    (Last Name, First Name. Leave blank if not applicable.)

To Company: _____
    (Who does "To" work for? Leave blank if not applicable.)

From: _____
    (Last Name, First Name. Leave blank if not applicable.)

From Company: _____
    (Who does "From" work for? Leave blank if not applicable.)

Summary (Write a short summary of the evidence contents):

_____
_____
_____
_____
_____
_____
_____

CODE SHEET
Grove Dumpsite Case

Document Number: _____

Number of Pages: _____

Date of the Document: / /

Type of Document: _____
    (Letter, Report, Memorandum, Brochure, etc.)

To: _____
    (Last Name, First Name. Leave blank if not applicable.)

To Company: _____
    (Who does "To" work for? Leave blank if not applicable.)

From: _____
    (Last Name, First Name. Leave blank if not applicable.)

From Company: _____
    (Who does "From" work for? Leave blank if not applicable.)

Summary (Write a short summary of the evidence contents):

_____
_____
_____
_____
_____
_____

2. Opening the Table and Entering Data

To enter the records into the database, select **File, Open, Table,** or click on the table's icon and click on the **Open** button. The Record Input screens for Paradox and Microsoft Access are shown in Figures 6.6 and 6.7.

There is a column for each field. The group of fields for each record is represented by a row. To begin entering data in the Paradox screen, you must click on the Toolbar button containing the pencil. As you enter the data, you need to be careful about capitalization and abbreviation. Decide ahead of time if you will use no capitals, initial capitals, or all capitals in a specific field. This is important because many search queries are case-sensitive—that is, a search for "box" may not locate "Box" or "BOX." Also, use only common abbreviations, such as the abbreviation that I used for the Oak Field Homeowners Association, "OFHA." Again, this is important because search queries for "City Manager" will not locate "City Mgr."

In fields that contain a person's name, enter the last name first. This will make sorting the records by the Name field easier. In Paradox, the Document Number and Number of Pages fields will display numbers with two decimal places. To remove the decimal places in these two fields for all of the records, right click in the entry box for each of these fields in the first record.

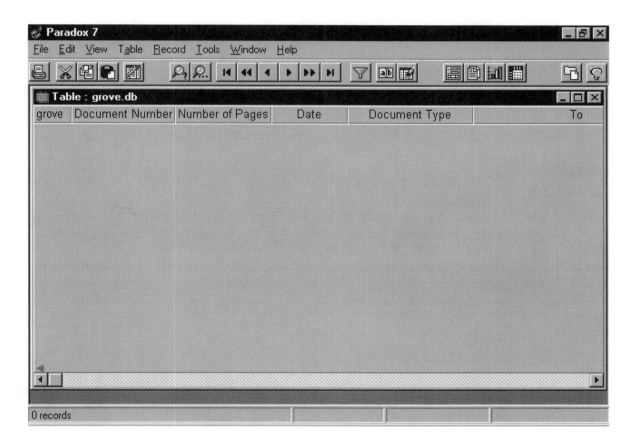

Figure 6.6 The Record Input Screen in Paradox

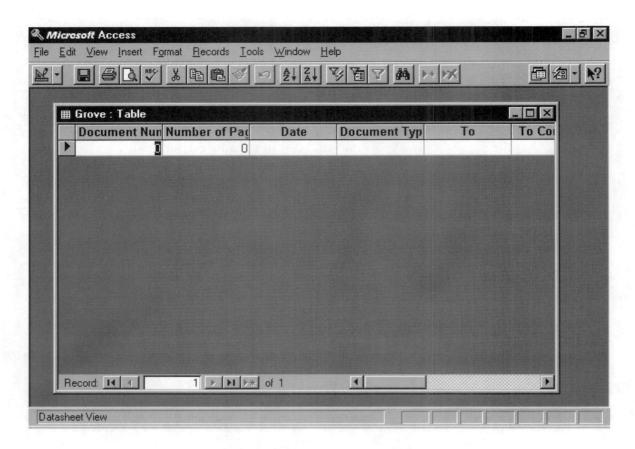

Figure 6.7 The Record Input Screen in Microsoft Access

From the menu that appears, choose **Properties.** In the Properties dialog box, choose **Format,** and select the **Integer** format.

To enter data into the Summary field, or any Memo field, you need to press **[Shift] + [F2].** This will take you to a screen similar to a primitive word processor. When you are finished entering the summary, press **[Shift] + [F2]** again to return to the Record Entry screen.

Enter the records for each of the evidentiary documents. The **[Tab]** key and **[Shift] + [Tab]** will move you right and left between the field boxes. The results should appear similar to the entries in Figure 6.8.

3. Saving the Records

As you enter each record, it is usually saved to the table file. To make sure that all of the records are saved, you should select a Save option after you have finished entering all of the records. **To save the entries in Paradox,** click on the Toolbar button containing the pencil. **To save the entries in Microsoft Access,** click on the diskette (Save) button on the Toolbar. To close the Record Entry screen in both programs, select **File, Close.**

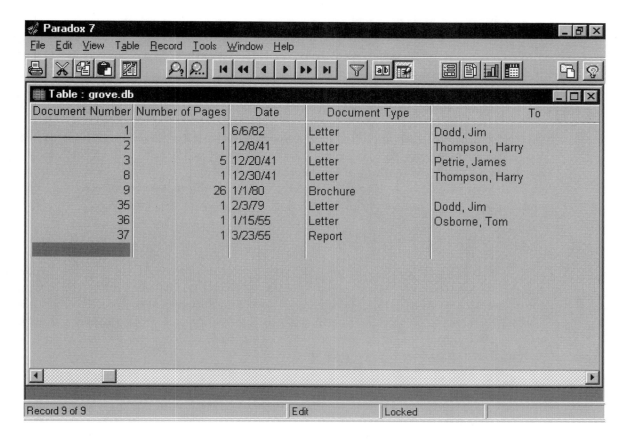

Document Number	Number of Pages	Date	Document Type	To
1	1	6/6/82	Letter	Dodd, Jim
2	1	12/8/41	Letter	Thompson, Harry
3	5	12/20/41	Letter	Petrie, James
8	1	12/30/41	Letter	Thompson, Harry
9	26	1/1/80	Brochure	
35	1	2/3/79	Letter	Dodd, Jim
36	1	1/15/55	Letter	Osborne, Tom
37	1	3/23/55	Report	

Figure 6.8 The Completed Records

4. Adding or Deleting Records

To add or delete records, you need to open the table.

- In **Microsoft Access,** new records are added at the bottom of the list of records by selecting **Insert, Record.** Records are deleted by clicking within the record and selecting **Edit, Delete Record.**
- In **Paradox,** you first need to click on the pencil (Edit) button on the Toolbar. Then, you may insert a new record at any place in the record list by selecting **Record, Insert.** Records are deleted by clicking within the record and selecting **Record, Delete.**

The table should then be saved and closed again.

D. SORTING AND INDEXING

Many times when you enter records into a database, they are not entered in any particular order. There are two ways to reorder the records, **sorting** and **indexing.**

1. Sorting

Sorting places the records in a new order. In Paradox and dBASE, a Sort creates a new table file with new record numbers arranged in the new sort order.

a. *Sorting in Microsoft Access*

Sorting is easily accomplished in Microsoft Access because there are buttons on the Toolbar to perform the Sort. In an open table, simply click in the field that you want to sort by and click the **Ascending** or **Descending Sort** button. To perform a Sort containing more than one field, select **Records, Filter, Advanced Filter/Sort,** and select the fields and the sort order from the drop-down lists at the bottom of the window.

b. *Sorting in Paradox and dBASE*

In Paradox and dBASE, each record has a unique record number that it is given when the record is entered. A Sort rearranges the records based on the sort criteria and creates a new file with new record numbers. To sort records in Paradox, open the table and select **Table, Sort.** Select the fields to be included in the Sort, give the file a name, and click on the **OK** button. Indexing, explained in the next section, is a more efficient way of ordering records in Paradox and dBASE.

2. Indexing

An index is a file that is established for reordering the records in a table. It is not a separate table file. There are primary indexes and secondary indexes. Keyed fields are primary indexes. The database will automatically order records in ascending order based on these fields. The Document Number field in our example is a keyed field. A secondary index is a Sort that is based on a single field or a group of fields. In **Paradox** and **dBASE,** you can activate these indexes when you are viewing a table to have the data automatically sort based on the index. In **Microsoft Access,** an index simply speeds up searches and sorting. To see sorted data on the screen, you will need to perform a Sort. A table can have many secondary indexes. You could create one for every field and be able to sort the records by any of the fields. However, you cannot sort a Memo, Logical, or OLE field. Combining two or more fields in an index is useful when you have fields such as Last Name and First Name. These two fields could be placed into the index, and then duplicates encountered in the Last Name field would be sorted by First Name.

Indexes are created in the screen where we established the structure of the table. With the table open on the screen you can get to the table's structure by selecting **View, Table Design** in Microsoft Access, or **Table, Restructure** in Paradox. To illustrate the creation of an index, we will create an index on the Date field.

a. *Creating an Index in Microsoft Access*

Indexes in Microsoft Access are used to speed up searches and sorting on the field. To reorder the records in a table, you will use the Sort features. An index can be created on a single field in Microsoft Access by clicking on the field name, **Date,** and clicking on the **Indexed** property box at the bottom of the dialog box. A drop-down list will display three options: No, Yes(Duplicates OK), or Yes(No Duplicates). We will select "**Yes(Duplicates OK).**" If you do not allow duplicates, only one record for each date would be displayed. To complete the index creation, select **File, Save.**

To create an index with multiple fields, click on the **Indexes** button on the Toolbar in the Design screen. In the first blank row, give the index a name, click on the field box, and select the first field to be included in the index. Move down one row, do not insert a name, click in the field box, and select the second field for the index. Continue this process until all of the fields that you want in the index are included, then click on the Indexes window close button (the **Control menu** button or the X).

b.   *Creating an Index in Paradox*

To create an index in Paradox, select **Secondary Indexes** from the **Table Properties** drop-down list. A list of available indexes appears, as well as a **Define** button. Click on the **Define** button. A screen similar to the one in Figure 6.9 will appear. Click on the **Date** field to select it, and click on the button containing the right arrow. In the **Index Options** box, select **Maintained.** This option will update the index as new records are added or deleted. The Unique option does not permit duplicates, and the Case Sensitive option sorts capital letters first. In the **Field Options** box, select **Ascending.** Click on the **OK** button, give the index the name **ByDate,** and click on the **OK** button. To create Indexes with multiple fields, continue adding fields to the list in the Indexed Fields box.

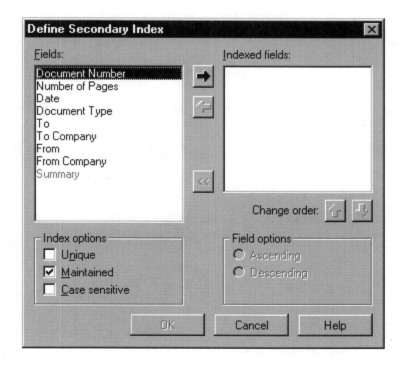

Figure 6.9   Indexes are created by choosing one or more fields, an index option, and whether the information will be in ascending or descending order

For each field, choose an Ascending or Descending order. Save the new table structure by clicking on the **Save** button.

To order the records in a table by an index, select **Table, Filter.** In the **Order By** box, click on the index name, and click on the **OK** button. Change to the **ByDate** index to see how this affects the table. To return the records to Document Number order, select **Table, Filter,** select the **Document Number** index, and click on the **OK** button.

E. QUERIES

A query is a search within a database. Queries are instructions sent to the database requesting records that meet certain criteria. For example, we may want to locate all documents written by a certain witness so that we will have the documents available at deposition. Many databases also contain filter options that will search for records that meet certain criteria while you are looking at the database table. We will discuss queries because they are used by most database programs.

The majority of database programs utilize "Query By Example." Query By Example is a query method in which each of the database fields is placed in a column. A search condition is placed within the column of the field to be searched. Paradox's Query screen is shown in Figure 6.10. The boxes

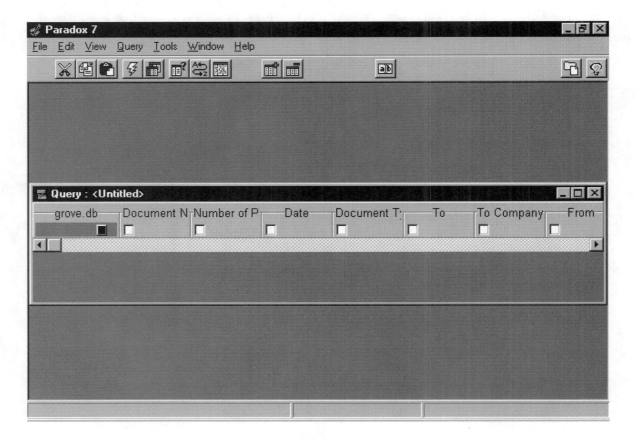

Figure 6.10   The Query Screen in Paradox

under each field name are there so that you can check the fields that you would like to see in your results.

1. Using Relational Operators

Relational operators are used to specify the data to be searched for with a query. The relational operators used by most databases are the following:

=	**Equals**
>	**Greater than**
<	**Less than**
>=	**Greater than or equal to**
<=	**Less than or equal to**
<>	**Not equal to**
Like	**For searches containing wildcards**

Database programs will have other operators that are unique to their programs. You can find these in the **Help menu.**

2. Combining Searches Using Connectors

Connectors are used to connect two or more search criteria. The most common connectors are AND, OR, and NOT. In Query By Example, the words AND, OR, and NOT are used for searches within the same field. For AND queries that use different fields, the search criteria are placed in the same row. For OR queries that use different fields, the search criteria are placed in separate rows. For NOT queries that use different fields, the word NOT, or the relational operator <>, precedes the condition in the field whose information is to be excluded.

3. Creating a Query in Microsoft Access

To create a query in Microsoft Access, click on the **Query folder** and click on the **New** button. Select **Design View,** click on the table name, and select **Add.** You may add more than one table to the query if you desire. Close the **Show Table** dialog box. The Query screen will appear as shown in Figure 6.11.

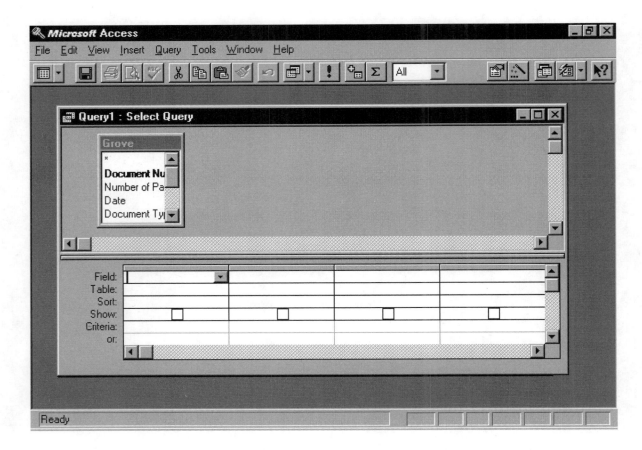

Figure 6.11   The Query Screen in Microsoft Access

To begin the construction of the query, you must decide which fields you want to see in the results. Usually you will want to see them all. To put field names into the columns at the bottom of the screen, drag the field names to the columns. You may drag more than one field at a time by holding down the **[Ctrl]** key as you are clicking on the field names. They can then be dragged as a group to the columns. After you have placed all of the fields into the query, the screen will appear as shown in Figure 6.12. The check marks in the Show row can be removed to exclude the field from the viewed results.

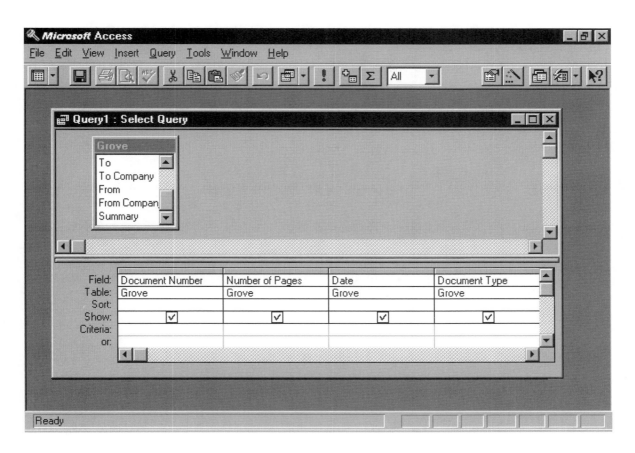

Figure 6.12   In Microsoft Access, the fields are placed into the query design
by dragging their names to the design columns

The Criteria rows are where you will enter the criteria for a particular field. There are different rules for how you enter a query into the Criteria row depending on the type of field you are querying.

Text   Items to be searched for within a Text field must be enclosed within quotation marks. A sample search is shown below.

               = "Letter"

Number   Numbers to be located in a Number field do not require quotation marks or any other qualification.

               >25

Currency   Do not use dollar signs in the search. Just use the numbers.

               > = 10

Date	When searching a Date field, the date must be enclosed within number symbols, "#."

<#1/1/97#

Time	When searching a Time field, the time must be enclosed within number symbols, "#," and include "AM" or "PM."

>=#12:00 AM#

Memo	Memo fields are queried with the "Like" operator, and must use quotation marks and the wildcard character "*".

Like "*vacant lot*"

Logical	Logical fields are called "Yes/No" fields in Microsoft Access. To search within one of these fields, the criteria will either contain the word "Yes" or the word "No."

Yes

OLE	OLE fields are queried in the same manner as Memo fields. They must use the "Like" operator, quotation marks, and wildcards.

Like "*vacant lot*"

To process a query, you will click on the button containing the exclamation point, **!,** on the Toolbar. When you have finished looking at the results, you will select **View, Query Design** to return to the Query Design screen. To practice entering queries, proceed to Section 5.

4. Creating a Query in Paradox

To create a query in Paradox, select **File, New, Query.** Click on your table name from the dialog box that appears. If your table is not stored in the default folder, click on the drive and folder selections to locate the file. Click on the **Open** button to open the Query screen. The Query screen can be seen in Figure 6.10.

To begin the construction of the query, you must decide which fields you want to see in the results. Usually you will want to see them all. Fields are selected by checking the box under their names. In Paradox, there are several different check marks available. They can be seen by holding down the left mouse button, or by clicking the right mouse button, on the box. Choose the check that is followed by a plus symbol. To place check marks with plus symbols in all of the field boxes, click on the box under the table name. A check mark can be removed to exclude a field from the viewed results.

The field box under the field name is where you will enter the criteria for a particular field. There are different rules for how you enter a query into the field box depending on the type of field you are querying.

Alpha	Items to be searched for within an Alpha field can be entered without quotation marks unless the text you are searching for contains a comma that can be mistaken for the AND connector. Two examples of Alpha searches are shown below.

> **= Letter**   **= "Smith, John"**

Number	Numbers to be located in a Number field do not require quotation marks or any other qualification.

> **>25**

Currency	Do not use dollar signs in the search. Just use the numbers.

> **> = 10**

Date	When searching a Date field, use the default date format. The default is usually Month/Day/Year. The ".." wildcard can be used to replace any part of the date in the search.

> **<1/1/97**   **= ../../80**

Memo	In a Memo field, you need to use the double-period wildcard, "..". This wildcard can also be used in other field types. For example, to locate documents where the words "vacant lot" are included in the Summary field, the search would be:

> **..vacant lot..**

Logical	Logical fields are called "True/False" or "Yes/No" fields. The default entry in Paradox is True or False. To search within one of these fields, the criteria will contain one of these words.

> **True**

OLE	OLE fields are queried in the same manner as Memo fields. They use the double-period wildcard, "..".

> **..vacant lot..**

To process a query, you will click on the button containing the lightning bolt on the Toolbar. When you have finished looking at the results, you will select **File, Close** to close the query results and return to the Query screen. To practice entering queries, proceed to Section 5.

5. Entering Queries

Several practice queries are presented below for searching for document records within the Grove table. The value of a database becomes clear when you have hundreds or thousands of pages of documents and one or more of them need to be located. When you find the record or records, you can then note the document numbers and retrieve them from the files or boxes of actual documents.

Search 1

We are taking the deposition of Jim Dodd. We have copies of all documents written by him, but we need to do a search for all documents written to him. To locate these documents, a search will be placed in the To field as follows:

Microsoft Access	= "Dodd, Jim"
Paradox	= "Dodd, Jim"

The quotation marks are necessary in the Paradox search because of the comma used to separate the last name from the first name. The queries are shown in Figures 6.13 and 6.14.

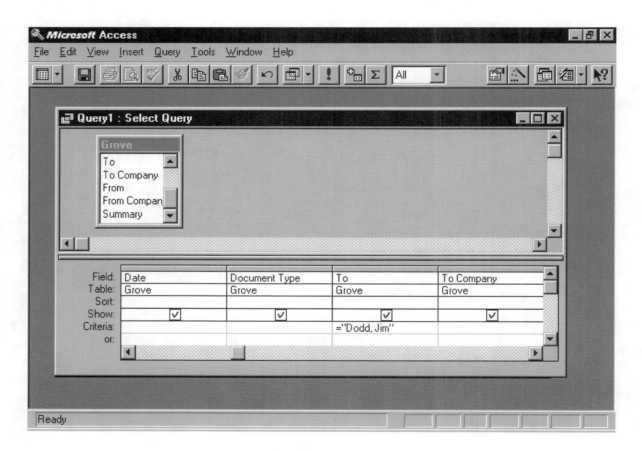

Figure 6.13   Search conditions are created in the Criteria row in Microsoft Access's query design

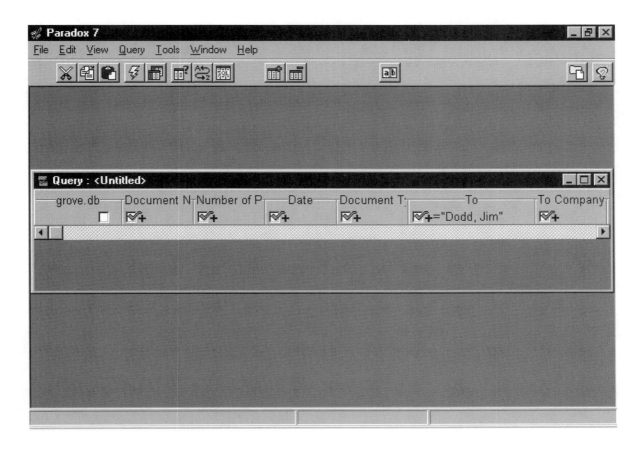

Figure 6.14 In Paradox, search conditions are entered into the field box
for the field in which the search will be performed

To process the query, click on the button containing the exclamation point (Microsoft Access) or the lightning bolt (Paradox). If a search does not locate any records, look at the way you entered the search. Did you misspell a word or use different capitalization? Did you leave a query in another field?

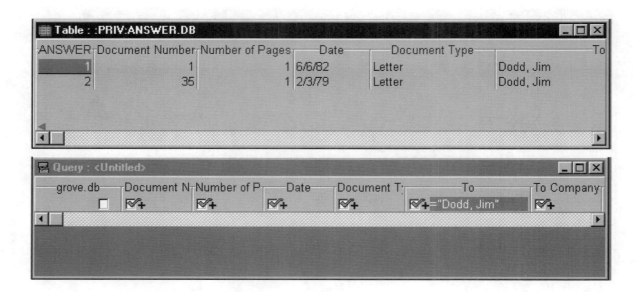

The results of the query are displayed above. Each of these searches and their results will be displayed using Paradox.

When you have finished viewing the results of the search, **return to the Query screen** as follows:

Microsoft Access   **View, Query Design**

Paradox   **File, Close**

Delete the search criteria from the To field so that we may try another search.

Search 2

Your boss is looking for the Oak Field brochure. You will locate its record with a search in the Document Type field as follows:

Microsoft Access   = "Brochure"

Paradox   = Brochure

Process the query by clicking on the button on the Toolbar. Review the results, return to the Query screen, and remove the search from the Document Type field.

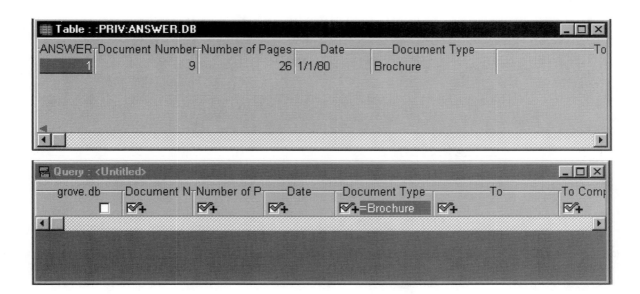

Search 3

To practice a query with two parts connected with the AND connector, we will look for all documents written in the 1940s. To search for a time period of dates, you must enter a search for dates greater than or equal to the minimum date, and connect it using AND to a search for dates less than or equal to the maximum date. This search will be performed in the Date field. In Paradox, the AND connector is represented by a comma when used in the same field.

Microsoft Access	>=#1/1/40# and <=#12/31/49#
Paradox	>=1/1/40, <=12/31/49
Paradox (wildcard)	=../../4..

Process the query by clicking on the button on the Toolbar. Review the results, return to the Query screen, and remove the search from the Date field.

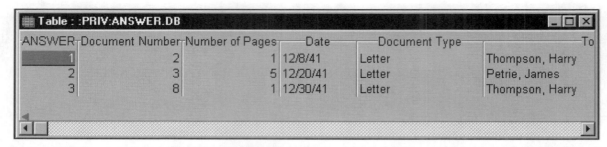

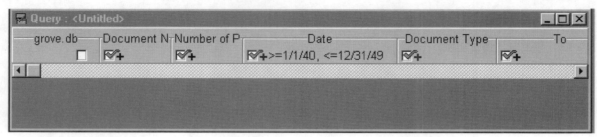

Search 4

To use the AND connector in different fields, we will perform a search looking for letters that contain more than one page. Searches using the AND connector and different fields will place the query in the same row. In the Document Type field enter the following search:

Microsoft Access	= "Letter"
Paradox	= Letter

Then move over to the Number of Pages field and enter:

Microsoft Access	>1
Paradox	>1

Process the query by clicking on the button on the Toolbar. Review the results, return to the Query screen, and remove the search from the Document Type and Number of Pages fields.

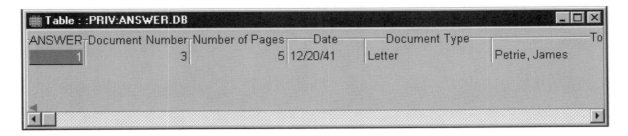

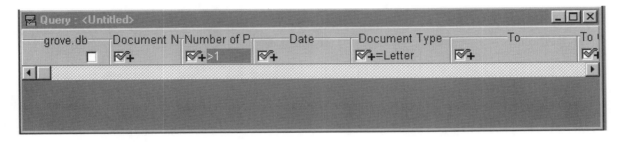

Search 5

To practice searching within a Memo field, we will try to locate the records of documents that talked about dumping the waste into the ocean. Move to the Summary field and enter the following search:

Microsoft Access	**Like "*ocean*"**
Paradox	**..ocean..**

Process the query by clicking on the button on the Toolbar. Review the results, return to the Query screen, and remove the search from the Summary field.

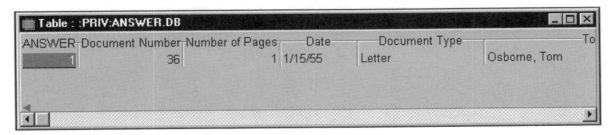

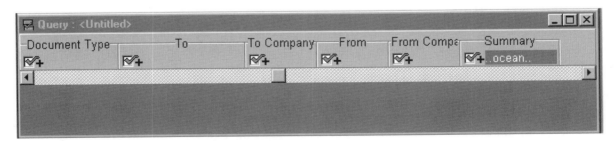

Search 6

Your boss would like to see the records of Documents 3 and 37. To create this search, you will use the OR connector in the Document Number field. Write the search as follows:

Microsoft Access	**=3 or =37**
Paradox	**=3 or =37**

Process the query by clicking on the button on the Toolbar. Review the results, return to the Query screen, and remove the search from the Document Type field.

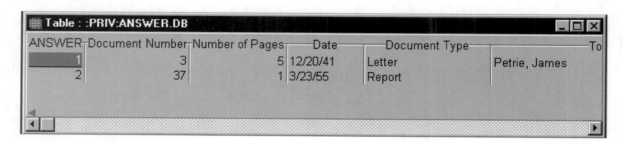

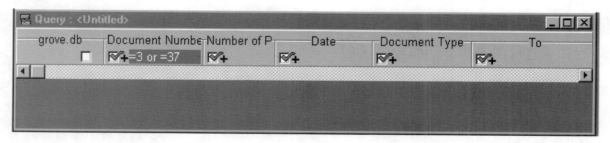

Search 7

The final search will demonstrate the use of the OR connector in different fields. We will look for the records of all documents to or from James Petrie. To perform a search in different fields using the OR connector, the searches must be placed in separate rows. Enter the following search in the To field in the first row.

Microsoft Access	**= "Petrie, James"**
Paradox	**= "Petrie, James"**

Press the **[Down Arrow]** key to move down a row. In **Paradox,** you need to place the check plus mark in the field boxes by clicking on the box under the table name.

Next, enter the same search as above in the From field in the second row. Process the query by clicking on the button on the Toolbar. Review the results, and return to the Query screen. We will save this query with a file name. Saved queries can be used again at a later time or can be printed in a report. To save the query, select **File, Save As** and give the query file a name. To close the Query screen, select **File, Close.**

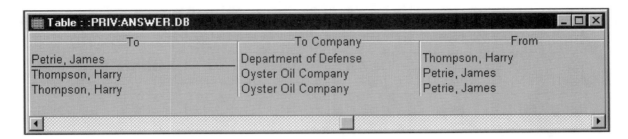

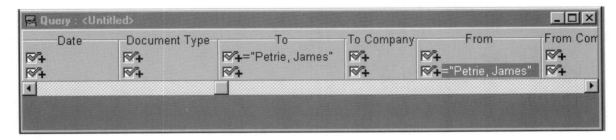

F. PRINTING

You may print the contents of a table or query file using a quick print option, or by creating a report. Quick printing options often use a default report with each field as a column. The printout often wraps on the page or creates multiple pages if the columns do not fit within the page width. This type of printout is often difficult to read. Quick printouts are nice when you do not need a formal presentation of the table information. A report is a way to print your data in a readable fashion and add text, graphics, and other features to make the printout look professional. When you design a report for a table, you can save the report to use each time you print data from the table.

1. Quick Printing Options

To create a quick printout of the data within a table or query, in **Microsoft Access** click on the table or query name, or in **Paradox** open the table or open the query file and run the query. Then, select **File, Print** or the **Printer button** on the Toolbar. The printout will appear similar to Figure 6.15.

Page 1

Document Num	Number of Pag	Date	Document Typ	To	To Company
1	1	6/6/82	Letter	Dodd, Jim	City of Oak Gro
2	1	12/8/41	Letter	Thompson, Har	Oyster Oil Com
3	5	12/20/41	Letter	Petrie, James	Department of
8	1	12/30/41	Letter	Thompson, Har	Oyster Oil Com
9	26	1/1/80	Brochure		
35	1	2/3/79	Letter	Dodd, Jim	City of Oak Gro
36	1	1/15/55	Letter	Osborne, Tom	City of Oak Gro
37	1	3/23/55	Report		

Page 2

From	From Company	Summary
Hicks, Clayton	OFHA	Letter to the Cit
Petrie, James	Department of	Order from the
Thompson, Har	Oyster Oil Com	Letter acknowle
Petrie, James	Department of	Letter directing
Field Developer	Field Developer	A brochure reg
Field, John	Field Developer	Letter expressi
Gedit, E. Dusun	Soil and Plant L	Opinion that the
Osborne, Tom	City of Oak Gro	Report stating t

Figure 6.15   A quick printout is a fast way to print data from a table, but
it does not produce a professional looking document

2.   Creating a Report in Microsoft Access

To create a report in Microsoft Access click on the **Report tab** and click on the **New** button. A dialog box similar to the one in Figure 6.16 will appear.

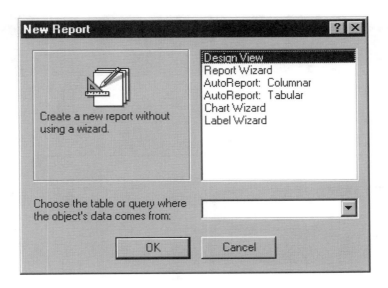

Figure 6.16 The New Report Dialog Box in Microsoft Access

In this dialog box, choose a report option and then select the file to be printed from the drop-down list. Choose the **AutoReport: Columnar** report and the Grove table for a nice printout. After the report is processed, you will see the results as shown in Figure 6.17. You can print the report at this point by selecting **File, Print** or clicking on the **Print** button.

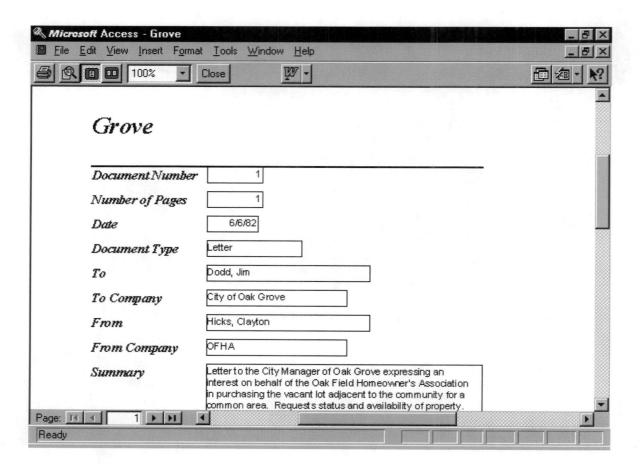

Figure 6.17 A Columnar Report in Microsoft Access

To customize a report, close the preview window so that you can see the report design as shown in Figure 6.18. Using the tools found on the Report Design button bar, you can customize the report. Your name can be placed in the header row by clicking on the **Text** button (containing the A), clicking inside the header row, and typing. Text can also be added within the detail of the report to help explain the contents of fields. Fields can be moved around by dragging them

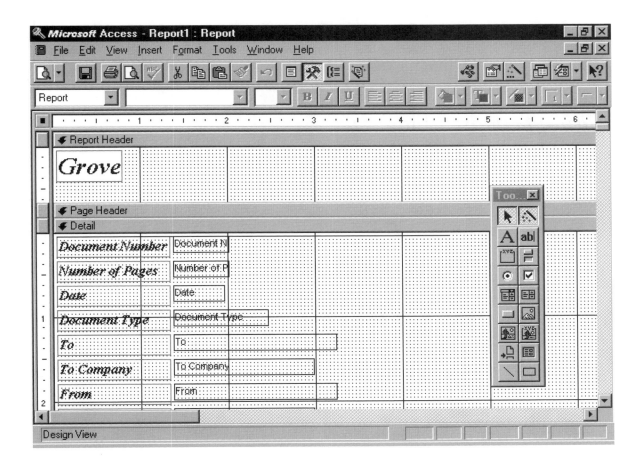

Figure 6.18   The Report Design screen allows you to alter the format of the report

with the mouse. The field names can also be changed by clicking on them and making changes. The new report can be seen by selecting **File, Print Preview.** The Report can then be printed. A customized report is shown in Figure 6.19. To save the report, select **File, Save As,** give the report a name, and click on the **OK** button.

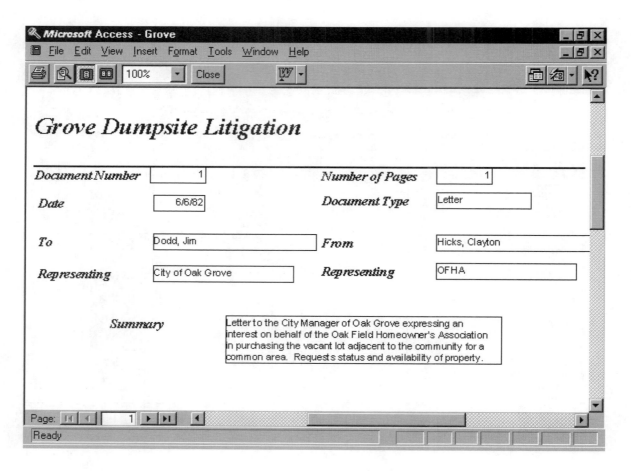

Figure 6.19 A customized report created by making changes within the
Design screen

3. Creating a Report in Paradox

To create a report in Paradox, select **File, New, Report.** In older versions of the program, you will be prompted for the table or query file name before you choose a report design. In the newest versions, you will choose the report design first. The dialog box that prompts for the report design is similar to the one in Figure 6.20.

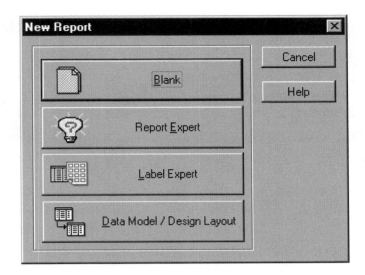

Figure 6.20   The New Report dialog box in Paradox prompts for the desired report design

For a nice simple report, choose the Data Model/Design Layout report. In newer versions of the program, you will then be prompted for a file name. Usually, the default file name display will show the names of tables. To see the names of the query files, you can select Queries from a drop-down list at the bottom of the dialog box. After selecting the Grove table, click on the **OK** button. Select the **Single Record** option and click on the **OK** button. After the report is processed, you will see its design as shown in Figure 6.21. You can print the report at this point by selecting **File, Print** or clicking on the **Print** button.

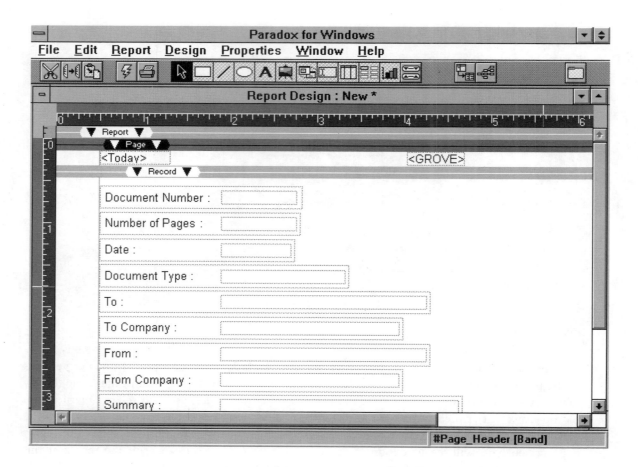

Figure 6.21 The Report Design Screen in Paradox

To customize a report, use the tools found on the Report Design button bar. Your name can be placed in the header row by clicking on the **Text** button (containing the A), clicking inside the header row, and typing. Text can also be added within the detail of the report to help explain the contents of fields. Fields can be moved around by dragging them with the mouse. The field names can also be changed by clicking on them and making changes. The new report can be seen by selecting **Report, Run Report** or clicking on the lightning bolt button on the Toolbar. You can return to the Report Design screen by selecting **File, Close.** To print the report, select **File, Print** or the **Print** button on the Toolbar. A customized report is shown in Figure 6.19. To save the report, select **File, Save As,** give the report a name, and click on the **OK** button.

G. FORMS

Forms are used to customize the input screens for record entry into a table. The process is similar to creating a report, but the form will be used to input data. When new records need to be added to the table, you can open the form and enter the data there.

1. Creating a Form in Microsoft Access

To create a form in Microsoft Access click on the **Form tab** and click on the **New** button. A dialog box similar to the one in Figure 6.16 will appear. In this dialog box, choose a form option and then select the table to be acted on from the drop-down list. Choose the **AutoForm: Columnar** form and the Grove table for a nice input form. After the form is processed, you will see the results as shown in Figure 6.22.

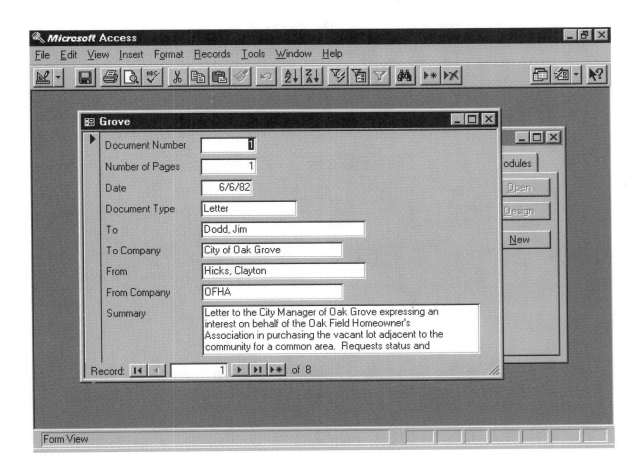

Figure 6.22 A Columnar Input Form in Microsoft Access

To customize a form, move back to the form design by selecting **View, Form Design.** Using the tools found on the Form Design button bar you can customize the form. Text can be added with the **Text** button (containing the A), clicking inside the design, and typing. Fields can be moved around by dragging them with the mouse. The field names can be changed by clicking on them and making changes. The new form can be seen by selecting **View, Form.** A customized form is shown in Figure 6.23. To save the form select **File, Save As,** give the form a name, and click on the **OK** button.

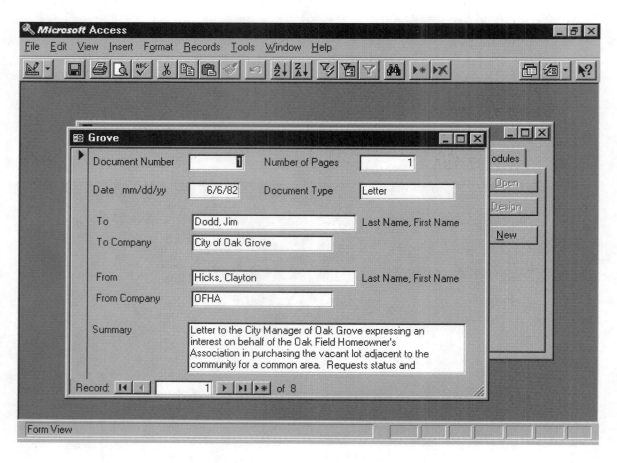

Figure 6.23 A customized input form can be created to assist persons entering records into the database

To use a form to enter data, open the form and click on the **asterisk** button at the bottom to move to a blank entry form. Enter the data as you normally would. To move to the next entry form, you can press the **[Tab]** key after the last field, or click on the **asterisk** button. To save the new data to the table, select **File, Save.** To close the form, select **File, Close.**

2.   Creating a Form in Paradox

To create a form in Paradox, select **File, New, Form.** In older versions of the program, you will be prompted for the table name before you choose a form design. In the newest versions, you will choose the form design first. The dialog box that prompts for the form design is similar to the one in Figure 6.20.

For a nice simple form, choose the Data Model/Design Layout form. In newer versions of the program, you will then be prompted for the table name. After selecting the Grove table, click on the **OK** button. Select the **Single Record** option and click on the **OK** button. After the form is processed, you will see its design as shown in Figure 6.24.

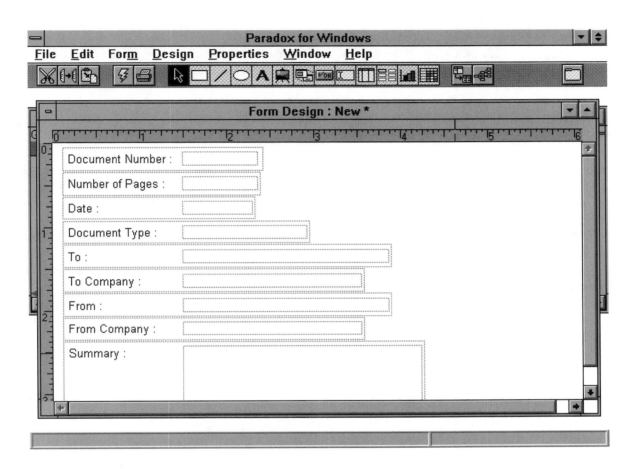

Figure 6.24 The Input Form Design Screen in Paradox

To customize a form, use the tools found on the form design button bar. Text can be added by clicking on the **Text** button (containing the A), clicking inside the form design, and typing. Fields can be moved around by dragging them with the mouse. The field names can also be changed by clicking on them and making changes. The new form can be seen by clicking on the lightning bolt button. You can return to the form design screen by selecting **File, Close.** To save the form, select **File, Save As,** and give the form a name.

To use a form to enter data, open the form by selecting **File, Open, Form** and select the form name. Enter the data as you normally would. To move to the next entry form, you can press the **[Tab]** key after the last field. To save the new data to the table, select **File, Save.** To close the form, select **File, Close.**

Summary

Windows summary database programs keep records of data in a table. To create a table, you look at the information to be stored in the database and establish the fields that will be necessary to keep track of the data. The group of fields forms the structure of the database. Each field is given a name, a type, a width (not with all fields), and can be keyed. A keyed field will be the field that the table is primarily sorted upon. After the field structure has been established, records are entered into the table.

Records can be entered by looking at the items themselves and entering the data or by reading the information from a code sheet. Code sheets are created to assist in the data entry. Once the records have been entered, tables may be sorted or indexed to appear in any order desired by the user.

Queries are searches run on the database to locate pieces of data. A query design screen contains columns labeled with the field names. To find a piece of data, you enter a query under the field name to be searched. Queries normally begin with a relational operator and can be connected to other queries using connectors. When the query is processed, the records within the table that meet the search criteria are displayed.

To create a printout of the records in a table or query result, a quick printout using **File, Print** can be created, or a report can be designed. A report creates a more formal presentation of the records. To create a report, a design is selected and altered with design tools. The report design can then be printed and saved for future use with the table or query.

To create a customized input form for entering data into a table, a form is designed in a manner similar to designing a report. The form is useful in helping people to understand how to input the data into the table.

Databases are valuable tools for keeping track of evidence and other information in a law office. Windows-based databases provide an environment that is pleasant to the eye and easier to understand than their DOS counterparts.

SUMMARY DATABASE EXERCISES

Exercise 1

If you were to set up a database to keep track of all of your textbooks for this course, what fields would you use? What type of field would each be? How many characters should each field hold? Should one or more of the fields be keyed? If so, which one(s)?

Exercise 2

Your firm needs a database to keep track of conflicts of interest. Conflicts of interest occur when an attorney or paralegal in the office has worked on a case for a client in the past, and that client turns up as the opposing party in a case for another client. With many attorneys and paralegals in an office, this can sometimes occur without anyone's knowledge. To avoid this embarrassment, firms run conflict of interest checks when retained on a case. The fields of a conflict of interest database would include the following:

Case Name

Responsible Attorney

Lead Plaintiff

Lead Defendant

Date Case Filed

Responsible Legal Staff

Other Parties

Prepare a new database table for the conflict of interest database. (Note: dBASE for DOS users will need to shorten the field names to meet the field name requirements for the program.) Enter the fields (the first field may be keyed in Windows-based programs). You can decide whether the Responsible Attorney field will hold attorney initials or full names. The Responsible Legal Staff and Other Parties fields should be Memo fields so that many names can be entered. Wildcards will be used to search the Memo fields.

After you have saved the database structure, open the database table and enter the first record as shown below.

Case Name	Hampton v. Peters
Responsible Attorney	Orwell, James
Lead Plaintiff	Hampton, Paul
Lead Defendant	Peters, Thomas
Date Case Filed	3/25/96
Responsible Legal Staff	Olson, Kathy; Marks, Steve; Issacs, Kevin
Other Parties	Hampton, Karen; Peters Construction, Inc.

Enter another record yourself and create a report of the data in the database table.

Exercise 3

Create an input form for the database in the previous exercise (you must have set up and saved the database structure in order to do this). Place the fields in different locations in the form. Modify the field names so that they will make sense to the secretary inputting the information. Provide explanatory text where necessary. Print the form.

Exercise 4

The following evidentiary documents have arrived in the *Yarrow v. Nelson* case. Set up an evidentiary database to keep track of all of the evidence (see example in Chapter 6 for field names and types). Enter a record for each of the eight documents into the database. Create a report of the database.

1

YARROW & NELSON CATERING

12345 Home Boulevard
Seaside, California 94444
(408) 555-1212

January 5, 1996

Tom Nelson
23 Patterson Road
Seaside, CA 94444

Dear Tom:

It has come to my attention from our customers that the amounts that you have been collecting on accounts are substantially more than the amounts on the invoices. I believe that you have been skimming money from the receipts of our company. Therefore, I am dissolving our partnership. Please return the keys to the warehouse by Friday.

My lawyer will be contacting you.

Phillip Yarrow

2

January 10, 1996

Dear Phil:

I don't know what you are talking about. The invoices are correct. Those customers must be trying to create problems. I will not return the keys to the warehouse because half of the inventory is mine. Call off your lawyer.

Tom

3

INVESTIGATION REPORT

Davis Investigations, Inc.

On January 11, at approximately 11:15 p.m., I observed an individual known by me to be Tom Nelson enter the Yarrow & Nelson Catering warehouse. Mr. Nelson proceeded to remove cases of soda, candy, and other materials and load them into the back of a rented truck. He left in the truck at approximately 12:30 a.m. and I followed him to a warehouse at 8844 Hideway Road, Seaside, where he unloaded the inventory taken from Yarrow & Nelson. He left this location at approximately 1:20 a.m. and proceeded to his residence.

Jefferson Davis, Investigator

4

YARROW & NELSON CATERING

12345 Home Boulevard
Seaside, California 94444
(408) 555-1212

January 12, 1996

Tom Nelson
23 Patterson Road
Seaside, CA 94444

Tom:

I know that you went to the warehouse last night and removed inventory. Our partnership is hereby dissolved pursuant to paragraph 14 of our partnership agreement. Return the keys to the warehouse immediately. Also, return the money you stole from the business.

My lawyer will be contacting you.

Phillip Yarrow

5

January 13, 1996

Phil:

    I have stolen nothing. What's mine is mine. Bring on the lawyers!

Tom

6

YARROW & NELSON CATERING

12345 Home Boulevard
Seaside, California 94444
(408) 555-1212

INVOICE

Date: 12/15/95   Rep.: Tom Nelson

To: Jim's Service Station
        945 Aspen Highway
        Seaside, California 94444

12 Cases of Soda @ $4.00/Case	$48.00
5 Cases Candy Bars @ $7.00/Case	$35.00
Total Due This Invoice	$83.00

7

YARROW & NELSON CATERING

12345 Home Boulevard
Seaside, California 94444
(408) 555-1212

INVOICE

Date: 12/20/95   Rep.: Tom Nelson

To: Jim's Service Station
        945 Aspen Highway
        Seaside, California 94444

10 Cases of Soda @ $4.00/Case	$40.00
8 Cases Candy Bars @ $7.00/Case	$56.00
Total Due This Invoice	$96.00

8

Jim's Service Station

945 Aspen Highway
Seaside, California 94444

January 22, 1996

Phil Yarrow
45 Beach Street
Seaside, California 94444

Dear Phil:

    We have been friends for many years, so I felt that I should bring this to your attention. I think Tom is stealing from your business. The invoices that he has been writing for my orders are for less than the actual amount that I am receiving and paying for. Tom says that it will just help us all out at tax time, but I don't believe him. I have attached the last five invoices so that you can check them. I have written the actual amounts that I received and how much I actually paid on each one.

    I hope that I am wrong about Tom, and if I am I apologize. But you have been my friend for a long time and I couldn't just ignore this.

Sincerely,

Jim Spencer

Page 1 of 6

Exercise 5

Using the database set up in Exercise 4, prepare a query that will locate all documents to or from Phil Yarrow. Save the query and print a report of the results. Run another query to locate all documents written in December of 1995. Save the query. Prepare a report of this query and customize the report by moving the fields around, changing the field names, and adding text to the report.

Turn in the two reports.

Chapter Index